# ELEANOR LANSING DULLES
*Chances of a Lifetime*

## ALSO BY ELEANOR LANSING DULLES

*The French Franc 1914-1928*
*The Bank for International Settlements at Work*
*The Dollar, the Franc and Inflation*
*Depression and Reconstruction*
*Financing the Social Security Act*
*John Foster Dulles: The Last Year*
*Détente* (in collaboration)
*Dominican Action—1965* (in collaboration)
*Berlin—The Wall Is Not Forever*
*American Foreign Policy in the Making*
*One Germany or Two*
*The Wall: A Tragedy in Three Acts*

# ELEANOR LANSING DULLES
## *Chances of a Lifetime*

## A MEMOIR

PRENTICE-HALL, INC., *Englewood Cliffs, New Jersey*

*To Emily–for the gift of friendship*

*Eleanor Lansing Dulles: Chances of a Lifetime, A Memoir*
Copyright © 1980 by Eleanor Lansing Dulles
All rights reserved. No part of this book may be
reproduced in any form or by any means, except
for the inclusion of brief quotations in a review,
without permission in writing from the publisher.
Address inquiries to Prentice-Hall, Inc.,
Englewood Cliffs, N. J. 07632
Printed in the United States of America
Prentice-Hall of Canada, Ltd., Toronto
10 9 8 7 6 5 4 3 2 1

Text Designer, Linda Huber
Art Director, Hal Siegel

**Library of Congress Cataloging in Publication Data**
Dulles, Eleanor Lansing.
Eleanor Lansing Dulles, chances of a lifetime: a memoir.
Includes index.
1. Dulles, Eleanor Lansing. 2. Dulles
family. 3. United States—Foreign relations—20th
century. 4. Diplomats—United States—Biography.
5. Educators—United States—Biography. I. Title.
E748.D867A33    327'.2'0924 [B]    79-23651
ISBN 0-13-246942-1

# PREFACE

The wooden bridge supported by chains crossed the Potomac near Little Falls and carried the horse and buggy traffic at the turn of the century. It was eventually replaced by the steel and concrete of Chain Bridge when I was about forty years old. The years between 1900 and the midcentury were times of changes and development for the city of Washington, D.C., and for the nation. As the small town, bordered by marshland, grew to a larger city, rich in cultural and professional resources, the country as a whole grew from a sprawling, loosely knit, industrial fledgling to a power that came to exercise technical and scientific leadership in the world.

The years from 1900 to 1980 saw the emergence of the United States as a source of military might and economic wealth as we took first place among nations, supplanting the British Empire in our financial, commercial, and scientific development. Meanwhile, after World War II we assumed a responsibility in foreign affairs we had not dreamed of in previous decades.

These were the years of my education and my learning. These were the times of professional work, of study—of struggle, danger, failure, and success. They were the years of many chances and of rich contacts with great personalities. The story of my personal adventures can cast light on the many changes that were taking place. My experience, which paralleled in time the era of extraordinary national change, can add some footnotes to history. I was fortunate to have had a part in the dynamic expansion of thought and action. When it became necessary to choose between alternative jobs or activities, I was increasingly aware of both barriers to advancement and the rare and exciting possibilities which could be seized. In the search for useful work, I did not turn to my brothers or others in the family for help. I sought rather for the support of my professors and colleagues in finding academic or government jobs. There were risks in every change I made and I know that another approach would have meant more money and higher rank—but on the whole I am satisfied with the course I took.

I worked for government for three decades in which new social, monetary, and diplomatic initiatives and crises called for creative effort and a high degree of awareness of the risk and possibilities. I taught economics for more than twenty years when the old theories were being reviewed by innovative intellectuals such as Jacob Viner, Joseph Schumpeter, Alvin Hansen, J. M. Keynes and Bertil Ohlin. During this long period I lived a life which was illuminated by new ideas of personal freedom. As the first and second world wars shattered the accepted patterns of behavior and changed many of the rules of family and civic life, I adapted to new conditions. Since I was directly involved in both these conflicts, as well as the war in Korea, I have a story to tell.

An autobiography is a demanding undertaking because it is based on the truth as one person sees it. This is my thirteenth book and the most difficult to write. And yet, this truth has to be cut to a reasonable length and breadth so the reader is not swamped in detail. How much does this pruning distort the clarity of the image? The readers can protect themselves by recognizing the inherent bias. More candor would add interest while reserve often raises questions which the writer does not wish to answer—this is a central dilemma. Life's joys and sorrows have a special meaning for the protagonist. The recounting of the tale is limited by good taste and calls on the reader for an effort at understanding. Assuming a degree of sympathy, I have not labeled my mistakes, nor have I underscored my accomplishments—most of the facts are there for others to judge.

I was aware of the swift pace of change, but not until the midcentury did the power of the nation and the challenge to action become clearly evident. The times brought new chances; many were open to me and I took them as they emerged. A life is not complete without venture into the unknown and I found both danger and opportunity in my choices. The situation was often complex. I should not have driven to the Soviet headquarters in *Baden bei Wien*, so they held me for interrogation. I should not have flown in an unpressurized plane over the high ridges of Mt. Everest. I should not have thrown hand grenades about the trenches of northern France.

In looking back over eighty years I have mixed conclusions. Clearly to go to France in 1917 and to Austria in 1945 were wise decisions. Certainly the acceptance of special responsibility for Berlin in 1952 was a good choice. These were three major decisions.

There were turnings on the way that meant less writing, less theory, and more action.

My thanks go now, not only to those who helped me write this story—though that debt is large—but to those who helped me live these exciting years. They go to my parents for their zest for people, for their awareness of nature, and for their will to serve. They go to my brother Foster for his immense courage in his search for a just and durable peace; to my brother Allen for his intense dedication to security and the essentials for national survival; to my husband, David, for his burning dedication to scholarship and the quest for truth; to my two sisters, Margaret and Nataline, for their continuing understanding and support.

Fortunate in the stimulating advice and counsel of friends whose ideas and knowledge helped me through the years, I can name only a few of the many. The list would include among others, Bertram Wolfe, Andor Klay, Winfield Riefler, Priscilla and Frank Allen, Karl and Martha Mautner, Elwood Williams, Seymour and Stacey Bolten, Anne Brunsdale, Cecil Lyons, James Riddleberger, Anne Crutcher, and Burke Wilkinson. John T. Mason, Jr., and Betty Mason, by skillfully preparing oral history transcripts of my story, were of enormous help to me as I brought this material together. This short list is but a fragment. I include, for their great and unstinted assistance, Charlotte Child, Doris Rich, Louise Des Marais.

Some have given me specific advice and some have helped by their judgment in times of critical decisions in living and writing. Only those who worked on the text during the later stages of checking and rewriting can realize the patience required and can properly weigh my gratitude for their tolerance and loyalty to me when I and they were under pressure. During hours of long and detailed examination and revision, the contribution that was made to my work by these friends and assistants was beyond measure.

# CONTENTS

John Welsh Dulles 1823-1886
m
Harriet Lathrop Winslow 1829-1878

John Watson Foster 1836-1917
m
Mary Parke McFerson 1840-1922

(deceased children Parke, Alice, Alexander)
Eleanor Foster Lansing 1866-1934

Allen Macy Dulles 1854-1930    m    Edith Foster 1863-1941

| John Foster Dulles 1888-1959 m Janet Avery 1892-1969 | Margaret Dulles 1889-1970 m Deane Edwards 1885-1970 | Allen Welsh Dulles 1893-1969 m Clover Todd 1894-1974 | Eleanor Lansing Dulles 1895- m David Blondheim 1884-1934 | Nataline Dulles 1898- m James S. Seymour 1900- |
|---|---|---|---|---|

John Foster Dulles 1888-1959
m
Janet Avery 1892-1969

- John W.F. 1913 m Eleanor Ritter
  - Edith
  - John
  - Ellen
  - Avery
- Lillias 1914 m Robert Hinshaw
  - Janet
  - David
  - Foster
  - Lila
- Avery 1918

Margaret Dulles 1889-1970
m
Deane Edwards 1885-1970

- Robert 1915 m Sally Alexander
  - Edith
  - James
- Richard 1916 m Vee Tsung Ling
  - Margaret
  - Joan
  - Lawrence
  - Edith
- Edith 1919 (dec.) m James Manning 1949
  - Deane
  - Thomas
  - Elizabeth
  - Foster
- Mary Parke 1922

Allen Welsh Dulles 1893-1969
m
Clover Todd 1894-1974

- Clover 1922 m Jens Jebsen
  - Clover
  - Allen
  - Joan
  - Per
- Joan 1923 m Eugene Buresch
  - Matthew
  - Alexandra
- Allen Macy 1930

Eleanor Lansing Dulles 1895-
m
David Blondheim 1884-1934

- David 1934 m Pamela Forbes
  - Frederic 1964
  - Edward 1966
  - Juliet 1969
- Ann 1937 m David Joor
  - Christine 1964
  - Susan 1965
  - William 1968

Nataline Dulles 1898-
m
James S. Seymour 1900-

- Marion 1930 m Norton Carson
- James D. 1935

Fifth Generation not completed for marriages or children

# ·1·

## CHILDREN BY THE LAKE

I stood up in front of the crowded political gathering in the Congress Hall in Berlin in September 1977 to deliver a message. It was twenty years after the opening of the building. When I had been responsible for Berlin Affairs in the Department of State, I had arranged the financing, helped with the design, and guided to completion this modern structure in the heart of West Berlin. It was designed and inspired as a symbol of freedom for those staunch citizens who, like Ernst Reuter, Louisa Schröder, Paul Hertz, Otto Suhr, Ernst Lemmer, and dozens of others, including the late Americans General Lucius D. Clay and Ambassador Robert D. Murphy, had fought for liberty. It served as a meeting place for leaders of the free citizens. It was sometimes called Frau Dulles' Hut and more often the Pregnant Oyster. Its nicknames came from the cantilevered shell-shaped roof soaring over the cluster of meeting rooms.

Now the sky-blue seats and speakers' platform were crowded with the older leaders and younger men and women who had stood firm for democracy. The memories of past heroes gave me courage to speak to this gathering—their example gave me voice and heart to recall the dangers that still menace their future and to speak of the opportunities that lay ahead:

> "Your city is vulnerable but you have resources. You are isolated but you have friends. You have had dark hours but also the dawning of a bright future. You have produced a strong industry. Your science and culture are shining results of vigorous efforts.
>
> "If some are discouraged they should think not only of past heroes but of leaders to come. When we come to visit you, we find not an ordinary city like hundreds of others, but an extraordinary center of active and determined achievement. ... "

This was my message twenty years after the start of the building, eighty years after I had begun my long journey to a distant goal.

Looking back from the vantage of 1980, I can see my early self as a different person and yet it is the beginning of me. Who is this child of eighty years ago?

In this book I shall try to tell the story of what happened to the little girl of 1900—what did she do as she came from the "Age of Innocence" to the present troubled, but exciting, years. I can look back with wonder on past events from the first airplane to the landing on the moon. I remember vaguely another century; and in 1901 I was standing in the dimly lit hall of my grandfather's house at 1405 Eye Street in Washington when the telegraph boy brought the cablegram that announced the death of Queen Victoria. I can recall the tragedy of two world wars, the fight for Social Security and for human rights. I was always concerned with international cooperation, and in this arduous work I came to know many towering figures of the century. For my part, I sought not fame, rank, or money, but to enjoy experience and give service. In eight decades I learned many lessons. There was action and I was there.

The child of this story, small, bespectacled, hair pulled back in two tight braids, doubting, wondering, looked over the wide stretch of Ontario's waters toward faraway lands. She was from the beginning seeking a mission she could carry forward. Some eighty years later there was evidence of a measure of satisfaction, a considerable fulfillment of those early wonderings and hopes.

The long and rugged path from Lake Ontario had led to Berlin.

Here by the lake the journey began. My early years by Ontario were to be of lasting significance to me as well as to my brothers and sisters. The Dulles clan was to live and work together for many years, often by the shores of the lake.

This was an overpowering family—outstanding grandparents, parents who both had firm opinions and strong principles, and two brothers and sisters with definite personalities, quick to take on the challenges of an active life. Foster, Margaret, Allen, and Nataline, when I was five in 1900, ranged in age from twelve to two years.

In 1894 my maternal grandfather, John W. Foster, built Underbluff, the first of several cottages by the harbor shores. These were to be a family center for almost a century. The red clapboard house with large circular porch reaching out over the water was home in summer for the Dulles family.

[2]

When I was less than a month old, I was brought to this house. As time went on I became very fond of this simple structure with its large living room, a kitchen for many purposes with woodburning stove, tin bathtub for Saturday night scrubbing, and hand pump to bring in the water. There was no gas or electricity, only kerosene lamps and candles.

The nearby windmill with its stark skeleton which brought our drinking water from the lake was both a symbol of the scale of living and one of several high points from which we could look down on the slowly growing community. We could count the wooden docks and see the boats, lapstrake Thousand Island skiffs, sometimes with oars, sometimes with small sails set to catch the prevailing west wind as they set out for the fishing grounds.

The annual migration from Watertown, where I was born, to Henderson Harbor by Lake Ontario each summer after 1895 was a major move. The main articles of household equipment went on a "load"—a large wagon carrying a stove, bedding, some pieces of furniture, trunks, and other useful and essential items. Usually the family went in a pony cart, in a surrey, or by bicycle. The dusty road with its deep ruts was eighteen hot miles of travel, but the trip was full of excitement and since we usually went in more than one group, there was a certain amount of competition as to who would get to the cottage first and who would have the most adventures on the way.

The first years of my life gave me unusual opportunities to look beyond the horizons of most ten-year-olds with glimpses of foreign lands and the problems that diplomats and missionaries were facing abroad. My grandfather was the dominant personality in our family circle. He was tall, upright, fair-skinned, and striking in any group with his bushy white side whiskers. His father, Matthew, at age seventeen had walked from the Hudson to the Ohio River in 1817 and built a log cabin for the family home at what is now Evansville, Indiana. General Foster, a Civil War veteran, had spent many years as our chief diplomatic representative in Mexico, Russia, and Spain. He had traveled around the world stopping in India, China, Japan, and elsewhere. He had been a member of the Chinese delegation at the Hague Peace Conference of 1907. It was inevitable that his young grandchildren should be aware of far-off places.

The travels of others in the family, particularly my mother and father, also gave a feeling of the reality of distant peoples and lands. We were particularly fortunate in this. Even though our financial resources were limited, my parents felt that funds could be stretched to give us a wide view of the world.

I did my first traveling in books, devouring Henry M. Stanley's *Through Darkest Africa*, Dr. Fridtjof Nansen's *Farthest North*, a book about "Hidden Shensi" in China, and several on Tibet and India. I also sat on the dock for hours with my friend Ross Thompson—the son of old friends from Indiana—each of us on a small packing case serving as motorcars with sticks in the cracks between the boards for gearshifts, navigating unknown lands in our conversation. But my attention was usually concentrated on the nearby activities of the family. My grandfather, appointed Secretary of State in 1892, was recognized as elder statesman but also as an outstanding fisherman. Like most of the summer visitors, he had an experienced boatman, Will Stevens, one of the best.

Henderson, bordering on the ancient seven-hundred-foot-deep lake, was noted for smallmouth black bass. Dark-scaled bass lazily circled in a current which brought the minnow schools and the baited hook. Will Stevens had his special holes chosen each day according to temperature and wind direction. He was an important figure to me and I know others respected his intuition. He was an upstanding man who said little, but, wise in the lore of the region, looked for weather signs and water changes. His thin, slightly stooped figure in brown corduroys was a beacon that I came to cherish as we honored his skill and his rare pungent words. He was my grandfather's boatman for more than two decades. He taught us children to sail. His meals on the shores of the islands could vie with any I have ever eaten. He cooked between rocks over driftwood fires, the coffee never to be equaled, the fish superbly broiled.

"Bacon finds its own place in the pan," he told me as I poked at the languid strips.

Will Stevens was at the same time superior to and typical of the year-round residents who cut wood, harvested ice, and worked on their boats and houses through the long cold winters. When the ice went out in the spring, it took some of the wooden docks and their repair called for cooperative work. Only reluctantly was the motorboat with its raucous noise and choppy wake accepted. Even sailing for sport was slow to come to this region. The summer visitors, not the local fishermen, swam for pleasure. It was mainly the people from afar who had accidents. The local people respected the lake's moods, and were cautious.

I was sometimes taken fishing sitting on a small stool between the two grown-ups who had wicker-back rest seats on the stern and midship thwarts. My task was to watch the sensitive tip of the rod and not to chatter. If I missed a strike, I was told to be ready to snap the rod upward and keep the line taut next time. Even with a large midday meal, I was hungry when I got back after a long day.

Since we ate at Warner's, a farmhouse owned by the Warner family from whom my grandfather had bought the land, the housekeeping in those early days was relatively simple. My grandfather would expect us to be lined up at the gate at 7:30 every morning to go to the nearby farmhouse. The family had a long table in the large dining room next to another for the Thompsons, and another for the Marcelluses and Pouchers, from Syracuse.

The talk between the tables was mainly of fishing. This was the major preoccupation, and the bass brought in were served for breakfast, lunch, and dinner along with chicken, steaks, and many vegetables in "birdbaths" and four or five kinds of pie—with salads, soup, and other fare which makes the modern restaurant seem very sparse indeed by comparison.

The Bay of Henderson offered ample space for childhood games and the rules were simple, although strictly observed. Certain times were set for swimming. The slippery raft was poled close to shore under parental supervision. The wooden docks were for throwing stones and catching minnows—occasionally a fish. Inland, exploring and berrying were chances to roam, the main requirement being to return by mealtime.

Nowhere could there have been a better place for lively growing children. The five of us and a few neighbors and farm youngsters were eager to race and climb and discover birds and fish and to learn of changing weather. As we grew older there were islands, some two, five, ten, and twenty miles over the water. They were for camping and adventure. This rich heritage, which is now being pushed to the edges of parks and reservations, was then free and open; largely uninhabited. Born before the twentieth century, I had the best of it. But much of the beauty is still there. The windy weather was an often stern master, and its unbridled force was a reality that taught us our place in a vast universe.

And then at night there was usually a time of calm when the west wind subsided and a breeze arose in the south, a land breeze. The still waters shielded by the bluff mirrored the shining constellations Orion, Cassiopeia, and the Big and Little Dippers, friendly to us in our childish imagination.

I still touch the stone and feel the strength of the boulders that storms and ice have left on my rock-strewn shore. One, the fabulous "big boulder," large as an elephant, has been brought by some ancient ice storm. It stands more than six feet high on the shore near our dock. It brings a mystery and a lesson that the unexpected happens. We who have been brought up at Henderson return to the lake for rest and for refreshment, not only in memories but also in recurring search for new and invigorating ventures on its deep waters.

I can recall the family circle on the wide porch by the mirror lake with the awning lowered against the western sun when I came back from France and World War I in 1919. I was asked to tell the tales of my adventures and I knew that with the telling I was again with my own people at home. Even more than the elements and surroundings, people form the developing purpose and will.

When Grandpa and his fishing companion came to the dock at eight in the morning, six days a week, waiting for the fishing boat, his seriousness of purpose was equaled only by the joy of the trip on the water and evening excitement of the day's catch. We all watched him set off and greeted him in the afternoon to see the fish he brought in. His white side whiskers contrasted with the pink of his skin, partly covered with powder to protect him from the sun's rays and reflection from the water. He and his companions were good fishermen, and a picture I cherish shows them standing with a display of thirty-six bass, the legal limit at that time.

Grandma was round and plump and her hair was always in place. She, Mary Parke McFerson, had married the young lawyer in Evansville, Indiana, in 1859. She was, as he said in *War Stories for My Grandchildren*, a "brave, true hearted woman." On a smooth "grandmother's day" she would go fishing and wore a large straw hat tied under her chin and a black alpaca dress.

Even when I knew her years later, she would fetch and carry for John, whom she called "Mr. Foster" before visitors. Grandma would go bathing on hot days, dressed with skirted suit, bloomers, and

[6]

stockings, dipping demurely beside the wooden dock while we splashed and shouted at a discreet distance, pushing each other under water.

Outside the water Grandma dressed much as she would in Washington, though her clothes were older. Under them she was sheathed in a stiff corset of the kind we used to call "Gospel armor." She was always cheerful and a true helpmeet.

I never saw Grandma in a kitchen. Madison, the butler, and Mammy, the maid, brought her breakfast or tea. She was a gentle woman and very reserved. Her comment in June 1919 on the peace conference was "Talk, talk, talk"—the most vigorous opinion I can recall.

Once or twice a week Grandpa would tell us children stories of his youth in pioneer days in Indiana and tales of the Civil War. We would sit on the long wooden bench decorated with Egyptian printed cloth and a few unyielding pillows, our restlessness checked by his vivid accounts and by the spell of his strong personality. The beaded curtain of the game closet would sway in the wind and an occasional slap would mark the intrusion of mosquitoes (there were not many).

Grandpa was not musical but he enjoyed the hymn singing and joined my father in conducting Sunday services on the lawn, to which neighbors were welcome. He also went to church in the village, riding in a surrey, and later, about 1905, in the newly acquired Packard after the influx of three automobiles into the community. We younger people walked back three miles over the fields, pausing on the edge of the bluff as we came home, looking down on our cottages and out over the far waters.

There is no doubt that we had a strong feeling of family loyalty. This applied to our solicitude for my great-grandmother, Eliza Read McFerson, born in 1816 (died about 1913). She had been widowed by the death of her husband in the Civil War. With three children to support she taught at Glendale Female Seminary. "Ma," as the middle child among thirteen, had been tutored by several of the twelve brothers in mathematics, Latin, history, and other subjects so she was well equipped for this work. We would be assigned in turn to play backgammon, anagrams, or cards with her.

We would sit under the kerosene lamp, with mosquitoes humming overhead, wishing we could be on the porch with the rest of the family, but aware of the importance of giving Ma some pleasure in her nineties after she had done so much in her youth, as a young widow and teacher, for her children and grandchildren. We were intrigued by the reverse morality of helping her take an improper advantage in games she wanted to win. We would look the other way when with her long silk skirt she would walk the croquet ball to the wicket. If we had managed this in our play together, it would have been called cheating, but for her we thought it fair. She lived to be ninety-six, almost blind and deaf but well loved for her spirit and her affection. After her death we found she had hidden bread and other food in her bureau drawer presumably fearing starvation.

As I look back over my mother's memoirs (privately published in 1934) I come to the conclusion that my grandfather's and grandmother's sense of righteousness and duty prevented my mother from being spoiled in her life of special privilege.

My father, Allen Macy Dulles, and mother, Edith Foster, had met in Paris in 1880 when Mother was sixteen. In love at once, Father had waited for her decision for six years. They were married in 1887. Their similarities and their differences were impressive. Father, slender, meditative, and imaginative, was a Presbyterian pastor. He worked in his large third-floor study in the house much of the time. He had been educated at Princeton University and seminary and also at Göttingen in Germany, a scholarly man.

Mother, more matter of fact and a strong executive, found the life of a minister's wife demanding, and five children called for considerable physical strength. The beginning was not easy.

In the Line-a-Day diary they kept for more than twenty-five years, one finds clues, but not descriptions, of life from 1886 on. In 1888 my mother, Edith, was in Washington, where she stayed with her parents, the John W. Fosters, at 1405 Eye Street, then the center of foreign embassies. Her early years of motherhood were extraordinarily demanding:

> February 23—Allen leaves for Detroit [where he was to be pastor of Trumbull Avenue Presbyterian Church].
> February 24—Allen arrives in Detroit. Edith in Washington.
> February 25—Saturday our first child, John Foster Dulles, born. Edith in Washington. Allen in Detroit. Heavy snow [the great blizzard of 1888].
> February 26—Allen assists in dedicating Trumbull Avenue Church, Detroit.

[8]

February 27—Monday Allen leaves Detroit. Edith ill.

February 28—Tuesday Allen reaches Washington. Edith very ill with fever.

February 29—Wednesday. Washington. Edith extremely ill. Doctor came.

March 1—Edith very ill, wandering.

March 4—Edith better, mind clearer. Some hope of recovery.

March 12—News from Edith in Washington fairly encouraging.

April 5—Edith leaves Washington, hearing restored, GLORIOUS. [My father's writing].

Mother was well enough in a few weeks to have Foster's "tintype" taken. Although Mother recovered from the puerperal fever which had threatened her life, by the following year she bore a second child, my sister Margaret. This time it was the baby whose life was threatened, and for months Mother cared for her day and night. Mother wrote, "She [Margaret] weighed only three pounds. The good old-fashioned nurse I had put her in the oven on a pillow, and with great care she began to gain." She told me the doctor said after Margaret was born that she must wait some years before having another child. "It was hard on your father," she said. This was the nearest she came to speaking of sex. (There was no vulcanized rubber to help with birth control in those days.)

Then Allen was born with a clubfoot. A fine surgeon in Philadelphia corrected it, and almost no one ever knew that Allen had had this birth deformity. I came along next, and was a tough little thing. Last was Nataline.

My mother was a woman who believed in action. My father was more contemplative. I can just hear her saying, "Now, Allen, we've got to do something about this." Or then she'd say, "Now, Allen, you've been working on that book for five or six years. Don't you think it's good enough? Let's publish it."

She ran the family. We kind of ran ourselves to a large extent. We were pretty independent. We were brought up from the beginning to be self-reliant and have our own interests.

Both of my parents were basically healthy. All of us liked to eat, to swim, to savor life. My mother was a woman of great vitality. She had lumbago and headaches and so on, but that didn't slow her down.

Henderson was the place where we shared most of our time as a tight family group. Father and Mother both loved the country and we went often to far shores for picnics.

Before we could go swimming on our own, each day Father dunked us deep to be sure we could manage over and under the water. He and Mother were good swimmers and enjoyed sailing and exploring the islands.

My memories of the early days are of fun rather than of discipline. Though Father was strict and practical in training us, he also wanted us to enjoy the good things of life. I remember when he stood us up in a row and taught us to eat oysters with varying degrees of acceptance. He also had us swallow pellets of bread to teach us to control our throat muscles. I can still swallow large pills without water.

I used to go to my father for help. I never felt the cold Calvinist atmosphere some write about. Our faults did not often give us a sense of guilt. When I passed my first decade, I turned to him as I felt a beginning of the tension I was to feel most of my life; the conflict between the desire for full enjoyment and the will to contribute to my fellowmen. The motive in any case included the determination to be *someone*. This urge to be significant, proud, and creative began to propel me toward hard work and a high standard of behavior.

I found it easy to understand my father's teaching and went to him when I felt I had "strayed from the path of righteousness." His punishment often seemed to be justified. My mother's reprimands left a longer hurt. I had enormous respect for her, but this esteem could not overcome a rebellion against her driving spirit which exerted pressure I was not ready to take. Once when she was sick in bed I telephoned for some groceries—she got up, called back, and changed my order from steak to chops. Only after I was married and witnessed her struggle to conquer loneliness and illness did I feel close to her.

Mother had had an extraordinary youth. We used to say "reared at the foot of kings." Because of my grandfather's foreign service, she was brought up in Indiana, Mexico, Russia, Spain, Paris, and Washington. Yet, when she came to live in upstate New York, she fitted well into the town and relished the country living by the lake. Toward the end of her life when she was nearly blind I would help her into the canoe and take her across to White's Bay where we would picnic to her joy, even though she could barely see the islands she loved so well.

A friend who knew mother well said she always seemed taller than her actual five feet five, since she dominated any group. But her sensitive mouth revealed a deep emotional reaction to people and events.

Her sister, Eleanor Foster Lansing, for whom I was named, had the same strong features and dignity of bearing. She was married to Robert Lansing. This handsome, highly qualified lawyer had been Secretary of State under President Woodrow Wilson after William Jennings Bryan resigned in 1915. "Aunt" as we called her, was extraordinarily attractive and central to our family festivities. She was much sought after in Washington, though not everyone knew her keen sense of humor. She once bought a whistle at the five-and-dime store. She put it in her handkerchief when she went to a state dinner. When she blew her nose, she also blew the whistle. A guest was heard to say, "It is a shame Mrs. Lansing is losing her hearing." She was highly amused. She also bought some imitation jewels and wore them—only once—for a real connoisseur of emeralds said, "Most extraordinary jewels, Mrs. Lansing." She retired them after that occasion.

At Henderson I cannot recall her going fishing, and she swam only on the hottest days. It was to "Aunt," during my college years, that I complained about the family dinner conversation. There was, I told her, absolutely no intellectual meaning to anything any member of the family said at dinner. The next day we all received written invitations to dinner at Aunt's. The invitations stated that each of us was to make a speech on the topic assigned by our hostess. Mother was to speak about gardening, Father on religion, Foster on diplomacy, Allen on history, and I was to hold forth on international finance. I can still hear the laughter, and I never complained again about the lack of intellectual conversation at Henderson.

Aunt loved croquet and card games. It was Aunt who gave me an Ackroyd dinghy in 1926 when I got my Ph.D. I went forty miles to Kingston with Will Stevens, who had a motor on his boat by then, and we towed back my boat, *The Scud*. It was a responsive, 14-foot, centerboard sloop, a wooden craft, which was still going strong fifty years later. I sailed her recently.

While Uncle Bert was Secretary of State, the Lansings lived in my grandfather's house on Eighteenth Street in Washington.

[11]

Grandpa had died in 1917; Grandma was dying of cancer. Aunt's main interests were the building of the new YWCA at Seventeenth and K streets and the Home for Incurables—in both of which she played a major part. But she did not confine her entire life to "good works." She was much sought after for diplomatic dinners.

After Uncle Bert's death, Aunt really did lose her hearing. She used to sit on the porch at her cottage in Henderson, gazing out over the water. I can see her on a chaise longue, fading away as if she willed it. She died there at Henderson in 1934.

Just as the family created a sense of stability for us, so the weather taught us resilience. Storms came out of White's Bay, two miles to the west. We watched the deceptive calm, the clouds moving toward us, the whisper of a wind, the first patter followed by white rain torrents preceding the winds. We learned to scoot for shore, if we were still sailing, to pull the boats high.

As the waves came rolling in, we watched them crash on and over the docks, the white caps marching in angry procession where there had been blue serene sheets of calm water. Two or three times a summer we had a "three days blow," the wind hauling from the west into the north, and "fishermen put not forth." We built our fires high on the grate, and went out to swim, struggling in the waves.

I never see a sunset without thinking of the family and of Henderson. I see again and again the congregations of clouds with shafts of sunlight, reflections of the brilliant reds and pinks in graying water. No one had to tell us there was beauty there. It drew us to the dock and to the porches, silencing our noisy chatter.

A pride of lions is defined as a group or family. Some might think of our clan in these terms. Aware of Foster's achievements, as statesman, in his later years when he was Secretary of State, people would ask me what influence he had on my early years. My answer is little or none. I was aware of his greater maturity and his unusual ability. He was more like a second father than like a brother. He was an acknowledged leader in our family activities, swimming twice across the two-mile-wide bay, sailing, fishing, camping. He was prone to practical jokes and staged a panty raid at a house party at Henderson when he was sixteen. He was good at tennis and all kinds of games. At sixteen he had a small catboat; we always called it *No. 5*, the name that was on it when it came to Henderson. He learned to be an adventuresome sailor. I have always thought that sailing—the art of seeking chosen goals in fair and foul weather—can be considered a prototype of the conduct of foreign policy. In any case as children we all learned that we must adjust to changing conditions that we could not control. Foster was a good teacher of sailing and helped us in our struggle with the elements to gain resilience and fortitude. The docking of the sailboat at the pier always roused in me a sense of apprehension as I waited for the shock of wood jarring wood. I relaxed pleasantly when Foster or Allen threw the line around the cleat and made it fast—the men seemed to take the lead.

I do not think we children felt a competitive drive, since we considered we were younger and less experienced. I was neither the best looking nor the smartest of the lot. With my bad eyes, some allergies, and a supersensitive reaction to my frequent frustration in competitive games, I set myself stubbornly to find some aims that could be sought by sheer determination and persistence. What these aims could be I was not sure. It was only when I was in high school and college that I felt a strong need for independence and was to strike out on my own with special interests and a leaning toward more radical ideas than Foster's.

There is only one instance of danger to Foster I remember— brought to my mind by a photograph of him as a boy of twelve being carried like a bundle of bones from our house in Watertown, when he was recovering from typhoid. I have a more personal memory of waiting outside the sickroom door when he was shivering and moaning after he had been given an ice bath to get his fever down.

Margaret came down with typhoid soon after Foster. The disease was said to come from the contamination of the Black River, which powered Watertown's mills. She came out of the sickroom bald as a billiard ball, but her hair soon came back in lovely curls. These I envied as Nellie, our faithful housekeeper, pulled unmercifully at my unruly braids. Nataline was subjected to a curling process by Nellie with her blond silky locks wrapped around a polished wooden stick. Margaret was my father's favorite and this seemed to me inevitable. She was very pretty and appealing, as well as intelligent.

I remember vaguely that Foster was attracted to a pretty girl who lived across the street. We teased him about her. She later became an aviator—if my recollection is correct. We all sang, "Come, Josephine, in my flying machine...," and very loudly another popular song, "Yip I Addie...I eh, I eh..."

Foster and Mother played a game calling for ingenuity and

causing surprise after one or the other had forgotten the last maneuver. The challenge was the exchange of a fancy engraved invitation which went back and forth for many years. Foster would send it to Mother in a box of flowers or disguised as a telegram and she would send it back fixed as a legal brief or in a magazine. This attempt to "catch each other out" went on for about twenty years. I would like to find this invitation now.

Margaret and Foster were pals and did many things together. I remember that in 1902 or 1903 while we were still in Watertown she was a convincing Portia opposite Foster as Shylock. He had a green, frayed raffia beard taken from a flower pot. Allen, often called "Allie," was the Prince of Morocco, I was Nerissa, and Nataline also had a speaking part as a messenger. This performance in our living room was one of my last vivid memories before we moved to Auburn.

Margaret was gentle and intelligent with a good literary sense. I think she knew I was sometimes lonely as Mother became increasingly busy with community work. She represented a transitional period between the very circumspect young generation and the freer oncoming boys and girls experimenting and venturing into a world often referred to as "flaming youth." The oncoming generation was breaking with tradition.

Later when Margaret became engaged to Deane Edwards and Foster married Janet Avery at the early age of twenty-one, their lives diverged. But there were still many family gatherings in upstate New York over the years and their children and grandchildren still come back to Henderson.

After Foster graduated from Princeton in 1908, he was home only for brief visits. Law, diplomacy, and his own family life with a young bride and infant children demanded the full measure of his energy. He seemed doubtful at times as to how his three sisters would manage their lives but gradually came to realize that they were capable of taking care of themselves. As I grew up I did not expect any advice or assistance. Thus by the time I was ready for college I was going my own way. We met occasionally for family celebrations and often at Henderson for summer vacations. Foster's influence was felt but only in a general way and did not affect my day-to-day decisions. By 1912 his sisters and his brother, Allen, were on their own.

Allen and Foster went cruising together in the open boat several summers. Allen also went with Father and Foster on a climbing expedition in Switzerland. I think he was under Foster's shadow until after college when he went to India to teach. He followed Foster around with great admiration and joined him whenever possible in fishing, sailing, tennis, and other games. The fact that when he was eight years old he wrote *The Boer War*— a slim but interesting book which my grandfather published—was notable. The proceeds at fifty cents a copy came to more than two thousand dollars. This remarkable achievement was reported in *The New York Times* and elsewhere but not much talked about in the family.

Allen was an important figure in my life. He helped me with various land and water ventures. He even tutored me in ancient history when I began to consider college entrance examinations. I found him companionable and saw some of the charm for which he was well known in later years. Ours was a fluctuating relationship. It ranged all the way from dislike and anger to a passionate desire for approval. My changing moods and his strong reactions to them continued throughout our lives and added pain and pleasure. His charm was irresistible and his intensity of rage was occasionally overwhelming, though not many people saw his tougher side. I know that there were months in our later years when I stayed out of his orbit to avoid the stress and furor that he stirred in me. Once he stormed when I parked too close to the door, another time he accused me of "blowing the cover" of one of his CIA agents—I didn't. His ability and his skill in handling people were real to me over the years.

He shared my interest in distant lands, as did the others. When I was in college he was in India, teaching in Allahabad. He came home by way of China. I did not visit China until 1979.

Nataline, more than two years my junior, seemed very young in those days. She was less belligerent than I and was accepted soon, as I remember it, into our childhood "clubs" and "secret societies." As we both grew older she seemed to me more of an age.

I was fortunate not only in my brothers and sisters but in the ancestors I chose. They were strong and purposeful.

My great-great-grandfathers, George Foster on one side and Joseph Dulles on the other, emigrated to the United States in the early nineteenth century—Joseph from Dublin, Ireland, to Holland hidden in a large butter churn to escape the persecution of Protestants. From there he went to Charleston, South Carolina. I think I was extraordinarily lucky— not only to have adventuresome forebears on the Dulles and the Foster sides, but also to have vivid memories of many of them. Some of Father's family, particularly Uncle Joe, Uncle Heatly, and Uncle Will, the three I knew best, sometimes joined us at Henderson. They and the three other of Father's brothers and two sisters were born in India, where John W. Dulles was a missionary in Madras in the first half of the nineteenth century. He and his wife took a sailing ship from Philadelphia on a six-month voyage that was full of raging waves and peril. They stayed in India until after 1850. I never knew them but their influence remained.

There are many pictures filed in my mind, mental snapshots of different festivities, family reunions, Christmas trees, birthday cakes, and Fourth of July roman candles splendid against the dark sky. If time tends to blur the dates and even the faces, the general color, glow, and sound of jollification remains and can be recaptured.

There were few episodes that I remember from my early years, although many memories flow through my mind like bits from a colored movie. One that still makes me tremble is the recollection of clinging to the limb of the hemlock tree that I had climbed and from which I saw no way to get down. Father came when I called and begged me to drop into his arms. For a considerable time I was too scared, and then, exhausted by my fears, I finally jumped and found his rescue was as good as his promise.

Another episode that I remember was when Allen, Nataline, and I were on the dock throwing stones to see who could throw the farthest. Nataline, aged five, figured that the bigger the stone the farther it would go and brought a large rock to the dock. When she tried to throw it, she couldn't let go so she fell in the water. Nellie and Mother came to our frantic calls. Mother ran out on the dock and jumped. She swam after the little pink child floating calmly out in the lake, buoyed up by the air in her clothing, and unaware of peril.

I remember, too, when my grandmother stood on the porch at Underbluff, wringing her hands. Foster and Margaret were out in the sailboat in a squall. Though she did not know much about sailing, she knew something was wrong as the boat heeled sharply. "They'll drown," she cried. Foster, too, knew it was an emergency and cut the sheet caught in a tangle and, quick to hold the short end, controlled the sail and brought the boat safely to the dock.

I recall some of the pain as well as the joys of childhood. The punishment for wrongdoing when I was six or seven was often an order banishing me to my father's study. I would lie on the couch and cry into an embroidered pillow that somehow seemed comforting. The green pillow, embroidered by a maiden aunt—a phenomenon that has almost vanished—had a free-swinging lady with golf club over her shoulder, and a long flowing skirt, almost hiding the golf ball on a lush green sward.

The nature of my sins is not clear in my mind. Disobedience, impertinence, and quarreling with my brothers and sisters are the only offenses I can recall, but there may have been other and worse breaches of the family code. There was an occasional spanking with the hairbrush.

When my father wanted to tell me that I had done something wrong, he would sit in the study and explain to me what was good and bad. He would tell me why something was wrong, and sometimes he would pray. I realized he cared a good deal about my understanding.

Naturally, when my father tried to explain to me, I tried to explain to him. We'd have a little Bible reading. Prayer put a burden on me. I had to please not only my parents but the Lord as well.

My problems were partly associated with the fact that I had worn glasses since I was six years old. This was unusual in those days. They were thick and jumped on my nose when I played with the boys. A child's face is not shaped right for glasses. I joined the others in baseball, football, duck on the rock, prisoners' base, and other sports, but my frustration was profound. It was reflected in nightmares of groping, tripping, falling.

In addition to this problem my hair was a constant drawback. It was long, black, unattractive. It delayed me in getting out and about in the morning. I had for a time a sense of impending doom that my handicaps would make my life continually difficult. I saw my younger sister, with her quiet ways and blond hair, as something of a millstone, for I was supposed to take her along with me. I often wished to strike out alone.

There were also times when I despaired of my future, and considered that my efforts were hopeless. One bitter occasion was when I took a knife from the kitchen and climbed the bluff over the lake at Henderson Harbor. Before I prepared to use it, I looked out over the wide stretch of blue water toward the unseen Canada forty miles away and in wondering about this great expanse of beauty, forgot the cruel fate that might await me in coming years. I decided to go quietly down the path to the cottage. Many children have climbed this path, only to return to face what life brings.

When I was seven I had a special present on my birthday. It was a shiny red bicycle. I got on it at once assuming I could do what the other children did and started down the walk. I fell immediately in a sad bundle of surprise and despair. I got on the bicycle and tried again, thinking it must be easy as so many children could ride. I fell time and again. For several days I kept at it. By the third I thought I was completely defeated but I tried again and in some miraculous way I kept my balance. The triumph was a delight. I wondered if other people had this same difficulty and disappointment before they had the fun.

In the first years of the century the boys and girls had long summer vacations, with no thought of working for pay. Even their parents took several months off most years, and the time between June and September was for recreation.

Most of the time we were more interested in external conditions than in our inner thoughts. It was a world that limited introspection, took us out of ourselves. Our activities were governed in large measure by wind and wave.

Sailing, swimming, fishing, picnicking were all better when there was a mild west wind. The usual calm at night and morning made the glowing colors brighter. The north wind was an exciting challenge and the south wind somewhat treacherous. These changing factors were highly objective and not the result of whim or mood. We respected them.

When we whittled small boats and set a square paper sail on them, we hoped they would go far to the outer shores. We sat on the dock dangling our feet in the water and watched them disappear. We watched for signs of storm in the blue of skies that we were later to cross in high-flying jets from the south to Montreal and Europe. When we went to the islands we could lie on flat rocks sunbathing—discarding long skirts, overalls, and civilized clothing in the warm sun. There was, in spite of old-time convention, a large degree of freedom.

[18]

The fact that we were minister's children did not lead to our behaving in a manner different from other children on the shore or in Watertown. Father and Mother were like their neighbors in their professional and in their social lives. The religious services held on the lawn or on the porch were considered pleasant occasions which other families shared. I thought it important to read the Bible and when I had finished considered one stage of my growing up had been accomplished. I skipped nothing—not even the begats. I took it seriously and enjoyed some of it. I did not think it told the literal truth. Perhaps when I was a small child I may have seemed pious to some, but I was also a regular in the community games. If we were considered to be different, I was not conscious of it. Our active sportsmanship probably helped to keep us in step with the other children.

I never feared hell and I thought heaven would be like Henderson but more so. Pink clouds would be comfortable to sit on, and pleasant people would drift by. I was sure I would go to heaven because my father showed me what I should do and said I was improving. Meanwhile, for many weeks in the year, I had Henderson.

Life in Watertown was agreeable but was more serious than in the country. The older children were in public school. Nataline and I went to Miss Rogers' Kindergarten and then briefly to Miss Porter's School. I was in a constant state of fear and embarrassment at kindergarten. Why, I do not know. But I recall that I could not grasp the significance of drop the handkerchief, which we played daily. The *where*, *when*, and *why* one *did* drop it completely baffled me. Our teacher never explained and I never dared ask.

Sunday in Watertown for a minister's family followed a regular pattern. We would all be scrubbed and brushed, given Bibles, take some of our allowance for the collection, and go to the First Presbyterian Church on the corner of Mullin and Washington streets. It stands still in its dignity with its sharp spire against blue skies and gray, a beacon for weddings, baptisms, and funeral services.

Our family pew was about the fourth from the front on the right aisle. We knew the people around us and bowed quietly when we came in, only occasionally speaking in a low voice. My mother sat on the end and with her fine contralto voice seemed to lead the singing but we all joined in—knowing many of the hymns by heart and watching the lovely tall soprano, Bessie Camp, in the choir. The church was usually jeweled with red, blue, and green flecks of sunshine pouring through the stained-glass windows.

Since Father believed no souls were saved after the first twenty minutes of the sermon, we picked up the theme before we were tired or restless. When we left the church, there were brief remarks exchanged with our neighbors but there was no coffee hour. We hurried home to enjoy the rite of ice cream making and licking the dasher and also the funny papers, which I think were a part of the *Journal American*—Little Nemo, Foxy Grandpa, and Buster Brown. The dinner was almost always roast chicken, mashed potatoes, sometimes spinach, and *always* ice cream with chocolate or maple sauce. The conversation was often related to the sermon and the rest of the day was the family's and usually ended with Bible games and reading. We never felt any hypocrisy in the religious note introduced into our reading and games. It all seemed natural, and the good food, including the supper we children helped prepare—usually corn pudding, veal loaf, thin bread and butter, and cocoa and cake—added to our sense of satisfaction and security. The repetition of menu and activities was not boring but made us feel always at home. Sunday evenings, summer and winter, we sang hymns, and the words and music burned deep into my consciousness. The emotion of those evenings was so poignant that even now I cannot accept easily the surge of nostalgia, the longing for those love-filled moments with my family. It contributed to my longing to get away and yet it brought me back to early values.

Winter in the northland was amazingly white, unpolluted by automobiles. We found the sparkling snow brilliant where the boys shoveled large piles to clear the walks. I sucked the icicles and also my red mittens, which hung from a string in the sleeves of my baggy blue suit. I hoped that my mother and Nellie would not know my long underpants were wet from melting snow and make me come in and change before the last hour of daylight slid away.

We were the first in the area to know about skiing. Allie's violin teacher from Norway explained the sport. Father made us skis out of barrel staves, before we could buy long ones at Spaulding's, the reigning sport shop of the time. Father also had a slide built from the upper porch into the backyard and up over the back fence. This attracted our friends for evening fun, and after a long day we found the cocoa ready in the kitchen to warm us to bed. We were glad we lived in the snow belt where igloos in the backyard often lasted for weeks and the fire in the grate glowed warm. This was Watertown in those days.

# 2

## AUBURN, A NEW HOME, 1904

In 1904 when we moved to Auburn my known world disappeared and new and awesome problems overwhelmed me. The fact that the family pulled up its strong roots of seventeen years in Watertown and journeyed seventy surface miles and seven thousand light-years away was for me a shattering experience.

It was, as my mother wrote, "a great wrench to leave Watertown... where four of our children had been born [Foster was born in Washington].... Then too, it meant leaving my sister [Eleanor Lansing], with all her friends."

My mother was forty-one years old, with five young children. Father, at fifty-two, teaching theism and apologetics, faced new demands on his time and mental resources. Mother told me later that she was really unhappy for the first three years in Auburn, although both she and Father had a nucleus of friends there. Her special position in Watertown, as the wife of the leading minister, had disappeared for a time.

Auburn was more of a small city than a large town. It was known for its state prison and its theological seminary. Its broad elm-shaded streets seemed to give it dignity—the town had shape and character. It seemed to me more sophisticated than Watertown. The late Samuel Hopkins Adams, who lived there, wrote of the charms and leisurely pace of the region around the Erie Canal. A number of its citizens became national figures.

This place was an important station on the underground railroad for escaping blacks under the guidance of the well-known Harriet Tubman. From here William Seward went to Washington to serve as Secretary of State and in 1867 to purchase Alaska for $7.2 million. Thomas Mott Osborne went into Sing Sing penitentiary as an inmate to become the leader of the prison reform movement. The Stewarts, the Seymours, the Woodruffs, the Averys, the Hoyts, the Gilchrists, and other fine families played an interesting role in the life of the community.

Mother eventually was taken into the literary club, the Fortnightly. Then in 1911 the *grande dame* of "society," Mrs. D. M. Osborne, sensing mother's ability, asked her to head the Women's Educational and Industrial Union. This institution had dormitories, classes, sports, and a summer camp, mainly for women working in factories. Mother became the leader of social work in the city.

Father had found us a spacious brick house on South Street, built by an architect who, I was told, because of financial difficulties, had to sell it. Foster and Margaret were away a good deal, Foster in college, Margaret soon to enter Bryn Mawr. I was at home with Allen and Nataline. The large yard and barn became centers for many of the young people after we had broken the ice that we found as outsiders from the north. The children's groups were clubs and "secret societies" which could only be joined after meeting tests of daring and passing the standards of the leading children. Without them one was isolated. Gradually our friendships developed.

The year 1904 was an election year, and Teddy Roosevelt swept in with a flourish. He aroused in Americans for the first time the realization that resources might run out and was an early fighter for conservation. I worried alone at night as to what we would do when coal was exhausted and all the trees had been cut down.

But these problems were superseded by more personal ones, the typical problems of a nine-year-old who is not only moved geographically from familiar surroundings but also moving away from the myths of childhood into the realities of a world outside the family.

My new troubles centered on school.

It was not until November 14 that my parents entered me in school. I was in the third grade, late, bewildered, and faltering in my efforts to cope with the strange, inhospitable public school on James Street. Physically, I had problems. I went into the halls and lost myself, unable to find the right door. I strained to see the writing on the blackboard, clear to everyone else, but invisible to me. My eyes were the main source of trouble, but there must have been others, because my mother's diary states I fell and hit my head, and I was operated for adenoids about two weeks after I started classes.

The third grade was taught by a stern, but able, teacher—Miss Rosenbloom. I admired her and feared her. Apparently I upset the inkwell, implanted in my desk, without knowing it. Miss Rosenbloom accused me of lying. This idea was completely shocking to me. No decent person ever lied.

Alone in my room at night, with the covers pulled over my head, I cried my heart out. After more than a week of this, my parents discovered my solitary misery and asked me about it. Enough of the story came out to prompt them to move me, along with Nataline, to Miss Robinson's, a small private school a block from home. The new school was not especially good, but at least the agonies of James Street School were ended. Later I returned to public school at the high school level and enjoyed it.

Since I was somewhat bewildered by the new surroundings, I sought a private retreat. The box in which the upright piano had been shipped was a favorite hiding place for me. I could lift the lid a crack to watch my older brothers and sister hunt for me, safe for a time at least, while they called me to supper or bed.

Along with the piano box in which I had hidden, there were other large boxes left from our move to Auburn and from them Allen, Nataline, and I built a two-decker house in the branches of a huge apple tree. It was a child's world into which adults would not intrude. And in it I knew only joy. There I took books of adventure and travel—to China, Tibet, Africa, the North Pole—the more remote the places, the more intense the excitement. It was more than fifty years before I flew around the world and saw the rivers, forests, and villages of my childhood reading. But when I reached Africa, I knew what a paramount chief with green face mask should look like, and he did.

At our new home I usually slept on a small porch outside my parents' bedroom. In the mornings, the steamer rugs piled high were frosted with snow, but I remained snug and warm until the inevitable moment when I crawled out, took the cold bath, and dressed for breakfast. At other times I slept in a south bedroom on the third floor—my father spent much of his time in a study adjoining it. He often worked through the night, going to bed at four, for a few hours' sleep. This was a room I loved, for when I opened my eyes in the morning, it was flooded with sunlight.

Mother recognized that I had problems adjusting to Auburn life. She decided that dancing school would help, so with somewhat youthful dresses and an evening wrap of heavy white loden cloth, which I hated, I went down to the banquet hall on Genesee Street to struggle with my feet and the larger feet of the equally awkward boys of the neighborhood.

My one close friend for several years in a pleasant group was

[24]

Mary Van Sickle—later Mary Waite. We used to go canoeing, skiing, and exploring together.

In about 1910 or '11 the girls in my special group secretly rented a room in a business block with their combined allowances and went there to smoke. Fortunately, or perhaps unfortunately, I was not included. I think they feared my conscience. This was one of the few times being a minister's child made a difference. When their strange hideout was discovered, they were sent away to various boarding schools, and my social life—just burgeoning—was shattered.

Father probably was stimulated by the move to Auburn, where he had many friends in the Seminary. He was a man of his time—but ahead of it. He was twice nearly expelled from the Presbyterian Church; once for performing a marriage for a divorced woman, and once for questioning the Virgin Birth. To the less fortunate he was merciful. He gave his overcoat to a shivering man in the street, continuing home in the cold. It seemed a simple, Christian solution to him for a fellowman's problem. He could get another coat— even on his meager salary, and with five children to support. Father told us not to put pennies in the collection plate. "You can be more generous in your charities," he said.

When a servant girl in our house was being courted by a farm hand who climbed in the window in the dark of night, Father dealt with the problem in a manner surprisingly sophisticated for the times. He recognized her charm and basic innocence, and without scolding or lecturing, he put her in the car and took her home to her parents.

Together, Edith and Allen ran the household, safeguarded finances, earned money, planned the future of their five progeny, accepting without question their varied responsibilities.

My father earned $3,500 a year in 1905 and 1906. Even in those days that was not enough to support five children without stretching it thin. In addition to his teaching when he was in Auburn he moonlighted by preaching and then took over the Second Presbyterian Church. My grandfather Foster was paid a handsome fee by the government of China in 1895. This made it possible later to give some money to my mother in addition to helping with the cost of our education. I am still somewhat puzzled as to how we managed and enjoyed so many advantages.

Children are often conscious of the money problems, though

these are seldom discussed openly with them. There were depressions in 1903 and 1907 and considerable talk about mortgage foreclosures. Some of the stories I was told were of families being thrown out of their houses because of their inability to pay. I imagined our having to leave our house and looking for a cheaper, smaller house. Such worries now seem incompatible with the amount of traveling we did, but they were real to me at the time. I heard my parents talking of borrowing from the bank.

Their diary tells of cooks coming and going. It was clearly expected that we would have two servants, often newly arrived girls from Ireland. We also had Nellie, who took care of Nataline and me. She was with us for twenty-five years and was like a member of the family, though she did not eat in the dining room with us.

The contrast between my early life and that of my late husband, David Blondheim, in the 1900s in Baltimore, indicates that by most standards we were "well off," the democratic euphemism for rich. David told me of being acutely hungry and the family worries about whether they could get bread. He did odd jobs to earn small amounts to help his family.

Meanwhile in Auburn we had a Scottish engineer, unemployed because he could not stay away from liquor, living in the barn, and other somewhat varied dependents getting food, clothing, and sometimes shelter from us.

Life in those years was expanding. We knew professors and workers and citizens all over town. We went about a mile to school on foot or on our bicycles. We found the Auburn Academic High School extraordinary in its faculty and teaching. Latin, algebra, geometry, and English were subjects that were made interesting. We all benefited from this opportunity.

Foster went from Watertown to Princeton University. He was writing his prize-winning essay in philosophy. One day he quoted William James to me. I was crying from disappointment at the age of twelve, because I had failed to get a jeweled hat pin I had saved my allowance for. "You are unhappy because you cry," he said, "not crying because you are unhappy." I was amused and laughed at his attention. This was about the time when he went with my grandfather to the Second Hague Peace Conference. He had there his first diplomatic accomplishment. He broke the protocol deadlock over who should call on whom first. He took cards from all the delegations and left them on each delegation on the same afternoon. No one knew which was first. He was nineteen years old and we felt impressed with his first mission abroad in 1907.

The houses on South Street have changed in the past decades. Business has crept up the road. The streets and gardens, where we spent our late afternoons and at dusk played prisoners' base and red rover are now filled with traffic and parking lots, even though the suburbs are still peaceful.

There must have been many sunny days in my youth, for I don't remember rain. But there was rain, it seemed to me, often on Memorial Day when the lilacs were in bloom. Their springtime fragrance bathed the porch where I would lie in the swing with a book and think solemn, sweet, and melancholy thoughts. I don't know whether there were five or six such days or only one when I happened to sense the sadness of life and breathe this gentle fragrance, wondering about myself and the world—perhaps it was just one time. Perhaps that was the year I was growing old and ceased to be a child.

# 3

# A WIDER VIEW—WASHINGTON AND PARIS

In 1908 Foster was graduated from Princeton University as valedic-torian and awarded a philosophy prize of six hundred dollars—a scholarship to study with Professor Henri Bergson at the Sorbonne in Paris. It was decided that Mother, Margaret, and Allen would also go to Paris. There was some question about Nataline, who was ten. Our parents feared she would miss Mother too much. Nataline told me years later that she cried, not because she thought they wouldn't take her to Paris, but because she was afraid they *would*. She was dismayed at the prospect of being parted from Nellie. Nellie didn't like me, but she was devoted to Nataline, who returned her affection.

But Nataline was taken and was, for a time, very unhappy without the faithful nurse, who had curled her hair, dressed her, fed her, and put her to bed for more than eight years.

Although I did not protest being left behind, I secretly felt that I was getting the short end of the stick. I was left with my Grandmother and Grandfather Foster in Washington in their house on Eighteenth Street, near Massachusetts Avenue.

I had been to visit my grandparents many times. We used to take a train to New York. Then we went on the ferry to New Jersey. From there we took another train to Washington. I have a succession of memories from way back—of Presidents, ambassadors, and officials, young and old. These memories cover eighty years. Some are antique and shadowy, some vivid and clear.

Often I had dinner with the grown-ups even when there were a few guests, though not of course when there was a formal party. I was usually quiet, listening fascinated to the conversation that was about the Washington world and foreign lands. One evening I remember, however, I broke with my tradition. There was a pause in the conversation and I said in a loud voice, "Theodore Roosevelt has very large teeth." My grandfather was not pleased. He sent me upstairs without my supper.

Grandmother Foster held regular "at homes," afternoon teas, when she received senators, cabinet members, and callers from many embassies. Many of these foreign friends she had known when my grandfather represented the United Satates in Mexico City, St. Petersburg, and Madrid. Grandmother Foster held the rank of cabinet minister's wife, and this meant, in the Washington of early 1900s, that she should receive callers one afternoon a week. She entertained a divorcée from Detroit whose husband was high in the new government at a time when the leaders of social Washington had not yet decided how to treat her.

Just after we left the North for Washington I learned of the Wright Brothers' record-breaking flights at Fort Myer. I was very enthusiastic about the future of flying. My grandparents said I could go out in the car to see the flight. However, we learned on September 17, as I was preparing to go, that Orville had crashed after three or four minutes in the air and his passenger, Lieutenant Thomas E. Selfridge, had suffered fatal injuries. They did not want me to see the bloodstained wreckage. They let me go the next day and I gathered grass from the site of the accident, a reminder that I kept for ten years.

In the dusk of evening, I would sit in the bay window of my fourth-floor room, and watch the lamplighter, and the carriages going to the British and Austro-Hungarian embassies on Connecticut Avenue, just opposite. In the twilight, I enjoyed a sweet melancholy, enhanced by the diversion of the carriages with their fine horses, liveried footmen, and elegant passengers.

The house, a four-story red brick, had a small half-circle drive off the street. At the entrance there was a billiard room on the left, a cloakroom on the right, and behind them, Madison's room. Madison was the butler and a devoted helper. He later worked for me occasionally in Washington. In 1949, when he was about ninety years old, Irene, my cook, asked him, "Madison, what do you do with all your money?"

He replied, "Spend it all on women."

Once I went with a friend Rachel Wood to see Madison's room in Foggy Bottom, the misty housing area near the future State Department. He had a silver punch bowl the Prince of Wales had given to my grandfather and autographed pictures of royalty. The room was filled with trophies.

The winter of 1908 and 1909 at Grandmother's, I'd go into the butler's pantry to see what Madison was doing and he would invariably say, "Lyrascatchamedlas." I never did understand exactly what he was saying, but I knew it meant I was to keep my nose out of his business.

But if Madison was somewhat short in his joking with me, Mammy, the black maid, was my dearest adviser, friend, and substitute mother. Mammy would let me manicure her fingernails. It must have been very painful, and why I wanted to do it, I don't know. I loved her very much, and perhaps this was my way of showing affection. That winter and spring I had Mammy mostly to myself. She had a room on the fourth floor, behind the door leading to the servants' quarters. It was there she explained to me what had happened when I started to menstruate.

"It isn't fair!" I said.

"Men have problems, too," was her reply.

I was mystified, but did not press the point. She was kind, but firm, and volunteered no more information than she wished me to have.

It was to Mammy I had fled during Dora Clover's birthday party. A distant cousin of Clover Todd (who was to marry Allen in 1920), Dora was an interesting girl. I liked her. But I was reluctant to go to her house on R and Eighteenth streets. I didn't know her friends. I had less social poise than Dora's dancing school pals. In an agony of shyness, I went to the kitchen, where the servants who had accompanied the guests were having a fine gossip. Mammy kept me with her in the kitchen until the carriage came to take us home.

From the house on Eighteenth Street, I roller-skated to Eleventh Street, where I went to Mount Vernon Seminary, and came to know well and to like a charming girl from the Japanese Imperial household. Now Mount Vernon is a woman's college, occupying a large campus off Foxhall Road in Northwest Washington. On my eightieth birthday, June 1, 1975, the occasion of the college's one hundredth anniversary, Mount Vernon awarded me an honorary degree—doctor of humane letters. It was a pity I couldn't don my roller skates for the journey there, but Washington is hilly, and I had a touch of the gout.

I was delighted when my father, who had accompanied Mother and the other children to Paris, returned and visited me from Auburn. I recall the Easter—not so much for its religious significance as for a lovely Italian pink straw hat.

Father told me he was taking me abroad in June on the S.S. *Rotterdam*. In ecstatic anticipation, I pored over the ship's plan, the queer little rectangles of cabins, stairs, and dining salons, with circles to represent the tables. What a miracle of a boat! Our cabin was marked in red.

The crossing was all I had hoped. I organized a group of youngsters and we ran the decks, raiding the trays of cookies, and drinking buckets of lemonade. There were no swimming pools on ships in 1909. We avoided harassing the passengers, but otherwise exploited the opportunities of ocean travel to the full. Father made no rules but that I must be in bed by 10:30.

Paris was magic. I adored every gargoyle of Notre Dame, climbing into the towers and throwing down cherry pits on innocent tourists. The Luxembourg Gardens, where I rolled a hoop, were delightful—gay with many children. Never will anyplace on this globe or in outer space be so glorious as Paris was to me.

We all returned together to America in the summer, and my serious education began in Auburn High School.

At fourteen I had vague and changing ambitions. Religion played a part and the urge to help someone predominated. I had no secure idea of my mental capacity. Exposure to chess, logic, and history did not persuade me I should be a student, much less a scholar. Some guiding motive came in September of 1909.

We were preparing for a fine celebration of the golden wedding anniversary of my Grandmother and Grandfather Foster. Everyone was to contribute in some way. I crossed the lawn on a beautiful day when the distinguished jurist Dr. James Brown Scott stopped me.

"Have you written a poem for your grandparents?" he asked.

"Here it is. It's short," I said.

He took the paper and read it slowly.

"You are going to be a writer," he said. "These are beautiful words."

That episode and that comment by a learned international lawyer stayed with me for more than seventy years. The incident seems to me to indicate the way in which older people can and often do give encouragement to the young, encouragement that stays with them through hard times and uncertainty.

[31]

When I was growing up, my social life, upset by the smoking episode that disbursed my group of friends, was further demolished when my one remaining close friend, Mary Van Sickle, fell in love.

Margaret seemed to me much older and had a different social life. She had a different set of friends. Nataline and I realized she had many suitors and we found them attractive; we had no strong preferences. It was not until after she was ill and left Bryn Mawr without completing the course that she announced her engagement to Deane Edwards. He was a student at the Seminary and a remarkably dedicated man. He was a descendant, I was told, of Jonathan Edwards, a distinguished clergyman. His family came from St. Paul-Minneapolis. We all liked Deane and respected him for strong convictions and kindly ways. He was also a good outdoorsman and sailor. When the war came, he enlisted as chaplain in the Army. The separation was a strain on Margaret but I don't think he was sent overseas. They were married in 1913. Their first child, Robert, was born in Auburn early in wartime.

Margaret was quick to realize that I should go away to school. She realized, although I think she never had the same problem, that I was pulling at the leash and that the great ability of my mother led to a sense of frustration in me, by the very fact that she was so strong of mind and will. I was, as many young people, seeking a separate identity and tended to contest the ideas of patterns of living laid down by the family, even though this difference was disturbing to me because of my devotion.

The choice of the small New England school Wykeham Rise was a good one. The Connecticut countryside was new to me and yet had the same attraction for me as Henderson Harbor. The principal, Fanny Davies, was an independent soul. She let the older girls call on her after lights-out, and took us down to the kitchen where we ate crackers and apples and drank milk.

Discipline was enforced by a point system, demerits being added up against the violator of rules, but the very mathematical nature of the score lightened the sense of guilt, and the end result was considerable mental freedom.

Classes were small and ranked with skiing and basketball in importance. I learned to get on with people from the South and West, and found the atmosphere healthy and invigorating. The inevitable examinations found me in fine fettle—with a sporting chance of getting into college. In fact, I won the First New England

[32]

Scholarship, an award of which I had never heard until the day the postman in Auburn gave me an envelope from Bryn Mawr College, with a check.

Looking now to the later years of my childhood I realize that one of the first times that I stood completely on my own feet and gained prestige was when I was sent with a friend, at the age of fifteen, to a summer camp in Maine. Here my swimming ability, particularly underwater swimming, my camping skills, and my zest for climbing, as well as my acceptable ability in competitive sports, gained me an award for outstanding contribution to the life of the group. The camp, near Camden, Maine, was run by Dr. Susan Kingsbury, who, some eight years later, was to offer me a fellowship at Bryn Mawr College. What I had won was more than a prize, it was the ability to compete with other girls away from home and completely on my own. There is no doubt that this success in the dim past fired my ambition and made me secretly aim for future awards. I found this experience in a new world was something that opened new prospects. I thought of being a missionary, giving solace and medical help to the "heathen," and I was inordinately curious about other people's business.

From schooling in 1913 I moved on to education.

# 4

# THE HALLS OF GRANITE—BRYN MAWR

In September of 1913 my father took me by sleeping car to Philadelphia and on to Bryn Mawr College. For this protective act he gave as an excuse his desire to visit his younger brother, Heatly Dulles, in Heatly's recently built Norman stone house, two or three miles from the college. I brought with me a small steamer trunk, a knapsack, a suitcase, and my sister Margaret's gaily decorated college songbook, one of my most treasured possessions.

The wrench of leaving the family again and being in a much more demanding and strange world than boarding school was made easy because a ready-made friendship awaited me. Living in a room near mine in Rockefeller Hall was Elizabeth Emerson. Her sister Helen and my sister Margaret were college classmates. For Elizabeth and me there was instant friendship. My first day at college was not a lonely one. I thought my tiny bedroom and small study delightful, and from the first day, loved to sit on the window seat and look through leaded windows at the ivy-covered buildings and tree-shaded vistas leading up to Taylor Tower.

The year 1913 marked the first of my associations, as student or teacher, with nine colleges and universities. I have emerged from my studies with eleven degrees—some honorary—and deep gratitude for the richness of the educational fare I enjoyed. However, at Bryn Mawr there began the continuing battle with the system older people devised, a battle not completely recognized, but leading me to some eccentricities in my work. Always there was challenge, always interest and a will to increase my capacity to face difficulties.

In college it was possible to sidestep some of the difficulties young people face. I found pleasant ways of making friends and wasting time, ways that militated against high marks. But they did not keep me out of the beloved library. As a child I found my father's library at the top of the Auburn house, with its twenty-foot table, books on all sides, and three bay window desks, was a place steeped in scholarship. He let me sit there while he worked at one or another of the desks. I first recognized the excitement of the quest for knowledge there. It prepared me for the book world of Bryn Mawr. In the library I watched the changing shadows and shafts of sunlight moving through the high Gothic windows, bringing shifting images as the light moved across high beams, blue star-studded ceiling, and gray walls. I read and I dreamed.

It is in the light of varied and contrasting recollections I now think of Bryn Mawr. M. Carey Thomas, the president when I entered, was a strong-willed, intelligent woman. She was the kind of creative person I admired, but she had an arrogance I had to fight. Bryn Mawr of my day was what she willed it to be.

Miss Thomas, struggling against heavy odds, had come to the conclusion that at most universities and among academic leaders, education for women was not considered important—few colleges would admit them. A Baltimore girl, she did her undergraduate studies at Cornell University. Then she went to Germany to study at Leipzig and on to the almost impossible achievement of a doctoral degree, *summa cum laude*, at Zurich in 1882.

Meanwhile, a gift of approximately $1 million from Joseph Wright Taylor had led to plans for a college at Bryn Mawr, Pennsylvania. Dr. Taylor left his fortune "to found an institution for the advanced education of our young female friends." The plans were general, and when Miss Thomas came along, she energetically shaped the course of the new college and set its standards. As dean and professor of English, and later as president, she never ceased in her struggle to make Bryn Mawr superior to all other colleges.

This assertive, snobbish woman thought the issue of entrance requirements a major one in her efforts to make Bryn Mawr *the best*. She had not set the original requirements and was stung by the criticism that they were too low. She heard this comment at a number of colleges, at Vassar, Smith, Wellesley, Radcliffe, and others, all of which she visited. She was only twenty-seven years old, but she persuaded the Board of Trustees to raise the entrance requirements. The exams were made much more difficult.

While high standards of scholarship always concerned her, so did practical details of study and living. She took a flexible tape with her to Oxford University in England, to measure the cloisters there. These measurements would determine the proportions of Bryn Mawr's library and cloister, with quiet walks and gray stone arches, images loved and cherished by many students over the years. She was adamant against requiring menial work by students. This work she claimed, would divert them from their important studies. She told us that at Mount Holyoke a student working in the kitchen had fallen into the boiling oatmeal kettle. She took care that we were well housed and fed. Tradition was established early. The atmosphere of Bryn Mawr today, both good and bad, can be traced back to this remarkable woman's painstaking work over forty years.

Bryn Mawr was needed in those years. Miss Thomas' experiences at Cornell, at Johns Hopkins, and abroad led her to understand the limitations frequently placed on advanced work for women. She was determined to further the development of women's education in such a way as to overcome the obstacles they found in men's institutions. She wanted to go beyond what was currently considered suitable. She was the first to establish graduate courses in a woman's college, and her faculty included such distinguished scholars as Paul Shorey, Woodrow Wilson, Charlotte Angas Scott, and Edmund B. Wilson. Even those who resented her pride and her disdain for what she considered lesser efforts recognized the value of what she did.

It is probable that if Miss Thomas had been born in the 1950s, her name would have been Ms. M. Carey Thomas. As it was, she dropped the name of Martha, and used Carey. M. Carey Thomas was among the few women who laid the basis for new attitudes on the part of other women, not only toward education but toward the vote, careers, freedom of choice to work and to marry, or even to "live in sin."

Bryn Mawr opened its doors on September 23, 1885, with Dr. James E. Rhoads appointed president by the Board of Trustees. I never met Dr. Rhoads and must attribute the college I knew to Miss Thomas. I can still see her striding to the platform in Taylor Hall, clad in her sweeping silk doctor's gown, reaching into the pocket she had added to it, in her respect for the practical, pulling out her handkerchief before she began to speak. She often startled the faculty and students with her forthright and unconventional pronouncements, dictating the codes and goals for us all. On one occasion, wishing to defeat criticism of unfeminine aims, and misstating her statistics, she boasted that 60 percent of the alumnae were married, and 80 percent had children.

I was to fight her, fear her, never to know her well, but always to admire her. She was headstrong, stubborn, inspiring—a leader who knew where she was going. The contradictions in her personality account in part for the dilemma that I have in evaluating my own experience at Bryn Mawr. For Bryn Mawr nearly ruined me. It came close to destroying my budding hopes to be a medical doctor and vague, but serious, intentions to write. I was not prepared for such strong medicine as I was given.

I have tried to explain to Matthew, one of my grandnephews, what my undergraduate work was like. He complains about his. My impression is that many of the problems he faces now existed in 1913, when I went to college. There has been a little change for the better, and occasionally some for the worse.

When my grandnephews and grandnieces start college, they think of learning new techniques, getting a passport to an interesting job. They talk of the debt of the college to the community. I was less sophisticated than they, and less demanding. In my time, I thought in terms of widening horizons, access to books and, perhaps, to wisdom.

The Bryn Mawr of 1913 was impressive but unsettling to an immature American girl. The aura of scholarship was there for me. The sense of belonging to those the faculty considered the elite was not. Only a few students had that comfortable feeling. I was not one of them. Most of its renowned professors treated me like flotsam and jetsam. Perhaps I was not orderly enough. My handwriting was not good. In my attempts to express myself, the words tumbled over each other. My marks were mediocre.

The English courses stood in the first rank in Miss Thomas' view and in that of many on the faculty. Composition was taught by a stern woman, Professor Regina Crandall. I came to like some of her qualities later, but they were hard to take as a freshman. On one of my "daily themes" she wrote, "This is an absurd attempt to cover the ridiculous with nonsense." My reaction to this was dark despair. My desire was based on a deep and secret sense of the possibility of human communication. I needed to communicate.

As a child I had found in poetry an understanding of the loves and griefs of many men. I could see the world they lived in and knew of the sight and sounds of their springs and winters, their passions and their sorrow. The mysticism of Blake with "Tiger burning

[37]

bright," the weird dreams of Coleridge "in reel and rout, the death-fires danced at night," Milton's lament over his blindness, Shelley's sorrow at Keats's death, Shakespeare's longing for his sweet friend, "more lovely than a summer's day," and Wordsworth's daffodils were all real and poignantly beautiful to me. To write one such poem would be the ultimate gift, an offering in return for the beauty I had seen and heard and felt.

It seemed to me seventy years ago, and it does now, that the beauty of words spun together in verse is a priceless heritage and that I would sacrifice almost anything if I could add to these treasures. This very personal feeling led me to want to write. For some reason I did not discuss this with my friends or with my professors. The shyness I felt was like that of a first love. The fear of failure was real—a sense that poor writing was shameful. Doubts as to how poetry could fit into a practical plan of living restrained me.

When I discovered that the college's elite, with different standards and values, thought I was a charlatan and a feckless person not worthy of their attention, I was deeply hurt. I did not share this disappointment with any of my friends. I could not entirely reject the judgment of those who had long experience and high prestige, but I felt instinctively that something better could have come of encounters between faculty and student.

In an oral history interview decades later I told of my solution to this problem. I said then:

> I was very much interested in the college newspaper. That was started the year that I went to Bryn Mawr, when I was a freshman, and I immediately decided that I wanted to be on this college newspaper because I wanted to write. Since the English professors didn't seem to like my writing, I thought I'd write for the public.
> *Q:* What was their criticism of your writing, the English Department?
> *DULLES:* It wasn't classical enough for them. I don't think they had any notion of how much I wanted to write. You could always pull apart a text that somebody else writes. They took great pleasure in doing it. They were very picayunish, they were very *précieuse* in their approach to language. It was Walter Pater, it was Swinburne, it was on a very—you know, hifalutin' scale, at the same time classical. They went on a theory, at Bryn Mawr in my day, that Shakespeare would get A and everybody else would get less than A unless they could write the way Shakespeare wrote. So you see, if you start with A for Shakespeare, you begin getting a scale of values that's rather hard for a

young freshman to meet. I think you'd find, if you talked to others who went to Bryn Mawr at that time, that there were many who felt this same chill wind of criticism that took the heart out of early efforts.

I remember their saying that my use of adjectives was perhaps too lurid, my phrases weren't sufficiently balanced. They were extremely critical. A certain amount of sarcasm was interesting, but beyond that point I found it rather disturbing.

The *College News* was fun and brought both friendship and practice in writing. The time came when the new editor for the *College News* was to be chosen. The board members came to me. Their story was convincing though disillusioning. "We know," they said, "you will work hard and unstintingly no matter what we do. Polly," they said, "will not keep working unless we appoint her as editor." They did and she did and I kept on working. I was learning cynicism at Bryn Mawr.

The courses that introduced me to new works of great literature I relished. As a failure in writing to suit the professors, I wrote for years for my own satisfaction. When I fell in love, I wrote less and experienced more.

Not every course was, like English composition, a stumbling block to me, and not every teacher unsympathetic. The classes that gave me some concept of real scholarship were those in physiological psychology. One was taught by Gertrude Rand and C. E. Ferree, whom Miss Rand later married. They were to become coinventors of a light sensor tester, acuity projector, and other optical and ophthalmological instruments.

Although Rand and Ferree were unpopular with many on the faculty, for Ferree was a gruff and ungracious man, I found their courses stimulating and valuable. We went through dozens of experiments before any conclusion was made. Partly because I was extremely energetic, and partly because my eyes were an unconventional shape—more oval than round—Rand and Ferree tried out their theories of color perception on me, using me as one of the classroom volunteers in experiments with the color wheel. We did thousands of tests. It was during my freshman year that Dr. Rand's work the "Factors Which Influence the Sensitivity of the Retina to Color" was published. By 1917, when I graduated, she had written

[39]

"Radiometric Apparatus for Use in Psychological and Physiological Optics." I was later to benefit from the research done by Rand and Ferree, research that helped to make possible the successful diagnosis and surgery performed for detached retinas.

The seriousness of the work of Rand and Ferree impressed me greatly. They increased my desire to engage in research later in life. But the numbers of experiments, and the oddity of some, led to a student reaction in the creation of the jolly jingle I can still remember:

> Light adapted eye,
> Dark adapted eye,
> Ferree veree
> Queer psychologeye.

Another provocative psychologist, Professor James Leuba, gave the course Decision, Emotion, and Will. A reputed atheist, he once told us that the reason the American people survived the enormous Sunday dinner customarily served in those years was that they went to church before eating it. Religious experience started their digestive juices flowing. He called himself an "empirical idealist."

I was in awe of tall, angular philosophy professor Theodore Delaguna. I had never seen a grown man cry in public before. He did. So intense was he in his feelings when he spoke of the sad deaths of the Brontë sisters that he wept. He was immensely human, completely unselfconscious, and carried our emotions as well as our intellects into the maelstrom of man's life in the universe.

I took biology because I had decided to be a medical missionary in China—China, because I was interested in the country, medical, because I was not sure my religious vocation was sufficient to justify mission work, except as a doctor.

In the biology lab work for Professor David Tennant, a skillful scientist and teacher, I carved away on the bone and gristle of a shark's head, uncovering the beauty and primitive delicacy of its semicircular canals. But I found working with the microscope almost impossible. I could not see the slides clearly.

In my sophomore year, my aspirations to a medical career were dealt a second blow. I failed my chemistry exam. Although I passed it on a retake, I felt increasing doubts as to my chances of success in medicine and decided to turn elsewhere. I did not know where. I grew used to the idea that I had no fixed goal and that I did not yet know how to be of service.

My work in psychology as a major helped me reorient myself. Yet I was distressed by the large amount of verbiage and overly sociological emphasis in this basically new field. I did not take any courses in history or in economics, which were to be my concern for more than fifty years.

As a minor I took courses in literature, which were not as frustrating as the composition had been. Some of the courses by Samuel Chew* were fine in style and perception. In one course we also read early Restoration drama. A group of Quakers from nearby Philadelphia protested that the plays were indecent. They were. Bryn Mawr continued the course, but the scripts were locked in closets in the rare-book room, and students using them for the course had to get permission to take them out.

My relatives in Philadelphia, Presbyterians, not Quakers, worried about my losing my religious faith at Bryn Mawr. They had heard that M. Carey Thomas was an atheist. My Uncle Heatly asked me discreetly and cautiously whether I was subjected to agnostic propaganda at the college.

"No," I said, "but we hear lots of interesting things."

Neither Uncle Heatly nor I could have forecast in what way my religion would evolve over the years as I reached toward an understanding of the universe.

College did not affect my religious beliefs directly, but it did lay before me so many new and startling experiences that I found it hard to reconcile my early beliefs and convictions with the realities that tested my faith. Conflict between early expectations and later troubles brought turmoil and uncertainty not easy to resolve.

When I went to the Easter Vigil Service at the Washington National Cathedral in April 1976 and saw the beauty of the rites at the altar, there was a message for me. And when I heard my nephew, Father Avery Dulles, the Jesuit priest and theologian, deliver the sermon, I concluded it was high time that I resolve my doubts and accept the mystery of my father's religion, even though I would never fully understand its meaning.

More than fifty years later I recapitulated my college experience in an interview that I quote here:

---

*I don't know what to do
 About Samuel Claggert Chew,
 He treats me like a lady
 And I don't know what to do.

My years in Bryn Mawr were rather peculiar. I went in, you see, with the highest fellowship and with very good marks. At that time, there were a number of professors at Bryn Mawr, which prides itself on its standards, who felt that it was not wise to have any student, particularly a freshman, think that it was easy to get good grades and get credit.

*Q:* It might be conducive to complacency.

*DULLES:* That's what they thought. So they decided to treat me and several other people with a certain amount of brutality, as I think of it. They tried to teach me that I really wasn't as good as they thought I thought I was. The result was that they put some scathing remarks on my quizzes and my various essays that I wrote, and nothing I could do seemed to please them.

This went on for some months, so I finally decided to turn my interest in other directions, which were already very attractive to me—sports, the college newspaper, and social work—and for the rest of my college life, until I ran into two or three professors who really thought I had some mental ability and I should be encouraged rather than discouraged, I spent about half my time, much more than I should have, going in to Philadelphia to the College Settlement, instituting what became the Community Center of Bryn Mawr which ran for more than a dozen years and which was set up according to my plan and run by people who I thought should run it, on a professional basis.

*Q:* This during your undergraduate days?

*DULLES:* During my undergraduate days.

*Q:* This is a leaf out of your mother's book.

*DULLES:* Well, I suppose it was her influence, really, that made me do it. But I felt that there was a lack of community activity and community feeling in this town of Bryn Mawr. I found that there was a woman on the faculty [Susan M. Kingsbury] who was very active. I talked to her about it, and I told her that I thought a recent Bryn Mawr graduate, Jane [Hilda W.] Smith, would be an ideal person to run the business. I found rooms where they could start classes in sports and various activities. There was no YWCA in the town or any group activity at all. The thing moved ahead, and I don't believe there are five people who know that I started it.

The social contacts of the new college environment overstimulated me. All kinds of psychological currents were set in motion by the talented, attractive women at Bryn Mawr. There were crushes and feuds. I dared not be too involved, yet was not entirely immune.

Fearful that some of the girls most interesting to me would be monopolized by others, I did not want to compete emotionally; neither did I want to be excluded.

Perhaps I did compete without realizing it. For some reason I do not understand, I slept on the floor for about two years. I took my steamer rug and pillow and went to the room of one or another of my friends. There I went to sleep, my rug on the bare floor. I lay diagonally on the rug so as to turn one corner up over my feet. I fastened the rug with a book strap. I had invented a sleeping bag. What I had started as a search for companionship continued, perhaps to manifest a degree of individuality or to establish a special identity. In time, I was recognized at Bryn Mawr, not as a scholar or a social butterfly, but as a student known for determination in pursuing extracurricular interests, and in my somewhat eccentric habits.

I lived with a congenial, though competitive, group in Rockefeller Hall. I did not try to get close to the "Big Beautifuls," who lived in Pembroke East and West, dressing and acting on a higher and more pretentious level—or so it seemed to me. My friend Marian Rhoads, later my housemate in Boston, was in yet another group—bridge-playing sophisticates.

I must have appeared inept to many of my fellow students. I felt and looked like a small-town girl. While many of them went into Philadelphia for the opera or the theater, and one out of five left for weekends spent farther away, I stayed on campus. I didn't have the money to leave. I did hear Caruso sing once.

But there were good times and good friends. I did better in sports than my physical endowments justified, particularly at swimming and water polo. I also played field hockey. The game was introduced at Bryn Mawr by "The Apple," Constance Applebee, now 106 years old, living in her home country, England. For the game we wore long corduroy skirts, which reached almost to the ankles. Our class wore red. The prized skirt was the one worn down to the nap—rather like today's blue jeans, which must be properly faded. We relished playing in the fall air, in the bright afternoons, running with spirit on the smooth green fields until dusk fell, and some had lost and some had won.

Freshman Night was a long-standing tradition, but the class of 1917 made a spectacular of it. The upperclassmen were occupied with a more important social function, and we had the run of the place. At other times, we were subject to a mild form of hazing, stepping off the sidewalks when older students passed, and showing respect on all occasions. Freshman Night we ran wild.

We raided the bureau drawers of sophomores, seniors, and even the juniors, who were our "sister class" protectors. We festooned the trees with underpants, slips, and stockings. We put toothbrushes in little patterns on the grass and wrote on the pavement, "Please don't pick the wild flowers as you pass." My own project was an attempt to remove the clapper from Taylor Hall's bell. It proved too resistant to the file I had brought. Assisted by "Scat" (Margaret Scattergood) and another classmate, I cut the rope. For more than twenty-four hours there was no sound from the bell. Later I heard that, since we were the only small, identifiable group, Miss Thomas contemplated expelling us. She relented, subjecting us to a stern interview. Our place in college history had been established forever.

These pranks must seem childish and absurd to today's students who worry about community relations, or are still revolting over political outrages and civil rights issues. But in 1917 we did not carry the world's problems on our shoulders. We were young and we had a sense of humor.

Much of the spirit of the ivy-covered walls and austere, classical halls of study would be rejected now. There was a lot of sentiment about interclass relations and the traditional hoop rolling and step-singing rituals, not enough to hinder serious scholarship but enough to fill much of our leisure time.

Toward midnight, when we had had enough of study, we gathered in one of the tea pantries to heat milk for "muddle," the thick sweet cocoa that filled an aching void and added pounds to already well-fed students.

We entertained men callers in the parlor of our dormitory, and the men we knew had been properly introduced to us. They were usually brothers of fellow students, relatives, or Haverford College men. A beau of mine from Auburn came for a weekend, spending the night in the village. Robert was a good friend, a quiet young man. I was impressed that he had taken the journey from Auburn to Bryn Mawr to see me, but otherwise his visit was unimportant to me. We had a pleasant time, neither frivolous nor ardent. I now think he must have been lonely, but I let him go home without any expression of affection. I was surprised when I learned he had been sent to a mental hospital later.

The reaction of growing women—and men—to the mystery and beauty around them has not been fully analyzed by those who are concerned these days with the rapid rush of young people to full physical expression of their emotions at an early age in love affairs or marriage. There is in most cases, however, a period, sometimes brief, sometimes longer, when their feelings are strong and demanding, stimulated often by art or the beauty of nature. They become attached to individuals who are understanding, responsive, and, sometimes, beautiful in their eyes. These relationships, whether vague and abstract, or more definite, lesbian or homosexual, are often encountered as a social phenomenon in schools and colleges. Sometimes they seem unhealthy but in any case they are frequent and significant. At a college that cultivates the finest in literature, that has constructed a beautiful campus with leafy corridors, stone arches, and cloistered walks, this expression of developing emotions is bound to appear. Given the relative isolation of the students from the world of business and stern realities of earning a living and competing in a rough world, the peace and beauty led to deep feelings among the young women. This was both a result and a cause of the relative lack of interest in men and the scanty contacts with their activities, which were distant from the campus. With the automobiles, air travel, and summer jobs the atmosphere has changed and the idyllic, dreamlike quality has largely disappeared.

Bryn Mawr girls of my day did not go to college to find a husband or meet a lover. I felt that there was too feminine an atmosphere and yet I did not particularly want men students in our relatively peaceful world. Nor did I share the feelings of the few who had frequent men visitors or who sought them elsewhere. I wonder now how well one can concentrate on studies with the constant awareness of the man-woman relationship in coeducational dorms and among married students. In those days we had to leave college if we married.

Members of the class wrote a play that presented a moral problem and a public relations one. As first outlined, the script called for the hero and heroine, who were engaged but not married, to spend a night together away from home. This breach of propriety was shocking. They were traveling by train across the continent. However, my classmates and I considered the possibilities of the then almost unknown development of air travel. A daredevil beau of one Bryn Mawr senior flew over the campus regularly, to demonstrate his prowess to his loved one. We introduced the airplane into the play script, shortening the protagonists' journey to a single day and preserving the high moral tone of the drama.

The worse social misdemeanor I can remember was smoking regular cigarettes by a group of girls in the basement of the gymnasium, near the swimming pool. Nobody had heard of pot.

Through the texture of the memories run threads of many colors. I recall vividly the variety of experience, the sights and sounds, the lights and shadows—the campus towers in the fall, the brilliant leaves of the maples by the hockey field and the flowering trees in the spring. But the people were more interesting than the scenery. There were some of my classmates who were to become well known—Lucia Chase of ballet fame, Helen Harris, a noted social worker, and "Blodgie" (Katharine Blodgett), who invented invisible glass at General Electric Company.

My special friends included "Blodgie," "Hemmy" (Elizabeth Hemenway), "Highty" (Harriet Allport), "Scat," of the Taylor Hall bell episode, and "Skipper" Emerson. I was called "Dooles," the name my father had at Princeton. It stuck to me for several decades. There were other delightful friends in our circle—gay, foolish, brilliant, intellectual, and full of mischief.

"Skipper" was to be one of my closest friends for almost fifty years, until her death in 1963. During the confusion of that first year, "Skipper" helped me immeasurably. She was a better student than I, but like me, she loved the beauty of the campus and charm of the surrounding countryside. We walked, we talked, and we joked. Our professors, we claimed—borrowing from Cicero—were "clothed in a little brief authority."

After class, when we met in the hall, we made use of Carroll's *Alice in Wonderland*.

"There's a lobster close behind you and he's treading on your tail," was a favorite of Skipper's.

"With what porpoise are you going?" I would ask.

Skipper had beautiful brown eyes and braided hair. She wore sandals and smocked dresses. Under her influence, I went on the only sewing binge of my life, making a long brown corduroy skirt. It was a triumph, right in style on the campus where students wore skirts and blouses. Also popular were blue serge suits with sailor collars, called for the maker, "Peter Thomsons." The skirts fell well below the knee, though not quite to the ankle.

Skipper and I had several classes together. Later she went further in biology, and I shifted to psychology. She became a medical doctor, after graduating from Bryn Mawr and Johns Hopkins University, and was married for more than twenty years to Walter Gardner, an economist at the Federal Reserve Board.

Although the Bryn Mawr of 1917 might now seem very conventional, even quaint, to modern students, we were still students and the winds of revolt blew up storms. There were two I recall—one over the "cut rule" for students and the other over the conditions of faculty promotion and tenure. There had been no requirement to attend classes. Then one was imposed. At about the same time, faculty members claimed they had not been given proper rank and tenure. They protested on the issue of their rights. The students who supported the faculty protested on principle. But both uprisings were based on a deeper one; neither faculty nor students could endure without rebellion the autocratic rule of M. Carey Thomas.

To protest the "cut rule" students sent delegations to Miss Thomas, threatening her with vague reprisals. She accepted the challenge and a momentous meeting was held in Taylor Hall. Helen Taft (Manning), daughter of former President Taft, and leader of the junior class, stood on the platform, face to face with the formidable Miss Thomas, and told her the "cut rule" was unacceptable. Miss Thomas' diplomatic skills were as remarkable as her capacity to intimidate. She said that Helen's ideas had long been in her mind and she had intended for some months to institute some of them. Like more than one university president of the late 1960s, this wily, experienced politician of the campus won at least half the battle. She gave up only what she had to, but she also received the student message, and the "cut rule" was dropped.

There was also student independence through evasive tactics, though not for me. One student invited her family down to Bryn Mawr for commencement. When they arrived on a lovely spring day, she told them, "Commencement is the most boring ceremony you could possibly imagine. You'll only see me for a minute. Why don't you drive to Valley Forge instead?"

They did. She never graduated and they never knew.

The world we were entering in 1917 was changing rapidly. Our education had been a solid one, but it was only barely adequate to prepare us for the upheaval we encountered. I told of my reaction in my interviews for the Columbia oral history program.

> ... when the war broke out, and at first I didn't see it coming. Then all of a sudden, the year that I was a senior—that was 1917—I realized that this was an immense and terrific thing that was happening. I didn't have much money and didn't travel much, but I got on the train and went to Washington, and went to my uncle's house [Robert Lansing]. My grandfather was still living but I thought of it then as my uncle's house.
> *DULLES:* I said to Uncle Bert, "What's happening? What's this war you people are starting?"
> I was very much shocked by a sense of world catastrophe at that time. That was the first time that I, and I would say most of my friends, had realized that we weren't living in a very safe protected world. I take it from my own point of view, because I was rather gregarious, that my friends also hadn't been paying much attention to world affairs. I don't say that we didn't read the papers but we didn't really give much thought to it. Our local concerns were so much more vital to us than anything else was. When I think of that in contrast to the college classes I've talked to in the last few years, and the immediate reaction to an international crisis that you get on the college campuses, it's quite impressive, as compared with the time when I was in college.
> *Q:* Yes. Much of it is due to improved communications.
> *DULLES:* Much of it, the radio, the newspapers, the whole atmosphere, and the fact that we've had soldiers overseas. Some of the young children that I teach now have had parents overseas, in the Occupation, and so on. At that time, the only contact with war really was the Mexican border situation, the Mexican war, and most of us didn't think much about that or take it very seriously.

I stood on the platform in academic gown and turned the tassel on my cap in June 1917, my twenty-second birthday just past. I left college without really understanding what history could explain and with a measure of bewilderment over creative literature. What I had gained was an appreciation of academic values and a respect for the tradition of scholarship. This was to be a major bond with my late husband, David Blondheim, who, as a renowned philologist, was a truly great scholar. If I think back to my triumphs in water polo and working on the *College News* with more enthusiasm than my encounters with the faculty, I would happily drink a toast to Bryn Mawr and smash my glass against its Gothic walls.

[48]

I left Bryn Mawr for France on June 9, 1917. In 1919 I was to return. Meanwhile the college will always occupy a place in my thinking of art and scholarship. It will always be a reminder of friendly companionship and bright memories.

The class of 1917 had its sixtieth reunion on a warm, sunny weekend. I hesitated because we were all getting old, but decided to go. Sixteen were there in good spirits and fair health. Seeing my dear friend the late Constance Wilcox Pignatelli, blind and courageous, was worth the trip. Margaret Feuer Plass, expert in African art, was a delightful hostess at our banquet. Helen Harris, well-known leader in social work in New York City and Pittsburgh, was our toastmaster. I drove to Bryn Mawr with my good friend of many years and a former staff member of the AFL-CIO "Scat" from Langley, Virginia. Dorothy Shipley White, expert on Charles de Gaulle and his career, wore her French medals. Here I was with the achievers at last. Eleven others impressed me with their frank and modest accounts of substantial accomplishment in philanthropic and business worlds. The members of the class had made their contributions.

# 5

# THE DEFENSE OF FRANCE, 1917–1919

When I went to the State Department to get my passport for France in the spring of 1917, I did not imagine that I was to be chased by a submarine, arrested by the French, and shelled by the Germans before the year was over. What I was expecting was to work for the refugees in Europe. The work had little relation to the education that had come to an acceptable end with my Bryn Mawr A.B.

It wasn't until the spring of my senior year that my eyes were opened to the ferocity of the fighting and the possibility of an Allied defeat. Until that time studies of past history and current science had fully absorbed me. But by April I realized that the war was our war—crucial to our future. I needed to see and hear and feel, to have a part in the struggle. Patriotism and a feeling that France and England were fighting for democracy combined with my need for adventure in a largely personal way.

That April 1917, when the United States declared war on Germany, I had dropped everything and taken the train to Washington. I was staying with "Aunt" and Uncle Bert—Robert Lansing was then Secretary of State. The talk of President Wilson's coming declaration of war filled the house with excitement. I wasn't able to hear the President speak. The seats allotted Uncle Bert were just enough for "Aunt," my mother, and two of Uncle Bert's sisters. But when they came home from the Hill, they told me of the tremendous surge of response to Wilson's speech. I went back to college determined to get in the fight.

My first thought was of running away from home, with a few dollars in my pocket. While harboring this immature plan, I ran into an old friend, Carlotta Welles, who was in Bryn Mawr visiting from her home in France. I talked to her of my plans and she told me that Helen Shurtleff, whom I had met in my brief visit to Paris in 1909, headed a committee working with refugees.

Mrs. Shurtleff's husband, Ernest, was pastor of the American Church in Paris. She had organized some of the church women, good Boston types, into a workshop. They were helping French and Belgian refugees from the north. Carlotta thought Mrs. Shurtleff could use my help.

I wrote at once. Her answer was a request for me to come as soon as possible. It occurred to me my parents might approve of my plan, so I wrote to them. They thought I should go. They had a great respect for Mrs. Shurtleff. They also sent me $1,000, telling me they hoped I could get along on it. Like most of the committee I would be a volunteer.

It was relatively easy to get a passport in May before regulations designed for wartime conditions went into effect. These were to make it harder.

Not long after receiving my passport I learned that Henrietta Ely, sister of a friend, Gertrude Ely, also wanted to go to France. She had heard of Mrs. Shurtleff. Henrietta wanted to bring her car and thought it might be easier to get permission to do so if she went with me. I doubt if it made much difference, but she did get the permit in time.

On June 9 we sailed on the S.S. *Espagne*, one of the small French Line ships. It was rumored that these ships were safe from submarine attack because the mail written by German spies was carried in their holds. In fact, none of the French Line ships *was* torpedoed.

Nevertheless, we weren't sure of our safe passage, and the crossing was tense, heightened by tales of other passengers who had already been in the war zone or in military work. One day we were taking a zigzag course on a smooth sea to avoid possible torpedo attack. About three hundred miles from Bordeaux on June 16, as we sat over our tea, we heard shouts of "Submarine!"

The people next to me pointed south. "There's a periscope!"

I could not see it.

I went to the cabin and discovered that one of the two life belts there had broken straps. In my desire to go down a hero, I offered the good one to Henrietta and fixed mine with safety pins, hoping it would hold for a short time.

The sailors were in panic, but the passengers remained calm. After we had assembled on the deck word was passed along that those with good life belts would board the rafts. Those without would go in boats. Thus in my dramatic self-denial I had doomed Henrietta to the more precarious raft.

The ship's guns were manned and for ten minutes we braced for the expected explosion. Another ten minutes went by. All was quiet. It appeared that we had been granted a reprieve. We were, after all, "carrying the German mail."

Tea was served. As we lounged in our deck chairs, congratulating ourselves on our courageous behavior, a loud explosion set off a mad scramble for the lifeboats. Short-order heroism was all we could manage. After several moments of pandemonium, we learned that the crew had fired at a piece of driftwood.

That night most of us slept in our clothes on deck. We could not bear the thought of being trapped below in a sinking ship.

The Garonne River and the port of Bordeaux were particularly beautiful when we saw them. We prepared our hand luggage for landing. I knew we would have to wait for Henrietta's car to be put ashore, but we wanted to get to the hotel at the earliest possible moment. A French immigration officer looked at our papers and asked us to step aside. He kept the passports.

I wondered why the special concern. I did know that Henrietta was quite a talker. A tall, authoritative woman from one of Philadelphia's best families, she had charm and an odd sense of humor. I knew that she had become well acquainted with a fellow passenger who was, I think, the French Minister of Education. What I did not know was that she had talked of Germany and Austria. Nor did I know that she had neglected to answer certain questions on her visa application, including queries as to the territory over which she had travelled since 1914—enemy territory. We waited an hour. When the passengers had landed we got our passports back. After we had settled in the Grand Hôtel de France, an officer burst into our room and demanded our passports. We learned we were under house arrest. Without passports we could not send telegrams or cash checks. We were being held incommunicado as possible spies.

Soon after we had handed over our passports, Henrietta was taken to another room for a long interrogation. I asked to see the American consul in Bordeaux. Vice-Consul George Young was in charge. I persuaded him to get in touch with Robert Bliss, deputy chief of mission in our Paris embassy. I told Young that I thought if the officials in the French Foreign Office learned that the niece of the Secretary of State was being held as a suspected spy, they might want to do something.

On the third day of our confinement he consented to telegraph. Our man in Bordeaux told us that Bliss had gone to the French Foreign Office—Quai d'Orsay—and requested our release. The French police were satisfied with the message they received.

By this time we had Henrietta's car. Vice-Consul Young suggested that he ride along with us to the edge of the city and start us in the right direction for Paris, no doubt to be sure he had seen the last of us. On the way out of the city our car struck an old man running for a streetcar. The vice-consul told us to go quickly on our way; that he would look after the man, who was shaken up but not injured. An angry crowd was gathering.

My confidence in Henrietta somewhat diminished when I asked about her driving experience. I learned that she could not drive in reverse. She had had three driving lessons and the use of the reverse gearshift remained a mystery. We could go in one direction only—forward—in her Ford touring model, and so we did, all the way to Paris. For three days I kept my left hand on the emergency brake.

Except for social occasions Henrietta parted company with me shortly after our first assignment from Mrs. Shurtleff. We were both asked to match pairs of shoes from an immense pile sent from America to the Shurtleff Relief Committee. Henrietta had decided this was not her way of winning the war. She persuaded the French Army authorities to give her a pass to the war zone and drove north. I later learned that she had become a one-woman clubmobile unit, dispensing cigarettes, first aid, reading material, and wit to the eager *poilus* in the war zone.

Meanwhile we were concerned with the thousands of peasants coming to Paris on foot, in trucks, and by train, from Belgium, northern France, and even from Germany. The French Government's relief measures were inadequate; our work and that of other relief organizations was desperately needed. Distress among the refugees was affecting the morale of the French soldier.

When I joined the committee in June, word of mouth had spread the news of our work. We were receiving scores of letters of request. We screened them to give priority to the most urgent cases, sending a committee member to interview the persons asking for our help, writing up a report of the interview, determining what help could or should be given. A month after I arrived I wrote to my mother that we had in the file 2,269 case records. They included requests for all the things that people forced from their homes with little or no luggage could need—just about everything.

I described the committee's center of operations, a combination of offices, workrooms, and storerooms, in a letter to my parents in October:

> All this week we have worked to put in order our new store room, taking things for babies out of the little shop which is to be kept entirely for the *ouvoir* and out of the office which is small enough when we are in it, without having any shelves for clothes.... We hope to be able to take enough of the things away so that we can have one room only for the fitting (alterations), with enough clothes on the shelves each week for the people that will come that week... the other room will be left free for the refugees to wait in, for the officer of the day to interview them when they come for their appointments, and for conference on Saturdays.
>
> This has meant endless loading up the car and then unloading around the corner, tying all sorts of things in piles of sizes and then crowding hundreds of these into appropriate shelves.... Esther Root [later Mrs. Franklin P. Adams,] is engineering the performance with me as assistant and we have been there, either alone or with helpers, all week. It is something to see the order developing out of chaos and I do not mind the work, especially when I can throw the packages on the shelves which is the nearest approach to basketball I have found.

Into this center of operations the thirty American women who were committee members came and went. The older ones were church members, the younger, students or tourists who happened to be in Paris before the United States entered the war, plus those like me who had arrived recently. We were all volunteers, except for a paid case worker and Mrs. Shurtleff's secretary, who bore the incredible name of Blossom Bloss.

After letters of appeal had been sorted, we had to see the families to determine their needs. Each morning I would take my share of letters for that day and a map of Paris and set out on the Métro. After six hours of searching for addresses, climbing stairs, and interviewing, I would return to the office and write up my reports.

By October I had the hang of it and wrote to my mother that I had visited eight families in one day, a record at that time:

[54]

Two of the families were living right over a factory in which they were making soldier's helmets. . . . We got there just at dark and all we could see below was the lights of the furnaces and the gleam of helmets and the men leaning over the fires. We voted on 49 cases in conference . . . that is really quite a lot to handle, especially when you consider that each family has about three to ten people in it.

I was making my calls in the red-light districts, four arrondissements in the Montmartre region, the real slums of Paris, with "step" streets and hotels in which prostitutes took rooms by the hour. I never felt afraid, nor was I bothered or insulted.

In another report to my mother I told her of calling on a woman with a five-year-old daughter. The mother had gone to Charlepont at her husband's suggestion to be near him and to live with her mother and small brother:

They had been caught there by the German advance and with five hundred other people had been forced to live in a barn for months, sleeping on straw and eating nothing but string beans, every day. . . . When they were sent to Noyon the mayor said, "We don't want these people. There is nothing for them to eat." "All right," said the Germans. "Line them up in front of the canons and we will shoot them." Some were actually put before the . . . fire.

"After we had been there some time," said the mother, "the Americans gave us some food."

"Oh, do you remember the little sugar," said the little girl to her mother, "and the little cakes!" [The food had been given by the Hoover Commission.]

When the French returned to the town, the government officials and soldiers used part of the house in which this woman and her child stayed. . . . One day a soldier came in—at first they hardly noticed him—but then the woman realized it was her husband, from whom they had not heard since the beginning of the war. He had walked about twenty miles that day and found them at last.

In the same letter I described a woman and her mother, the mother with a cataract in one eye, the daughter unable to work because her mother got lost when she went out. The mother's husband had been run over and the daughter's husband had been drowned.

Every day the reports we had filed the night before were reviewed at a meeting. Where possible, we found unfurnished lodgings for families with small children, and gave them the bare essentials, beds, tables, and a couple of chairs, and *batterie de cuisine*, kitchenware. We referred to this outfitting as *broc, pot*, and *sceaux*. Where there was a need for clothing, we had the families come for a fitting in our workrooms, giving the children their black aprons, *tabliers*, for school. Every refugee child wanted these simple black jumpers, for without them other children would think they were different. There were layettes for babies. We employed some of the refugee women to make or alter the clothing.

To those who were undernourished we gave canned goods, flour, sugar, milk, prunes, raisins, rice, and similar staples. To a few we gave money to travel farther south. A doctor worked part-time at the center. Along with our aid, all refugees received *allocations*, government welfare. This small sum was given promptly by the French Government.

Other work in the center included wrapping packages for the relatives, husbands, and fathers, who were soldiers, prisoners, disabled, separated from their families. Some of this work was time consuming and dirty. Some of it was frustrating. Government regulations abounded as only the French can make them abound. The wrapping of prisoner packages had to be according to regulations, with stiff paper, twine that hurt our fingers, the contents including only exact amounts of chocolate, bully beef, and other sanctioned items.

Packages had to be dispatched at seven different places, depending on the circumstances of the recipient. The categories differed— prisoners of war, blind, soldiers in hospitals, etc.

Another regulation prohibited the storage of gasoline in large containers. So, working in filthy garages once a month, we had to decant all the gasoline from the large barrels into small jerricans. We needed the fuel for our few cars, donated by our volunteers.

In our efforts to raise money, we wrote home, telling stories of German atrocities. There was one memorable atrocity—a woman was reportedly taken by the German soldiers and nailed to the wall of her home. The soldiers took her children away from her and threw rocks at her, according to the report. A week after we dispatched this story in our letters we discovered our source was a pathological liar. There was not a word of truth in her account. Our later reports were verified before we wrote about them.

In these months there was so much to be done, so little to do it with. Early in November I wrote Mother:

We hope to have a doctor give a good deal of time for the families to whom we are giving food. They come from Germany in such bad health now, worse than before. The children are all sickly and the women too weak to work.... We also want to be able to move some of the families who are tubercular out to the suburbs. The [Paris] sanitariums are so full that we cannot get the sick ones in. The only chance to save the children is to move the families to larger, airier quarters. We are doing a good deal of installing now. It takes about 500 francs to set up a family.... There is any amount of work to be done. We have more than we can handle....

But the rewards for me were beyond measure. I could see the people I helped. Rarely has a group functioned more simply, economically, or wholeheartedly than our committee. The several thousand families aided were few compared with the total number of displaced persons, but to each was given aid within our means on a carefully studied basis. Meanwhile we waited anxiously for the promised American military help.

I had reached France in mid-June of 1917. Late that same month the first American military group, a battalion of the 16th Infantry Division, entered Paris. These men from Texas marched to the Invalides, and then on across Paris to Lafayette's Tomb. I was on the Rue de Rivoli, watching. The French went wild. They broke through police lines, throwing their arms around the Americans, pressing flowers on them, and creating pandemonium. A Frenchman standing near me turned and asked, "Where do these soldiers come from—Brazil?"

It took me a moment to realize that he thought of America as one great big continent. Which nations or states were Les Etats-Unis he did not know, or care. In the months that followed, the French were to learn during the bitter winter and spring of 1918 that it would take more Americans than a few battalions to save France.

These were times of great anxiety and hard work. For me life alternated between long hours on committee business, the exciting tales of war, and occasional fun. On July 15 I wrote my mother a story I had heard about an American ambulance driver.

A Bosch airship had been shelling his post and he went out to try and get a picture of the shells exploding around it. He was out in the open field when he noticed that the German airship was coming down. He had no place to run.... The Bosch got out, armed with pistols, and the ambulance driver asked him to surrender. The German fired his pistols at the incendiary bombs in his machine, threw his hat on the ground, and surrendered!

In a letter to my sister Nataline, I reported the big celebration of every Saturday was a hot bath. On Saturday, July 14, I had also gone out to dinner and to a movie, *Oliver Twist*. On the fifteenth I went to church, and after lunch, to the Gare de l'Est, where I frequently worked on my day off, serving beer and wine to the French soldiers. The canteen there was supported by American money, and staffed by American and French women. In my account of that Sunday, I wrote: "I feel quite qualified to take a permanent job of that kind if it ever becomes necessary.... I suppose I washed, or dipped, almost 1,500 glasses."

In my horizon-blue tailored uniform with Sam Browne belt, I caused some amusement among the soldiers, who gave me considerable advice on how to be a barmaid. Bryn Mawr had insisted that all graduates read and speak French, but had not included bartending.

Among our minor sports of 1917 was finding where, within legal limits and with what money we had, we could get good French food. Some of my compatriots also scrounged black-market supplies. When anyone received a check or package from home, she would give a party. We were often joined by brothers, fiancés, and friends from the American Field Service and the Lafayette Escadrille. An occasional American soldier on leave, like my cousin Jim Bourne, also joined us.

It was at one of these gatherings that I met an Escadrille pilot, Jim Fiske, from Boston, who had fallen out of the pilot's seat in his plane, but managed to catch one of the struts, crawl back on the wing, and hold on as he glided to a safe crash landing; a fellow pilot landed nearby to bring him back.

The Escadrille was an elite flying foreign legion, equipped with fabric-covered airplanes, a machine gun mounted in front for the pilot to fire while he tried to outmaneuver the enemy. World War I was to be the last I knew of in which gallantry was shown to one's enemy. Pilots would drop wreaths over the spot where they had shot down an enemy flier.

We felt deeply involved in these struggles. I had a tremendous desire to get to the front. Permits were hard to get. There was a forward zone which could not be entered without a *carnet rouge*. The military always had specific orders.

That summer of 1917, Uncle Bert's two sisters, Emma and Kate Lansing, had come over with an advance contingent of the Red Cross to work in a canteen for the soldiers. They were in Epernay, west of Verdun, within a few miles of the trenches. Kate and Emma served meals to soldiers in the front lines who were allowed to come out of the trenches for a brief rest after being under heavy shelling. My aunts worked on round-the-clock shifts. They helped the soldiers with their correspondence and did other tasks to relieve the mental tension of men almost constantly under fire.

I managed to get a permit to go to their post. I took the train along the Marne to the canteen within a stone's throw of the trenches which French troops were desperately holding. Pressure on their lines had been increased by the revolution in Russia, which released troops of the German Army withdrawn from the Russian front.

The area I visited was flat, with burned-over trees, the earth gray with mud and ashes. It was late fall, the weather dark and dull. There was a silence I had not expected after the fever of Paris with its flood of refugees and soldiers on leave. At this forward post, no one talked about whether we were winning or losing. Although we could hear a number of explosions not far away, they were not continuous.

The sight of wounded men being brought in on stretchers and taken in ambulances to the train, the tired nurses, and the weary look of the soldiers at the canteen made a tremendous impression. I was shaken and depressed, not because of the drama, but because the fighting seemed to be an endless, meaningless business. I stayed thirty-six hours, watching and helping Aunt Kate and Aunt Emma, already in their fifties, working so calmly and efficiently in that place of danger.

Danger became somewhat less remote for me by 1918. Air raids on Paris were stepped up by the Germans. Although there were not many fatalities, if you were hit, you were dead. I told my mother in a letter of July 29:

> I was spending the night with Rootie and Crocker [two friends on the Committee] ... the great searchlights kept playing around the sky. ...
> There were seven airplanes I saw at once, little red stars dodging about. ... Three times we heard explosions. I suppose it was the anti-aircraft guns, but it may have been bombs.... After the first few

minutes it seemed like a wonderful display of Northern Lights and falling stars, not like war.

Regulations regarding air-raid alerts stated we were to go to the nearest shelter. I had some strange encounters with pajama-clad Frenchmen and wailing wives in the furnace rooms of several apartment houses used for shelter.

The air raids were soon overshadowed by a more disturbing threat—"Big Bertha." We later learned there was more than one of these huge guns which could fire seventy miles toward their target, Paris, but they continued to be called Big Bertha. My introduction to this new danger came at a staff meeting one morning. A Frenchman rushed in to show us a piece of metal, still hot. One of the first shells had fallen a half block away.

At this time I was living on the eighth floor in an attic studio apartment on Boulevard Raspail. It was difficult to sleep, and once awakened by an explosion, I would start waiting for the next. They occurred at twenty-minute intervals, a delay apparently to let the bore of the gun cool. At the beginning of the interval, I would think, "Just another ten minutes to go," then, "Just another five minutes." It was worse than the air raids.

My first attempt to protect myself against this threat of annihilation was to put on my hat. However, before long I made a more sensible adjustment on the theory that the shells only destroyed the top two or three floors of well-built apartment houses. I moved to a *pension* with four floors above my room and slept soundly.

The effect of the bombardment and its impact on Parisian morale came up in a strange conversation I had twelve years later when I was in Bonn. I boarded in the house of a *Justizrat* (a judge), learning German. One night an ex-officer of the German Army came to dinner. Someone mentioned that I had been in Paris during the war. The officer asked if I could tell him where the first shell from the big guns had fallen. I said, "I can. It landed on my doorstep."

He was pleased to know and I was glad to tell him. Here we were at dinner, former enemies, but somehow it was strangely gratifying for both of us. He had been responsible for aiming a Big Bertha so many years before. This ironic episode brings home to me the irrationality of humans fighting humans.

[60]

We took a grim interest in these shells. At the committee's center we worked out the pattern of shelling on a map. We were able to do this because we were making calls all over the city. The bombardment did get on our nerves. Every once in a while I felt I had to spend some time out of the area of the shelling, and on occasional Sundays I would borrow a car and go south of Paris.

However, neither I nor my fellow workers ever panicked. Thousands of Parisians did. Around Easter of 1918 when the Allied line broke to the west, and the Americans massed in the east could not close the gap immediately, the trains filled with refugees coming to Paris. There were too many to take care of in the city. We tried to get them out with a little food and care in the train stations and warehouses where they slept. The great city that was the heart of France was threatened.

I could understand their fear, but did not feel it myself. I knew the Americans were coming in large numbers. It seemed to me that the Parisian women, unlike the peasant women I grew to know so well in my work, did not have enough stamina. Peasant women stayed at their homes and with their land until the Germans forced them off physically, putting them in trucks or marching them down the road. When I went to see them, they would pull up their blouses or roll up their sleeves to show me the scars and wounds. They gave graphic descriptions of how they had been shelled, of when and where they had been bombarded and how it had felt.

Thousands of soldiers poured into the city along with the refugees. Families fled to the south on packed trains. Censorship and official silence led to rumors, and eventually all of us thought that Paris would be lost. Hundreds of homeless slept on the station floors. Mattresses and blankets were spread in the railroad stations where we worked day and night. I worked mainly in the Gare de Lyons. There were births and deaths, members of separated families wandering through the station looking for each other. All were victims of hunger, weariness, and despair. The suffering seemed fathomless. We worked without sleep through the crisis. Then in May 1918 the Allied line stabilized and Paris was safe.

Earlier, in March, while the shelling of Paris was at its height, Mrs. Shurtleff got pneumonia. I decided she should be moved into an apartment away from the area where shells fell. After work I spent the nights there, caring for her. Part of the treatment was "cupping," which I learned to do. A glass cup was inverted and a lighted taper placed under it. When the air in the container was exhausted, the taper was withdrawn and the cup clapped quickly over the skin. In the vacuum created, the skin was sucked and became a bluish color. This relieved congestion. Antibiotics were then unheard-of.

Mrs. Shurtleff had lost her husband the previous summer, exhausted herself working during the worst of the Paris bombardment, and now was faced with increasing pressure from the Red Cross, which sought to take over the work of all the smaller organizations. I took her down to La Rochelle on the ocean for three weeks after she recovered sufficiently from pneumonia and then to Bordeaux, where she took ship to escort her husband's body back to the United States for burial.

The committee was threatened with extinction. By the summer of 1918, the Red Cross had arrived in full force in Paris. Advance units had been taking over most of the Hôtel Crillon, and the organization was offering paid jobs to many volunteer workers. At the same time it was cutting off the capacity of small organizations like the Shurtleff Relief Committee to import supplies and raise funds.

It is difficult for me to describe with impartiality my disillusionment with the Red Cross. Within a few months the full force of money, equipment, cars, personnel, and rank was brought to bear on our operation. I could not prevent their decision to drop the aid to families dependent on us. I turned for advice to the Society of Friends.

A number of old friends of mine had been working with the Quakers. On November 1, 1918, I joined. I was assigned to a forward unit, or *équipe*, on the Marne at Mareuil-le-Port. I left Paris on November 11, the day that marked the end of World War I. I wrote to Mrs. Shurtleff, who was back in Boston, that it would have been wrong to break my promise to report to my post on November 11, but added wistfully, "I'm afraid I missed the day of my life."

While Paris was going wild, I was standing on a railroad platform at Château Thierry, waiting to change for a local train at eleven o'clock, the moment the Armistice was signed. Not far to the north was Belleau Woods, where hundreds of Americans had died in desperate battle, more casualties than we had suffered in any other area of France.

[62]

All the way up from Paris I had seen gun emplacments, shell holes in fields, little groups of graves. Near Dorman, another station on the Marne, my friend "Scat," from Bryn Mawr days, and two other members of the *équipe* were there to meet me in an old truck.

We celebrated that night, opening unexploded shells and taking out the gunpowder to make small bonfires. The gunpowder did not explode, but burned brightly. Although there was plenty of champagne in the cellars of the village, we didn't drink any of it. It was hardly the celebration I might have had in Paris.

In a letter to my parents written that Armistice Day, I described Mareuil:

> This is the most fascinating little place, a small town of about fifty families. It is typical Marne country.... there is a little wood behind the house and some pine trees about. The town is on the regular military road.... The *équipe* has just come ... things are just being settled ... Scat and I have a room upstairs in the *Mairie*. The shell hole in the roof has been mended and the window panes replaced by heavy oiled paper.... We are cleaning up the house, used for some time to quarter soldiers ... for two of the other workers, and for our sitting room and kitchen.... We sleep on army cots.

Two days later, I had received my assignment, a nearby village on a hillside, which I reached by bicycle. Every house in the village had been hit by shellfire, yet all eighty families who lived there had returned to their damaged homes. Obviously I wasted no time getting to work, for I wrote to Mrs. Shurtleff that night:

> I'm going to get a list of all the people and a plan of the town from the *Mairie*. Then I am going to visit every family, find out their needs.... and we will send them packages of clothing.... Nothing could be more interesting than to get to know all these people. I love it.

At Mareuil our staff included an Irish girl, Dorice White, handsome, literate, temperamental, and a tireless worker, an Englishwoman who was systematic, earnest, and emotionally stable, two other Americans, and me. Later more personnel were added. We worked with a group of young men, conscientious objectors, who had been taken on by the Quakers because of their religious beliefs. They lived across the river and helped with the heavier work. They put together the prefabricated one-story wooden houses we were building for the refugees and villagers whose houses had been destroyed. We frequently ate with the men workers and shared tasks with them as well.

With this small staff our daily responsibilities were much like those in Paris, with the *équipe* determining the people's needs. But our system included a store where we charged nominal amounts for the goods distributed, since there were not enough supplies and we wanted the recipients to choose what they considered important.

We sold at very low prices bedding, hand tools, clothing, shoes, kitchenware, and, when spring came, seeds. The peasants came in and registered with us before being admitted to the store. The selling was an arrangement that was to be the origin of a plan I proposed twenty-five years later for the United Nations Relief and Rehabilitation Administration (UNRRA) in 1944, and which was used after 1948 to create *counterpart funds* under the Marshall Plan. Prices were about one third of the retail value. Even with the selling there had to be a degree of rationing because our goods were of high quality, though simple, and no such items could be bought in the winter of 1918.

On store days, about twice a week, the men and women would line up in an expectant throng outside the schoolhouse, where we spread our wares on long tressel tables. There was a gay mood and the French householders were happy to be building for the future. The children came for their little black aprons, glad to fit again into the conventional pattern. The peasants were very particular about bed linen and especially about the *duvet*, the fat feather bed that always fell off my stomach as I rolled over in bed. At first they would not buy our sateen to cover the feathers because it was not red. We told them green was the color of hope. Then they crowded the tables eagerly. We had hundreds of pairs of shoes and good tools. I learned the names of the French carpenter's tools, bit and brace, chisel, screwdriver, as well as the names of household items. The money taken in went back to the central groups to help in the purchase of more supplies.

We did our visiting from town to town on bicycles. We would start out after our *café au lait*, in the dusky mist of early morning, and go to the village that had been assigned. We would estimate the need, ferret out special cases, tell the people what we had in the store. Even in those days, in some of the least-damaged towns, we would be given a glass of champagne, brought up from the peasant's small cellar where he kept bottles full of the fruits of his own vineyards. We would hear the tales of the invasions in 1914 and 1918, the story of wounded, dead, and *disparus*. Everywhere we were received as friends and left the families with a sense of confidence.

The house assigned to our group had a kitchen, a living room, and four small bedrooms. The floor was of red tile, the furniture simple, and the main charm, a wide fireplace. In the large iron stove there was a *bain-marie* to heat water.

We rarely returned from our villages until dark and were glad to find that Lucienne, one of our neighbors, had prepared our supper. There was soup and cabbage, cheese and coffee, potatoes, bread, and sometimes meat and butter. After supper we sat by the fire, talking about the day, writing up our special cases, often reading poetry.

During the first two months I could not sleep at night because I was cold on my canvas army cot, no mattress, and was billeted in the schoolhouse in the mairie, windblown because there were no panes in the windows. I did not complain because I was accepted by the Quakers, who had been through worse hardship during the days of fighting. I thought I could hold out from day to day. It was a cold winter, and I wore socks several layers deep, often inside very large boots. For much of the work I had to stand on the stone floors of unheated rooms. Then I wore wooden *sabots*, which kept my feet warmer, but we all developed chilblains.

Finally they got me a bed in the little house, with a mattress, and I could sleep. The snow-covered hills above the Marne, the purple smoke winding up over the stone house in the glow of sunset, the twisted streets, and the primitive churches with their massive stone walls, all added to the beauty which I shall always think of as France. I came to understand the people of the Marne as I have rarely understood the Parisians.

These were the French who had won the war. But they could not imagine that in winning at the cost of their young men, thousands buried at Verdun, the Argonne, at the Chemin des Dames, they had already lost the war that was to come in 1940. The *grands blessés* with their crutches and empty sleeves and the piles of rubble were the living testimony to the horrible price of victory.

That price was not yet realized on December 14 of 1918, the day their new hero, President Woodrow Wilson, entered Paris. Crediting Wilson with bringing the war to an end, they lined the streets by the thousands to cheer him. I was there.

It was my first postwar visit to Paris, a month and two days after the Armistice. Although I missed the great celebration of November 11, history passed before my eyes as I stood on the balcony of the Hôtel Crillon, overlooking the majestic Place de la Concorde.

Van Sanford Merle Smith, one of the American staff officers, held me up so that I could see the seething crowd below and Wilson's open Victoria driving slowly through the cheering mob. I met Uncle Bert there. He was followed shortly by Foster and Janet and Allen from the legation in Berne, Switzerland. Foster, a major in the Army, had been working as assistant to Vance McCormick, head of the War Trade Board, and dealt frequently with Bernard Baruch of the War Industries Board. Allen had done outstanding work as a young foreign service officer doing intelligence work in our legation in Switzerland. All were working on the peace treaty draft. They arranged for me to stay at the Crillon, where even the historic events I had just witnessed did not decrease the importance of my first hot bath in weeks.

Although I did not share the tremendous optimism of the liberated French finally freed of fear of conquest, I did view Wilson's proposals as important and constructive. My lack of experience in political matters did not prevent me from taking a keen interest in the conference which was to begin in Paris and end at Versailles.

A number of trips to Paris for several purposes—to see my relatives, to make purchases, and to get a few hours of rest—brought me into the middle of a very disturbing and puzzling clamor and debate. It was immediately clear to me that there was a large amount of disagreement, ignorance, and a fierce political struggle going on. It was not clear what personalities and ideas would dominate.

The remoteness of Wilson from his staff was physically and psychologically apparent and I heard details of this from the husband of a former co-worker, who was in the Wilson entourage for routine duties and security. He said the isolation was even worse than we supposed. The effect on my aunt and uncle was not discussed, but I saw the depression and the frustration in their silences. My brothers were busy with their work and did not talk about the overall situation with me but I knew they found the conflicts ominous.

I was to make several visits to Paris, all of them brief because of my work on the Marne. What I heard during my visits was very disturbing. One of Wilson's aides told me the President's health was not good. Wilson became increasingly disturbed and difficult as he discovered he could not convince the English, French, or Italians, partners with the United States in the Big Four, of his views. Each was more interested in what could be gained for his own nation than in Wilson's concepts or his plan for a League of Nations. Wilson's health was failing. Like Roosevelt twenty-five years later, he was psychologically isolated, but was to make decisions with the power of the United States behind him. He had majestic ideas, but by 1919 he was a sick, and sometimes confused, Chief of State.

In February Wilson returned to the United States to address the Congress. He made no progress at home, where opposition in the Senate was increasing. Back in Paris, his mood did not improve. Most disturbing to his aides was his unwillingness to consult with others on the American delegation. My uncle, who was extremely reserved, never gave any indication of his distress, but Aunt became ill with skin trouble, caused by the worry over the frustration of her husband, cut off from the President—his advice ignored.

The four main representatives, along with Secretary Lansing, were Henry White, General Tasker H. Bliss, Colonel Edward M. House, and Joseph C. Grew. While they held regular meetings, they never knew whether Wilson would follow their advice or go off on a tangent. Wilson was sure he was right and dealt personally with the three Allied Prime Ministers, England's David Lloyd George, France's Georges Clemenceau, and Italy's Vittorio Orlando. The result was a disaster in European relations—a disaster in the twenties and the thirties and way beyond.

Foster was mainly concerned with reparation clauses. He was convinced that the Germans could not pay large sums. At twenty-three years I had strong opinions based on my knowledge of devastation in the northern provinces of France. I argued that there must be some way of compensating the French peasants. I had not studied any economics then, and did not know the difficulties of transferring wealth. When I asked, "Can't you at least send the German cows to France?" Foster tried to explain to me that shifts of real wealth would be disrupting to economic systems.

Foster and John Maynard Keynes, the famous British economist, worked together on restitution, reparation, and related financial problems. When Keynes found he could not prevail over the demanding political leaders and realized that Germany would be asked for more than could be produced and transferred, he resigned and returned to England. Foster thought Keynes could have had more influence by staying.

I did not meet Keynes in 1919. I did in 1944 at Bretton Woods, New Hampshire, where the charters of world financial institutions were framed. He wrote the first brilliant and persuasive book on the mistakes in the World War I settlement, titled *The Economic Consequences of the Peace*. Although it was a very good book, I later found his statistics, put together in the fall of 1919, exaggerated the time and the amount of material aid the French required for reconstruction. In fact, the economy of France was quickly restored. But the loss of the flower of French manhood was irreparable.

Foster stayed on and continued his fight to minimize to some degree the demands for enormous reparation payments from the Germans. He wrote a strong brief against the inclusion of British military pensions in the bill to be levied on Germany.

Allen, brought from Switzerland where in the legation he had collected and transmitted information on Germany to Washington, was assigned, among other things, the task of drawing the boundaries of the new nation, Czechoslovakia, and other countries in the Danube area. There was a degree of fumbling in much of the pretreaty work. It is said that Wilson did not know where the South Tyrol was when he agreed to let Italy have the area. The experts were ignored for the most part. The politicians fought a shrewd battle for postwar power, not recognizing the danger of breaking up the Austro-Hungarian Empire and humiliating Germany.

A horde of representatives from a multitude of nations streamed into Paris. Even the device of separating the Big Ten,* and later the Big Four,† from the larger group had not ended the confusion. Specific issues such as the League of Nations, German disarmament, and financial retribution were lost in a whirlpool of political intrigue in which Wilson vainly tried to swim.

I knew little of the major struggles, but in discussing with Foster the need for quick and adequate reparation for France, I

---

*Big Ten: Woodrow Wilson, Robert Lansing, David Lloyd George, Arthur James Balfour, Georges Clemenceau, Stéphen Jean Marie Pichon, Vittorio Orlando, Baron Sidney Sonnino, Kimmochi Saionji, Count Nobuaki Makino.

†Big Four: Wilson, Lloyd George, Clemenceau, Orlando.

pointed out to him concretely the nature of losses. I also heard the talk of starvation for Germany and knew that Uncle Bert had finally persuaded the leaders in Paris that continuing blockade and ensuing starvation of a helpless, prostrate Germany was neither humane nor good politics. This was one of his contributions to Europe and the foreign policy of the United States.

We had German prisoners working for us on the Marne. They were young, friendly, and helpful. They appreciated the treatment they got from us as well as from the French peasants in the villages where they helped to clear away the rubble of war and carry out simple building projects.

My trips to Paris gave me some understanding of the difficulties of achieving a settlement. The mistakes made in the Paris Conference in 1919 were to affect my entire life and the lives of my children and grandchildren. I witnessed the conference as from a distant seat in a large amphitheater, and only sensed in general terms the magnitude of what was taking place. Having talked to a dozen of the participants, I was to remember the controversy for more than fifty years. It foreshadowed future oppression, atomic warfare, and global threats and misunderstandings. If I was too young then to get the full meaning of what was happening, I was not too young to hear and in part to remember.

One later episode at Henderson relating to this post-Versailles conflict I recall. It was at the time of President Wilson's illness in 1919. It was a warm day in early September. Uncle Bert asked me to go to the Warners' farmhouse with him. He wanted to telephone long-distance and for some reason he wanted my company. We had no telephones in the cottages. I remember the small officelike room just inside the porch—linoleum flooring and a few chairs. We stood by the wall telephone while he asked the operator for the temporary White House in a midwest city—I think in Iowa. He tried to talk to the President but Tumulty and Edith Wilson would not put him through. As Uncle Bert told me, William Bullitt, with whom he had talked in Paris, had reported to the Senate a story of a conversation that distorted his view. He wrote a letter later to Wilson, but I remember, as we walked back to his cottage, he was upset because he could not speak to the President. He was not against the League but he thought Wilson's tactics wrong. The record was never set straight. He had tried to help Wilson with honest criticism but his advice was resented.

A few months later Wilson, again resuming some of his duties, wrote a strong letter asking Secretary Lansing to resign. My uncle was a disciplined, well-trained government servant and never criticized Wilson in public.

Going back to 1918, life on the Marne was only slightly touched by the political drama in Paris. News was scarce and I was fully occupied with my daily work. We continued our sales of materials and tools, extending our activities into the badly shelled and bombed areas.

In the early winter two friends bicycled with me to Rheims. We were the first American civilians to enter the town after the Armistice. We rode north from Mareuil over roads pocked with shell holes, spending one night on the way in a half-ruined hotel at Ville en Tardenois. The three of us shared a big bed on the second floor of the hotel surrounded by broken walls and debris. During the night the back half of the house next door fell away. When dawn came we looked down on a pile of rubble where the wall had been. After a brief breakfast of the warmed-over provisions we had brought with us, we went a few miles farther, to Rheims. We found the cathedral in ruins, its roof open to the sky. Soldiers had slept on piles of straw and had started a fire that badly damaged the sculpture on the facade. But the stained-glass windows had been taken out for preservation, each piece of glass numbered and labeled. We hoped desperately that reconstruction could somehow be achieved. It has been.

The devastation throughout the region was so overwhelming that it sickened us to ride through it. No one who had not seen the miles and miles of churned-up fields and piles of rubble where villages had been could imagine the psychological impact. We knew that many soldiers were buried in these piles of bricks and stone. The war of tanks and trenches had a horror that lasted long and that had an intensity of suffering that can be compared with the holocaust of Hiroshima. It is hard now to imagine World War I in all its waste and misery.

I was able, somewhat recklessly, to explore a number of the dugouts and trenches in which the doughboys and *poilus* of 1918 had lived for months of fighting. I had heard that there was a piano in a deep trench in the Argonne. Searching for it, I went down about forty feet underground, descending three flights of steps which were never in a direct line. The construction was to lessen the danger that a hand grenade lobbed over from enemy territory might fall to the bottom and explode. The shafts of the trenches were reinforced with timbers, like coal mines. I never did find the piano, but discovered cooking utensils and other evidence of the many days of living underground.

Foolishly, I picked up and tossed away a number of German "potato masher" hand grenades until my friends dissuaded me. We looked for souvenirs—pistols, spent shells, military insignia, and belts—and we took an almost childish pride in collecting the flotsam and jetsam of the grim struggle. I had learned from returning soldiers that there were some points on the front where the men had talked with the enemy and made rude jokes across the muddy stretches of "No Man's Land." Verdun, to the east, was where thousands died to fulfill General Robert Nivelle's command, "*On ne passe pas.*" "They shall not pass" was more than a slogan and the enemy did not pass.

When, in 1919, we drove north to see if we could return refugees to their former homes, we passed Amiens and went on to the Vimy Ridge, to the Chemin des Dames, and to Lille. This was the region where the British line had broken twice. Thousands of fine young men were buried in their blood, covered with rubble and mud. A few spikes of trees here and there stood in once fertile fields. Empty trenches zigzagged across the barren waste. The silence was more horrifying than the earlier sound of battle which I had heard when I went to visit my two aunts at the front. I felt sick and lost among the ghosts and broken bones, the shards of warfare and its desolation.

In the spring of 1919 I went north again, for the Shurtleff Committee. After the Armistice the Red Cross had begun to pack up and go home. The Quakers were finding funds hard to get. When I heard that Mrs. Shurtleff was returning to take some of her refugee families to their homes in the devastated areas, I rejoined her committee and we set out in two station wagons to see where we could reestablish the peasants who had fled to Paris. Often we would see a curl of smoke coming out of the rubble in a place considered uninhabitable. It was a sign that another staunch farm couple was living underground, waiting to cultivate the fields, which could not be effectively restored for several years.

Accompanying Mrs. Shurtleff and me were Hilda Williams,

"Scat," Atherton Curtis, and two other committee members. It was a strange experience in which we all tried to conceal the strong emotions that swept over us. We were personally uncomfortable, sleeping in half-ruined inns, but this was a minor matter. Our thoughts were on our main purpose—to resettle as many refugees as possible.

The tension was broken by the meticulous habits of Mr. Curtis, who had helped the committee throughout the war. He was a wispy, fastidious vegetarian, very concerned with sanitation. He had brought his own bed sheets. At one inn, when he discovered there was but a single towel for three of us, he said, "I would like the middle. The ends are ambiguous."

We reported to the refugees of the conditions of their land and homes, but they still wished to return. It was time to resume the tilling of the land, to restore the pattern by which they had lived for generations. We could take but a few, and these we set up in their old villages, with the minimum necessities of life. Our work and our resources were nearing the end.

While we had worked constantly there was little time to think about ourselves and our personal lives. Only later, as spring began to pass into summer, did we feel the pressure less and begin to look at each other as individuals. We realized that each of us had talents, aspirations, and different personalities. As the separation that we knew would break our wartime camaraderie neared, the affection, attachments, and deep involvement with each other became more intense. Yet we all knew we would have to adjust to so-called normal living. We found various ways of adapting to old and new patterns of life. There were some of us who could not face the change. Two or three of my group became Communists and went to Russia. Engagements were broken. One girl walked off into the forest and took poison, probably because of a departed lover. The sense of returning to a humdrum life disturbed and distressed us. I can understand today the opportunities, the challenge, and the dangers faced by members of the Peace Corps. The life we lived and, for a few of us, the death we faced were similar in their strange excitement.

My letters show that in moments of emotional stress I had a dawning desire to go home. I indicated in writing to my mother and father an awareness that I was needed at home. My grandmother was ill and I began to have illusions of a capacity to be a homebody, a returning guardian angel for my family. I saw myself helping my mother, caring for my small nephews, Robert and Richard Edwards, seeking to ease the burden of my sister Margaret who was still weak from the aftereffects of the flu. She had been a near victim of the first widespread epidemic of influenza.

I sailed for home with Mrs. Shurtleff on June 7, 1919, six days after my twenty-fourth birthday, on the S.S. *Espagne*, the same ship on which I had reached France two years earlier. Almost any price would have been too little for me to pay for this experience in France. When the haggard soldiers in gray-blue uniforms marched down the Champs Elysées, I was at Henderson. As I remembered the *poilus* at the Gare de l'Est, the *grands blessés*, the trenches in shattered woods, the rubble, the grief, and the victory, I wept.

I was lonely for the French, for the peasants with their passionate concern for their land, their vineyards, their rabbits, their kitchen utensils, their beds and the linens that covered them. I missed their blunt descriptions of all of life's sensations, their dry wit. My feelings for French officials and shopkeepers of Paris was less fond. The officials in the city were so petty. The shopkeepers wrapped vegetables in newspaper, and even with this they used as little as possible, fussing over every request, measuring the string with which they tied the package. But I missed them too, missed my daily conflicts with them, my schemes to foil their disregard of me and of their rural countrymen.

I had changed. When I first worked in Paris, I had had a real problem deciding whether I could permit myself to join friends who went to the opera on Sunday, and not to church. Then I had played cards on Sunday with a guilty feeling. With the Quakers I had joined in prayer meditation services daily, in our get-together I had learned surprising as it may seem, to smoke. I had also learned to enjoy the company of men without thinking that I should or must fall in love. I had talked and danced with many men and felt comfortable in their presence.

My family took the new and outward evidence of change in me in their stride. I smoked Fatimas in front of them. I went to the Henderson village barber and had my hair cut. Yet during the summer at Henderson I felt very much a part of the family again. It was not until I went back to Auburn that I realized how restless I had become after the excitement of the preceding two years. I thought of the song title, "How Ya Gonna Keep 'Em Down on the Farm?" because I, too, had seen Paree.

### JULY FOURTEENTH 1919

Far away the soldiers are marching
Like great strong waves is the sound of their feet
I only hear the lake waves breaking
And the swifter pulse of my own heart-beat
While the heroes are marching.

Through desperate hours and dreary winters
We longed for the dawn from war's dark night
In Paris triumph's banners are waving
Clouds flame here with standards of light
For the heroes marching.

Down from the forts of the Aisne and Verdun
Tramp the soldiers who held to the end
I know those men, I know their leaders
I see gray mist at the far road's bend
As of heroes marching.

Down from the front in the blue of battle
Grim, yet gay with sweethearts' flowers
Soldiers march and shall march forever
As we think back to the world's dark hours
And the heroes marching.

Over the earth there steals a shadow
I think of France and my hills grow dim
But my heart thrills to the song of glory
As into the west to the future's rim
The heroes are marching.

*(written by Eleanor Dulles, July 14, 1919, at Henderson)*

# 6

# INDUSTRY—FROM STEEL TO HAIRNETS

The long search for goals that had begun earlier was renewed in my return from war work in France.

An unexpected offer of a fellowship at Bryn Mawr in 1919 led to a tentative decision to consider industrial management as a career. In this field I assumed I could gain financial independence and perhaps opportunities for leadership in industry. It was worth a try so I went back to college.

The training and experience of the next three years were to prove worthwhile as education, but not directly, as circumstances developed, to start me toward the goals I was to seek in later years. I earned my first M.A. degree.

I accepted the scholarship from the Social Economy Department, headed by Dr. Susan Kingsbury. I thought there might be a career in industry with action, drama, and eventually power in the heart of America's economy. Heavy industry appealed to me and so did the idea of a woman making a breakthrough in a man's world.

This new course of training was related to the manpower requirements of World War I. Bryn Mawr had opened a special course in 1917. I thought this would lead me into the *real* world, somewhat as the battlefields and danger in France had made real demands. I wanted to make my way in a world where hammer struck anvil and sparks flew.

The students with whom I worked were a motley crew. They intended to move on to management jobs, to supervising younger workers and climbing the promotion ladder. We lived and studied apart from the other stately graduate scholars who walked the cloisters as I had once done. Now we rose early and went to our practice jobs and on industrial survey trips, and argued in seminars that followed. Our meals were hurried and we fell exhausted into bed each night.

Philadelphia had many factories, some of which were attempting to make their management more scientific and to control the flow of materials in effective ways. Some were less progressive. Unionization was increasing, causing considerable ferment among workers and management. We debated questions of training, incentive, monotony, safety, and a host of problems as we sought to understand what motivation led to good production and how to analyze the mistakes that led to waste.

The possibility of understanding the state of affairs was enhanced by the ideas of women who had actual experience. Outstanding among them was my professor, Anne Bezanson. Miss Bezanson was a former farm girl from Nova Scotia. She had come to Cambridge, Massachusetts, to work in the Gillette factory. At Gillette, one of the top management officials, William E. Nickerson, had decided she was a person with extraordinary promise and he gave her generous scholarships which enabled her to study at Radcliffe and Harvard, where she earned her Ph.D. She had come to the academic world of Bryn Mawr with unusual insight into American production methods and factory conditions. She was never assimilated into the ivory-tower atmosphere of the college. Her quaint diction and remarks on the superficiality sometimes evident at Bryn Mawr did not make her loved by her colleagues though understood and appreciated by her students. They could relish her biting sense of humor about everything except herself. She had an odd kind of arrogance as when she boasted that she had twenty-eight pairs of shoes and might buy more. She was a large, broad-shouldered, slow-moving woman, forthright in her instruction, specific in her advice. It was well known that Miss Bezanson and her department head, Dr. Susan Kingsbury, hated each other and kept as far apart as a small campus permitted. Miss Bezanson thought the social economy teaching was phony, although she appreciated guest lectures from real experts like Dr. Alice Hamilton of Johns Hopkins University and Lillian Gilbreth, who was cohead with her husband, Frank, of a well-known engineering firm. Two of Dr. Gilbreth's children were later to make her even better known as the mother of twelve, the heroine of *Cheaper by the Dozen*.

Miss Bezanson was just the person I needed in my search for a career. I still relish thoughts of her vigorous personality in the somewhat incompatible setting of Bryn Mawr. She took us on our field trips to factories and assigned us for one day a week working in an office or a shop. We noted a number of the high-level plant officers were on the defensive in a society increasingly critical of harsh policies and indifference toward workers. Their claims of improvements in efficiency, reduction of accidents, and rising wages were frequently as much excuse as explanation. The war had changed many attitudes in all people, and the postwar years were like the decade of the 1960s, shaken by change and revolt. This postwar restlessness brought heated debate to our seminars as we pooled our experiences and came up with many varied criticisms.

My first work assignment at the Atlantic Refining Company was a boring desk job. I was to interview job applicants and there were not many in a company with a fairly stable work force. But it was a first assignment, and I felt somehow I had a part in the vital industry, as if I were helping to govern the flow of oil in the great tanks outside my office window.

My second job was more interesting. The W. R. Scott Company sold its industrial advisory services to manufacturers seeking production quotas, controlling raw materials, and standardizing operations. The simple ideas on which their advice was based were feared by workers and sought by managers. In some cases the new procedures exerted increasing pressure on the worker for more output. In some instances the aim was to cut down waste and regularize conditions, making work easier. While in most cases the workers would gain, they were fearful of exploitation and condemned all time and motion studies. The analysis of tasks and recommendations for *rationalization* presented interesting problems, which were highly instructive to me.

As part of our Bryn Mawr course, we wrote reports on our work experiences. These were thrown into the seminar pot to help us make comparisons, to assess the performance of employers and workers, and to visualize how we would run the shops once we had the opportunity. We often had a chance to interview applicants, as well as to study training, rating, and wage systems. Of the twenty women in our group a few chose retailing rather than factory work. Retailing would almost certainly mean better salaries and rapid advancement. Those of us who chose industry did not expect equality with men—only near equality. We knew the work would be hard but we hoped the door to better opportunities was opening.

Our summer assignments were for full-time work. It was then that I went to the steel mill in Bridgeport, Connecticut. I had investigated the possibility of employment on a railroad but found the women were only employed as window washers and women were not wanted in management. Perhaps if the railroads had employed more women, the trains would be in better shape now. Certainly the companies have almost given up window washing. In 1920 I was glad to settle for the American Tube and Stamping Company.

Miss Bezanson had found me the job—a temporary one as assistant to the employment manager, Robert Bradley. He was a good-looking, blond, Ivy League type who probably earned five times my sixteen dollars a week. But I think he was bored with his job and glad to have my company in his office. I was to do some interviewing, to study the cases of accidents in the plant, and get out the company paper. He seemed to have failed to develop any real job for himself, nor did he find any significant work for me.

I worked first in the office, where I became editor of *Steel Craft*, the house organ, and was assistant employment manager. I wanted to run one of the rolling mills. It was gigantic. They told me it was the largest cold rolling mill in the United States. I finally persuaded Mr. Bradley to let me work on one of the punch presses.

The shed in which I worked opened onto the mill. Men passed me with "shapes and forms," billets and forgings, ready for milling. They carried the heavy iron and steel on shoulders gleaming with sweat, shouting and cursing at each other, adding a few decibels to the crash and roar of the machines. The sense of power swept over me as I sat, insignificant, at my machine in the dark and dirty workshop. Already I knew that this world of industry was not mine to conquer. I began to see that brute strength in the mills and male dominance in the office were to rule. Where they left off money and ownership would prevail.

The air was dusty, the floor uneven and unpaved. Here I sat before the press, tripping the pedal with my foot while I pushed a piece of metal under the cutting tool, repeating this process with a sustained rhythm. My first task was to machine round boxes in which I cut holes for the springs that were part of a Victrola (the precursor of the modern record player). My second job at the press was making holes for the screws on coffin handles. Although the work was tiring, with dirt and oil dropping around my press while nearby machines roared and pounded, it was more vital than staying in the office. No skill was involved. It was just push in, take out, pile up. The hours were eight a day for five days and four on Saturdays.

My sixteen dollars a week was an office salary. The women in the factory got twelve dollars.

On my right a bright-looking, small, Polish girl worked at a brisk pace; on my left, a tall Scandinavian woman. During breaks I tried to talk to them, but they were wary of me, probably because they knew I had come from the office. I did learn they lived with their parents and their principal interest was men, with or without marriage. Until they married they worked, contributing to the family income.

Later, when I worked in the assembly shop putting together small batteries, we labored in a quieter atmosphere. The women talked then, but what they said was incomprehensible to me. I had not heard the colloquialisms they used but guessed that most of the conversation dealt with sexual activity.

I visited the shop across the river, part of the company's Bridgeport operation, and saw the pouring of molten metal into molds of sand and clay. I saw the puddlers stirring the red-hot "porridge" with long poles to make the ingots carried past me as I sat at my punch press. What was the plan for these hurrying men? How did they know where they were going? Who supplied whom with material? Experience seemed the only answer and it seemed no one had thought of changing the scheme of things for a long time.

Tough old birds broke in the few new workers. Even now I can see the men on lathes, bent under a spotlight, oil dripping on the cutting tool as the blue steel shavings curled away from the block of metal they cut. Their precision came from a long apprenticeship. A mistake could put in jeopardy months of work and valuable raw material. Everywhere there was dust, dirt, oil, steel shavings, big billets, and heavy forgings, most of the heavy ingots piled without apparent order. I still do not know if the confusion everywhere was as irrational as it seemed. Perhaps it was like a writer's study where papers are strewn about but where there is a kind of system that only he understands.

But there appeared to be little order in this chaos, and some years later I learned the plant went bankrupt. While I was there I never saw one man from top management looking through the shops. I took the reports of accidents and knew that a man had fallen into the molten metal and had become part of a large ingot as it cooled. I knew that men had lost arms and legs. We worked at improving safety, urging the workers to take precautions, but they were reluctant and casual. They took off their goggles whenever the straw boss left.

Whatever production planning there was at American Tube and Stamping, it was not in accord with the theories I had studied at W. R. Scott in Philadelphia. The lack of organization and control in Bridgeport was not unique, nor was the firm's bankruptcy. It occurred during a transitional period for American industry, between standardization and moving-belt production, which came later.

The Dennison Company, famous for its paper products, where some of my Bryn Mawr classmates were working, was well organized. But many other firms were not. The size and complexity of operations had increased, but the necessary controls for the flow of material and supervision of personnel had not. The small punch press at which I worked was incongruous in the total operation, which included tons of heavy equipment.

In Bridgeport I lived in a cold-water room with one small window. There was nothing to please the eye, inside or outside. I did my laundry in the washbasin, ate a fifteen-cent coffee and egg breakfast, and walked a mile to save car fare. Lunch at the factory cafeteria was not bad, and cost about twenty-five cents. I usually had dinner at the YWCA for about eighty-five cents—good food—better than I could get now. From my sixteen dollars a week, I spent five dollars on my room and eight on food. That left three dollars for soap, car fare, postage, telephone, movies, etc. I bought no clothes, had no medical expenses, and can't remember buying a book. I was too tired to read.

On Saturdays I went to the Fairfield beach. For a small entrance fee I could change into my bathing suit and swim in the Sound. It was a good summer in spite of some privation. I was excited by the new environment, interested in strange problems, and getting answers to questions on plant conditions.

When I went back to my family at the end of the summer, the clean, comfortable cottages at Henderson seemed to me the *unreal* world. I was happy to be there, but I did not forget the smoke, the fumes, the noise of the vast and vibrant sheds. And I still thought perhaps I wanted to work in industry.

This was the summer when Allen, who was still in the Foreign Service, came home on leave and met Clover Todd. She was visiting in the nearby Thousand Islands. He fell in love at first sight. He told Mother he had been very restrained and did not propose to her until the third day of his visit. She was a charming blond and kept her lovely spirit throughout her life, a delight to all of us.

The Todd family had never heard of anyone named Dulles. Professor Todd was teaching at Columbia and in order to see if there was anything good to say about Allen he looked in the library catalog. He found Allen Welsh Dulles, *A History of the Boer War*. "The family must be intellectual," he said, not knowing the author had been eight years old in 1901. "Perhaps he is all right, but is Allen an old man?"

Clover and Allen were married in a few weeks and all of us were delighted. I saw a great deal of her in Washington and missed her after her death, in 1974, one of the painful separations I have suffered.

When I went to New York to get a job in the fall, rising unemployment throughout the nation complicated my search. In the postwar slump of 1920, I searched the Help Wanted ads and walked the streets, looking for a job. I was not desperate, since I could always go back to Auburn and live with my parents, but the drive to be independent and find a career was one I could not resist. I wanted a professional life. Somehow I had to work it out on my own terms.

I lived at the YWCA hotel in Manhattan while I registered at employment agencies. An advertisement for a financial job tempted me to attend several group preparatory sessions for applicants. A very smooth, good-looking man told us eager job seekers that we could sell stock and bonds to small shopkeepers, beauty parlor operators, barbers, and other merchants. We were to give them certificates that would represent shares in a company that owned shares in other companies.

"All these small businesses have a few hundred dollars in the cash register," he told us. "They will buy the bonds."

"What will they know about the firm behind the firm?" I asked.

"It doesn't matter. You get a good percentage."

There was no Securities and Exchange Commission in 1920. I rejected this offer.

Another of the early offers I rejected came from a brassiere factory. It was too much to face, after the flaming blast furnaces and enormous rolling mill of the past summer, to work on women's intimate underwear. However, I found an advertisement of an opening in a Long Island City factory that interested me. They needed a forewoman to supervise some two hundred girls. I thought they would also need an employment manager and took the subway and the old elevated railway, the "El," to the address of the loft.

It proved to be a hairnet factory. The sharp-nosed, bald-headed manager looked at me dubiously. He had just employed a round, blond, blue-eyed super-doll for the job. But he needed a payroll clerk he said. I told him I would be a payroll clerk if he would also take me on as employment manager. I started at eighteen dollars a week and stayed for almost a year.

More than half my day was taken up with interviewing job applicants. There were hundreds of them in the early part of the week, fewer toward the end. Our rate of turnover was fantastic. We had a full working complement of about three hundred girls and five men for heavy work. We would employ as many as fifty or sixty women a week, and half of them would be gone after the first payday. This meant a loss for each girl of about three dollars in wages held back—a common practice in industry at the time. The women did not protest; they simply disappeared.

Their work was sorting, grading, and packing hairnets. The nets, made of human hair, came from China. In theory the ones without holes were nicely packed and sold to the good drugstores and five-and-dime stores—Woolworths, Harrises and Kresges. Sorting was done, but when the flow of incoming stock was interrupted, the rejects were taken out of the storeroom and put in the envelopes, even for the better stores, thus making a mockery of the original elimination.

Apparently consumer complaints were slow to get back to the stores, and producers could get away with such practices. The manager was puzzled as to what I was after. He suspected that I did not intend to spend my life in a hairnet factory. He probably wondered if I had some faint reform ideas, but he did not worry overmuch and asked me no questions. He saw the money coming in. I kept my eyes open and my mouth shut.

As payroll clerk I took my data mainly from time cards, recording employee earnings. At the end of the week I made out two tables. One showed the earnings, which I transcribed on the pay envelopes. The other was a frequency distribution of the number of ten-, five-, and one-dollar bills, the quarters, dimes, nickels, and pennies, to be paid out. This one went to the bank.

When the sack of money came in, the manager and I locked ourselves in a room and filled the pay envelopes. If we were a penny over or a penny under, my blood ran cold. It meant either that the envelopes were marked inaccurately, that we had put the wrong amounts in, that my table for the bank was wrong, or that some of the money had fallen on the floor. We would go through every envelope again. These were tense moments for me but I made only a few mistakes in the year of my work there.

For some weeks all went well. My salary was raised to twenty-five dollars a week, in two steps. I actually saved a little money each week.

As the result of my interviewing, I knew that we had some able girls in the place. I worked out a wage incentive system with a sliding scale for production above the standard amount. If the girls increased their production by 20 percent, their wages increased by 15. If they doubled their production, their pay went up more, but it was never doubled. The management gained more than the girls, but the girls did not lose anything by the increased effort. In fact, I thought they enjoyed their work more and took a sporting interest in a sense of competition.

Then the trouble began.

The manager said he was worried that some of the girls were too smart. They were earning sixteen dollars a week and might earn even more. This would never do. They would get "cocky" and unmanageable.

The answer was easy—for him. He slowed the flow of hairnets. Production dropped. The best workers left. We still had more applicants than we could handle at eight o'clock on a Monday morning. Some would come for the few dollars they could earn in one pay period—less than twelve dollars. Others with more responsibilities, older and with families to support, would hope for longtime employment. The place was light, clean, and quiet. The girls could joke and gossip among themselves. It was not a bad place to work except for the labor policy. We were in competition for workers with the National Biscuit Company across the street.

At Christmas there was to be a tremendous party. When I told my sister-in-law, Janet, about it, she wanted to come. I had heard of

[83]

other factory parties and convinced her she would be bored. Fortunately she accepted my advice. After an hour of cookies and lemonade, bottles of harder stuff appeared and the men disappeared into stock rooms or private offices with some of the prettier girls. I did not stay for the finale.

That year in New York I was lucky in having Emily Huntington sharing a room with me on Staten Island. I had met Emily in 1919. She was to be my close friend for more than fifty years. The first time I saw her I was on the Paoli local, a commuter train from Philadelphia. On the train was a handsome young woman wearing a blue serge suit and Knox straw hat.

I thought, "I hope she's getting off at Bryn Mawr."

Emily did get off at Bryn Mawr. She was taking the same courses as I, after completing her undergraduate work at the University of California at Berkeley. She was to return to Berkeley to become a professor of economics until her retirement in 1958. The year we shared a room, Emily worked at Procter and Gamble.

Every morning at five o'clock we made coffee and toast and set off in different directions. She took the train to Port Elizabeth and I rode the now less used Staten Island Ferry and the subway to Long Island City. I loved the ferry ride when dawn came up over the bay and the city shone in the early light. Tugboats and steamers passed the lumbering, comfortable boat while I tried to pull myself together for a long, hard day. I think the entire trip, including the subway, took about an hour and cost ten cents.

As I look back to the ten months in the hairnet factory, I wonder why it did not seem more strange to me. My experience came at a time when production in the United States was undergoing a profound change. While it did not equal in importance the industrial revolution of one hundred years before, when the factory system dominated the British economy and spread to other European countries, it was an important new phase. The result of time and motion studies was more planning and control. Worker opposition led to a great surge for organization of labor, workers' compensation, and systems for airing grievances. Yet the subdivision of tasks into small segments, which diminished the scope of their jobs, led to workers receiving higher wages as output increased. The struggle of union and management early in the twentieth century brought shorter hours and higher pay. For women conditions of work gradually improved.

[84]

Women in increasing numbers preferred the factory to house-work. I gave considerable thought to this trend, talking it over with my classmates. Social workers were inclined to differ with me, but I came to believe that women liked factory work because the supervision was impersonal, they were paid for their labor, and their minds were left free to roam as they worked, for much of the work was repetitive.

My interest in the question of monotony in work was aroused by widespread discussion during these years. A whole day might be spent turning a series of screws or in a repetitive cutting operation with no knowledge on the part of the worker as to what he might be doing in relation to the finished product. I concluded that monotony is not as abhorrent as some think. Many workers welcome the security of repetition and resist change. The ones who crave variety and excitement escape into more venturesome types of work than the assembly line.

However, it is fortunate that over the years, as more people seek higher education, the new techniques remove many standardized jobs to computer-controlled processes. In the time I spent in industry the change led to a notable reduction of the heavy labor. A smaller number of people suffered the deadening fatigue and drudgery which for centuries had made of men beasts of burden. American industry was always oriented in the direction of labor-saving methods. Progress has been uneven, but heavy manual labor has come to occupy a smaller fraction of the work.

My months in factories—studying, teaching, and working—have made me conscious of the changes, the balancing of costs of men and material, the losses from labor turnover, the importance of mobility, the choice between leisure and earnings, the problem of regimentation and sacrifice of initiative. I am grateful for my close view of the industrial base of our society. The problems I studied then helped me understand industry in England, and reconstruction in Germany and Austria in later years.

There were two major results of my work at this time. I learned from direct observation much about American factories and wage earners in a transitional period. There had been only partial adaptation, before 1920, to rationalization and the assembly line. The unions were weak. Machines were reality. I also learned that industry was not to be my life's work. I might gain authority and expertise, but I would not find the kind of creative work I sought. I wished broader contacts and a more stimulating intellectual world where causes and effects were of major concern in economic development. Moreover, I sought more influence over events.

The obstacles to meaningful work I saw were faced by other women. Even the well-known expert in industrial medicine, Dr. Alice Hamilton of Harvard, was not respected when she first began to tour factories. When a friend Phil Drinker, an expert on industrial dust hazards, took her on a tour of inspection, someone yelled, "Get that lady out of here!"

Only gradually was her work accepted. I knew without such a special competence it would be even harder for me to find an interesting life in industry.

I decided to get to the root of some of the economic problems and to follow the advice given me two years before by my teachers at Bryn Mawr. By the spring of 1921 I had about eight hundred dollars in the bank. I calculated that with a yearly income of four hundred and help from my parents I could go abroad to study. My direction was becoming clear to me.

*Eleanor, about five years old, in Russian costume (1900)*

*Dulles children, right to left: Foster, Margaret, Allen, Eleanor, and Nataline*

*Eleanor at desk, reading, about 1908*

*John Foster Dulles, 1891, three years old*

*Allen Welsh Dulles, 1901, eight years old*

*Eleanor in Bois de Boulogne, April 2, 1918*

*Office workers in S. Glemby Company, hairnet factory,
Long Island City, 1922. Eleanor at desk near typewriter*

*Emily Huntington and Eleanor in German kayak in
front of Linden Lodge, Lake Ontario, August 1932*

*David S. Blondheim in study at Johns Hopkins University (circa 1930)*

*Eleanor Dulles with Mollie Dewson, testifying before Vandenberg Commission on the Social Security System, 1937*

# 7

# STUDENTS IN BLOOMSBURY, LONDON

In the damp murky dawn of London winter in 1921, I stood on the corner with my friend Emily waiting for the No. 77 bus. This lumbering red vehicle took us to High Holborn and the Strand, near the London School of Economics. As I waited so many mornings I was glad my coat was so stiff and strong (it could almost stand up by itself), shedding the rain which fell from my blue felt hat.

My year in England began a new experience. At twenty-six I had been still without a profession. Then, in 1921, I reached a decision. I would lay a solid basis for economic studies and go on for a Ph.D. in economics. My undergraduate work had not included economics. As a graduate at Bryn Mawr I studied industry and labor but with no base in theory. I recognized, even before Professor Bezanson suggested it, that I needed to read and study and listen. By going to London I chose an institution where the level of thinking was high but where the competitive struggle in the classroom was at a minimum.

It was largely coincidence, but perhaps not entirely, that I began a serious study of economics at a time of ferment and change. New techniques of measurement and control were being devised. The whole body of thinking with respect to business cycles, monetary policy, labor economics, and social security was being challenged and revised. It was in the years between 1920 and 1940 that many great economists took over the task of revising and expanding classical economics as expounded by Adam Smith, David Ricardo, and Alfred Marshall, for example. The doctrines applicable to economic systems had been altered by increasing mechanization, rapid transportation and communication, and the myriad scientific developments that came between the two world wars and that were to continue into the computer and space age. The rules of basic relationships were developed by the early economists. However, some of the refinements built upon them, relating to the business cycle and monetary policy, have been expanded and adapted to a more dynamic world. For example, the quantity theory of money has never been discredited. However, by adding the meaning of velocity of the circulation of money, changes in the practical approach to monetary policy have occurred.

Although much of the new thinking in economics was attributed to Keynes, with whom I had a brief correspondence in these years, there were some thirty or forty outstanding thinkers and philosophers who redirected much of economic practice and some of the basic policy. It was my extraordinary privilege to meet a large number of outstanding writers and teachers. It is worth mentioning a few to illustrate the caliber of men who were changing ideas in business and government policy in Europe and the United States. The list includes T. E. Gregory, Edwin Cannan, Sir William Beveridge, F. A. Hayek, Gottfried Haberler, Henry Clay, Charles Rist, Milton Friedman, Robert Nathan, Lord Robbins, Arthur F. Burns, Paul Douglas, R. H. Tawney, Alvin Hansen, and Jacob Viner. My preoccupation with economic problems was actively stimulated in London and continues until this day.

Emily Huntington and I took steerage passage on S.S. *Homeric*. It was not a student or tourist accommodation. It was just plain steerage, buried somewhere below the waterline, with both stateroom and dining room innocent of portholes or outer ventilation. The food was of a lively character. On one occasion the meat moved on the plate. We were young and healthy but Southampton looked wonderful the day we sighted it.

An old friend, Nan Tynan, had asked us to live in her small flat. We had first met Nan at Bryn Mawr, where she studied on a scholarship granted by President M. Carey Thomas. Nan was one of the two women on a major Government War Commission on Industry and a former worker in the Telephone Union in England— a real trade-union type. She was tall, dark, somewhat ungainly. Her speech was cultivated, almost literary in tone. Her friend Gerry Foster, who was a scholar, had greatly expanded her horizons, limited by an all too short period of schooling.

The flat had two small bedrooms and a tiny living room, with a coal fire which gave out more dirt than warmth. For a shilling that strange English contraption called a "geyser" would change the ice water in the bath pipes to boiling, but it required remarkable agility to avoid being scalded. I didn't mind the cold but what did worry me was the soot. It was on my pillow when I awoke in the morning, on the milk in the jar we put outside for deliveries in the morning. I was not surprised at the drab quality of the food, for we spent only a few shillings a day.

Since students at the London School included many British civil servants, daytime lectures were repeated at night. I took night courses and in the afternoon I spent long hours at the British Museum in the spacious, domed reading room. The light was dim, the chairs comfortable. A goodly number of my neighbors at the desks came in out of the cold to sleep in peace. When I grew weary of books I would go out to the halls to see Lord Elgin's marbles, "liberated" from the Acropolis in Athens.

A special lecture, which was an unusual privilege, was given by George Bernard Shaw. Surprisingly it was on the British Post Office. It was the only time I saw him.

I also spent much of my time in the museum working on a long, rambling, meditative epic poem on the Russian Revolution. This tremendous class struggle puzzled me and stimulated me to creative, or so I thought, effort. My mother, who had been in Russia in 1880, told me of the life there, where the rich ate lavishly, wore luxurious furs and jewels, while a hundred million of their countrymen had scarcely enough to eat and wear. To me the Revolution was inevitable. The distribution of economic wealth was intolerable and I felt burdened by the inequity. I have never come to terms with the injustices of life, not then, nor now, but even in the 1920s I was not a good revolutionary. I was appalled by violence and killing.

The school had already begun in what was to be an honorable tradition, the combination of a classical, theoretical economics with sponsorship of social security insurance programs. There was attention also to means to stabilize or improve economic relations. In the school one took a degree, no tests. If a student wanted a degree, attendance was not by roll call, quizzes, or exams, but by payment of fees. It was presumed the student listened to at least some of the lectures. I signed up for sixteen courses!

Alternating with lecture periods, "reading periods" were devoted to learning either in books or by other means. During one of these periods, Felix, the brother of the author Christopher Morley, introduced Emily and me to Toynbee Hall, one of the world's leading settlement houses. The staff asked us to do a study. Emily and I agreed and went every day for several weeks to four London boroughs to study home workers. In the East End, a slum area near the India docks, I climbed tenement stairs, talked to the aged, decrepit, and crippled women who made paper flowers, sewed buttonholes, and did other piecework in their flats.

Homework had already been recognized as evil by the trade unions in New York. In London, Emily and I asked the workers what they earned, what they paid for food and rent, how long they worked each day. We would canvass different buildings, then meet at noon in a fish-and-chips place for lunch or a cup of tea. We saw the worst of Stepney, Shoreditch, Poplar, and Bethnal Green, where the crowded poor lived in inexplicable complacency.

During another reading period, we turned to British industry for material. I was investigating wage systems, and Emily was studying apprenticeships. We thought it would be good to come back to Cambridge, Massachusetts, with the equivalent of an M.A. thesis.

We wrote letters to some eighty firms in England and Scotland. We said we were studying British industry and would like to observe steel, cutlery, textile, chocolate, printing, and other factories. We found the names of plants in directories. One of our professors, James Drummond Smith, helped us. Seventy-five of the eighty firms answered our letters, inviting us to come.

Our hosts in the factory towns met us often with a chauffeured Rolls-Royce. They were taken aback when they saw us. We would alight from the train, clad in our blue serge dresses and sailor hats. But the directors were amused by our imaginative endeavor and they gave every possible help. Charles Reynolds, owner of a lock and chain factory outside Manchester, invited us to stay in his home for several days.

We admired the workmen, many superb in craftsmanship, who were finding it hard to accept the dash and waste that characterized the speedup system of twentieth-century production. The American methods in industry that I had studied were alien, and the belt line that fragmented production was demeaning. As their skills became less significant the men were out of step with the New World, and Great Britain suffered from competition. I felt the loss of economic strength, which was a sad turn of events for the world.

Our trip was a success. We learned about industry and came to the conclusion that the nation that had given the world the Industrial Revolution a century before had subsided into placid competence with little striving for increased productivity or accelerated output. Quality was achieved at enormous expenditure of time. Even then I wondered if England could hold its own.

My familiarity with industrial problems was to stand me in good stead in postwar reconstruction in Austria and in Berlin. In that time it was a beginner's exercise in research.

Not all free time was spent so seriously. There were weekends at The Bell, a small inn at Aston-Clinton, near Oxford. In those years outsiders were not taken frequently into the clubs and homes, so we were especially grateful to Nan for introducing us to the literary people who gathered there on weekends. I regret I have not kept up with these creative people. I associate them in my memory with Lytton Strachey, the great biographer, but I don't think he ever came there himself. A pleasant interlude, also, was our visit to Oxford. We went with Felix Morley to visit his brother, Frank, and friends at Oxford. Professor Drummond Smith invited us to his home for dinner. Most of the faculty gave their brilliant lectures and disappeared.

One English home I shall never forget was where Sidney and Beatrice Webb, well-known Fabian socialists lived, worked, and maintained an intellectual social center. Their living room was simple, comfortable, and full of books. Sidney sat on a little stool poking the fire while Beatrice served tea. She was a tall, well-built woman. He was small, almost gnomelike. They were both active in reform groups and labor meetings. It was the year of their major work, *The Consumers' Co-operative Movement*, and a year before Sidney, later the first Baron of Passfield, was elected a member of Parliament. He had been active in the development of the London School of Economics.

The Easter break was spent bicycling with friends in Cornwall and Devon. I remember looking over a cliff at Tintagel to see a young man and maid pull pillowcases over their heads to disrobe discreetly for a swim in the sea.

Tired by the ups and downs of the road, we would stagger into the small inns, often to be told they were full. With difficulty we would wangle a place to sleep. Every day brought us quaint old towns and rocky shores, clear air, and a fine change after our noses had been in the dusty books of London.

It was in March 1922 that Charles Lindbergh took his first flying lessons. I did not know of this beginning but I did know of the

Wrights and was excited when I learned that there was a commercial plane flying the Channel. I had always been interested in aviation. I wanted to cross the Channel.

Emily and I had a moment of hesitation when the proposed flight was delayed after the hangar in Brussels burned to the ground. I wondered if my father, who was not well, would be very upset if there was a failure to reach the far shore.

The plane with four or five passengers taking off from Croydon was a small, flimsy affair. I noticed the pilot looking jerkily from side to side, peering out of his open cockpit. Emily turned gray. I was uneasy. As I remember, it took almost two hours. When we landed in Brussels we had a sense of relief, even of achievement. Hardly anyone we knew had flown.

Sometime in the fourteen months since we had landed in England we had sandwiched in a short trip to Italy. I also sailed for home for a brief time in March. My mother wanted me with her when my father had to have an operation. How all these travels and studies were managed in this short period I don't know, but they were crammed into a wonderful year. The London School justified itself to me with its fine professors and its scholarly atmosphere. This was the time when I knew what I wanted. I wanted a Radcliffe-Harvard doctor's degree.

In 1923 I had very little concrete evidence of qualifications to offer the economics community in Cambridge, Massachusetts. Although I knew some of my professors in London would vouch for me, there were no means of getting economic prerequisites on my record. At that time official registration for women was at Radcliffe, although graduate economics courses were all taught at Harvard.

President Ada Comstock (later Mrs. Wallace Notestein) and Dean Bernice Brown (later Mrs. Cronkhite) knew of my work at Bryn Mawr and I thought they might be predisposed in my favor but I also knew that the year in London had been a gamble. Fortunately it all worked out. Radcliffe and Harvard accepted me. I, and Emily, too, thus became candidates for a doctor's degree.

In 1923, and before 1925 when I received my second M.A. degree (the first had been from Bryn Mawr), I went to five courses at Harvard. They included Professor Charles J. Bullock's History of Economic Thought, and for several months Plato and Aristotle, with French, German, Austrian, and English thinkers crowded into the last three weeks. Then there was Monetary Theory under Allyn A. Young, Statistics under Edmund E. Day, Economic Theory—the world-famous "Ec ll"—and Psychology under Professor William McDougall. "Ec ll" was taught by the monumental figure Frank W. Taussig, the pillar of the Economics Department. Taussig was dogmatic, classical, and orderly. Most of his course work was identical from year to year with a few new cases introduced.

The class included about thirty men and six women and discussion was good. One classmate, a Swedish student, Bertil Ohlin, was later to be awarded a Nobel Prize. I have talked to him often since then, but my memories of him center on a tall blond man jackknifed into one of the classroom desks, the size suitable for third-graders, his knees almost up to his chin.

My other courses included Statistics. Psychology was my minor. My M.A. thesis dealt with testing of job applicants in industry and new systems of hiring, placement, and job rating. Professor William McDougall was my adviser. I earned a credit for Professor Abbot P. Usher's Industrial History by reading and taking the examination.

Allyn Young was the most flexible, creative, and inspiring of the professors I studied with at Harvard. I took a course from him again, in 1924-25, after completing my M.A. He attacked crises with new ideas in the field of international finance, a field of inquiry that was expanding rapidly as international trade and foreign exchange values grew in importance. Sweeping new ideas were being presented by British economists, particularly J. M. Keynes and R. W. Hawtrey. The movement to emphasize money had begun after the inflation in 1921 and 1922 became rampant in Germany and Austria. It was recognized that although the "quantity of money" could never be left out of account, familiar analysis did not explain contemporary catastrophic change.

The courses at Harvard differed from those in London. We got to know the professors well, their specialties, their prejudices, and their feuds. The Taussig method in the renowned "Ec ll" called for keen debate with the student put on the defensive in the exploration of a theoretical proposition. These outstanding professors were available to graduate students, whereas the undergraduates were in another world taught by young assistants. Taussig was a grand-fatherly person, demanding yet benign, his reputation and books known worldwide. He had a deliberate manner with a touch of sarcasm. Anyone who came through his examination with A's was well on the track for the awesome "general" orals.

Emily and I along with a score of Ph.D. candidates had cubicles in Widener Library, dusty with the research material of decades of scholars. We could hold quiet discussions with our colleagues, put the most useful books on our desks, and live a life of study and contemplation. It was a serious time but one that I thoroughly enjoyed, shadowed somewhat by the fear of failure in the impending General Examination—terrifying orals before the university's greats. We sympathized with each other and deeply regretted the failure of any friend—a failure occurred perhaps once in ten examinations. We could repeat and some did, even three times.

I think that when I got through my orals I felt more than at any other time in my life that I had achieved honorable status and proven my ability to go on in professional life. I have always thought that Harvard's graduate courses were the best in economics. Radcliffe made this possible for women, but there were neither women economics professors nor classes on the Radcliffe campus. Only our fees funneled through the Radcliffe offices.

When Emily and I went to Radcliffe to study economics, we vowed we would not become enmeshed in feminine feuds, such as we found at Bryn Mawr's graduate dormitory in 1919-20. There restless and unsatisfied women cooked up intrigue and spent hours gossiping about each other. We decided to live in Boston. We found a basement apartment on Mt. Vernon Street on Beacon Hill, later moved to Charles Street, and then to West Cedar Street. We had a short walk to Cambridge Circle and a quick subway ride to Harvard Square.

The basement apartment on Mt. Vernon Street had windows at the street level. We had china, bedding, and army cots, but no chairs. For weeks we used packing cases. Then we found a hotel furnishings store where we bought Windsor chairs for ten dollars each. They were good for fifty years. I remember standing in line from seven o'clock to nine when Woolworth's had a sale of stew pans for ten cents apiece—"one to a customer." We felt very independent and entertained some of our fellow students for dinner.

The second year we moved to West Cedar Street. There were three of us, Marian Rhoads, my former Bryn Mawr classmate, Emily, and I. We had a larger apartment and more furniture. Marian, a small, spirited person, worked at the publishing house

Ginn & Company. She was witty and well read. We made a congenial threesome.

One summer, I think it must have been in 1924, the authorities let us use Weld Boat House on the Charles River. I started on a wherry, which is a fairly heavy rowing boat, and moved on to a sixteen-inch shell. Never had I felt so close to the water. The two oars, I soon learned, had to be kept in balance. I did not upset but I came close to it when a late afternoon thunderstorm loomed over me as I raced to the landing stage.

When we had time and money, a group of us would go to Durgin-Park restaurant across from Faneuil Hall. There I had the most filling meals of my life—large steaks and Sally Lunn bread and potatoes and fabulous strawberry shortcakes. I don't remember wine or cocktails but can recall large steins of beer. We fraternized with the men students but as far as I knew none of our small group of women students fell in love.

The "orals" were one of the hardest ordeals I had faced. I felt the strain but I did not fall out of the low window in a dead faint as did Harold, one of the male candidates. Nor did I rush from the room in panic as several other students did.

The examination over, I had to choose a thesis subject. That choice was destined to affect all my future.

I set two criteria. First, I wanted the most stimulating adviser and that was clearly Allyn Young. Second, I wanted to do my work in a country to which I was attached—France. Since Allyn Young was very concerned with the decline of French currency, which was showing signs of weakness, this fact pointed the way.

Foster had been interested in the currency problems that emerged after World War I. As a lawyer he had been asked to work on the German international payments difficulties. He was soon to be counsel for the new Polish loan. Several investment firms also solicited his help. He was surprised when I told him my plan to study the French franc.

"You might as well cross the Atlantic in a rowboat," was his comment.

Foster's prediction proved partially correct. The route to Paris and the final stages for the Ph.D. were not easy. My studies from 1925 to 1927 were to cover many aspects of French life. What were the probable limits in fluctuation on the exchanges? Did the value of the franc, in France, in terms of prices, correspond to its value in terms of other moneys? No full-scale study of modern currency had been made. A decade before, Keynes had written about the Indian rupee. Seymour Harris, at Harvard, was working on the assignats, the currency used in eighteenth-century France.

The grant for my Ph.D. was initiated by Radcliffe in conjunction with Harvard under the Bureau of International Research of Harvard and Radcliffe Colleges. My first grant of $1,500 was given with the understanding that I would later develop my thesis into a published work. The bureau made a second larger grant of $2,500 in 1926 after I had finished the thesis to finance my return to Paris. Macmillan was the publishing house for *The French Franc* and later, in 1930, for a second book, also for the bureau, *The Bank for International Settlements at Work*.

I reached Paris in 1925—the Paris of Ernest Hemingway and F. Scott Fitzgerald. I spent two years there and though I never met Hemingway or Fitzgerald some aspects of *"la vie de Bohème"* were mine—ascetic and exciting. During the first year my parents added to the grant enough money to allow me almost $200 a month for all my expenses.

I was introduced to a portrait painter who knew of a room for rent below hers in an art school, Cola Rossi. It is still there on the Rue de la Grande Chaumière near the student quarter, just around the corner from the Dôme and the Rotonde on Boulevard Montparnasse.

The building in which I lived was over a passageway to a courtyard, and beyond this were studios. Through the wide cracks between the floorboards it was possible for me to observe those in the halls below. I bought some linoleum to cover the cracks. There was no plumbing in the rooms, but in the stairwell there was a saloonlike door, behind which was a toilet. The seat was a wooden ring, and footrests were provided for balance. A woman came into my room once a day with a pail of water for washing. There was a window facing on the street and one electric light plug into which I connected my lamp. In the fireplace I burned *boulets* (egg coal) with *résineux* for kindling. This was my only heat. The rent was an easy ten dollars a month.

From the long window I could see artists and students in the street below and hear sidewalk merchants crying their wares. In the early morning I watched the women washing the streets. They put rags in the gutter to guide the flow of water from the hydrants.

Nearby was the Women's Student Club on the Rue de Chevreuse. I could take a bath at the club. My friend Kitty Merrick lived there and I ate an occasional meal with her.

My favorite dancing partner was Jake (Herbert Jacobs), an American journalist from Milwaukee. He was later to be a biographer of his friend Frank Lloyd Wright, the architect. Eric Voeglin, an Austrian philosopher and economist, was one of our group. I had met him earlier in Austria. Susan, the portrait painter, and Margaret, the singer, were close friends.

Our social life was casual and spontaneous. It broadened my perspective and formed a colorful background, refreshing after hours of research. We would get together for discussions at lunch or dinner, in cafés or in our rooms. We worked hard from morning until late afternoon and sometimes all night. Most of us fell in love with someone and were swept by emotion. We did not indulge in drugs or heavy drinking, but suffered broken hearts.

We usually ate inexpensively in *crémeries* and at small restaurants. If any one struck gold—money from home—or got an occasional paycheck, we would go out on the town, to the Moulin Rouge or Le Bal Tabarin, near the Place du Tertre.

Foster and Janet came to Paris frequently and would take me out to dinner. I remember I gave several parties in Foster's name, when he sent me checks for Christmas and special days. Our philosophy was to use unexpected funds for splurges, rarely for necessities.

Once in summer four of us went to Laperouse, an expensive restaurant by the Seine. We looked at the menu and counted our money—five or six dollars. The entrée cost five dollars. So we ordered hors d'oeuvres and divided each into four pieces and had coffee with just enough money to cover the bill and a tip. At the next table were some Americans who observed this. When the check came, one of them came over to the table and looked over my shoulder to read the bill.

Customarily in the autumn of 1925 I got up early, made coffee in my room, and drank it with bread. Then, since the room was cold, I went to the Rotonde or the Dôme. The Dôme with its round tables was more interesting socially, but the Rotonde offered a singular advantage for a Ph.D. aspirant. It had rectangular tables. By sitting on a bench and using three tables, for the price of a cup of coffee I could spread out my papers. The café was warm, light, and not until midafternoon was there a crowd to deprive me of space and quiet. I usually had a second cup of coffee, but it was not necessary. The management was agreeable about my extended use of their furniture.

I registered at the Ecole de Droit, a part of the Sorbonne, and spent a few hours in the dark and dusty halls just off the Boule Mich. Going to lectures was not required, and was not conducive to learning. Professors read the text of the books they had already published. A handful of students slouched on the wooden benches, paying only slight attention to the speaker.

At that time the students were restless, but not in revolt. I had, and would have now, great sympathy for French students during their sporadic protests. They got a raw deal, and still do, as President Valéry Giscard d'Estaing is being told. The system hasn't changed much and I would not advise anyone to attend the Sorbonne except for the pleasure of living in Paris.

The professors I wanted to know I met outside the university. Charles Rist, the foremost French economist of the time, had been at Harvard and had written, with Charles Gide, a comprehensive book on French economic thought. He was later to become president of the Bank of France. The Rists used to ask me to their house in Versailles. Twenty years later I worked with their son, Leonard, in Vienna, where he was head of the French financial division, a part of the four-power occupation forces.

My main work involved the gathering of statistics at the Morgan Bank, at the National Treasury, the Bank of France, the Bibliothéque Nationale, and the Finance Ministry. The French, reputed for mathematical skill, had the official wholesale commodity prices written on large cardboards, two feet by four feet in dimension. If a figure was corrected for some reason, paper was pasted over the old figure. Their manner of handling such essential data was astonishing to me. Recording the statistical data on these awkward cards was an almost incomprehensible procedure.

The *inspecteurs de finance* were young, well-educated men of the elite—attractive and destined to be the high officials, probably undersecretaries, of the French Treasury. They would discuss problems with me and try to help me in getting reliable statistics. My accumulation of material grew. My room was full of paper folders, piled by the foot of the bed. Metal file holders would have been a luxury.

Early in my research I went to the Morgan Bank to see Dean Jay, who was Foster's good friend. He told the clerks to help me and they gave me the quotations for the franc. From there I would go to the Bibliothèque Nationale and check the bank's figures against those of the *Journal Officiel*. The bank clerks insisted they didn't make mistakes, but I felt I had to check the quotations. I found only one error.

The Bibliothèque had electric lights by the time I worked in it. For many years it had been without such illumination. There was fear of fire. At three o'clock every afternoon a man with a disinfecting spray would walk up and down each aisle where people were studying. The chemical solution was to keep us from getting the plague!

The orthodox theory of monetary value was then based on the quantity of money, particularly bank notes, in circulation. This total was assumed to govern the value of the franc. Little attention was paid to the velocity of circulation or to important psychological factors. My study showed that the number of notes in circulation increased *after* the value declined and as the result of the rate of turnover of funds in existence—that was best described as the velocity of circulation. Thus, I maintained the psychological consequences of political uncertainty, and the anticipation of rising prices, were causal and determined the rate of inflation of the currency.

The more mechanistic approach was the classical one applied to any currency being studied. Moreover, the international value in world prices was supposed to correspond fairly closely to the value on the exchange markets in New York, London, and Paris. Study showed me that the franc was falling much faster on the exchanges than was justified by wholesale prices, and the retail price level lagged still further behind. In this period the increase in the public borrowing was both an index of deterioration and a mechanism depressing the value of the franc. The extensive government use of short-term *bons* was particularly unsettling, since the public reaction to unfavorable conditions led to the nonrenewal of the investment. This practice put more money in circulation at the same time that the lack of confidence put pressure on the government to find additional resources.

Thus the increase in public debt brought political instability, the loss of confidence, and the flight of capital. The urgent sale of francs reduced their value on the exchanges. The internal currency value was different and lagged behind the decline on the exchange market. Consumers spent more cash as their purchasing power suffered. The increase in money in circulation followed increase in velocity—the rate of spending.

The complex interaction of psychological factors, which were noted in the main financial journals, and the extreme sensitivity of speculators to capital movements eventually led to panic in 1925 and a sharp decline of the franc. The franc had been weak in the early twenties, but it was not then evident that it would collapse to half its value.

Conditions worsened. In one month, December of 1925, the French Government changed hands four times. People lost confidence in the leadership and there was a catastrophic flight from the currency—a selling of francs.

Then the strong man, Raymond Poincaré, took over as Premier, and his capacity for bold action to reduce expenditures was evident. He was able to gain the immediate confidence of the French people and to hold the value of French currency by determination and moral strength. The franc rebounded on the foreign exchanges and also improved in the internal commodity market. The flight of capital ceased.

When I had studied with Allyn Young, he was exploring new ideas. The basis of the more sophisticated velocity theory (the rapidity with which units of currency are passed from hand to hand) was psychological—the attitude of the public and popular forecasts of what their money might be worth. If the buyer thought the price of goods would double, he would begin to hoard. When goods are hoarded, there is real inflation.

*The French Franc*, the book that evolved from my studies at this time, led to the idea that the velocity of the circulation of money and short-term bonds was determined by political and psychological factors. Keynes was to comment on my book in a letter to me saying it was an outstanding contribution to monetary theory. He had been exploring these theories for some time.

I observed the fate of governments, listened to stormy debate in the Chamber of Deputies, watched the people clustered in nervous groups outside the banks, and heard loud debate in cafés. As I gathered my reports and figures, it became clear that the commodity export and import balance did not greatly affect the exchange rates. The rates were governed by the movement of "hot money" to New

York at a time when the United States was accumulating gold. It was also clear that costs of production had almost no short-run influence on prices. Commodity prices were controlled by the value of the franc in dollars and pounds, and by the timing, scope, and nature of speculation.

My book, *The French Franc*, was never a best seller, but it served a purpose in monetary theory and in the analysis of value that was part of the mounting wave of new economic ideas. The Ph.D. thesis that was to form the backbone of the book was in chaotic shape when I rushed back to Harvard in March of 1926 to meet the deadline for submission. I had a wealth of material, but had not realized how undeveloped the written text was until I saw Professor Young. He riffled through the box of text, unwilling to discourage me, but convinced, I learned later, it would require months of rewriting.

"I can rewrite it in ten days," I told him.

I did not know what a struggle it would be.

Fortunately, I located an expert stenographer. She worked with me from ten to twelve hours a day and we rewrote the entire thesis.

On April 1, at 4:30 totally exhausted, I stumbled up the stairs to Young's office and gave him the text. The deadline was five o'clock.

"You made it!" he said. "I never believed you could do it."

Next came the oral examinations, three weeks off. In a trance from fatigue, I reviewed notes on old and new monetary theory. The day before the examination my mind went blank. Emily asked me questions and she was horrified. I did not recognize the names of the most renowned economists.

"Let's go for a walk," I suggested.

We walked around and around the Brookline reservoir.

"I've done it before," I told her, "and I can do it again."

Without reading another note, I went into the examination room and faced the professors, who were ready with a barrage of questions. All I had learned in the past four years came back to me like a spring flood of refreshing water.

I was awarded a Ph.D. in economics in June 1926. I was also given the fellowship promised me, and with more than two thousand dollars for living, I sailed back to France.

I had no sooner settled down to expanding the thesis into a book when an astonishing confrontation with two distinguished Columbia professors took place.

Professor Robert Murray Haig and Professor Harvey Rogers

came to call on me in the little room at Cola Rossi. They were in Paris with a group of their colleagues, under a large grant to study the French economy. Their reasons for calling on me were astonishing.

Haig said, "You are here on a small grant and working alone, studying the nature of French inflation. Professor Rogers is working with our group and can do a more searching and complete job. We want you to turn over your notes to us and we'll carry on your work as part of our comprehensive project. I'm sure Professor Young will approve."

These men were years senior to me. Their reputations were established. I found it hard to believe that they would make such an approach to intimidate a young scholar and a woman as well.

When they left, I wrote to Allyn Young. I said I did not want to give up the material over which I had worked so hard, nor the theory that I had developed. Within days I had a cabled answer from Young: "Stick to your guns. Don't let Columbia men change plans in any way."

*The French Franc* was published in 1929 by the Macmillan Company, close to the date of Rogers' book. Allyn Young said in the introduction:

> Miss Dulles's book has a twofold significance. In the first place it is history. It gives an account of an important episode—or series of episodes—in the recent history of France. In the second place, it is an essay in monetary theory ... the reader will find that Miss Dulles draws no sharp line between her account of the various specific factors which shaped the fortunes of the franc and her analysis of the quantitative relations between the variations of the currency and the fluctuations of other economic phenomena. This...is one of the principal merits of her book.... The stress which Miss Dulles puts upon psychological attitudes, particularly as they manifest themselves in speculative operations, is, I believe, not disproportionate to their real importance.... The results of two years of residence and study in France show themselves not only in Miss Dulles's knowledge of details and in her command of sources of information but also in her interpretation of the character of the problem with which she deals. That problem, as she sees it, is not merely a matter of the changing quantitative relations of certain economic variables. It is first of all a problem of public policy, and it is a problem which is related to the interests of the country and of its people in many different ways.... Miss Dulles has made good use of that opportunity.

This introduction was one of the last things he wrote before his death.

Every time I see *The French Franc* on my library shelf, I have thoughts about my supporters and my activities as a scholar, when fewer women were in the field of finance. At that time there were several dozen women economists, many of them working on labor problems, minimum wage legislation, consumer standards, and social betterment. There were fewer in finance, foreign exchange, business cycles, and international trade. These subjects interested me then and I continued to pursue them.

# 8

## DAVID IN PARIS, 1925

I first saw David at a table in the left corner of the restaurant Pré-aux-Clercs, at the corner of Rue Bonaparte and Rue Jacob. Two friends, the Jaffes, were there. They had told me several times that I would find David congenial—that he had a lively mind and was a real scholar. I was busy with my research and was not in a hurry to add new friends to my small circle. However, when the Jaffes arranged lunch, I agreed to come.

My new friend plunged into the center of the subject I was working on. Professor Blondheim, the philologist, asked me what I thought of the gold standard. "I think it is quite unnecessary," he said.

I rose to defend the system. It had been at the heart of international monetary relations for decades, serving as a mechanism for the flow of funds, giving confidence to traders, I told him. The discussion waxed lively over soup and veal and green salad. I see us in my recollection venturing in spirited argument, hardly aware of our surroundings. It was intellectual fun.

As we drank coffee David said, "Will you have dinner with me tomorrow night?"

"No," I said. "I'll be on my way to Turkey."

"When do you come back?" he asked.

"On January tenth, on the Orient Express."

He pulled a little notebook out of his pocket and wrote down the date. This was a moment I thought I forgot, but one I was to remember for more than fifty years.

On the January day I returned I struggled up the stairs to my Paris room. David stood on the threshold with a bunch of flowers.

When I met David in Paris he was forty-one years old. I was thirty. He was almost completely bald. He had a very sensitive mouth and clear, brown eyes. He was short, though taller than I, and well built.

When I first knew him he wore stiff, high collars. In the summer he wore a straw boater, in the winters, a soft felt hat.

Later I persuaded him to wear soft-collared shirts, but he was always conservative in his dress, not overly concerned about style, but with consistent regard for correct appearance. His pince-nez glasses added to a first impression of seriousness.

My friends said he was a good-looking man; they responded to his warm smile. David was a high-strung man, and in periods of stress he showed it. While he didn't bite his nails, his tension was obvious. Often as he sat he would swing his right foot up and down.

I was not interested in his appearance at our first meeting. What struck me was his quick wit and lively conversation. In pouncing on an idea he showed an immediate awareness of what I said. I was immediately conscious of a keen mind and well-directed questions. It was apparent that while quizzing me, he himself did not make any pretense of knowing more than he did of my subject. He never did. His manner was urbane, between the extremes some people reach. He assumed that whatever subject was being discussed was comprehensible if it was handled in a reasonable way.

Thus it came about immediately that we got into a conversation about monetary theory; a discussion that was professional in the level that probed the issues. He led the discussion into my field of study, not his. I later learned this was his way. He wanted to broaden the scope of his knowledge. He was conscious of the fact that linguistics can be a narrow line of work, but at the same time a field in which the best scholars insist on a knowledge of other disciplines.

In the conduct of his studies David had worked for months on groups of words, such as heraldry, chemistry, coinage, or medicine, or perhaps words in metallurgy, "ships and shoes and ... sealing wax." Whenever he began to collect a new category of words, he was anxious to know about the field. I had brought economics to lunch in December—by being an economist—so he presumed I knew something about my speciality. He had met my hosts, the Jaffes, at the University Union on Boulevard St.-Germain. The Jaffes were working with a group of Columbia University economists; they were amused at the dialogue. Their work interested David, and when they offered to introduce him to me he saw it as an opportunity to learn more of economics.

The day after the meeting with David, I started on my trip to

Turkey. I felt an unanalyzed sense of elation. I associated it with the prospect of a vacation, but I realized that it was more ethereal and more exotic. Something in the quality of life had changed. I felt the breath of new adventure, not in Turkey, but in France.

After going by train to Marseilles, I boarded a small Greek steamer bound for Istanbul. Nataline, my younger sister, was teaching in the American Hospital there and in spite of a heavy work schedule, was having a gay time with the American naval and diplomatic young men. The voyage to the Bosporus was to take ten days. There were no planes in those days. My mood was the mood of spring. The world was very bright, the air, balmy. I was ready for what lay ahead. I knew no one on the ship. Many of the passengers were seasick, though the lift and fall of the waves was moderate.

As I walked the deck I met a Greek banker who spoke French— no one on the ship spoke English. Together we watched the moon come up over the silken, wine-dark sea. The ship skirted the coast beyond Athens and Mt. Olympus, to Salonika.

The banker, Hagianou (if that was his name), came to me before we reached port, "You must go ashore with me in this old city."

I made a vague excuse. He came back to me. "I know what you think," he said, "but I promise I will respect your reserve. I want to show you some of the ancient buildings and sights you could not find by yourself. Trust me."

I decided it was worth whatever risk there might be and said yes. When we got near the port he said, "Don't land with the others. Wait for me."

When the others had gone ashore, a small boat drew alongside. The crew lowered a number of heavy bags into the boat. My banker friend turned to me: "When the last shipment of gold went overland, it was all stolen and one of the couriers killed. You will understand that I have a responsibility. I have to take this to the bank myself."

It was pitch-dark when we landed. On the dock Hagianou turned me over to a tall, handsome Greek who spoke neither English nor French, and he disappeared into the darkness. Somewhat taken aback, I followed the stranger, who took me to a hotel, introducing me in whatever fashion he considered appropriate.

My room had three doors. I inspected the locks. Half an hour later I opened to a knock and took a message from a bellboy. The note was an invitation for cocktails, signed by four American foreign service officers, from four different capitals. All said they were friends of Nataline's. They had looked at the hotel register.

[106]

I went down to meet them. They were very curious as to what I was doing there and it amused me to be mysterious. I was not worried about what they might think. I sat with them over ouzo until my Greek escort came to take me to dinner.

From dinner we went to the nightclub where, not long before, in a fatal accident, the King of Greece died of a monkey bite, which he suffered during the floor show.

Up early the next morning, I explored the churches and mosques in the city with Hagianou. The boat was to leave at two o'clock. When Hagianou took me to the quayside, he handed me a bunch of lilies of the valley, and bid me godspeed. The short interlude was the only time I saw the gallant man, but he wrote me a charming letter. The episode fitted my romantic mood.

Going down the coast past the ancient monastery and through the Dardanelles, I saw the British ships rusting on the beach, victims of the ill-fated battle, and came to the city of minarets—Istanbul. My sister was at the pier to greet me.

Though Nataline had a responsible job in the hospital and was busy, she was enjoying the Christmas season with a host of friends, many of them on the staff of Admiral Mark Bristol, United States High Commissioner.

Istanbul was the most exotic city I had ever visited. I can still picture the small balconies on the minarets where the mullahs called the faithful to prayer. I wandered the crooked streets, having difficulty getting back to the part of the city where I stayed. I rode the streetcars and in one case got completely lost. I found a sailor who knew French and he guided me to a streetcar going to the Pera Palace Hotel, where Nataline was to meet me.

Nataline, after her hospital work, went with me to a reception or dance every evening. She gave me good advice about drinking. "Stick to Scotch," she said, "and drink it slowly. There are long, festive times ahead."

Mrs. Bristol, the admiral's wife, loved parties and gave one almost every night. There were attractive bachelors in the Foreign Service and the Navy—plenty of dancing partners. I visited Roberts College, where many well-known Middle Easterners received advanced education.

One Sunday some of us drove eastward to the Black Sea. Wizened old men smoked their hookahs outside small mud huts. The landscape was barren but mysterious and somehow exciting. My entire stay was a festive period. I had time for sight-seeing during the day and dancing, talking, and drinking at night. I was interested in the Turkish economy and glad to get a break from my work in dark, cold Paris. Still there was an unacknowledged magnet pulling me back. When Nataline's friends took me aboard the Orient Express, I was ready and willing to return. Jefferson Patterson, a young diplomatic aide, took the same train and was a good companion while the train crossed the barren landscape, which was wild and mountainous in some places. We got off at Sophia for a few hours and dined at the Ritz.

I shared a compartment with a strange Frenchwoman who told of having committed capital crimes while living a high-level social life in France. I do not know whether she was really a murderer on the run or whether she was an amusing liar. That was life on the Orient Express.

The dinner with David that I declined in December I enjoyed in January. As I shook off some of my mental limitations, I concluded there was no better place than Paris in which to grow older.

Though the winter was cold and dark—sometimes uncomfortable for those of us who lived on the fringes of financial subsistence—the mists were beautiful and the vistas stretched out in generous lights and shadows. There was a pearly shimmer at sunset and a gleam of soft light on the Seine. The bridges were arched gracefully through the mist and the bookstalls by the quays dusty and fascinating with moldy books and old prints.

When in 1976 I was there again, I knew I was a stranger and no longer a citizen. But in the twenties I knew the heart and soul of the city. My memories even now are not those of a tourist but of one who could relive the life of the boulevards and see the shine of the glowing autumn and the tender flowers of spring.

In 1926 David and I walked the streets together. We saw each other almost every evening. After a day's work we were eager for talk of history, of literature, of Paris, and of life. We occasionally met with friends. Our life varied. Because David did not want to forget when someone invited him to dinner or asked to borrow a book, he would take out a postcard, write down the information, and address it to himself. At the first postbox, he would drop in the message. It would come back to him in twenty-four hours.

When I knew him well and we had had one of the minor disagreements that people do have, he turned to me and said, "You know, you are so *attractive* when you're angry! I just can't tell you how lovely it makes you!"

And I burst out laughing.

He could break my mood almost instantly.

He was a gentle man. I remember his meeting with the child of a couple with whom we had dinner. Their little girl was already under the shadow of a serious illness. He sat on the sofa reading to her for more than an hour. He was not condescending, but interested and courteous toward children.

He knew Paris well and took me to old quarters and cafés. The Luxembourg Gardens were locked at night but we walked around them, scores of times. It was a shadowy, quiet area. I began to sense the direction in which my feelings might propel me, fascinated and somewhat fearful in anticipation. And above and beyond my personal feelings was the recognition that David was the most dedicated scholar I had ever known—honest and unwavering in his search, rigorous in his standards, scornful of shoddy work. The extent of his knowledge was enormous, his efforts unremitting and tireless. Admiration came even before love.

The man I came to know so well was to alter the foundations of my life's structure in the winter of my thirty-second year. We explored the *cité*, the Boule Mich. On one of these evening walks in the shadow of Notre-Dame's deserted moonlit square, David put his arms around me and kissed me. I was shaken and surprised. I had a sense of expectation, but even so, I had a profound shock. David hailed a cab and told the driver to take us to the Bois de Boulogne at the other side of Paris. For some time we drove around and around. I was face to face with a realization that overwhelmed me.

As I became more encompassed by our relations I realized my independence was threatened. One day I told David I could not see him anymore. I felt an inexplicable fear of losing my hard-won identity and of neglecting my professional aims. I went in hiding to a friend's room in a hotel across the street. I could watch my door from her window. I did not know whether I wanted him to come or not, but as it grew dark I wept. All night I cried. In the morning, exhausted, I went home and waited. In the evening David came. We went for a long walk and I felt comforted. My fear had vanished—how could I be afraid of this man?

It was not long after this time of trial that David told me of a beautiful cathedral town some hours from Paris—Vézelay. He wanted to show this to me but he made clear that he thought this weekend should mean a fulfillment of what each knew the other felt, a desire for a night without separation. I thought it over for some days and then said I would go.

At this time I had no wish whatsoever to get married. I had nothing against marriage but was truly interested in my work and rarely lonely. I had an adequate social life. I also knew that any kind of marriage requires adjustment and compromise. One cannot get married and live the same life as before.

However, the year 1927 was a turning point in my life. After a few weeks I knew I was in love. I did not at first realize the strong emotional currents that would carry me along. My first enchantment turned to feelings that were almost uncontrollable.

As I recall those days in Paris and David's continuing effort to get to know me and give me pleasure, I realize that it would be hard for young people today to understand my shyness, my ignorance, and my lack of readiness. I had not felt the need for close personal contacts with men, though I knew many in my work and in social and outdoor sports. I was the product of a simple, innocent environment, and my account now of those bygone days is accurate. I *was* the person who reacted in this naïve way. The circumstances were possible, for they occurred. The person was real, for it was I who lived these days and nights of excitement and of discovery.

As David came to the conclusion we should get married, he too faced problems that made him ponder. He had close and cherished relations with the Jewish communities in New York, Philadelphia, and Baltimore. He was very fond of his sister, Grace. They went every summer to St.-Moritz in Switzerland together. They understood each other in many respects—for years if one of them was depressed the other would hold a "celebration." They would give a party for two and proclaim the intelligence, charm, and many admirable qualities of each other, extolling them without restraint.

David knew that Grace would have strong feelings against his marrying a Christian. His sense of racial loyalty was deep and pervasive but his adherence to Jewish rites was not as demanding as that of his sister. He had been married and divorced. He had a son, Hillel, who went to Jerusalem and became an honored physician there. David was older than I and was somewhat surprised to find me inexperienced and naïve. We respected each other's reserve. I did not go to his hotel nor he to my room. But our walks became longer and longer, our feelings more intense.

I suppose I have stayed in more than six hundred hotels in my life and travels, but one of the few I remember was the one in Vézelay, where David and I slept, fifty years ago. The hotel was somewhat dingy, but clean, the large double bed had a thin mattress and a time-worn *duvet* for a cover. The element that was both important and inconvenient was that the bathroom was down a long hall. I don't know what the choices of inns were, but I know David wanted one where we were unlikely to meet friends. He knew I was fearful of a casual encounter. I think he was apprehensive, too. He had only recently realized how inexperienced I was. By Sunday morning I came to understand the extent of his consideration and concern, his disappointment that our time together had not brought the response that he knew was possible and that was to come later.

The churches at Vézelay and nearby Auxerre were notable for their ancient beauty, but only the greatest mutual consideration made it possible after the difficult night to enjoy them together. We did. To me this experience signified more than a cathedral viewing. I had made up my mind that I was going to act with greater freedom and awareness of our genuine devotion to each other.

I would like to tell my grandchildren and my nieces and nephews about my weekend in this cathedral town in France, long, long ago. My two days at Vézelay with David taught me more about love and understanding than I had learned in the previous thirty years. I also learned the true nature of David, the man I was destined to marry. I learned that love enhanced by tenderness is the outward expression of deep commitment which can make an overwhelming tide of emotion an incomparable experience. This knowledge cannot be gained in casual encounters. The various difficulties that made our relationship turbulent and yet that gave it an extraordinary vitality probably seem strange to modern young people. The variety and challenge of my life so far had shielded me from romance.

What can I tell these young people today? What I can say is that casual experiences are no revelation of what they may achieve later. The physical aspects of love are important but they are not enough to bring fulfillment. David and I, in that simple room in the old French inn, failed in the full expression of our deep attraction. But we went on to full and glorious response which could survive time and could even surmount separation and death.

We both loved France and had traveled over it a great deal. We continued to do so, together. When we visited a new town, as soon as we had decided on an inn, David would set off for the bookstore. I went with him, luxuriating in his enthusiasm. He was passionate about books, consumed by a desire to buy every old dictionary he found. He would ask to see the books in the attic or the storeroom. Thus, when David died he had a valuable collection of dictionaries, all purchased on a very limited income.

His library included dictionaries from Czechoslovakia, Romania, Bulgaria, Hungary, Turkey, and many other countries. He also had old texts on Romance languages, and the Talmudic studies of Raschi.

One night David was taking me to the Comédie Française to see a very fine classical play. We got news that Lindbergh was flying the Atlantic. I remember standing in the Place de l'Opéra, after an early dinner, wondering whether we should go out to Le Bourget, or whether we should go to the theater. Something told me that the traffic on the Le Bourget road was going to be rather heavy that night. My sister Nataline, who happened to be in Paris at that same time, decided that she would go out to Le Bourget, but we decided to go to the theater.

They had an electric display sign somewhere near the Place de l'Opéra, on the other side from the Café de la Paix. We watched this, and it said: "Lindbergh over the Atlantic... nearing French coast..."

We went into the theater, and when we came out, the crowds were shouting in the streets, and the sign said, "Lindbergh has landed."

But for him to get from Le Bourget into the American Embassy was almost harder than flying the Atlantic. It was a very exciting moment and very vivid in my mind. The drama of it was something fantastic. Nataline was caught in the crowd. She did see Lindbergh but she couldn't get very close. I think she spent about six or eight hours on the road.

After work we spent two or three hours walking along the quays or around the Gardens. Often we went to the Isle and Notre-Dame. He talked of his work, which was mysterious and arcane. He asked me many questions about my research. He was a good listener. Sometimes he talked about his childhood in Baltimore, which had been difficult and poverty-ridden. His father and mother and only brother were dead.

Johns Hopkins opened the door for him to a wider world. His trips to Europe on scholarships gave him an ease and a companionship he did not find in Baltimore. Parisians were broad-minded and tolerant. There was no noticeable anti-Semitism and much respect for scholarship. He used the offices of the American University Union on Boulevard St.-Germain and we frequently had coffee opposite the Union at the Deux Magots, frequented by writers and professors. David gave me a number of books, including a beautifully bound copy of Shelley's poems, which is on the shelf near me now.

After our trips to local bookshops in France, we would go out for a superb meal. The restaurants were neither expensive nor famous, but the food was extraordinary.

This initial falling in love in Paris was only the first battle in what turned out to be a prolonged struggle. We became engaged and unengaged. When I thought it was settled, something unsettled me—undoubtedly the original reluctance to compromise persisted. The trap was not tender and attempts to evade it were distressing for both of us, in spite of moments of sheer joy.

In the stages when we were engaged, David was eager to introduce me to the eminent professors with whom he worked. He knew well the thirty most renowned philologists in Europe. In France, he knew a dozen or more, among them Antoine Thomas and Clovis Brunel.

I recall a party, given for Antoine, celebrating the anniversary of one of his famous works. These men liked David, but some wouldn't speak to each other. So David would take me out for coffee, or for a glass of wine, with each of his French friends and introduce me to them, one by one. The more I saw of his world, the more it pleased him.

Although he was proud of his research and fascinated by it, he would exclaim at times, "It's the most impractical, unproductive area of work imaginable."

I refused to believe it. I told him, "You find new truths. Anybody who finds new truths is leaving something of value for future generations."

When my parents came to Europe in the early spring of 1927, the manuscript of my book was already in fairly good shape. They stopped in London first and I went over to see them. On the way back to Paris, I said, "Oh, by the way, I'm engaged."

I had written home about David. After ten years mainly away from home, working with people my parents did not know, living abroad, I had stopped trying to describe friends they had never seen. It was just too complicated and time-consuming.

I saw that my father was taken aback. He asked about my fiancé, and I told him David was an eminent Jewish scholar.

He asked me if I did not think there would be problems, as a Christian, marrying a Jew. I told him that David, though deeply loyal to his heritage, was not an Orthodox Jew. Father did not press the issue. The following day my parents suggested I bring David to dinner.

The invitation, given so hospitably, frightened me. I timidly asked David, "Would you have dinner with my parents?"

"Of course," he said. "If they are your parents they must be wonderful people."

They were staying at the Trianon Palace, a lovely hotel in Versailles. The other guest at dinner was the economist Charles Rist, with whom I had conferred frequently. Mother had told me that most people dressed for dinner, and I mumbled something to David about dressing. He told me he would wear his dinner jacket. As we rode out on the train from Paris together, I kept looking sidewise at him, and noticed there were stripes down the side of his pants.

"Other people don't have stripes down the side of their pants," I thought. "This is terrible!" Since that night I have never seen a man in dinner dress without noticing the stripe on the trousers.

When we arrived, I saw that Professor Rist's trousers also had stripes.

The dinner went off beautifully and Father and Mother told me they found David charming and interesting.

The date for the wedding had yet to be set, and I was still afraid to give up my independence. David had already told me that he wanted me to continue with my work. He was glad I was planning to go on with teaching. He thought it a good profession and flexible enough to be compatible with marriage. He also said he assumed I would retain my own name in all professional endeavors, after our marriage.

"Eleanor," he told me, "you can't start publishing as Eleanor Blondheim. Your four books, all the published articles, your teaching contracts—these are all under your own name. Keep it."

This is why my name has always been Dulles.

# 9

# TEACHING FROM THE 1920s

My first assignment in teaching was a strange experience. It was as instructor in 1921, at the new Bryn Mawr Summer School. President Thomas said that the school for Women Workers in Industry was the result of an idea she seized upon when on a camel trip in the Sahara. It was a forerunner of other schools that emerged elsewhere soon after.

The plans for it were worked out with her cousin, Alys Russell, Professor Susan Kingsbury, and Dean Hilda Smith, usually known as Jane Smith. The program was put together quickly and the fact that I was chosen as teacher, when I had never studied economics, was an oddity I have remembered with amusement. True, I had studied and worked in industry, and I also knew of the educational standards in approaching an important subject, but as for economic texts, I was in total darkness. The names of the classical works served as a beginning, and not until I had engaged in brisk arguments with the students did I realize how inappropriate to them was the description of "the system" as a well-oiled machine, producing, distributing, and consuming the goods that were needed. In a short time I was to learn the realities of friction and lack of adjustment in the economic world. The lessons were more valuable for me than the theory of wages and rent that I first tried to expound to my puzzled students, schooled in a brutal world. These workers were in too much of a hurry for immediate gains to turn to abstract studies, but at first I tried to give them the classics—in small doses.

The encounter, in 1921, was a beginning of my awareness of the importance for an economist keeping in touch with the real world.

It was a hot summer. The Philadelphia area's humidity was not then eased by air conditioning as now, nor was it made more palatable by the vast divergence of views of many of the instructors and guest lecturers. One was Paul Douglas, a tall, handsome, articulate professor, later senator from Illinois. He loved to swim and came often in the 1950s with Emily, his wife, to my swimming pool in Virginia. He was the author of a monumental study of wages and was well reputed as a liberal. Because of his ability and leadership qualities he was talked of as presidential timber in 1951. But he was not put forward after he had a hysterical episode in the Senate at that time. A. J. Muste, a Methodist minister also at the school, had more revolutionary views than Paul. He was a fiery speaker.

At an early stage, Eleanor Roosevelt, the wife of the President, took an interest and visited the campus on several occasions. She was much impressed with the educational potential and also the improved communication between workers and employers that she anticipated from the project. She devoted increasing amounts of time to students and to workers as she saw her friendly participation in some of the meetings was much appreciated. I doubt if she realized how far the young would go in violence if their first efforts were not effective. I was surprised at the militant spirit of some of the labor leaders and secretly a little astonished that few students felt any gratitude for the generosity of the college in providing the board and teaching free. In 1921 I was just beginning to realize the deep unrest in the American labor movement and the growing determination of women to gain their rights, both as workers and as women.

The students soon were seen to fall into two groups. The majority wanted to learn how to fight the system and organize for battle. The minority looked on the studies for personal advancement. They hoped to find their way into the managerial class. Many excited gatherings under the trees in the hot summer nights were dominated by the more aggressive young women who had already found strength in organizing. I was quickly put on the defensive—presumed to be a capitalist.

The effort was exhausting, but valuable to both those asked to teach and those who came to learn. The first year of the school was the most exciting; it stimulated educational efforts elsewhere. The courses continued through other summers, enriching the labor movement in a variety of ways. It sent me back to the books, but it also taught me practical lessons—more about human nature than about theory.

My next exposure to teaching was in 1924. My motive was mainly economic. I was taking the familiar way of graduate students to supplement small resources. I taught at Simmons College on the Fenway in Boston. In 1924 and then later after my return from

[116]

research in France the students were docile young women who took their notes and listened, or dozed during my exposition of traditional economic theory. They were incurious and unambitious, not visibly interested in subject matter. Since those days there has been an admirable development in Simmons College.

I was under the direction of the pugnacious and amusing head of the Economics Department, Sara Stites, an outspoken liberal. Sara had imagination and initiative. She brought as lecturer the notable Socialist candidate for the Presidency, Norman Thomas. I remember the strong flavor of his personality as I talked with him. I knew he had been in prison, but I was shocked by his gray pallor and air of resignation over the world's inequities. He was easy in his conversation and talked informally about labor problems and economics. Six times, before his death in late 1968, he was on the Socialist ticket for President.

At Harvard women were treated politely and even in a friendly manner. All the graduate economics courses were taught at the main campus by the prestigious Harvard professors, but there was no professional equality. After the men got their doctor's degrees those who had done well were offered a choice of staying at the college as instructors or going elsewhere with strong recommendations. For the women, the possibilities were more limited. There were no women faculty members at Radcliffe in those days, I was told. When Bryn Mawr offered me a job, in spite of some of the difficulties I knew I would face because of conflicts between the Economic and Social Economy departments, I accepted. From 1928 to 1930, and from 1932 to 1936, I was on the faculty.

When I was asked by my friend Louise Watson to advise an investment consulting firm in New York, I accepted. Louise, a Bryn Mawr graduate, had a fine reputation in the world of Wall Street. When my Wall Street association was known in the thirties, I was reprimanded by Acting President Helen Taft Manning, the daughter of William Howard Taft. She said I was to give more time to the students on weekends and that teas in my apartment would be a useful part of my work at Bryn Mawr. This shocked me, for I thought Wall Street activities in 1928 were concerns from which I should gain experience, not only for my own sake but for my students. Helen Manning did not insist, so I continued trips to New York. Helen had very definite ideas. She was a strong administrator and an impressive teacher of history.

[117]

The practical emphasis of the industrial work with students in factories and stores, begun during the war, struck a new note at Bryn Mawr. The college had always emphasized the classics and there were few on the faculty who knew that economics was expanding in new directions. Some of the old theory had ossified in a framework of relationships that did not take account of rapid, short-time readjustment. In the period after World War I, the speed of economic change accelerated with new technology in production and communication. There was large-scale, popular speculation in stocks, with values changing rapidly.

Basic patterns of economic causes and effects persist—valid as the law of gravity—airplanes that fly do not gainsay the law of gravity. Short-run changes that affect our daily lives must be related eventually to the lasting relationships.

Dealing with students was a special problem. Many of them were dazzled by short-run spectacular changes and "get rich quick" ideas. At Bryn Mawr, since my courses were in two antagonistic departments—Economics and Social Economy—I began to learn diplomacy.

The academic community looked down on the students learning the techniques of management for their professional future. The professors in the more classical courses expected to get a dependable perspective in traditional studies and texts.

The management group were on the average older women from various colleges. They had at Bryn Mawr, as part of their program, jobs in factories and in stores. I knew my students well and we talked freely. It was not always easy to find positions for them with interesting work, but we always managed. In the summers of 1928 and 1929 I visited them in their places of work—the Hood Rubber Company, the Midvale Steel, Leeds and Northrup, Dennison, and other concerns. They wrote frank accounts of their mistakes and their accomplishments in the workshops. They noted a degree of puzzlement on the part of fellow workers as to their aims for future professional work.

Having placed them in varied plants and stores, I had to make certain they were getting some meaning out of their work and to protect the cooperative college-factory relationship on which the course was based. Most of them went on to good jobs. Part of their preparation on the campus came from special lecturers. Among our star guests were Dr. Alice Hamilton from Johns Hopkins University, the expert on industrial medicine and hazards, and Lillian Gilbreth, the efficiency engineer.

To keep my students in the academic course alert, teaching required a vital effort to make a dry subject come alive. I wanted to stimulate a real contest between teacher and taught, and not to be batting a ball against the wall in an empty gymnasium. Bryn Mawr had small classes at the advanced levels, perhaps eleven or twelve students, and of these special students, about half were genuinely interested, so I felt I had some influence on their future work and ideas. But even in the best of circumstances, the numbers of people I could reach at that time were extremely limited.

In the twenties leaders in the field thought they could moderate the economic swings by forecasting and monetary intervention by government and banks. They were convinced the trend of prices and wages would go up over the long run, but not steeply.

This mood of confidence among the experts led to the increase in speculation. The rush to invest in that period is one of the most interesting phases of the inter-war years.

Institutions, particularly investment trusts, forerunners of the more sophisticated mutual funds, bought large blocks of securities. They pyramided one holding company on another, with control from the investment-minded manipulators more than from production management. Everyone seemed to be getting rich overnight.

I was impressed with this fever but I knew there was a flaw in the structure of paper wealth. I remember teaching a class when the Wall Street excitement was running high. I asked each student to pick a stock value for a theoretical speculation. Their assignment was to tell me what it would be worth the next month. After each student picked a security, each invariably forecast an increase in value.

My personal struggle in the economic arena included playing with my original investment of $8,000 or $9,000 and building it up to about $28,000. In this gamble I learned some valuable lessons. Before I took a vacation trip to the West Coast to visit Emily Huntington in 1929, I cut my margin borrowing to practically nothing. When the stocks began to waver in September, and then to plunge, I was not in debt. I made a little money—not much—in spite of the crash.

In these years the brilliant British economist John Maynard Keynes, whose ideas I presented to my classes, saw a weak link between funds going to the consuming public and flow to the producers of goods. Some of the purchasing power was sterilized. Since he was one of the few economists of the time who could write English clearly and concisely, he had a greater influence than others. Keynes stressed purchasing power as a force in controlling the volume of production.

Many of the Bryn Mawr faculty took an active interest in the stock market, becoming "instant economists." They joined the "get rich before lunch bunch," entering the exciting marketplace. One of the great losses to the nation that came with speculation was the reluctance to work at their normal professions on the part of those who could make large sums in speculation.

The failure of the banks could have been prevented by emergency action early in 1932. The President-elect, Franklin Delano Roosevelt, had been unwilling to collaborate with President Hoover before the new administration took office. The action in the four-month interval between the election and the inauguration of the new President was inadequate. President Hoover took an important step when he set up the Reconstruction Finance Corporation (RFC), but financial losses seriously undermined the foundations of plans for future production and impaired the capacity of individuals who counted on contingency funds to help them in times of need. The loss was greater than might have been in other changes of administration because in that year the new President did not take over until March 4.

The worst losses of the subsequent depression were not immediately after the market crash but two years later. I have always credited Secretary of Labor Frances Perkins, who worked with Roosevelt when he was governor of New York and who came to Washington with his administration, for creating the work programs and other measures that helped limit the extent of disaster and stimulated recovery, which finally got under way in the mid-thirties.

In my teaching at Bryn Mawr in 1928 and 1929, I had already tried to do the difficult task of combining the wisdom of philosophers and scientists of the past, when the instruments of control were limited, with the flexibility required by the rapidly changing techniques of machines and calculators which would change the world in the distant future. The airplane and radio were just becoming significant elements of economic life. The computer was emerging from early beginnings, and the potential of television, rocketry, and space travel was still ahead. Clearly some modification in the rules of the marketplace were needed—but the fundamentals of production and exchange still had to be kept in mind.

After my twenty-six years of working for government I went back to teaching in 1962, first at Duke University in North Carolina and then at Georgetown University in Washington.

In my last decade of teaching I was able to give more emphasis to the international aspects of economic policy and considered my courses more political science than economics. This trend was congenial and led to a flexible analysis of contemporary problems in aid, trade, and investment. I found the growing opportunities and responsibilities of the United States fascinating. I was glad to see our increasing leadership and involvement abroad. It seemed to me the students reacted eagerly to the dynamic nature of the subject matter.

I was not so happy with the strong mathematical influence extending to the nth degree the statistical material now so richly available. It seemed to me then and it seems now that the psychological elements in industrial decisions and patterns of consumption were submerged by some contemporary analysis.

In any case teaching has always kept me in touch with exciting current happenings and shifting policies. I also enjoyed the stimulating questions and in many cases friendships of the young students.

[121]

# · 10 ·

## INTERNATIONAL BANKING—RESEARCH IN SWITZERLAND

Teaching and research crisscrossed my other work—always interesting—over a period from 1921 to 1971. In 1928 I became somewhat restless. I wanted to continue research abroad. I was fortunate in being granted a new fellowship from Radcliffe and Harvard's research bureau. It came to a tangible result in my history of the origin and early months of the international bank in Switzerland. While I worked on a book published under the title of *The Bank for International Settlements at Work*, I acquired more knowledge of Europe, of the rising Nazi movement, and of the changing structure of the international financial system. Planning to resume my teaching, I continued learning.

My request for research support stated that I would explore some of the economic problems close to my earlier work on the French franc and investigate weak spots in the international exchange system. I said my inquiry would be a study of the transfer problem. This had become urgent because in the years after World War I, unprecedented sums of money moved from one currency system to another.

When I went to Europe with the new grant in 1930 Germany was experiencing great financial difficulties. There had been a temporary suspension of the transfer of funds. In 1929 an international conference, organized by the United States under the chairmanship of Owen D. Young, president of the General Electric Company, came forward with proposals, called the Young Plan, that outlined the nature and scope of a new bank, *The Bank for International Settlements* (BIS). It was designed to facilitate the payment of reparation by Germany and also to create new machinery of wide usefulness.

I had followed these developments in Europe and thought there was an opportunity for interesting research. It should probably be centered in Germany. A vacation seemed in order as I faced demanding work in the attempt to resolve difficult financial problems. Many in Europe were apprehensive about future exchange adjustments.

Meanwhile I developed the idea that I was a little tired of bicycling uphill in Europe. I figured out there was only one way you could be sure to go downhill all summer. That was to get on a river. So I thought I would head for the rivers of Europe.

I talked to various people, because it's my experience that if you talk to enough people, sooner or later they'll tell you where you can buy a giraffe or where you can find a new kind of banana or something. So I talked to a lot of people, and finally came across a woman who said, "Well, why don't you get a German folding boat?"

This sounded good. She gave me a little description of the German folding boat, and she may even have mentioned one of the factories that made them. In any case, my friend Emily and I took a ship, because you didn't fly unless you were a Lindbergh or something like that. We were off to find a boat to fold.

I remember our putting together this boat in the shop, on a very hot day, perspiration streaming down our faces. The man who sold it put it together first, then knocked it down, then we put it together with some difficulty. Emily was a little bit nervous, but she had a surprising amount of confidence in me. I still wonder why she had.

We took this boat down to the dock on the river. In this case, it was the Neckar. The Neckar flows from Stuttgart to Heidelberg, then on into the Rhine. We got the boat together. We put it in the water. Then we were off. If you think of a boat in the river, there are no brakes, and it has a special problem: if you want to get out of the boat, how are you going to stop it?

We had the books with us that told us what to do about various things, and Emily sat up in the front with the dictionary on her knees, and I had the book of instructions on my knees, and we had double paddles. Every once in a while I'd say, "There's something dangerous ahead." I'd say, "It begins with *stau*, but I don't know whether it's a separable word or not."

So we went down the Neckar with her reading the dictionary, I reading the instructions and the maps, and we really had a wonderful time. Now, the Neckar, as any good boatman knows, is not one of the most difficult rivers, so it wasn't as perilous as it sounds, but we still felt pretty shaky. The boat is almost as sensitive as a shell, so you

[123]

can't really throw your weight around. In many places you cannot paddle as fast as the current. If we turned around and tried to paddle upstream, we'd still be going downstream.

We went along for two or three hours. Finally I said to Emily, "I'm tired, I've got to get out."

She said, "How can you?"

We really didn't know if we'd ever get out of the boat until we got down to Rotterdam. But eventually we found a spot where we could get into a side stream, and I threw myself panting on the bank. Of course we always pulled the boat out. We ate a little of the food that we had with us (we always had some food), and considered that we'd done a rather heroic stint, but after a brief rest, we got in again.

We did the Neckar and went down to old Heidelberg, encountering some *Wiederwellen* (white water), whirlpools where the waves curled backward, and we shot through safely.

From Heidelberg we went by train to Bavaria. I had had the romantic notion of going from the source of the Danube to the mouth in the Black Sea and miscalculated my distance by about two thousand miles. But we did find a place called Donaueschingen, "the source of the Danube." There the river was about ten feet across and eight or ten inches deep. We walked from there to Sigmaringen, a fine old town, east of the Black Forest.

Then at Ulm, we found the Danube flowing about ten miles an hour, between stone-walled embankments. Young men launched their boats and disappeared in a flash down the river. After watching them, we looked at each other, pale and apprehensive. We went to a café and drank beer to think.

The Danube was not swift all the way. There were places where it curved back and forth in lazy loops. At the Donaudurchbruch (the Danube Breakthrough) there were high cliffs with a German temple, the Valhalla, on the rocky heights, a terrible structure—hybrid Grecian-Medieval. It suited the pseudo-heroic mood of many Germans. Near there we spent a night in a monastery, where the rats outnumbered the monks.

At the Regensburg Bridge, built by the Romans, the river rushed through arches about twelve to fourteen feet wide. The rushing water swept us through like a shuttle on a loom.

Emily and I went through various types of territory and finally got to Passau on the Danube, where a big, new dam had been built, one of the biggest dams in Europe. Passau is at the confluence of the

[124]

Danube and the Inn River, on the border of Austria and Germany, rather an interesting place.

Now our time had run out, so we had to take our boat to pieces, put it in our rucksacks, get on a river steamer, and go down to Vienna. After a week Emily went back to California and I went north to Bonn. But I was not finished with *faltbooting*.

This was the time when I first became aware of the Nazi movement. Stimulated by the strenuous outdoor life, but apprehensive of the hysteria among the young people, I set out for Bonn to begin my research. We had met many young German men on the rivers. They were belligerent, they were revolutionary, and they were anti-American, anti-English, anti-French, anti-everything, except Germany. "The German soul must be re-created, the German imperialism must be strengthened, we must have our place in the sun, we must have expansion, we must have *Lebensraum*," and so on. This was Nazism in its beginning, when it spread from Hitler's small group to the younger generations, and then gradually crept up through the older generations.

All I could do was to catch a word here and there, and get the feeling of this tremendous zeal and pent-up energy that was expressed by these young men. I say men because at that time there were practically no women on the rivers. The girls hadn't taken up *faltbooting* and I might also add as a footnote, I think we were the first Americans to be in a *faltboot*. There's an article in the *National Geographic* about *faltbooting* that a woman—Mrs. Carleton Parker— wrote after talking with me, and it's always been considered that she was a pioneer on this, but she got most of her ideas from me and then later went on the river. She was a very attractive woman. Her husband was quite a figure, an industrial psychologist, and she was very much interested in industrial problems. I met her after my boat trips, in a hotel in Geneva.

My vacation over, I went to work in Bonn, reading in the University library of that sleepy provincial town, later to be the capital of the Federal Republic of Germany. I choose that town because I could consult there with Professor Joseph Schumpeter, the eminent Austrian economist, who was living there prior to going to Harvard. I lunched with him on his terrace on the Rhine. I told him of my voyages in a German kayak down the Neckar, the Danube, and then on the Rhine to Bonn. The river trips had given me a chance to talk to many young men, welcoming Hitler as a leader, so I asked Schumpeter his views of the situation. He was apprehensive.

In September, knowing a little more of the language and considerable about the mood of the nation, I went to Berlin. There I shared an apartment with Mildred Wertheimer, who was reporting for the Foreign Policy Association in New York. We saw a great deal of our mutual friend Dorothy Thompson, who was writing for American papers.

Although Berlin was interesting with its fevered struggles for power, I came to the conclusion that I would find much more financial material in Basel, Switzerland, where the new bank was beginning to function. So after a few weeks in Berlin, armed with a score of letters of introduction, I shifted my base and arrived on the doorstep of the new institution to begin the second phase of my work. *

The letters, addressed to President Gates W. McGarrah and to Vice-President Leon Fraser, I presented first. They were very cordial. Fraser told me he would assign me a room in the bank and have all but the confidential papers routed over my desk. He said that in many respects I would be treated like a member of the staff.

Two days after this first interview Fraser called me in and said this plan would have to be canceled. He had received protests from the representatives of two member banks. They said they were not going to permit an American spy to report to the U. S. Government and the Federal Reserve Board. I presume that the two were Japanese and German.

I knew that the relations of the United States to the bank were unique. We had refused to join as members. Three American banks, The First National Bank of New York, The First National Bank of Chicago, and J. P. Morgan and Company, had joined the group and held shares. The Board of Directors who set up the BIS had elected McGarrah as president and Fraser as vice-president to enhance the U.S. involvement.

At this time, Foster was in Paris working on some aspects of financial assistance to Germany. Foster had, by 1930, made his mark in the world of international law. He had represented American creditors who had underwritten German securities. This and other work, including his responsibilities for the Kreuger and Toll bond-holders, brought him to Europe frequently.

---

*For more discussion of Berlin days see Chapter 15, pp. 179-183.

I felt that his comments on my situation might be helpful. I telephoned.

"Come to Paris Friday," he said.

I took the sleeper and went to the Ritz where he and Janet were staying. I joined them at breakfast, and asked, "When can we have a conference?"

"You don't want to be bothered with business," Foster told me. "We're going to have a wonderful dinner. I'm going over to Foyot's (one of Paris' best restaurants, now closed) to plan the meal."

"I came up here to talk to you about my work, and if you haven't the time, I will take the 3 o'clock train back to Switzerland."

"You wouldn't miss the dinner, Eleanor?"

"Oh yes I would."

He looked surprised and said, "Then I'll see you at four this afternoon."

Then I went out with him to Foyot's on the Left Bank. There we discussed a certain type of pigeon we were going to have for dinner and the old chartreuse that comes with cobwebs on the bottle from the deep cellar and the exact salad and the soup. Then he went off to do some business and I went off to tend to some errands on my own.

When I saw him at four and told him my story, he said, "Well, I guess that means you can't write the book."

"I'm not looking for advice on whether to write the book. I want your view on *how*."

"It will be difficult."

"I know. If you have any constructive suggestions, please make them."

He continued to be skeptical.

I had told Foster about my difficulties because I liked him—I liked both my brothers and wanted them to know what I was doing. The conversation didn't ruin the dinner for me or the others. It was a perfect meal. Afterward I took the sleeper back to Switzerland.

Although my funds were limited, I had to live in the first-class hotel where most of the directors and economists coming to the bank were staying. So I took the cheapest room at the Three Kings, on the Rhine, and ate only breakfast there.

The hotel was dramatically situated on the edge of the rushing waters, but it lacked charm. I came to hate it—stiff, formal, elegant, and pretentious. These lonely weeks seemed like months. No one spoke to me. The dour waiters and maids did not have an extra word.

I ate alone, I walked alone. I sat alone in my dark red hotel room. I clipped newspapers. I went to the a ⁺ museum to look at the ominous cliffs and chasms in Holbein paintings. Occasionally I would go to the zoo and even less frequently eat in the fine restaurant, the Schutzenhaus—but alone. I would go to a concert to hear fine music but always alone. These days made me more dependent on friends in later years.

In the reading room of the hotel just over the Rhine I would take the long bamboo rods holding the newspapers of France, Germany, England, and Switzerland and sit for hours, hearing the roar of the river and seeing its whirlpools. Occasionally I swam in a wire-enclosed area where the water swept through with astonishing force. I swam alone.

The Balois people in the town spoke a special dialect. They would listen to my German and then take off in the local dialect, which I could not understand. The old families of the city were surrounded by a wall of tradition. They were a proud exclusive society. Basel is a picturesque city for a few hours, perhaps for a few days. After a short visit the outsider goes to the mountains or to the lakes.

After eight or nine hours of work, I would go to the movies. I saw some fine German films including *The Blue Angel*, with Marlene Dietrich and Emil Jannings. I could sing—"I am enveloped in love." I saw it three times.

I haunted the halls and salons of the hotel in search of a friendly economist. I asked one prospect about the weather.

"Rain," he said.

Then I got the break I was looking for. I asked a scholarly-looking man, short, serious, and pleasant, a question about the current exchange rate. "Would the pound hold?" I asked.

He answered in a friendly manner. He was the Austrian expert on monetary matters and was eager to talk about financial prospects. He realized I was not a novice. He asked me to come to his office.

The new friend, Hans Simon, had been assistant to Joseph Schumpeter, whom I had consulted in Bonn. Simon was a brilliant man, keen in his analysis, fertile in imagination. He was about fifty at the time. He and his charming wife invited me to their house, where I had my first social evening in many weeks. He had never been a Nazi, and later when he was in Vienna he was warned to escape since he was a Jew and was going to be picked up. He fled over Spain to Portugal. Finally, in the early forties I was able to help him get to the United States.

The day after our first conversation, with hope and fear, I called on him. He took me to the office of his colleague, Marcel van Zeeland.

Marcel asked me to come to his office the next day. While I was talking to the two men, Fraser came in. He was amused to see me there.

"I hope you are finding some interesting material," he said. He did not discuss my project, but his tone gave the clue to the others that we were friends. I could see the doors opening to me.

It was not long before I knew all the staff members and had easy access. I also came to know the directors who came to the monthly meetings. I remember particularly the extraordinary Pierre Quesnay from Paris. Karl Blessing, the German economist, later the head of the Bundesbank, remained my friend until his death in the early seventies.

When it was no longer necessary to stay in the hotel, I moved, sharing an apartment with two charming secretaries, one Belgian, one French. We had a lot of festivity after a long working day. One night we gave a party for the younger members of the staff. After a generous amount of Rhine wine, we decided to play hockey with umbrellas and a can of soup. It was a new development in the field of sports.

The next day we were called on by the Basel police. They told us that unless we could carry on our social life in a more restrained fashion they would ask us to leave town. With the exception of carnival time, Basel is a very austere, Calvinistic town.

During the pre-Lenten festival of Mardi Gras, I left Basel since no work could be done. The people in the city drank all night and most of the day.

Back in Basel I had long discussions with Hans Simon, who had worked out a proposal to facilitate transfers at par. Larger transfers would carry discount or premium.

I still found the city dark and gloomy in the winter months, and used to take my skis and go into the Black Forest above Freiburg in Breisgau, and ski in the *Feltberg*. One weekend I went up on the train, and asked a group of pleasant-looking Swiss if they knew of a good trail for a beginner. They told me there were no trails suitable for beginners in the weather that weekend, and none for anyone who intended to ski alone.

"I've got my skis," I told them, "and I'm alone."

I wasn't after that. They took me up into the woods, halfway up the *Feltberg*, through rather narrow trails among the trees, to a log cabin where we spent the night, sleeping on straw, breaking the ice in a little spring for water, and sharing our food. I always travel with chocolate, bread, and oranges to quench my thirst and keep up my strength. They had potatoes and bacon. After breakfast they showed me a trail I could follow up to the *Hebelhaus*, on the upper slopes. It was one of the best weekends I had while I worked at the BIS.

The group in the bank was extraordinarily able. They brought together information gathered in the areas of the participating banking systems.* This was considered by the directors in monthly meetings and summarized in the yearly surveys of the world's economy. Per Jacobsson from Sweden did an impressive job in putting the facts together. I found him instructive and stimulating. But I did not realize that he also valued my work until we met fifteen years later in Vienna. He was assigned the task of analyzing the Austrian financial situation.

Hans Simon made no progress in convincing his colleagues of his special plan for assured transfers, but he helped on many recommendations as to other action in the European money markets. To a degree his ideas were forerunners of the European Payments Union established under the Marshall Plan and using the BIS as agent.

The original purpose of the bank, to transfer reparation payments, did not set limits to its scope. It had been the hope of the people who established it to have two coordinated branches in the Washington institution, similar to those of Bretton Woods—the International Monetary Fund and the Bank for Reconstruction and Development. If the Basel bank had succeeded and extended its membership, the economic history would have been different.

---

*At the outset the representatives of six national banks and a consortium of three private U.S. banks were present. The number of representatives on the board grew to ten almost at once and then over the years to thirty nationals. See Eleanor Lansing Dulles, *The Bank for International Settlements at Work* (New York: Macmillan, 1932), p. 587.

England went off the gold standard in September 1931, and Credit Anstalt failed in Austria. The Vienna and Berlin banks closed for several days.

Trouble was set off by a mutiny in the Royal Navy, which upset the British political equilibrium and frightened financiers. The pound fell. There were several black days with banks closing in many centers.

To me, the adjustment of the twenties and early thirties, the collapse of the New York stock market, and political threats from Germany were sufficiently frightening.

The idea of economic opportunism as contrasted to economic morality opened the way for Hitler's plans for centralized control of the finances of Germany. The depression deepened. It is difficult to conduct rescue operations with public funds, without changing from the free enterprise monetary system.

I remember arguing with my friends, and with my brothers, in 1933, that we should go into the economy as a government and rescue the insurance companies, mortgage companies, and banks. In the end we paid the cost of the depression and let many financial institutions collapse. Then we had to control prices, help thousands of jobless, and assist institutions to recover, spending from a budget in deficit.

Government intervention is a hot subject. I recognize that in the field of social insurance and public utilities there must be government action, but the extent of such activity has essential limits. The early thirties were dark years of turmoil and change.

What I had been working on in France in the 1920s was now spreading in an uncontrollable wave through the major areas of business and finance. The worker was having his say and he had the community of consumers with him most of the time. The will of the little man was being expressed through government and its many institutions.

In 1932 I returned to the United States to finish the text for *The Bank for International Settlements at Work*. The Harvard and Radcliffe bureau insisted that I cut the manuscript in half. After substantial cuts in the 950-page manuscript I retyped the text with narrower margins and on thinner paper, and managed to have it approved for publication.

I remember standing in a telephone booth in Harvard Square,

cramped, tense, and dropping papers on the floor, as I called the head of the committee. He said they had met earlier in the afternoon—and they recommended publication—all 500 pages. (The third I threw away should have been kept.)

What I had accomplished is best said by a review that appeared in *The New York Times* (July 23, 1933):

> Miss Dulles' conscientious effort to treat every aspect of the bank's work is the story of how those bright hopes and sanguine expectations were blighted and turned into disillusionment, at least as far as the debtor nations were concerned. But she makes it clear that this was not due to the deliberate unwillingness of the bank to oblige, but to its real inability to help because of the limitation imposed by the statutes governing the institution. The fundamental issues were decided, after all, not by economics, but by politicians.

The wonderful cooperation of the members representing many nations—seven at the beginning, thirty later—taught me some lessons. I was convinced that, particularly in specialized agencies, international cooperation was feasible. The efforts of the International Monetary Fund (IMF) and The International Bank for Reconstruction and Development (IBRD), the World Health and World Food Organizations, were foreshadowed in Basel. Where technical skills, professional ability, and specific goals were central, the difference in nationality and even major political conflict became less important.

During almost sixty years of professional work, I have been concerned with practical economic problems a considerable part of the time. I have found the channeling of some $3 billion of government funds to the restoration of Austria and the rebuilding of Berlin probably the most satisfactory part of this experience. This sum was partly Marshall Plan dollars and aid money and some was counterpart schillings and Deutschemarks. I admit that my theoretical studies have played a part, but I think there was something illusive in economic doctrines. I liked the world of ideas, but I found the buildings, the monetary arrangements, the laws, and the specific and tangible accomplishments gave me more sense of achievement than the abstract—the Marshall Plan, rather than the theories of international trade.

[132]

As a result of greater concentration on the specific programs, I do not feel at home in the "micro-macro regions," the new models and econometrica. I do not understand all the current lingo. Computers often leave me in a "do not bend or staple" jungle. But they still must deal with *demand*, which is inexorable, and the *supply* problems, which call for work. Adam Smith is still a closer friend than the fascinating modern witches and wizards.

One of the least satisfying tasks I undertook reluctantly in 1933 called for the writing of the book *Depression and Reconstruction* (University of Pennsylvania Press). I began it on the insistence of the late Joseph Willits, director of the Wharton School. He wanted the two of us to undertake a cooperative study and write the book together. Unfortunately for me, he left the University of Pennsylvania to take an important post at the Rockefeller Foundation. I was asked to continue the work on my own.

The resulting publication has some useful analysis, but as a single-handed effort to attack an enormous problem it was not impressive. Its publication came at a time when most economists were more concerned with concrete measures to end the Depression than they were with theory. Professor Simon Kuznets of Columbia, who read several chapters in manuscript, warned me that it would not exert a significant influence. I learned much from my work in preparing the text and from my close association with the gifted staff of the Wharton School's Research Department. Here serious, sharply focused studies were painstakingly developed.

When I joined the Social Security Board in 1936, I was to struggle with many of the practical aspects of government which hemmed in our economic programs. My dealings were with the laws that prescribed the benefits to be paid to qualified individuals, and the taxes to be collected to pay the costs. Because of my writings in finance, foreign exchange, and international banking, I was asked to analyze the reserve fund and fiscal measure adopted. Even as I moved into the field of political science my economic specialization continued to claim my attention.

Eight years later I worked for government in the development of the system of monetary exchange and investment usually referred to as the Bretton Woods system. The name was taken from the New Hampshire location of the conference that established the IMF and

IBRD. Here again, political power and practical matters such as the relation between central banks and government played an important part.

When I joined the State Department, in which work was divided into political and economic groups, it was natural that I should find myself working on the financing of the United Nations Relief and Rehabilitation Administration (UNRRA), and on the preparations for the Bretton Woods conference. J. Maynard Keynes had been good enough to write to me about *The French Franc*. I did not meet him until the Bretton Woods conference.

It was gratifying and stimulating to have carried my training and writing into a field where significant constructive work could be done. I was on the International Secretariat and burdened with preparation of daily reports, but I did have time for useful discussions of the probable postwar financial situation—and methods of avoiding severe distortion of the emerging postwar economies.

Techniques of measurement and economic doctrines have changed drastically since my early reading and research. I sometimes feel adrift when I attend conferences. In the whirling mass of quick decisions people with strong will and little knowledge dominate a large segment of business and of government. As I review my past experience and the existing complex of current relations, in spite of some limitations, I am still an economist.

When I became engaged to marry David, I was destined for a lifetime of college teaching. I had taken the necessary steps and considered it a good line of work. Although my plans changed when I entered government in 1936, I still continued to think of it as an interesting and useful profession. I returned to it in 1962 when I left government. Altogether I taught for more than sixteen years. Much of the rest of my time as a writer was directed toward the history of foreign affairs since 1942.

# MARRIAGE BY COMMUTERS

In Paris, for many weeks I had faced the choice between marriage and independence. The freedom of France made an intermediate resolution of the question temporarily possible.

Back in the United States in 1927 a decision became more urgent. I continued the struggle to resolve the problem. On my return to Harvard with my manuscript on the French franc ready for publication, I was in a quandary. I was increasingly aware of my love and need for David and at the same time of the growing importance of my career. I went first to Boston and Cambridge.

David said he was coming to Boston. I wrote him that since I shared an apartment with two women, Emily Huntington and Marian Rhoads, he would have to find someplace else to stay. But he came anyway, before going back to Johns Hopkins to resume teaching.

David had urged that we marry as soon as both of us returned from Paris that summer of 1927.

"That would interfere with my teaching," I told him.

Economics was my profession and I had agreed to teach it. I was determined to support myself. I intended to do so, for the whole year.

David's answer was that any college would understand if a woman got married that her working plans would change and her employers would release her.

I disagreed.

"I'm going to teach the whole year. I won't leave after one term."

This was the only time in my career in which David held to the conventional pattern of expecting a woman to fit her career to the needs of her husband. I knew that adjustment was inevitable, but I was not yet ready. He wanted me to do research and writing in Baltimore. But I felt I was fully obligated to keep my contract and that our marriage should be postponed. I now think David was right in assuming that breaking the contract would not have been held against me if marriage were the reason, but then I did not.

My protest over changing my plans was really part of a war against marriage on my part. I even developed a strange arthritic condition. I could scarcely walk, couldn't go up and down stairs. I cried frequently.

Emily said I must go to a nursing home, as there was no one to take care of me at the apartment. She also suggested I see a psychiatrist. I did both, with my generous parents contributing to medical expenses. The psychiatrist listened a lot and I talked a lot and after thinking over how much he charged and how little he did, I told him, "I don't need you. I can make up my own mind."

He said, "You are right."

As soon as I decided *not* to get married, my mysterious malady disappeared.

When I went from Simmons to Bryn Mawr, David and I met for weekends. Few of my friends saw him. We had a wonderful time alone together exercising great discretion.

In 1929, when I received a grant to write the book on the Bank for International Settlements, which was a perfect excuse to escape again from facing the facts, I was not ready to marry David, nor had I found a way to get along without him. Moving to Europe seemed to provide a temporary answer.

When I was working in Switzerland I became further convinced that marriage was not yet for me. I wrote David that our relationship would have to end. I simply could not face the commitment of marriage. He answered in a wonderful letter that he would abide by the conditions I wanted to set.

I answered, "There can be nothing. It is too upsetting to make a partial adjustment. I can't see you or write."

He wrote back again that he would do as I wished. He may have known I would change my decision.

In the months when I worked in austere and melancholy Basel, I would go to Geneva and stay with my friends Gerhardt and Mary Jentsch every few weeks. One day when I was working in the League of Nations Library, I saw a copy of the Paris *Herald Tribune* with a story of a reception at the American University Union. Among the guests listed was Professor David Blondheim.

I put my papers in my briefcase and left the library. I went back to the apartment and told Mary, "I've got to take a walk along the lake."

She went with me for three or four miles. We did not talk much, and when we returned, I wrote David. "I don't know if you are still in Paris or not. I saw in the paper that you were there last week. Also I don't know what your situation is. Perhaps you are married or engaged by now, but I just thought I would write you and say that if you were here, I would be very happy."

Within a few hours, I received a telegram, asking, "Where can we meet and when?"

The message continued with the suggestion that we might go to Colmar, near Strasbourg. We did and I do not remember anything about the town of Colmar—just the tremendous joy of reunion.

We spent that Christmas, 1931, with Mary and Gerhardt at Andermatt, in Switzerland. It was probably the best Christmas I ever had. The four of us stayed in a small inn. No one else we knew was there and we were completely happy in each other's company. We walked and talked and three of us skied. David offered to learn to ski but I advised against it.

One excursion remains in my mind. I went with Gerhardt and a guide up a long mountain trail, starting before dawn. With sealskins on our skis, we toiled up the slope for five hours. Then we struck ice on a pass and had to inch our way up and over to a tiny inn, where, at dusk, we were served hot wine and bread and cheese. By the time it was dark I was aware of the difficulty of the return to the valley. Descent was by starlight with no firm hold on earth or sky. I followed the faint tracing in the snow and the filmy figure of the guide, flying in dark space. The mystery, the fear, and the speed transported me to an unreal world. Then, when I was at the point of exhaustion, the lights of the town sparkled below and there was the warm inn and David. I shall not ski again in the high mountains nor find again the warm welcome of David.

In January my work was finished and I had to go home. David and I met in Paris first, before I took the ship, the impressive *Leviathan*, to New York.

At this time (1932) Foster and Janet, married for some twenty years, had the joy of complete congeniality of tradition, upbringing, education, religion, and many mutual friends. They had met David in Paris in 1926 when we had both been there. They knew—better than my parents—of our deep devotion and intimate relation. They also knew of David's intense preoccupation with his work and my defiant independence and determination to pursue my career.

When I told Foster that David and I would be married, Foster wrote me that he could see a dozen problems that would make marriage difficult and complicate professional life for each of us. He did not visualize me adapting to the formal conditions of marriage. Tradition, mutual friends, professions, temperament, he wrote, all must be taken into account. Foster wrote that he admired David, but he also knew I would have difficulty adjusting to marriage.

His letter stunned me. I was touched that he had written this long and intimate advice. My father had died and Foster was now the head of the family. That he felt responsible I knew, but that he thought I had not considered all these matters upset me.

I wrote Janet that I had considered the problems Foster discussed for more than six years and that I was determined to face what lay ahead. I hoped Foster would understand. He did.

In the years to come, Foster's son became a Jesuit priest. A nephew married a distinguished Chinese scholar. A niece married an Austrian; another niece, a Norwegian, and a brother-in-law became a Mormon. Foster's granddaughter married an Afghanistani.

I was not the only one who chose to take my own course.

One of the most poignant episodes I remember from 1932 was the evening David took me and his son, Hillel, to dinner in New York. Hillel was about thirteen years old, a charming, well-educated, good-looking youngster. We ordered with great care, the boy taking an interest in the meal and in me. Then David told Hillel that we were engaged and planning to marry. The sudden change in Hillel's face, his voice, his attitude, was heartrending. It seemed he was willing to accept me as a friend, but as a relative—this would be disloyal to race and religion. It was pitiful to see his shock and despair. He could not eat his meal and sat silent while we tried to keep conversation going.

I saw Hillel twice again. He is now a talented doctor in Jerusalem. I do not know his wife, but I have been told they are a very congenial and happy family with several children.

In early December of 1932 David and I again announced our engagement. I was teaching at the University of Pennsylvania and Bryn Mawr College and he at Johns Hopkins in Baltimore. He telephoned me late one evening and said, "We can't get married."

I answered, "We're going to get married. We're going to do it."

We talked for over an hour. Nothing was settled. I was so upset I called Caroline Robbins and her husband, Joe Herben, friends of mine living and teaching in Bryn Mawr, and asked if I could come out. I took a taxi for the fifteen-mile drive.

I talked to them for several hours. They knew David. It was after midnight when I decided to take a train to Baltimore. Joe called David to tell him I was coming. When I reached Baltimore Station, David was waiting for me. We shook hands in a very formal greeting.

David asked me if I would care to take a walk. We went around and around the reservoir. He turned to me and said, without a smile, "I heard a funny story the other day."

He told me the story, and I burst out laughing.

"You know," David said, "I have to marry you. You have such a marvelous sense of humor."

It took some planning to arrange our Washington wedding at my aunt's house, for we discovered that we had to have blood tests in the District of Columbia if we were to be married there. That meant both of us would have to be away from our classes and stay in Washington for several days.

Our solution was to be married in City Hall in Philadelphia, where neither of us had to be residents. Then we went to Washington and were married again.

The Judge at City Hall was very friendly. David said he thought the service was probably Episcopalian. After the ceremony we were presented with a certificate covered with cupids and flowers, the most elaborate marriage certificate I have ever seen.

David had to return to Baltimore for classes immediately. My friends at the university, Anne Bezanson and several others, took me out to dinner and home to spend the night. David was back in Baltimore by then. I taught my classes the next day.

At the end of the week I went down to Washington for the second ceremony. We gathered at my Aunt Eleanor's at Sixteenth and S streets. Margaret and Nataline thought our mother was not strong enough at the time to have the wedding at our Auburn home. She had a bad heart and arthritis.

My sister Margaret's husband, Deane Edwards, was a minister. Deane and Margaret came from Bronxville, New York, so that Deane could conduct the ceremony. Since David had a deep respect for Jewish tradition, although he did not attend the Temple regularly, my request to Deane was that he "do any kind of service he thought suitable, with Jesus included, but it would be nice if he left *Christ* out of it." It was an understanding and sensitive service.

After the ceremony and luncheon, David and I went down to the Lincoln Memorial. Back at the Lansing house, we met Deane and Margaret, and the four of us traveled in a compartment on the train to New York. David remarked that he thought it rather unusual to have the minister accompany us on our honeymoon.

We spent the night at the Biltmore and took the Empire State Express the next day to see Mother in Auburn. After a few days there we each went back to our teaching jobs. I kept my two-room apartment on Spruce Street in Philadelphia, and David and I rented a small apartment in Baltimore near the university. I went there on weekends. David came to Philadelphia when his weekends off from teaching were longer than mine. We used to go out to Bryn Mawr on Saturday evening to talk and play roulette with some friends. Joe Herben, who had helped me in December, like David, was a philologist, and the two men had many esoteric jokes. It was a small, congenial group. Our life was pleasant and we had a quiet social life in Baltimore and Philadelphia.

Both of us were mature and totally committed—to each other and to our future together.

From the first days our interest had been intellectual; only after we got to know each other had the emotional attraction been added to a deep understanding of the life of scholarship. We found the life in two cities meant that our long days and nights over the weekends did not prevent our absorption in our research and teaching for five days a week.

It was obvious that when it was decided we would have children—two we thought—that I would have to make some further adjustment in my schedule by carrying a lighter load, but this did not seem impossible. Throughout the eight years of our close attachment we had adjusted our personal lives and our interests.

I do not think life could have separated us.

Money was a problem and was the nearest cause of disagreement. I told David he could not afford to buy expensive old dictionaries, which were his passion. I tried to be practical. The love of books was so strong in David that I think I made him too careful in spending.

[140]

We really were hard up. Johns Hopkins had instituted a system of holding back a large portion of the salary of the professors, but the income tax was imposed on the nominal salary. Moreover, David's son, Hillel, had been granted support by the court. The amount to be paid was based on David's nominal salary. What he had left for his own living was only about $1,500, not enough for food, clothes, and rent.

Meanwhile my salary was $5,000, but it too was cut by special adjustments. We had the expenses of two apartments and travel back and forth. I don't think we suffered physically, but we suffered mentally with constant worry.

Very shortly after we were married the bank in which David had small savings failed and he was left with no reserve. These problems were the only ones I remember, and we did not talk about them at length. Our apartments were small but well located; we needed few things.

In 1933 we went abroad during the summer on a delayed honeymoon. David went to Paimpol in France and collected pictures of the local ships used by the *Pêcheur d'Islande* of France. He also collected photographs of the building in which Pierre Loti had lived, and of the home of the heroine, Gaud, of a Loti story, for a textbook on which he was working.

On our return to the United States we continued to teach, and I became very interested in David's plans for a great French dictionary, comparable to the Murray *Oxford English Dictionary*. He had explained to me the lack of such a work—*Larousse*, used by so many Americans, was not a dictionary in the sense David meant, but a small, handy word book. The first present he ever gave me was a copy of *Larousse*.

He had also told me one reason for the lack of such a major work was the many differences of opinion among linguistic scholars in France. It left little chance for cooperation necessary to carry on this huge task. After discussing this we decided the way to get the enterprise started was to have the beginnings in the United States and then present the first year's research material to the French, inducing them to go on with the program.

As a first step, David had a committee appointed at the meeting of the Modern Language Association. He made himself secretary—a chairman, vice-chairman, and treasurer were then chosen. After this start he enlisted the support of most of the universities with notable chairs in philology. These professors guided a number of linguistic students into the fields of research where they would write *fiches* in many sectors of the French language. The small piece of paper with the word, its meaning, its first uses, became part of the building stones of the final work. The students would get their theses and their degrees out of this work, and the foundations would be laid.

David got a small grant from the Carnegie Foundation to cover incidental secretarial expenses. By this device the thousands of *fiches*, which underlie the final definition and history of French words, were collected under the guidance of the best professors in the United States.

David sought no credit, and except among experts, he never received any recognition for this plan. It amused us to engineer the project and it was well under way at the time of his death.

Our marriage was a far better one than either of us had hoped. David was less nervous and I did not feel trapped. When I suggested that we have a child, he said, "Fine, but not one. Two—at least two."

We realized that our freedom, with its complete absorption in work for several days a week, and in each other for almost half the week, would be changed. But we wanted children, and so we planned to have the first one in August, so the birth would not interfere too much with our work. I also knew I could have a lighter teaching schedule with less research as I gained more seniority.

In January a test proved I was pregnant. David was so pleased and proud. I had seldom seen him as happy.

"Her name is Eleanor," he told me.

"She's a boy," I answered, "and his name is David."

The weekend of March 17, 1934, we planned to be together without company. The weather would be good for walking, a time for talking about summer plans and about arrangements for the baby. It was to be uninterrupted. It was, in fact, a wonderful time. On Sunday night David took me to the station. We said good-bye on the steps of the train. I telephoned him when I got back to my Philadelphia apartment.

Ever since our marriage, the only cloud over our horizon had been financial. Our outlook for the future had been influenced by our hopes that each of us would get academic advancement. David decided that he would write some textbooks for additional income. He disliked writing them, because they called for a different kind of research from that which really interested him. However, the texts he did—*Carmen*, *Hernani*, *de Maupassant*, and *Colombo*—were good. Royalties on them were paid to me for more than thirty-five years after he published them.

The texts were meant for high school and also for beginning college students; they were French texts, with a system of lesson assignments, explanations of idiomatic phrases. The annotated text stressed phrases out of the ordinary, enabling the student to appreciate and use the language with subtlety and grace.

However, in spite of this supplementary income, we really were in a very difficult financial situation. We didn't expect it to remain that way, or we would not have felt justified in having children. But David wrote the texts, and I found a suitable house for rent around the corner from where I worked in Philadelphia. We assumed that we would manage.

Foster asked me why I did not tell him I was short of money, and had offered me money when David and I married. But my sense of independence was strong, and David's even more so. We felt that to manage on our own financially would be one of the signs of wise planning and proof to ourselves and our friends that it was a good marriage. We did not discuss our difficulties with others, and I think no one suspected how hard pressed we were.

My $5,000 annually from my teaching at the University of Pennsylvania and at Bryn Mawr was enough for me. David did not want to accept any cash from me anyway. After he had paid all his necessary expenses, there was almost nothing for the purchase of books. This situation put tremendous pressure on him. He had not given up hope that the university would give him extra work, or somehow mitigate this difficulty.

Even now, more than forty years after David's death, it is possible to reconstruct with reasonable accuracy how he spent the last eight or nine hours of his life. He went to the dentist in the morning, where he had a painful treatment, partially eased as he was given gas.

From the dentist's office he went to the university to speak to one of the top administrative officials about possible alleviation of his financial difficulties. The answer was that the university was in serious financial need, so no relief in the immediate future could be expected. He had hoped rather desperately that the answer would not be a definite no.

He was also worried about the next payment owed to his former wife, and had considered taking the matter to court. But he dreaded the publicity, and disliked the thought of having the university community aware of his problem.

From the administration office he went to his study, to meet with one or two students for consultation on their work. At noon, he stopped in the library to see the librarian, a kind and pleasant woman, whom he asked to have dinner with him that evening.

He returned to his study to eat his sandwich and apple, which he always brought for his lunch. After lunch he usually took a short rest on the sofa in his office. About 3:30 he left his office and walked home.

An article in the June 1934 edition of *Modern Language Notes*, published by the Johns Hopkins Press in Baltimore, stated:

> The editors of Modern Language Notes express their sorrow over the sudden death on March 19 of their colleague, David S. Blondheim. Born in Baltimore in 1884, he was long closely associated with the Johns Hopkins University as student and teacher. He received his A.B. degree there in 1906, his Ph.D. in 1910; he held the Romance fellowship in 1909–10, was a Johnston scholar in 1913–14, became a member of the faculty in 1917, and was made Professor of Romance Philology in 1924.... While the articles and reviews that he published in leading Romance journals, the dissertations he directed, and the undertakings he helped to organize show that he had a wide range of interests, including the history of culture and of literature, syntax, etymology, the constitution of texts, the lexicography, his main contributions to knowledge were in a single field, that of Judeo-Romance. Here he continued the work of Arsène Darmesteter and became the leading authority in the world on the subject.... It is most unfortunate that he was unable to finish his study of Raschi's Biblical glosses....
>
> Romance scholars will all feel the loss of his stimulating and exacting scholarship, and he will be especially missed by those who depended upon his vast knowledge and sound judgment in matters of linguistic history. He had a remarkably keen mind, and extraordinary knowledge of languages, and a great zest for exploring the regions that had seldom been visited before his time. American scholars may well take pride in his achievement. They will deeply regret the loss of what in twenty more years of labor he might have accomplished.

In addition to this summation of David's brilliant scholarship, the Modern Language Association of America published a bibliography listing his seventy-four published works, with this editorial introduction.

> In recognition of the distinguished services of Professor David S. Blondheim of the Johns Hopkins University, deceased on March 19, 1934, the following bibliography is printed as a notable contribution to scholarship in the Romance languages and literature.

David's sudden death was announced to me in the late evening of March 19, when I returned to my apartment from work. I went immediately to Baltimore. I had just seen the sun set in a brilliant evening sky as I walked from my office in West Philadelphia to Spruce Street. At the telephone call I was numb with shock.

I did not know the reason for his death. More than forty years later I still do not know. Thinking, pondering, wondering for all these years have still left me with the mystery and unsolved questions.

What is clear to me is that for a period of eight years I had a wonderful relationship and that in the end for him there was peace.

# ·12·

## SOCIAL SECURITY AND FINANCING OLD AGE

My life changed completely in 1936.

My son was born in October 1934. I had struggled to keep my mind on this important event and to seal off the wound of my husband's death from the task of daily living and from my job. I had moved to a house around the corner from my office in the Wharton School. I had no interest in social life. I did not go to cocktail parties, concerts, or the theater. I had a good Canadian woman to help with the baby and I worked as hard as I could to keep my mind full of impersonal matters.

My friends were concerned because I was living in a psychological shell and cut off from outside interests. They thought I should somehow be jolted out of it. They talked to Professor Walton Hamilton, who had just gone from Yale to Washington to head research at the newly established Social Security Board. He offered me a job.

A telegram asked me to come to Washington at once.

I did not know then that in government language "immediately" meant "Hurry up and wait." I packed a few things and asked my sister Margaret to take care of my son, David, and went to Washington that weekend. Margaret was living in a suburb of New York with her husband, Deane, and her two younger children.

I reported for duty on Monday at the scantily furnished loft temporarily assigned to the new agency in downtown Washington. I found at once what I later learned was typical—government rarely prepares for new employees. There was nothing for me to do, and the man I was to work for had no time to figure out my job. There was no place for me to sit and I was one of several with no desk to work at. I joined the confusion. Hamilton, the chief of research, a large, handsome, professorial man, finally talked to me and I knew I would have great freedom to move into unknown territory. I liked Hamilton enormously and was eager to work for him, even though I was never sure whether he was talking to me or someone behind me, or even someone not there.

The other young men and women wandering around in the large, crowded area were as bewildered as I was. I realized then, as I would on several later occasions, that I must invent my job.

I took some hours off and found a house at Thirty-third Place in Cleveland Park. Then I went back to Philadelphia, where I gathered up my child. Settling in to a new life and work was demanding and stimulating. The temporary assignment of 1936 was to last almost seven years.

During those years there was an important event in my life: I adopted a baby girl, Ann. She was a continuing delight. I built a New England-style house, made a host of new friends, and worked in an expanding and creative social insurance system. I gradually developed a stronger interest in life, and my outlook became more normal as events thrust me into an exciting community of New Dealers. This group included Arthur Altmeyer, Edwin Witte, Jane Hoey, George Bigge, Mollie Dewson, Ewan Clague, Colis Stocking, John Jay Corson, Rachel Wood, Ida Merriam, and John G. "Gil" Winant. Winant was a dreamy soul, lacking in decisive qualities, large, rambling, and charming. He was to offer me a job in the International Labor Office in Geneva, where he was established in 1938 when I went to the finance meeting. I could not make out what the job was, so I declined.

I can still remember when I invited Wallace Murray, an old friend and a conservative foreign service officer, for cocktails. He drew me aside to say, "Your friends are so excited and so jovial. They are all talking about their work. The house is vibrating. The sofa is rocking with their laughter. They are earnest and humorous at the same time. I have never seen anything like this in Washington."

In my work as an economist, heretofore, I had never thought of government workers other than as hacks or military men. Few affected the lives of ordinary citizens. Government had some functions to perform: defense, customs, justice, immigration—routine and necessary work, little else. I was to learn otherwise in 1936. The establishment of the Social Security system marked an important advance in the protection of American citizens. Other countries, notably Germany and England, already had comprehensive programs. We had lagged behind. Our economy, which had thrived on

[147]

open frontiers for the first two hundred years, had reached a new phase in the 1930s. The disastrous unemployment and the change from a rural to a more dominantly urban society left large groups in want. Neither family care nor individual savings could protect the old and the needy. Those economists and social workers who had fought for social insurance found the public demand and executive leadership supporting their proposals.

The Social Security Act became law in August 1935, but the machinery for registering those who would benefit, establishing the terms of eligibility, giving them identifying numbers, and providing funds to meet the new obligations still had to be worked out. The new recruits among whom I worked had a complicated task involving both the federal and local governments.

There were three main branches to the system. Old Age Insurance was to be federally administered and financed from payroll taxes. Unemployment Insurance had to be passed state by state and was required to meet standards set by the federal government. Public Assistance was to be financed in part by Washington and in part by the state and local programs. The total package was complicated and unfamiliar.

The research we undertook was specific and directed to practical measures. For the Old Age Insurance we originally took into account the "covered" wages (wages which were counted for contributions to the system) of some 20 or 30 million workers. This income was taxed—the employers and employees paid an equal amount. These tax collections were placed in a Reserve Fund. The wages were reported by employers and made a permanent record on the basis of which annuities were to be paid. The important part of the *insurance* as contrasted with the *assistance* programs under the act was that there was no *means test*. The pensions were paid as a matter of right to those who had contributed. Similarly, the state-by-state unemployment insurance was not paid to the needy but irrespective of income to all who had contributed the requisite time period. The means test, an investigation of income and assets, is both expensive to conduct and unpleasant for those being investigated.

It has always been difficult for the general public to realize the difference between government insurance and welfare. Since it was compulsory, they thought of the system as a high-grade welfare program. They did not then, nor do they now, equate it with private

[148]

insurance. Some complain that they do not get out more than they put in, which can be true if they come in to the covered group early and die soon. There is also a great deal of mystery about the Reserve Fund.

To help evaluate our law, my colleagues and I examined the well-established and smoothly functioning insurance systems in other countries. I had studied the pension systems in Europe for Professor Allyn Young in the summer of 1923. We realized then an important part of our work was to make the aims and requirements clear to the average citizen.

Those who were on the Right of the political spectrum hated Franklin D. Roosevelt and the growing interference by government in the life of the average citizen: to them this was a foretaste of socialism. Those on the Left welcomed the new measures but complained also, for they did not think the program went far enough. The dynamism of the central government in these years of difficult adjustment was unanticipated and, to some, shocking. The new measures were only gradually accepted. Yet even the more conservative have been unwilling to tear down this new structure.

There are flaws and imperfections, but no Chief Executive could do away with the pensions or allow the public assistance programs to be substantially curtailed. Now when critics promulgate doubt in the minds of present or potential beneficiaries they are causing irreparable damage. The fear generated is a destructive force, upsetting those who do not fully understand the protection they have been granted.

The reason why the economy has gone through the difficulties of the early seventies without panic, and why consumption has held fairly steady, is that almost every family has access to Social Security payments. Those who remember the street scenes of the 1930s when bedraggled and desperate men and women sold apples to gain a pittance know this fact better than some of the younger generation. Recently, in spite of high prices and unemployment, the stores were crowded; Christmastime was a busy and prosperous one in 1975, 1976, 1977, 1978 and 1979. There was a sense of optimism that kept the productive system operating. Painful individual budget cuts have not disrupted national life.

The cushion provided by the Social Security benefits and the belief that somehow government would prevent disaster such as

[149]

occurred in the 1930s has buoyed up the spirits of many. I hear many complaints, but I am rarely given time to explain the intricacies of little-understood provisions.

The grounds for criticism are that the insurance is underfinanced. There have been changes in the structure of the labor force and also in the population, altering the ratios between contributors and beneficiaries. The provision for cost-of-living adjustments was not originally in the plan and throws the actuarial calculation out of whack. The solution that is likely to be adopted is to include a government contribution to assure the payment of benefits. This change would not be a serious distortion of the system. In fact, many nations have this arrangement.

What is central is the basic requirement that there be contributions by the covered workers so that the insured carry a part of the burden. The young benefit not only in the distant future but *now* because their parents and grandparents have some dependable income.

Even in the early years there was much material to work with. Social Insurance both demanded and provided a large increase in economic data. The records, set up in Baltimore, coded and summarized the wage statistics for millions. The Hollerith cards were used on an accounting machine. They were the forerunners of the more sophisticated computers of today, and while not as fast, gave totals of wage payments useful to answer a number of questions.

Since I was not assigned to specific tasks, I decided to make much of the information available by issuing a *Social Security Bulletin*. This was originally for the Board and then as time went on available to a wide group. This compilation was a by-product of our consideration of changes we thought should be instituted. The *Bulletin* presented the facts available from figures on old age wage contributions and from the welfare programs of the states. I set up a series of tables, with the help of my assistant, Florence Beal, and we circulated the monthly *Bulletin*, which proved useful in policy and planning.

In 1938 Ewan Clague, then director of the Research Bureau, wrote me a letter commending this product and assuring me of its future:

> At this time when we have just issued the first copy of the Social Security Bulletin as an official publication of the Board, I wish to express to you, both on my own account and on behalf of the Bureau,

our sincere appreciation for the work you have done during the past two years.

It was you who originated and developed this publication from a simple desk handbook of statistics to the regular monthly bulletin which it has now become.

Our collection of data was of particular value to a newly established Income Committee. For the first time in government, leading economists including Milton Friedman, Robert Nathan, Paul Douglas, and Hildegard Kneeland, along with other colleagues at the Board and from universities, worked to bring together statistics on money income—gross national product (GNP).

In examining the picture, I saw the anomaly of provisions governing the federal contribution to the states under the public assistance program. Because of the matching arrangement in contributions from the state and federal governments, new inequities in the transfer of money from federal to state treasuries arose. The welfare payment program was a supplement to the insurance system.

Since states were reimbursed within limits in amounts proportionate to what the states paid out of their funds to the poor, the "poor" states were actually getting less from the federal government than the "rich" states, who paid more. The citizens of poor states paid *relatively* more—not absolutely—in income tax than the rich states. For example, if West Virginia was giving, in public assistance, five dollars to a recipient per month, and receiving matching federal funds, and if New York State was paying thirty-five dollars per recipient, New York would receive much more in matching funds from the federal government. The dollar difference between the grants to the states was taken out of general revenues, from national revenues, so it was possible that a "poor" state such as West Virginia paid into the federal treasury money that went to finance a New York State welfare program. This situation had to be remedied.

The more we studied the situation, the more we needed to know of per capita income. We found many questions but few answers. The eager, dedicated scholars among us soon discovered that there was not enough statistical information to guide the administration of the program.

Robert Nathan, now head of Nathan's Associates, a management concern, came to me for a job. He had been a young research assistant when I first went to the Wharton School in Philadelphia. I thought he would contribute to our studies. But our administrators said he was too young for a $3,600 job, so he went to the Department of Commerce and was given $5,000. He and Milton Friedman were leading members of the income committee on which I also worked.

Many of the statistics gathered routinely as a result of tax collection, contributions on wages, and related provisions under the Social Security system had never before been available.

The total picture produced became an extension of statistical history developed by Professors Wesley Mitchell and W. C. Mills at Columbia University. The work was pushed back into the past and projected into the future so by the end of the 1930s we could talk in specific terms about the limits of insurance and welfare legislation and future administration.

As far as old age pensions went, the data comprised a large sample. Less than half the people of the United States were covered then. Teachers, ministers, service employees, were at first ineligible under the act. We worked energetically to increase the coverage; it came years later.

One of the threats to our program in this formative period was the inquiry initiated by Senator Arthur Vandenberg of Michigan, who was said to favor the abolition of the whole system. A commission was set up by a Senate committee and the Board. It consisted of one third labor, one third employers, and one third representing the public—its members included newsmen, bankers, and professors.

Mary W. Dewson, in her recollections entitled "An Aid to the End"* points out that Morris A. Linton, president of the Provident Mutual Life Insurance Company of Philadelphia, and an opponent of Social Security legislation, was on the council. But, she writes:

> ... no one could run away with a Council containing men like Gerard Swope, Marion B. Folsom, E. R. Stettinius, Jr., and William S. Knudsen, representing the employers, and economists such as Alvin H. Hansen of Harvard, Paul Douglas of the University of Chicago, J. Douglas Brown of Princeton and Edwin E. Witte of the University of Wisconsin, or a banker like Henry Bruere.

---

*The manuscript sent to me was designated *General Services Administration*, National Archives and Records Service, Franklin D. Roosevelt Library, Hyde Park, N.Y. A copy is also in the Dewson Papers in the Schlesinger Library, Cambridge, Mass.

The council spent fourteen months digesting statements, figures, and theories, wrote Miss Dewson, and then met to decide on advice to give the Congress. She adds:

> ...Altmeyer chose Eleanor Lansing Dulles to talk on what many thought the most vulnerable point, the size, character, and disposition of reserves. Twenty-two of the twenty-five members of the Council were present and not one man's attention wandered for an instant from her profound, lucid statement.

My profound, lucid statement was the result of very hard work—a defense of the stipulations in the act. I recall being awed by the assignment to give this defense. I even remember the blue dress with a white ruffle at the neck I wore, and my hair, newly curled by the hairdresser. I remember, too, how I studied the outlines of my talk the night before so that I could make a presentation with little reference to notes. It was pleasant to have the compliments of the council and to know that I had found in Washington a useful and interesting job.

During the hearings we learned that somebody was monitoring them and telephoning Senator Vandenberg. When Vandenberg realized that all three sectors of the council approved of the plans, he withdrew quietly his concern for the problem—so quietly, in fact, that few people remember now that Senator Vandenberg once tried to abolish the Social Security program.

The staff not only met the challenge of the hearings but decided to make them a springboard for amendments to extend the act. Public assistance (welfare), which was a floor under the insurance program, was to be administered by the states. Unemployment insurance, another form of income protection, would come into effect only as each state voted its own law.

The entire old age benefit financing is federal. This makes sense because, as the program got in full operation, the covered individuals might have lived in a number of different states. I am typical of the wandering American worker. I have worked sixty years in six states and several foreign countries. I now receive Social Security benefits based on contributions in several states. Eligibility for old age benefits might come for many in a place different from where the individual had paid contributions.

In 1938, because of the emphasis on finance in my work, I was asked by the Board to go to Geneva as its representative. An international conference was being held to discuss financing social insurance payments. The conclusions revealed little that was new, but the exchange of views, particularly with the British, French, and Germans, was pleasant and instructive.

After the meeting, I went back on the S.S. *America*. My friend Winfield Riefler, a much admired economist, was also a passenger. Together, we made a foursome with a handsome widow from Baltimore and a sprightly gangster named Joseph, from New York. The four of us sat at the same table in the dining salon. One evening, while we were dancing, a man not in "our group" asked the widow to dance. The gangster, enraged, drew his gun. We were frozen with fear. Win, rising to the occasion, elbowed him out on the deck and managed to cool him down. Meanwhile the attractive widow fled to her cabin, where she remained until the ship docked. Then we spirited her off.

All of us experts had been summoned to Washington in 1936 from various colleges and research institutions to meet an immediate need. Emergency arrangements were required to get the Social Security program under way quickly, so dozens of us were "blanketed in" to the government service. We were presidential appointees.

My letter of appointment read:

Madam:

You have been appointed by the Social Security Board to the position, grade and salary indicated below, effective April 6, 1936:

| | |
|---|---|
| Bureau | Research and Statistics |
| Position | Senior Economic Analysis |
| Grade | P-5 |
| Salary | $4,600 per annum |
| Station | Washington, D.C. |
| Nature of Appointment | Excepted Appt. Act of 8-14-35 |

Late in 1937 it was decided to regularize the situation by putting us through an unassembled Civil Service Examination. This required us to submit evidence of our training, experience, writings, and degrees and to fill in Form 57, which was the predecessor of Form 171 and the entryway to Civil Service.

It was then that the blow fell. I was rejected by the commission. My accomplishments in the past eighteen months were being passed over and my work was to be terminated.

This is Mollie Dewson's account of this jarring experience:

... The law setting up the Social Security Board had required its high staff appointments to be made from Civil Service lists because the form of organization had to be worked out before job requirements could be drafted. Some 150 experts had been appointed of the type which does not take an open examination but submits books and pamphlets they have written and other evidence of their previous work. After two years, when things were in running order, the Board arranged to have these appointees examined by the Civil Service Commission.

Our business management became quite stuffy when Eleanor Lansing Dulles of the research division, sister of John Foster Dulles, was rejected. But of course, there must have been a reason for rejection although none had been mentioned, so I called on the Commission and found that because Eleanor Dulles' eyesight was very myopic they feared the disease was progressive and when unable to see, she would become a burden on the government. I said that, "Eleanor Dulles would be more valuable blind with someone to read to her than most workers who see," but I would report my findings. Later, I produced detailed medical evidence from Johns Hopkins, where she had been treated for years, that her myopia was arrested, and she was accepted.

These early exciting years reached a peak when we went into the Ways and Means Committee on the Hill with amendments. The hearings revealed to me the difficulty of instituting new financial measures and the safeguards with which tax and revenue bills were surrounded. Our efforts were directed mainly to the extension of coverage to workers and professional people who were not in industry but who needed protection for their years of retirement. Only a moderate enlargement of scope was accomplished in 1938. The long debate necessary to convince the committee taught me much about the workings of government and the patience and persistence needed to bring about change.

We economists got deeply involved in the nation's financial problems and came to know much about the economic differences from region to region. Our teamwork in those early months was

[155]

inspiring and I never found even the long hours and exacting statistical work burdensome.

By 1939 the high hopes of those of us who had helped initiate the Social Security program were partly realized. The states were falling into line on Unemployment Compensation and were cooperating in Public Assistance—aid for dependent children, the needy, and the blind. We were becoming aware, however, of some of the shortcomings of the program and wished to press on to equitable provisions. Studies of health insurance possibilities had been initiated.

Changes in the pension formula based on actuarial calculation were debated within the Board. Differences of opinion between experts came to the surface, and some of the typical problems of government bureaucracy emerged. I struggled with the weaknesses that had become apparent and urged simplification of the complex provisions.

My experience then and since has convinced me that government agencies should not be run by clever people. They like to play intricate games. They do not mind complicated arrangements which baffle millions of people affected. I cannot say now, having been on the outside for almost forty years, what should be done to make the financial requirements comprehensible, but I knew then and I am sure now that the formulae were obscure and that the public was confused. If I am in a fog, it is understandable that those who have not worked in the system should be dubious about the relation of contributions and benefits. There is much written in 1979 about the need for changes. Some of these were advocated in the thirties.

One gap in our knowledge was the lack of data on state and local financial conditions. Since the tax collections and disbursements of many states were not reported, it was impossible to judge what burdens these jurisdictions were assuming. We knew that the needs and resources of the different localities varied widely, but we could not say how much. A study was undertaken in my division and carried on for more than five years by my able aide, Selma Mushkin. (Our advisers and consultants included Mabel Newcomer, Paul Wueller, Theodore William Schultz, and Harold Groves.) They collected, collated, and organized millions of items. The large volume that we produced—about the size of the Manhattan telephone book—was called *The Fiscal Capacity of States*. It presented the

[156]

first nationwide compilation of taxes and gave a basis for judgments of what funds could be collected. This work led to continuing reports on these important facts. The study was a basic source book for scholars and public officials.

In late March 1940 Professor Charles Rist, who was then, I believe, President of the Bank of France, came to see me in my house on Chain Bridge Road in Washington. I had seen him many times in Paris and elsewhere. He could not stay for dinner but he let me give him a Scotch and soda.

He sat on the sofa in an attitude of deep despair. He said, "I have been to the key people asking for help. They do not understand that the situation in France is desperate. They do not realize that it is likely that France will be overwhelmed in a few weeks. We will be lost to the Allies unless something is done immediately. I can find no prospect of help. I do not think I have gotten through to any of the leaders here."

I felt a real affection for this intelligent and wise man but I could do nothing but show my compassion. I had no friends at that time who had the power which he sought to influence. He left for two or three more interviews before flying back to Paris. France fell to the Nazis in June.

After my first three years at the Board there were changes in the top-level personnel. Ambassador Winant and Mollie Dewson had left. Two of my bosses were brilliant men, but difficult to work with. They had a love of maneuver and a lack of responsiveness to views of the staff. I and my colleagues ran head on into the strong person-alities of Arthur Altmeyer and Isador Falk. It was then I learned for the first time the degree to which it was possible for authority to stifle ideas and prevent free discussion.

There was continuing struggle by the staff to simplify the formula for old age benefits and to broaden the coverage. An example of these suggestions was the "double-decker" system, designed to provide a general basic amount per aged person plus an increment where taxed earnings justified graduated additions.

My first awareness of disagreements between me and top Board members came in connection with a study of income, which my division prepared. Using material gathered by Dr. Hildegard Knee-land, we had taken per capita income figures that had been compiled

[157]

by regions. We had extrapolated them into income averages, state by state.

When we were very well along, we showed the text to Miss Kneeland. She explained that we could not use figures this way. When I brought these facts to my supervisor, Dr. Falk, he said we should publish the report and add a footnote at the end, stating the figures were of a special nature.

I protested that this would fool many people, since the format of the report carried automatically the assumption that the figures were reliable. A note at the end saying they were not would be confusing. This was my first serious break with the top-level officers and was the beginning of a subtle campaign against me, which convinced me that I must leave the Social Security Board. Rumors were planted among members of my staff, and I was accused of slandering young men, some of whom I had actually recommended for promotion. I might have ridden out this storm, but I found many obstacles were set in the way of considering the simplification of the old age system I advocated. Some of us found the situation intolerable.

World War II erupted while the social insurance system was being gradually expanded at this time. I concluded I had reached a dead end in my work. I found I could not accelerate changes in the system or modify the formulae. It was some months later that I left the Board. War work was of growing importance, so I accepted a job with the Board of Economic Warfare in April 1942.

Just what should be done now, in 1980? Because of changes in population structure and the labor market, it now seems likely that a change to a three-party financing will at some time be necessary. It would not be disastrous. It would be a modification of the original philosophy, introducing into it a welfare element that need not be objectionable and would not diminish the dignity and rights of the recipients. It would not bring a means test or the probing of private financial status.

The social insurance system is good, sound, and dependable. It will not fail. It may be modified in ways that I favored in 1938. The reserve fund as it now stands with billions of dollars will not need a supplement for some years.

The original idea behind the Social Security Act of August 1935 has been largely obscured by the expansion of welfare programs and the extension of benefits so that the contributory principle is little recognized. The early plans were outlined in imitation of European programs, which for several decades had been in operation and which were an accepted part of many national economies. The thinking in this country has never willingly absorbed or understood the welfare state or the degree of government intervention in the economic life of the average citizen in Europe. Now some forty years after the initiation of the system there are complaints of varied nature—too little is paid, too much is collected, and the financing is inadequate. Many of the criticisms cancel each other. They originate in the desire to have the old, the disabled, the dependent taken care of by *someone else*. Perhaps the general taxpayer is the one to carry the burden.

The times when there was no old age insurance the aging parents would live in the large farm or crowded apartment of the children. Either that or go to the poor farm. Now, in many cases, the retired people can live in their own quarters and manage with small savings and moderate monthly insurance checks to leave their children to devote their earnings to their growing family. It was this relief for the oncoming generation that was the aim of the new system, made more urgent by increasing urbanization. The fact that some people die before they draw pensions is not a weakness of the system but inherent in the insurance principle that spreads the burden and keeps the yearly cost diffused among the large mass of workers. Many think they would save and invest without having the pressure of government, but if some would do so, there are many who would dip into savings in an early emergency and find themselves with no funds when they retire. There are few young people who, if given a choice, would prefer the financial support of their parents to the impersonal and widely shared expense of the nationwide funding.

There will be no ready acceptance of the present system, even with its flaws and inadequacies, until the idea of the absorption of the burden by the entire working population is understood. Other nations have insurance for these risks, and we can learn of its benefits and advantages if we face resolutely the alternatives that would hit the younger workers hard in their years of rising responsibility. The payroll tax is a lesser burden than that which many individuals would carry.

The Social Security programs have many facets. My comments are addressed mainly to the Federal Old Age Insurance. The pensions and the unemployment payments, plus the other benefits, help maintain purchasing power in times of recession and thus exert a stabilizing influence on the economy.

My thoughts turn in the direction of old age benefits because I worked mainly, though not exclusively, on that system. Also, I now get a monthly check.

The Social Security Act was the first major recognition of the volatile nature of industrial society, the weakening of family links, and the results of labor turnover in the United States. By the Great Depression of 1930, we had passed the traditional frontier in American society.

I left Social Security in 1942 because I did not believe in the method of establishing eligibility and pension levels. When I had lost my fight within the organization, I thought it best to find another place to work.

I had children to support. My efforts to redirect policy had been frustrated. Those with different views had power. I thought it would not do to let these clever people destroy me as a government worker, but before I left there were two years of fear and frustration. I was anxious to find more useful work elsewhere. I did leave to join the war effort; my reasons were in part a subterfuge, but I had no regrets.

# · 13 ·

## NICHOLAS

I cannot remember when I first met the man I shall call Nicholas in this book. But it was sometime late in 1936 with a group of intellectuals working on European problems. Nick had a subtle, ironic humor and a touch of sarcasm as he commented on the American rich and poor. He was bitterly against Soviet communism, having been born in Russia and having seen communism at work. He was employed by a specialized agency where his knowledge of the Russian language was of help with measures relating to our security.

I found him stimulating and saw him often. He came to my house in Cleveland Park, where I lived for a year, and later to my house on Chain Bridge Road, opposite Kemble Park. We discussed social philosophy and the possibility of simplifying modern life. He wore slacks and blouses and his hair was longer than that of my more conventional friends. He was probably the first hippie in my life.

As I got to know him better, Nick told me it was foolish for me to go on living alone when my husband had been dead for more than three years. I soon realized that he was urging me to share my life with him on a free and easy basis. I found him attractive and what began as an intellectual exchange grew gradually into affection. I did not think I wanted to marry him, but I did share many hours with him as our attachment deepened.

There was a strange psychological problem that bothered me. My devotion to David had been complete. I did not want to think of David and our love as primarily a physical bond, and could not analyze my feelings. After I entered an intimate relationship with Nicholas, I realized that the physical part of my relationship with David had been in a measure additional to my deep devotion to the man of learning and compassion. It had not been the determining factor in my decision to marry him.

As I came to know Nicholas better, I was relieved of part of my confusion about the past. I saw another part of life through Nick's eyes. My new relationship with him did not diminish my sense of loss of David as a person.

The revitalizing of some aspects of my emotional life after three years of virtual paralysis was a great relief as well as pleasure. Such an evolution of my attitudes may seem strange to present-day readers. But I suspect it was the result of the fact that ardent and overwhelming love came to me only when I was thirty and that its loss when I was thirty-nine was a profound and enduring shock. By the time I was in my forties I gained a degree of balance and could approach the world of men with a growing sense of freedom. For almost nineteen years Nick was to play an important part in my emancipation from past inhibitions.

In the spring of 1937 we wanted a brief excursion together. We drove down to Williamsburg, Virginia, in my red Ford convertible. It was a jubilant and at the same time tumultuous two days. The woods were fragrant with honeysuckle and we wandered through them, stopping on grassy slopes to enjoy each other's company and feeling spring as our response to each other set our pulses racing. The outdoor world and our joyful feelings occupied us more than the treasures of Williamsburg. These two days are luminous in my memory. We got back to Washington at midnight Sunday, after two nearly fatal automobile encounters—near misses at high speeds. Nick came to my house often in the months to come.

The war broke out in Europe two years later and Nicholas worried about his mother in Poland. I thought he should go to look to her safety. It was hard to be parted, but both of us recognized his obligation. I knew from his story of his early days that his mother was a fine woman. She was no longer young. Nick left for Europe sometime in 1940.

Not long after, Nicholas' mother escaped to Switzerland with his help. He stayed on trying to settle the family affairs. But in 1941, after the United States declared war, he was trapped in Poland. He was in constant danger, for the Soviets considered him a Russian, not an American, citizen. After some perilous days he escaped—walking with a Polish friend through wild country to Lithuania. The river that formed part of the border presented a serious risk, and when he and his companion, a man slightly taller, walked into the water, they held their packs high. They did not know the water's depth. Each step took them deeper until the middle, where the river leveled off. They still had their heads above water and made it to the other bank.

I was living in my house on Chain Bridge Road in 1943 when Irene, my faithful cook, telephoned me that I had a cable. It was from Kaunas, Lithuania. Meanwhile I had heard from his mother in Switzerland. She did not know where he was. I sent her an urgent message, telling her that he was safe. I also got in touch with our consulate, endorsing Nick's request for help. It was some weeks before he managed to travel to London, where he became attached to the Polish government-in-exile.

All these uncertainties and dangers were disturbing and I was most anxious to see him but only a few friends knew of my concern. At least when he got to London we could communicate with each other. His financial situation was precarious. I sent a substantial check, which he later repaid.

I was not to see Nick again until 1945 when I went through London on my way to Austria. I thought it would be best for him to get back to Washington if he could. I could do little for him in London. I had my job to carry out, and we both felt our responsibilities to work for our governments in time of war. I went on to Vienna. He stayed in London.

It was late 1946 when Jack Erhardt, political adviser to General Mark Clark, asked me to go with him from Vienna to London. He didn't know I had several reasons to be pleased—reasons he knew nothing about, including seeing Nick, even though briefly. It was hard to have so little time, but I was only there for three days—and my official purpose was to consult with my brother Foster who was meeting with the Council of Foreign Ministers, the group negotiating the German and Austrian treaties.

When I got to London, it was wonderful to me to find that Nick and I had remained close in our feeling for each other. I questioned his pessimism about the future of Austria and I urged him to go to the United States. We agreed that if I could, I would come to England later for a ten-day vacation.

This chance did come in the late spring of 1947, and I was able to spend ten days in Cornwall and Devon, beautiful country with roads worn deep by oxcarts between hedgerows where the camphire and the bluebells hung in bright clusters. We visited old inns, castles, and churches. I had a friend living in my house in Austria

[163]

and through her I kept in touch with the children. I was free from work and worry for a time. I wished the idyllic hours could be stretched longer. However, I was in the midst of work on the reconstruction of the Austrian economy, still barely surmounting war losses and the Soviet seizures of factories and produce.

In the spring of 1948 I went to the United States on home leave via Southampton. When I came back with the children, we met Nick in London. After a few hours of respite Nick joined us and we went on to Pevensey, where the Battle of Hastings was fought in 1066. From there we drove to Dover and took the Channel boat. I said good-bye to Nick as we took the ferry.

The children were fond of Nicholas, partly because they knew him as a friendly adult and not as a person who changed his tone of speaking and acting with the young. He was kind to them, but I knew he was not anxious to have the responsibility of children. I was not ready to commit myself to him on a permanent basis, even though we shared many interests.

After I had settled back in Washington in 1949 Nick came to America. I went to New York to meet him. A friend loaned me her apartment and we had several days there before I returned to work. He came at once to Washington and found a job related to the one he had held before. He never worked with the OSS or CIA.

I was building a house in McLean, Virginia. He went with me several times to see the progress of contruction. When I moved out to Virginia, he came frequently. He loved my cook Relly's goulash and lentils. We had talked at length about the ideas of French and Russian philosophers. He had a wide knowledge of political science and literature and was interested in the early notes of a book I was working on—a book I never finished. I was analyzing the possible viability of some type of communism in a capitalist world. We agreed that serious flaws in the present capitalist system posed a challenge for its acceptability by oncoming generations. We had more questions than answers, but these discussions were very stimulating to me.

On weekends he sometimes brought friends with him when he came to see me. My swimming pool was a special summer attraction. Most of the time, however, we spent alone, after the children were asleep and when there was no intrusion from the outside world.

[164]

In the summer of 1954, Nick and Henry, a friend with whom he lived for a year, drove to Henderson and we had some good canoeing and sailing. Before Henry's departure, Nick and I took him on picnics at Sandy Beach and walked in the dusk on the magnificent hard, sandy shore. Nick stayed on and we spent some hours on my island, Six Town Point, where there was a shingle beach and a small cabin, used often in the fall by my nephews for duck hunting. It was a lovely spot for swimming and sunning. The children and many of my family were at Henderson for the summer. Nick liked the atmosphere and easy informal life. He shared my love of the outdoors and the casual life in the country.

In Washington over the years we visited several of his Polish friends. I admired the ambassador, Cyanwiecz, and his wife. We talked of the tragic helplessness of Poland and the many-sided blame for the failure to protect the country and its people. Nick thought the mistakes in policy could have been avoided. I was not so sure, with the complex problems of war in the Pacific and Atlantic and the errors made at Yalta, that there had ever been a real chance for Poland.

Although we continued to enjoy each other's company, by 1956 a note of strain had been introduced. I was not sure whether it was because some of Nick's friends were not as congenial to me as the ones he had at first or because I found his political ideas exerted a pressure that was difficult for me to take. I did not defend everything that was being done by the Eisenhower administration, nor did I agree with all of my brother Foster's ideas, but I felt I understood why the policy was as it was. I felt a loyalty to Foster's ideals and proposals that I could not always explain because many things that I knew were too "sensitive" to discuss with nongovernment officials. Some were complicated and might be misunderstood if I talked about them.

When Nick left one Saturday afternoon, I had reached the conclusion that we were disturbing one another and that we should break off our relationship. I thought we exerted pressure that was wearing us down. I did not think we could be helpful in the circumstances or really enjoy each other's company.

"I owe you a great deal—I'm grateful, but I do not think we should meet again," I said.

It was a strange emotional situation. Each of us recognized that something had changed in the last few months. I never knew exactly what it was. I felt freer after I had made my decision—sad, but not devastated. I was very preoccupied with my home, my family, my brothers, my work on Berlin. I had a busy life.

I saw Nicholas one night when I was driving on Connecticut Avenue and he crossed in front of my car, but he did not see me. I felt a shock which I could not explain to Julia Ward, a college friend, who was with me. She did not know the story.

He wrote me when Foster died in 1959. My life had lost a precious element, but it was lost before I said good-bye. He died of a heart attack in 1979. I saw him several times in his last year.

# 14

# WAR AND POSTWAR PLANNING, 1942

I was standing on Rachel Wood's doorstep Sunday afternoon, December 7, 1941, when she said to me, "Come in quickly to listen to the radio. The Japanese have bombed Pearl Harbor!"

My children were only seven and five years old, but they caught the sense of outrage and shock. The news kept coming in machine-gun pattern as word from the Pacific was broadcast. The next morning, on the radio at the Social Security office, I heard President Roosevelt's declaration of war.

The sense of national peril added to my incentive to find another job—work closer to the national defense and in the field of foreign affairs. I was not openly seeking a new position, but when one was offered to me in the Board of Economic Warfare (BEW), I asked for an immediate transfer.

Although some of the work there was effective, methodical, and concrete, particularly that on export and import controls, most was strange and unstructured, shot through with bureaucratic feuds and confused by comings and goings of experts and administrators. President Roosevelt and some of his associates were fighting his former close associate, Vice President Henry A. Wallace, who was head of BEW.

A typical episode confronted me one day when the chief of my division, Louis Bean, asked me if I would prepare a paper for Wallace. Wallace had an idea that tourism increases friendship and, hence, peace—a thesis I questioned. He wanted an analysis and a chart to show what would happen as the standard of living rose after the war and more people traveled, looking for a correlation.

I said to Louis, "There's only a narrow range in which the amount of tourism can increase without lowering national income. If you push these elements to the extreme, the result will be a situation in which a large share of the working force travels abroad, while the national income goes down, because workers are not producing goods. You will come to a point where the curve reverses itself and income plunges downward."

Bean, an indomitable statistician, famous for his election predictions, was very annoyed. He said, "Eleanor! You wait until this war is over and I'll show you can correlate anything with anything and get useful results."

I was pleased when I was offered a job in the Department of State by Dr. Leo Pasvolsky. The State Department had always seemed glamorous to me from early days when in 1902 I rode in with my grandfather, John W. Foster, with his horse and carriage. Forty years later I felt that I could carry on the family tradition if I worked there.

There followed some months in the grim pile of rock at the corner of Seventeenth and Pennsylvania Avenue, the State, War, and Navy building. After working in the new Social Security Board, this work taught me about traditional government. I learned about channels, jurisdictions, clearances, classification, stilted languages and stutter words, and 8-by-14 inch dispatches. There were changes to a more modern style as the old ways proved too slow. The Social Security Board had been more free flowing.

The Special Division was a new unit staffed mainly by professors with a few government employees and businessmen. It was breaking new ground, working in a near vacuum toward invisible goals.

Pasvolsky, chief of the Special Division, had a brilliant analytical mind. He had come from Russia in 1905. He held degrees from Columbia University and from the University of Geneva. He had gathered a staff of twenty or more trained economists and political scientists.

At first it seemed to me that Pasvolsky was playing a game of chess. He was resolved not to be swamped by details in drawing economic and political plans.

All of our papers were in rigid framework of four choices and concluded with recommendations. Problems in various countries of Europe and the Far East began to demand specific answers.

One officer, Professor M. M. Knight, objecting to the system, said the postwar draft treaties that we outlined were like Mother Hubbard gowns, designed to fit any country and no country. Even though some of our work seemed abstract, it later proved useful. For instance, Pasvolsky and his staff produced the outline of the United Nations Charter in the Dumbarton Oaks meetings, a charter that has lasted for many years. In the course of its preparation Foster was called to Washington several times to help in the drafting.

For the first time anywhere, after any war, elaborate planning for peace was carried on. We prepared a host of papers for countries in Europe and Asia, covering political structure, education, finance, transport, industry, power, refugees, labor, and other major aspects of postwar national life. These papers became the basis of a series of directives to be used after surrender.

As the outline of the United Nations took shape, some of us working mainly on economic reconstruction thought of the urgent requirements for immediate actions to prevent starvation and provide for displaced persons. The United Nations Relief and Rehabilitation Administration (UNRRA) was proposed to provide relief.

There was a small group that met in the evenings to plan the new agency to care for the destitute and the refugees. I remember the names of only a few of the individuals among them: Roy Veach of the Treasury Department and Vera Micheles Dean of the Foreign Policy Association. Vera came down from New York as a consultant to the State Department. We sketched the outline of a cooperative international agency that would pool resources and coordinate assistance where it was most urgently needed.

The ideals that guided us were the result of a spirit of collaboration, which, as it developed later, could not be realized. The contributions were almost exclusively from the United States, and the control of supplies and funds was in considerable measure by the communists. American public opinion and Congress became highly critical as this situation became clear.

We explored the extent of relief needs of a devastated Europe. When the plan crystalized, it was included in the official complex of postwar policy and brought into existence after international conferences in Atlantic City and in Bretton Woods. I was asked to work on the financial arrangements.

I was also to act as secretary for the interdepartmental committee on plans for the tens of millions of displaced persons. These were mainly people who had been moved across national borders as forced labor or put into camps. In this connection I recommended the development of counterpart currencies. This plan resulted in the building up of large funds in local money.

Counterpart currency was similar to the device the Quakers had used when I worked with refugees during and after World War I. We sold the tools, the seeds, the blankets, and other items at low prices. Then we used the money taken in to buy more goods and to sell. The result was that the funds revolved over a considerable period. In the case of UNRRA, many of the relief supplies were sold, with the government receiving the money to provide more relief. Some of the counterpart currency is still available in Berlin now, twenty-five to thirty years after the first transactions.

There has been considerable criticism of UNRRA because American money got away from American control and other nations did not carry their share. In some cases funds were spent to support Communist parties and governments under Soviet command. Although the workings of the system were not perfect, it is fortunate that some measures had been worked out in advance, and that camps for thousands of displaced persons were set up quickly.

Another financial problem I worked on in the Special Division was that of international banking and exchange control. The horrendous inflation and confusion in the years after World War I had been studied by many economists. We were determined that the sequence of excessive inflation and subsequent destructive deflation that occurred in the thirties should not be repeated again. We felt that unemployment and the social demoralization attendant on it were some of the main causes leading to the Second World War. Some of us on the Committee felt that the important reforms needed should take into account the merits and flaws of the Bank for International Settlements. My previous detailed study of the Bank for International Settlements gave me the nucleus of ideas on which I could draw up a plan. My draft called for an inclusive international bank to stabilize exchange rates and smooth the flow of funds between money markets. It was also to offer short term loans. My plan was scarcely noted. Another had emerged in Washington, designed by Harry Dexter White.

White, who was close to the Secretary of the Treasury, Henry Morgenthau, Jr., had considerable prestige in Washington. In 1941 he was known as a sharp, able, aggressive government executive. Not widely liked, but generally respected, he was later to be accused of being a Communist party member. In 1948 he died of a heart attack on a train returning to his summer home in New England, after testifying to charges made by the McCarthy committee.

At the end of 1942 the White Plan had been accepted in American Government circles as the American proposal which was to deal with external restrictions and temporary balance of payments assistance and to be called the Exchange Stabilization Fund. Meanwhile, a plan with the same broad aim but of a completely different concept calling for the establishment of a world currency union and tantamount to the establishment of a world central bank was prepared under the title "International Monetary Union" by John Maynard Keynes in England. Lord Keynes was authorized to discuss his plan with the American officials and there was considerable debate between the British and American experts both in Washington and in England. A plan was also prepared by the Canadian financial officials which in many ways was a compromise between the two positions. After intensive discussion between the U.S. and U.K. Treasury officials, who in turn informed their Governments of their ideas, a joint U.S./U.K. position was issued in early 1943. It was this joint statement which formed the basic paper for the Bretton Woods Conference. In July 1944, after a week's preliminary meeting in Atlantic City, the financial planners met at Bretton Woods in New Hampshire for three weeks of discussions and negotiation.

I was a member of the International Secretariat, which served all the representatives of the forty-four nations attending the Conference. My particular job was to prepare, in the middle of the night, minutes of the previous day's meetings for distribution at breakfast each morning.

My supervisor, Leroy Stinebower, of the State Department, was an exacting taskmaster. I found myself after exhausting daytime debates in the First Commission with a pile of notes which I had to turn in as a summary, subject to Stinebower's approval. Sometimes I would despair of satisfying him, but I learned a great deal from his corrections. By two or three a.m., I would rewrite the summary, including his changes and additions to my material.

I had to be up at seven o'clock to be sure of getting a swim in the hotel pool before the day's work began. I remember a Czech, an Egyptian, and an Indian sweeping past me as I swam the length of the pool a dozen times before breakfast. I wondered if they too had worked all night.

The setting for the Bretton Woods Conference was an attractive, large, old-fashioned hotel in the New Hampshire mountains. We were free of most interruptions from other work and intensely absorbed in the Keynes-White struggle for acceptance of the plan each had designed. There was time for all of us in the Secretariat to describe our theories and give suggestions to the other experts on reshaping the world of international finance.

Even before we went to New Hampshire it was clear that the conference was to be a duel between two strong men, Harry White of the United States Treasury and J.M. Keynes who led the British delegation. The idea of having two institutions probably originated with Keynes. Keynes had in mind a development bank which would assure developing countries of capital to support their growth as well as to stabilize their export earnings for primary products. The planners could not agree whether one of the institutions (the Fund) should also deal with trade matters and accordingly they agreed only on a resolution indicating that in due course an international trade organization should be established. Negotiations about such an institution went on for three years after the war but the agreed constitution of that organization was not ratified by the U.S. Senate and, instead, trade matters were handed over to a separate temporary organization called the General Agreement on Tariffs and Trade (GATT), which has become a very important instrument of trade policy of the world in the postwar years.

There were many elements to be negotiated in Bretton Woods even though the basic approach of each of the plans had been accepted as setting the framework for two related financial institutions. Political issues such as voting rights, contributions to supply funds, and the quotas for the accommodation of countries drawing on the resources were matters which required long hours. Some of the technical details of rules for operations and codes of behavior were demanding.

The two plans as they developed were complementary and different in their scope and aims. The White Plan—the Fund—was designed to facilitate short-term transfers of money and keep the exchange fluctuations within tolerable limits. It provided for changes when these rates were out of line with trade and investment.

Lord Keynes' plan was the establishment of a world clearing union with certain automatic credits and debits to each nation and a separate International Bank for Reconstruction and Development. The American loan of U. S. $3,750 million to the United Kingdom was a completely separate deal not related directly to the institutions, to allow the United Kingdom to regain its economic footing as quickly as possible after the war.

During the meetings White, who sat one place from me, insulted the other delegates in asides clearly audible. He was particularly abusive about the Indian delegate. The air was electric as Keynes and White sparred with each other—Keynes, the English gentleman, White, the rough and sarcastic American.

During the negotiation the Soviets took great pains to ensure that an international organization greatly influenced by the Americans would not interfere in their domestic economy and their right to establish the exchange rate of the ruble as they wished. The rest of the Conference went along with it, primarily because they felt that the ruble exchange rate did not affect world trade. In considering quotas which determined the resources available, it was agreed the the U.K. quota would be U.S. $1.2 billion, while the Russians were offered U.S. $750 million. In the negotiations, they insisted that they should be equal with the British and on this the Conference well nigh failed. At the last dinner, at long last the Russians indicated that they had got an agreement from Moscow to accept a U.S. $1.1 billion quota (to which they were obviously not entitled on the basis of their participation in world trade and payments). It was accepted as a signal of cooperation with the rest of the world. In the end, on idealogical grounds and on the basis of his plans for Eastern Europe, Stalin informed Ambassador Harriman in December 1945 that they would not ratify the agreement. As he said it, "for a while, we would like to go our own way."

Now, thirty-five years later, news stories are written under headings like, "Why Has the International Monetary Fund Failed?" The answer is that it has not. It has survived thirty years of tremendous pressure. It has instructed new nations in international finance. It has developed new and ingenious ways of transferring large international payments, and special drawing rights (SDR) have added to international liquidity.

In spite of serious difficulties, the Fund has helped to keep international trade flowing. Similarly, the IBRD has done much to supply emerging industrial economies with capital—not enough, for there is never enough, but significant amounts. The directors and experts of both institutions have worked together in a world where economic relations have been distorted, but have not come apart completely. These institutions continue their work and manage to support harassed monetary systems.

[173]

In the later years I met some of the delegates to the Bretton Woods Conference in India, in the Philippines, in England, in Washington, and elsewhere. The sense of accomplishment we felt remains.

The fifteenth annual report of autumn 1945 from the Bank for International Settlements (BIS), the institution I had studied so intensively in Basel a decade before, has interesting comments on the Bretton Woods agreement. It refers to the conference with forty-four countries represented, which preceded the acceptance of the "Articles of Agreement of the International Monetary Fund and the International Bank for Reconstruction and Development." It states that the most important provisions were those that promoted foreign exchange arrangements and were designed to prevent competitive depreciation.

The Fund resources must not, it stated, be used to meet a large or sustained outflow of capital, but must be consistent with the purposes of the Bank, and the particular aim is to avoid restrictions on payments and transfers of current international transactions.

The Fund was not to be considered by itself, but in conjunction with the IBRD. It could, according to the 1945 BIS report, undertake three kinds of operation:

(i) it may make or participate in direct loans from its own loan fund;
(ii) it may make or participate in direct loans by means of funds which it will obtain through borrowing (thus borrowing funds in one market and lending them elsewhere); and
(iii) it may guarantee, in whole or in part, loans made through the ordinary channels of private international investment.

The BIS report concluded:

... There would seem to be general agreement about the need for an institution formed for the particular purpose of stimulating international investment. After all the unhappy experiences with regard to the loans and credits granted in the 'twenties and the beginning of the 'thirties, it does not seem possible to count on a revival of unaided private lending.

The major aspect of IMF and IBRD, the creation of Bretton Woods, has been the constant and serious consultation between central bankers and financial leaders, and the recognition in all decisions that the value of money, the interest rates, and fiscal policies in all countries impinge on one another. Here in concrete and specific forms, the *one world* concept takes on a reality not found elsewhere. It is possible for those who helped create the Fund and the Bank to criticize their own work, but on the whole, they can be proud, as I am, to have participated in the creation of these institutions. In 1969 I was glad to be one of a group of fifty persons who attended the twenty-fifth anniversary of the Bretton Woods Conference. I would like to be at its fiftieth anniversary.

The three years after I left Social Security and before I went to Vienna were transitional. I traded some of my abstract idealism for fighting pragmatism. I began to see how I could get influence and find funds to support programs. It was at this time that I discovered Cassandra's law. This law, which I found in a moment of cynicism, was to the effect that whenever you find a new constructive program ten people rise up to tell you it can't be realized. The response to Cassandra's law involves risk taking. For some reason, though I wished to survive professionally, I had an appetite for risk taking. This did not emerge at once. I did not have much opportunity for innovation and creative work until I got to Vienna in 1945.

# 15

# EUROPE IN TURMOIL

In 1943 one of my main concerns was the controversial German committee. There was a division of opinion in the group and I was often in the minority. Though we did not realize it at the time, Roosevelt was soon thwarting the work of the experts and had decided to follow the lines recommended by the Treasury Department. We fought over the issues of reparation, reconstruction, reform, and occupation directives, not anticipating the imposition of a tough *Directive 1067* limiting German activity, and little dreaming of the agreements that were to be reached at Yalta in February 1945.

I had in mind the mistakes made in Paris in 1919, which I had barely understood, and the economic and political catastrophes of the 1920s and 1930s of which I had considerable knowledge. What I did not realize was that Roosevelt would go his own way in 1944. By the strange irony of Roosevelt's death in April 1945, some of the recommendations he had rejected were adopted instead of the Morgenthau Plan. The proposal was to reduce Germany to a decentralized rural nation. The change was revealed in the major speech delivered by Secretary Byrnes in Stuttgart on September 6, 1946. The lessons we learned in the early months of occupation in Germany and in Austria made us realize in 1946 the Soviet intentions.

Why have I worked for the rehabilitation of Germany for more than twenty-five years? It is not so much that I love Germans, whether Prussians or Rhinelanders, Saxons or Bavarians, more than other people or nations, but working on the German Committee in the State Department was a turning point in my mental journey. I moved from the hatred and fear of Germans in my youth to a better understanding of German people as they emerged from the war. The whole journey from one point to the other covered a time span from 1909 to 1979. The German Committee of 1943 was a way station at which I changed course, to support the building of a strong and reliable ally.

I knew when I was young of the tragic acts of Germany in the War of 1870 and in World War I in 1914. As a child I read with tears the story, "The Last Class," in which Alphonse Daudet reflects the emotion in Alsace-Lorraine as the Germans invaded in 1870. When I went to Paris in 1909, Hélène Herzog, the family tutor, told me her personal tragedy of relatives killed in the army. She was middle-aged when I knew her. I was fourteen.

Later when I was in France between 1917 and 1919 I heard stories of atrocities in northern France and Belgium, some of which proved false, but which strengthened my feelings of fear of Germans. This was the time when I knew the American flyers in the colorful Lafayette Escadrille. They were risking their lives as freedom fighters.

Now, looking back for some sixty years, I find that my early impressions of Germany were of a belligerent and difficult nation, but early in my work in the State Department and for a large part of my life I was to be concerned with helping Germans. I was to realize in 1943 that we could not have a healthy Europe with a distorted and diseased Germany at its core—that a constructive foreign policy and cooperation between nations could bring an effective working relationship between Germany and her former enemies.

I was acutely aware of the horrors committed by the Nazis and I knew that Hitler's support by many Germans was in part the result of the errors of Allied policy after World War I. I knew there had been a resistance movement. Some of the heroes of July 20, 1944, were still alive. Young people were coming along, untainted by National Socialism. It was my belief that a constructive policy toward Germany would help save Europe and win a lasting peace.

My first visit to Germany was a walking trip in 1922. Both my friend Emily Huntington and I wished to improve our facility in the German language. German and French were requirements for the doctor's degrees we sought. We wanted to get the examination out of the way.

The Quakers who had been in Germany after 1919 gave us the name of a possible traveling companion, Irmgarde Fabre Dufour, a German girl who loved hiking. The three of us planned a backpacking trip through the Bavarian Alps. Irmgarde was a tall twenty-year-old, blond Brunhilde. We liked her and admired her Amazon-like strength, but we were in awe the first time we saw her standing on the craggy cliffs in the mountains, reciting Goethe in a loud singing voice. The sounds echoed from opposite cliffs, like a call to arms. For this peculiar exercise Irmgarde was appropriately clad in a long, flowing cape.

Emily and I were less striking in appearance, though now that I think of it, our costumes were hardly conventional. We had purchased some men's trousers— "plus fours"—the voluminous pants tucked into knee socks, like those worn by Bobby Jones, the great golf champion of the 1920s. With these we wore cotton shirts and denim jackets. At one of the crude mountain shelters in which we slept on the journey, Emily and I had to push the bed up against the door to prevent some young men from forcing their way in. We were of the new generation of "wander birds."

We were later accosted by a priest in Berchtesgaden who told us we could not go through the town in our "trousers." He suggested we take the back streets to get out of town before any respectable townspeople saw us. Irmgarde was more conventionally clad. We talked to her about her philosophy and that of her family. We found her profoundly influenced by the defeat of Germany and the desire for national power at a time when inflation was destroying the social structure.

The hyperinflation of the early twenties brought intense suffering and economic disaster to the Germans. Emily and I witnessed the desperation but we had the advantage of rising exchange value. The dollars we took with us bought millions of reichsmarks; our small funds stretched to great lengths. Our experience was mixed. We recognized the beauty of the landscape and also the tragedy of the German ordeal, as people struggled for survival.

It was eight years later that the political results of these bad years in Germany became clearly evident. Irmgarde's excitement in the inflation period took on the more specific lines of aggressive nationalism.

While I was reading Economics in Bonn in the late summer of 1930, I began to see the political trend that led to war in 1939. My trip with Mildred Wertheimer in a *faltboot* on the Mosel river was revealing. Sitting in the high vineyards and looking down to the curving river, we drank wine and ate bread and cheese. We admired the countryside and sometimes we stopped at the canoe clubs. There we were impressed by the strength and vitality of the young Germans we met.

[178]

But a recurrent feeling of apprehension, close to the feeling of the past, came again. Mildred, who was Jewish and bilingual in German, heard the young men talking about Germany and its future. Their talk was Irmgarde's refrain—but more ferocious. Mildred told me her conclusion—that they were on the verge of revolution or war.

The new revolutionary types Mildred heard were belligerent—anti-American, anti-English, anti-French. They talked about restoring the German soul, of finding a place in the sun, of expansion, and of *Lebensraum*, themes that foreshadowed the beginning of Nazism.

We saw the movement spread from Hitler's close associates to the younger generation and from them through older generations. On September 14 there was an election in Germany and Hitler gained enough votes to have a significant representation in the Reichstag. This was the turning point.

My trip with Mildred was a startling education. Even though I remembered Irmgarde, I was shocked to hear the handsome young men we met along the way talking of blood running in the streets of Paris, and of the joy of revenge. As an undertone I heard of unemployment and industrial depression.

At that time, President Paul von Hindenburg was an important figure, Hjalmar Schacht, a leading economist. Schacht was influential in the economic world, born, I believe, in Brooklyn, reputed to be a financial wizard. Chancellor Brüning was bowing out at this time. Foreign Minister Gustav Stresemann was gone. Aristide Briand, the French statesman, died in 1932. I've always felt that history and contemporary thought have neglected him, because if he had lived we might have found ourselves far on the way to European unity. He really had a concept of the united Europe and had a vision that might have inspired other people to join with him.

While I was in the Rhineland that fall I talked with Wolf von Dewald, an outstanding editor of the *Frankfurter Zeitung*. He explained to me the threat of Hitler, the rising tide of revolt.

In October of 1930 I joined Mildred in sharing an apartment in Berlin. One day she came home from an interview, shaking with panic.

"What happened to you?" I asked.

"I went to the National Socialist Headquarters—14 Hedemanngasse. I asked for the man I was going to see—Joseph Goebbels.

One of the men in the outer hall said, 'You're Jewish, aren't you?' I told him, 'I'm American.' Then all of them asked me, again and again, and I finally said I had another appointment and ran out. The men followed me down the stairs, hissing and booing. It was horrifying!"

Mildred and I often entertained our two friends Dorothy Thompson and Margaret Goldsmith, also a writer. Dorothy had been married for two years to the American novelist Sinclair (Red) Lewis, and was now free-lancing. She had left her job as chief of the Central European Service for the New York *Evening Post* and *Philadelphia Ledger* the year she married Red, but still covered Berlin and acquired the background that was to serve her well.

She became one of America's most perceptive columnists during World War II. Margaret was also American, but working for English journals.

Dorothy and I made an appointment for an interview with Goebbels, Minister of Public Relations. The appointment had been made well in advance, but on the day before we were to meet Goebbels, Dorothy said she had a meeting with an editor of *The Saturday Evening Post* and could not break it. I was disturbed. I wanted her help—her German was much better than mine—but decided to keep the appointment anyway.

Americans can now identify the brown Nazi uniform associated with the sickness that swept over Germany and engulfed a world in war. Hundreds of films and television stories have made this possible. But the young jackbooted men who opened the doors for my appointment that day were unfamiliar and shocked me. Their military precision as they led me through a maze of dark corridors filled me with uneasiness. They turned me over to an officer who indicated a hard bench against the wall. I sat and waited. Another officer escorted me into a large study to face a handsome blond man. I knew it wasn't Goebbels, but I was anxious to learn whatever I could, so I began to ask him about the economic program of the National Socialist party.

Then I heard a sound behind me and turned to see the gnomelike Goebbels, also in uniform, about six inches behind my back, listening to this conversation. When I looked at him, he silently left the room. I left, too. That was my only meeting with Goebbels.

Later in October Dorothy Thompson and I interviewed Hjalmar Schacht. I had known him through my brother, because Foster had a keen interest in the financial problems of Germany. Dorothy had an appointment at the Hotel Bristol at ten o'clock and I had one at eleven. Schacht told both of us he was joining the Nazi party, a fact not yet known.

He was a tall, broad-shouldered, Prussian type, with an explosive temper. In the interview with me he got so flushed and excited that I was afraid he would have a stroke. He called President Roosevelt, banker Owen Young, and Benjamin Strong, the head of the Bank of England, by insulting names. They were thieves, scoundrels, liars, wretched, and worse, he shouted.

I knew a good deal about Schacht before I went to Berlin. It was his policies that brought the German currency to near zero in value in the twenties and occasioned the virtual cancellation of the reparation obligation. The payments were greatly reduced. Foster knew him in these years mainly because of his association with the German loans and the Still-Stand Agreement that lifted some of the burden.

It was Schacht, too, who created different types of marks for different purposes and reestablished the German economy. His machinations made possible the accumulation of large stockpiles to support the war Hitler planned.

On my return to the United States more than a year later, I tried to get my friends and family to recognize the looming danger of Nazism. Few would listen to me or were impressed with my warning; Foster listened.

When in 1943 I found myself on the German Committee in the Department of State, I recalled various past experiences and had a number of firm convictions. In the committee there was a battle between two factions. The majority wished to see the country restored, purged of extreme ideas, and under the leadership of moderates. A minority wished the nation reduced to a low level of production and a highly decentralized government.

I made my views known in the committee, calling attention to the mistakes of the Versailles Treaty. My opponents insisted that the negotiators at Versailles were dolts; thus a consideration of their decisions offered little if any guidance. But the experts I had met in

1919 on those trips to Paris to visit Uncle Bert were not all foolish and inexperienced. Most were extraordinary men, caught up in a political network of forces they could not control. Certainly there was something to be learned from their futile struggles for a durable peace.

Those of us on the German Committee seeking such a workable policy were to lose this paper war temporarily when President Roosevelt was persuaded to move toward a Carthaginian peace with the theory that a weak Germany could not threaten other nations.

If Roosevelt had not died shortly after the Yalta three-power conference of 1945, Germany would almost certainly have been dismembered and reduced to an agricultural country, with only light industry, and without the potential of Ruhr production. Roosevelt had overruled our committee, but events overruled Roosevelt. When he died his influence gradually faded, although his wartime courage left its mark. His confusion over postwar Europe was to be rectified by General Lucius D. Clay, Secretary of State James Byrnes, Dean Acheson, and others.

Directive 1067, written in 1945, did in fact govern the early months of the occupation with its repressive measures. Only as the miserable conditions of Europe, as well as of Germany, and the urgent need for coal from the Ruhr developed, did the change come.

Secretary Brynes was then working with General Clay on the Stuttgart speech of September 6, 1946. This promoted the new aims and lenient methods of the occupation in the western zones by Britain, France, and the United States. Thus Bizonia and later Trizonia were created, the Soviets refusing to join. This turning point for the German people preceded the Marshall Plan by some months, but it made possible the development of constructive measures and brought effective, democratic-minded Germans into positions of significance.

In time I came to know large numbers of Germans as persons. I met and talked with Ernst Reuter and Konrad Adenauer, Paul Hertz and Frau Leber, Willy Brandt, Fritz Erler, Theodor Heuss, Carlo Schmid, Louisa Schöder, Bishop Dibelius, Heinrich Krone, and scores of others. These were not the brash young men I had known in 1930, but people of experience and spirit. If I were to tell their stories, stories of their resistance to oppression, it would fill volumes.

_Four Power pass identifying Eleanor as Lieutenant_
_Colonel in occupation of Austria, 1945_

_Eleanor and Mary Curnias (Pircher), going into Vienna_
_in 1945 in Hitler's car during occupation of Austria_

*Eleanor in Baltimore, helping load wheat as relief for
flood-devastated Balkan areas in 1954*

*Lightning strikes unfinished Congress Hall in Berlin,*
*July 4, 1957, after building was dedicated by the Benjamin*
*Franklin Foundation (Schirner Pressebild-Agentur)*

*Symposium at opening of Congress Hall, Berlin,*
*September 24, 1957. Group includes Melvin Lasky*
*(standing); left to right, John Fischer, Fredrich*
*Torberg, Virgil Thompson, Professor Ernst Fränkel,*
*Willy Brandt, Eleanor Dulles, Thornton Wilder, and*
*François Bondy*

*Eleanor and Konrad Adenauer with interpreter Heinz Weber at farewell reception in Bonn, 1963. (Copyright by Presse-und Informationsamt der Bundesregierung)*

*Arnold J. Toynbee after lecture at Free University, Berlin, with Frau Ernst Reuter, Chancellor Andreas Paulsen, and Eleanor, May 6, 1959*

*Foster Dulles, January 1959, under umbrella held by
Chancellor Adenauer at Wahn Airport near Bonn, Germany*

*President Eisenhower and Winston Churchill, former
British Prime Minister, visiting Foster Dulles in Walter Reed
Hospital during his last illness*

Looking back, I realize the German Committee was the most important and controversial of all on which I served. The effect of our papers was limited but they were theoretically useful. Their applicability was lessened not only by the President but by the Soviets. The Russians prevented cooperation between zones and they gutted many factories in Berlin and East Germany. More attention in our planning should have been paid to the past experience of 1919.

As it turned out, the Soviet's harsh action hastened the time when the Western Allies altered initial positions. In 1947 those who favored demolishing German industry were out of office, and no one argued for a reduction of German economic capacity. Factories were already flattened by bombing, and the cold winter of 1947 made the need for Ruhr coal throughout Europe glaringly apparent.

While these developments and changes in attitude were taking place, I was in Vienna working in the office of the U.S. occupation's political adviser, John G. (Jack) Erhardt.

In March of 1947 I was asked to go to Berlin to confer with Foster. He was one of a group of Americans along with the newly appointed Secretary of State General George C. Marshall, and James W. Riddleberger, going to Moscow to endeavor to write the terms of treaties for Austria and Germany. Austria, which was considered "the first victim of Hitler's aggression," was under a more beneficent regime and was ripe for reconstruction.

What I saw in Berlin, which was still part of the whole Germany, was almost total devastation. I stayed with Elizabeth Holt (Mrs. John Holt), a well-known American art historian. Elizabeth, who was working with the occupation committee on Women's Affairs, showed me the city. The S-Bahn, the elevated railroad winding through Berlin, gave us an overview. Elizabeth showed me where the Russians were moving machinery out of the factories and piling it on freight cars.

On one of our excursions we also had tea with a friendly sculptor who lived in a building minus its entire front. Large canvas serving as a temporary wall was shutting out the view of the street, but not the cold winter wind.

The sculptor had very little tea and a tiny stove to heat water, but Elizabeth had given him some food.

[183]

During this visit I also met some of the women leaders of Berlin, including Frau Reuter, whose husband was to be the renowned mayor of the city, and some of the men and women who had been in the German resistance. Special among these people was the late Annedore Leber, a writer and philosopher, whose husband was imprisoned and then hanged for standing out against Hitler. Frau Leber had suffered in hiding.

We who were in Vienna followed the German situation carefully and noted the changing opinion among the American occupying forces. The Austrians, like the Germans, were starving, and we endeavored to get food and fuel to them in those years of extreme misery from 1945 through 1947. Temporary relief financing was passed by Congress, and some army supplies, already in Europe, were used. But Germany got less, and at a later date.

At the time of the Soviet blockade of Berlin in 1948, we in Vienna were again shocked into watching the German situation and considering our own vulnerability, as the cutting off of access would be easy for the Russians.

Before the blockade was lifted, I was ordered back to Washington and, in late 1948, was associated with German and Austrian affairs in the department. No progress was being made on the German treaty, and the Austrian treaty was crawling at a snail's pace. I was only occasionally brought into German affairs during the next three years.

Then in 1952 the work that I consider the most significant of my professional life began when I was asked to organize what became in effect the "Berlin Desk."

Jimmy Riddleberger, head of the German Bureau, had the idea that someone should be specifically responsible for the city of Berlin. This work has continued, off and on, for twenty-six years, and I have recently made some suggestions to improve the image of the city which, if successful, may carry my ideas into the 1980s.

It seemed to me that the Berlin of 1952 was in a different world from that which I knew in 1930 and 1947. The whole spirit of Germany had changed. There were few traces of the nation that I feared and disliked in the 1930s. It was active politically, with a larger percent of the people voting than in the United States. There were three effective parties and some smaller ones, sometimes influencing government at the local level. Its statesmen, Willy Brandt, Helmut Schmidt, George Leber, Carl Carsten, Walter Kiep, and dozens of others, were articulate and reasonable. The treatment of minorities was moderate, its financial policy effective, its educational system liberalized, and its standard of living high.

The beginning of the German component in NATO was in 1954. It was built over twenty-five years, into an important element. I think back to the evening when the new German Army was planned in my swimming pool in McLean, Virginia.

Recently I checked my memory with Teddy von Kessel before he died. He was in the German Embassy in 1954, under Ambassador Krekeler. That year, Jimmy Riddleberger came to me with a request. He said the German generals, in Washington to discuss their military contribution to Europe's defense, were stiff and uncommunicative. Jimmy suggested it might ease matters if I would invite them for supper and a swim in the pool.

They came—among them Minister von Kessel, Generals Heusinger and von Manteufel, Minister of Defense Theo Blank, and Colonel Fett.

I pressed them to have a swim before supper. They started to refuse, but I gave each a pair of swimming trunks and before long they were bobbing about in the pool, along with five Americans I had invited. The formality was gone, the conversation was easy, and the dealings between the two groups went famously. This was the beginning of the postwar German Army.

As an ally, Germany is strong and dependable. From the days of Adenauer to the present, it has been cooperative with the United States. Minor differences indicate the independence of the nation but do not cause serious friction. It has begun to take a responsible part in the adjustments that must be made in the Middle East, in Africa, and in China. It has shown strength and leadership in the European community.

For me this is a new nation, a new people, and although I prefer some of the American tradition in education, women's affairs, and our own sense of humor, I have enjoyed my work with Germans over the last thirty-five years.

# 16

## VIENNA—FOUR POWER OCCUPATION, 1945

The convoy of seventy-six ships was on its way to Britain in April 1945. Four destroyers were in station at the "death corners." My two children and I were aboard a Liberty ship, the S.S. *Marine Fox*. We were on our way to Vienna, Austria, where I had been assigned as financial attaché. The war was not yet over.

Several years before, the leasing of destroyers to Britain meant, as Churchill said, that Britain was not alone. The bridge of ships across the Atlantic became increasingly important, and, when Pearl Harbor brought us into the war, the volume of tonnage—war materiel and food—grew. By fifties and hundreds, Liberty ships gathered to sail in flotillas, protected in part by destroyers as they entered the danger zones. German submarines were sought out and destroyed. Some ships were lost but most survived. These naval ventures were to lay the foundations of victory.

My son, David, who was ten years old, described our convoy— probably the last convoy—in his diary:

> We boarded the boat at 8:45, April 25th. We sailed at 4:30 a.m. on April 26th.
>
> In the morning I went up on deck and I saw that we had started and I saw two or three other boats. I then went to the dining room where I had a lovely breakfast. The boat is a rather large, new transport type of cargo boat. The life preserver is worn at all times on board. It has a signal light and a whistle and a queer knife.
>
> Then I went to the upper deck where I saw the two Grumann Avengers and the gathering of a convoy. We went to the bow and saw the ack-ack guns. There was a practice fire drill for all hands.

The children enjoyed every minute of it and they "entertained the sailors," wrote David. They were excited by gun practice, by talking to the captain, and even by the knowledge that submarines were nearby. However, the Atlantic crossing was more nerve-racking to the State Department staff and officers' wives on board. We knew our lives were in danger.

In midocean the radio reported the first rumors that Hitler was finally defeated. These were followed by reports that submarine "wolf packs" in desperation and rage were wildly attacking ships at sea. We were near the Channel and were told we would make an emergency stop at Weymouth, near Land's End, rather than continue to Southampton. In the harbor we were met by small launches and dumped unceremoniously in midafternoon on the dock.

After several weary hours, somewhat bewildered by the confusion of the unscheduled landing, David, his sister, Ann, eight, my niece, Joan Dulles, who had accompanied us as the children's governess, and I arrived in London. Our train pulled into the dark city at 4 A.M. A friend from the Embassy took us to the Park Lane Hotel.

The next day was V-E Day—the day of England's glory in the victory. As soon as we were awake we joined the crowds in Hyde Park outside Buckingham Palace. A young English schoolboy with a camp chair helped David up beside him. Arms around each other, they watched the two little princesses and Churchill greeting the crowd from the Palace balcony.

As David said, "Churchill made a speech. It was very short, but it said what most of us felt . . . We must not shirk from our task."

The park was full of rejoicing people, all day and night. Bonfires burned, people danced and sang, and the ruined buildings glowed with light for the first time in many months.

The days of fighting in Europe were over. A period of real and spectacular reconstruction in England and in Europe was beginning. I had to leave London to join my outfit, leaving my children in Joan's hands to come to Vienna later. Regretfully, I flew off without them to Italy where "Austria forward" was stationed.

General Mark Clark was to head the occupation forces. He and his armies had landed at Anzio, Italy, and occupied the lower part of the Italian peninsula while plans for the eventual occupation of Austria were still under way. The State Department's Austrian contingent was to join Clark's staff and move from Caserta to Salzburg, Austria, as soon as the region was cleared of enemy troops.

[187]

We did not know in April when we would be able to enter Vienna, but we were impatient to get to the capital of Austria to begin reconstruction.

The "political" work was headed by Jack Erhardt, the diplomatic representative attached to General Clark's staff. Erhardt—a large, burly man, who chewed gum incessantly—was sometimes brusque and interestingly unpredictable. He had a warm sense of humor. As a type he was much like Will Rogers—an amusing talker.

Mark Clark was very different, a "spit and polish" martinet, proud of his appearance, his soldierly bearing, and his military record. I never saw General MacArthur in Tokyo, but from what friends have told me, I would guess that they both ran their outfits with the same style—strict discipline, spotless white gloves for MP's, lots of ribbons and full-dress display, from the top ranks all the way down. People had to toe the line. Clark was well suited to Austria at that stage. The defeated Austrians were suffering from a deep-seated inferiority complex. They'd been crushed by the Nazis in 1938 and then associated with them in disaster. They had lost their capital assets, their pride, their territory.

Clark went in with determination and style, a tough, conspicuous figure, and the Austrians got what they needed then, assurance that the period of uncertainty would end. Clark went by the book, and if the Austrians would cooperate they would know the time for rebuilding was at hand.

Jack Erhardt was able to work effectively though unconventionally with Mark Clark. Every now and then he would say, "General, if you do that you'll make a fool of yourself."

Clark would say, "What do you mean? What do you mean?"

Erhardt would laugh and say, "Oh, go ahead if you want. Make a fool of yourself—you'll be the laughingstock of Europe!"

Erhardt knew instinctively how to guide the general. Most of the time he would let him take a strong line with the three allies and the Austrians, and support him. Every once in a while, he'd say, "That's ridiculous, you can't do that." His criticism was never heavy-handed and Clark would usually take his advice.

We came to respect Clark's wisdom in that he negotiated with the Russians over access through their zone. At the time, the delay in going into Vienna seemed to us unnecessary. By August the essential agreements were made, and the staff, in small parties, entered the city. Some have said the plans for Vienna were better than those for

Berlin, but I think the difference lay in the Soviet appraisal—they placed a higher value on north Germany than on Austria.

In any case, the establishment of the occupation apparatus, security, and basic economic arrangement could not be completed overnight. Clark handled these matters well. The conditions prevailing in 1945 are difficult to imagine now. There were no railroads, no buses, no civilian planes, and the extent of guerrilla fighting was menacing but not known exactly. The communications were in chaos. Distress was everywhere. The responsibilities of the occupation forces were of immense proportions, more difficult than we knew at the outset.

The military plane on which I traveled from London landed at Naples, near Caserta, in May of 1945. The late Carmel Offie, American head of mission there, met me and took me to the headquarters. It was in a huge gray palace about the size of the Pentagon in the rural area outside the crowded town. Almost a thousand people, both military and civilian, worked in it.

Carmel told me that the group I was to join had just gone north. I could join them in Florence. On the way a stop in Rome would be possible. In Rome I stayed in a hotel for the Women's Army Corps—WACs. But I spent most of my time with my good friend Ambassador Alexander Kirk. He was, years before, aide to my uncle, Robert Lansing. He had been in and out of the Lansing house in Washington in the early 1920s. When last I heard of Alexander Kirk, in 1970, he was living in a windowless building in Arizona, because he believed in "creating his own atmosphere." A sensitive and artistic person, he was residing in the exquisite Barbaroni Palace in Rome. During my stay there, he gave a wedding reception for a junior staff member, Robert McBride, and his wife. There were only a few hours for me to see the Vatican, the Forum, and many magnificent sights. I left in two days for Florence.

I did not know that we would languish for days, idle in a tobacco factory with nothing to do. We commuted from the Minerva Hotel to our "offices" in the empty factory. Every day we gathered in the damp, empty sheds, without work, sitting at long benches trying to find some useful tasks.

Only our chief, Erhardt, had the appurtenances of a bona fide government man—the In and Out baskets and a real desk. He was conferring with General Clark about the work to come. The rest of

[189]

us were drones, theoretically studying German and reading occupation directives.

After two weeks of this, we threatened to strike unless we could see something of Florence, largely spared from the war's devastation. We won two days to sightsee. I managed to visit the Uffizi and Pitti museums, and had glimpses of the city. I bicycled on Sunday in the hills. However, I had already satisfied a little of my desire to know the city by getting up early and seeing some of the beautiful churches. Churches open early.

On my fiftieth birthday I was sent to Lugano (Leghorn) to get my military identity card. It showed my assimilated rank was lieutenant colonel. This classification was granted so that if I were captured by the enemy—then the far-off Japanese—I would receive field grade officer treatment under the Geneva Convention. I was thus at a higher rank than the twenty women secretaries with whom I shared billets but received from the men the treatment accorded a woman secretary. On my way back from Lugano to Florence, I stopped long enough in Pisa to climb the Leaning Tower. After our two weeks in Florence, the group went on to Verona; Austria still seemed far away.

In the city of Romeo and Juliet our group assembled each day in a muddy area which was a former concentration camp, with duck boards across the slippery paths. The buildings resembled run-down cheap army barracks. I found the continued inactivity frustrating and went to Jack Erhardt.

"Let me go on to Salzburg," I said. "Some of the men are working there. I hear the area is mainly cleared of Nazis."

"All right," he answered.

Fearing he would change his mind, I hurried to the Office of Transport and told the man in charge I was supposed to report to Salzburg and needed written military orders and authorized transportation. I was in luck.

He said, "A Captain Little is going to Austria tomorrow in an open jeep. Take your bedroll, duffel bag, and knapsack and report at 0600." I was gone before Jack could give me another thought.

The ride was over the Brenner Pass, a steep mountain road, pitted with shell holes. It was many hours later when, weary, we arrived at the shattered town of Salzburg. We went on to the twenty-five-room, two-story villa of Heinrich Himmler, infamous master of concentration camps, instigator of millions of gas chamber murders of the Jews. He was already dead. A captive of the British, he had committed suicide on May 23, biting the vial of potassium cyanide hidden in his cheek before his captors could interrogate him.

There were still signs of executions at the bottom of the garden; a group of buildings with barred cells were pockmarked with bullets. The main house itself was not damaged. It was a pleasant refuge for less than a dozen State Department officers. I enjoyed a brief stay there. We had good conversations, exploring political and economic questions for which we needed answers in our coming work. In the daytime we were in a temporary office, a partly ruined building in town.

One evening after dinner I said, "I'd like to go for a walk. Will any of you come?"

My dinner companions insisted it was "too dangerous."

I went anyway and as I was walking in the forest I saw some men hiding behind the trees. I turned back quickly toward the villa. I knew this area was supposed to be the last bastion of Hitler's SS troops and was not surprised. I did not know whether the men were Nazis, Austrians, or Hungarians. As the Russians came up the Danube, hundreds of Hungarians came into Austria, hoping to be captured by the Americans. I never did find out who the men were lurking in the shadows.

A week after I moved into the villa my stay was cut short. Erhardt's deputy, James Orr Denby, said, "This is a boys' club, Eleanor. You can leave in an hour. You must stay in town with the women secretaries. We don't want you here."

I knew the other residents of the villa did not feel as he did, but decided not to argue the point. I packed up and was driven to the Pitter Hotel in Salzburg.

The Pitter was half destroyed, but it was a good observation point in the center of town. I remember looking out at the building across the street. The front wall was completely gone. Four Austrians on the fifth floor had put up a card table, placed some kitchen chairs around it, and sat down. The house was open like the front of a child's dollhouse, and if they had moved their table three feet, they would have fallen to the street. But they were enjoying a social evening by candlelight. There was no electricity and even kerosene lamps were unavailable. Despite the suffering, the Austrians still sought pleasure.

Once in Austria, I began to search for the economic data that would give us information on what was left of industry, what was important

[191]

to the economy, and the nature of the price and wage structure. There was not much statistical data and few books and reports were available, but we had to know about conditions relevant to separating the Austrian economy from the German system.

It was clear that the Austrians were starving. There was nothing to buy in the shops. They would search for cigarette butts in the streets and look through the garbage. I learned that there were potatoes and cabbages in nearby Bavaria. Since Germany was kept to the subsistence level, I thought it would be good to get some of this food into Austria. I persuaded the authorities to let me go to Frankfurt accompanied by a friendly Texan Major Hughes, to negotiate with the U.S. military command. We had about two hundred Hungarian horses to offer as a bargain.

We flew into the ravaged airport at Frankfurt am Main on July 21. The army plane landed on the metal strips and we walked through the mud to some waiting jeeps. We were billeted across from the roofless rain-drenched railroad station. Although most of the floor was ankle-deep in water, several hundred refugees from a concentration camp farther east were huddled in the drier portions.

The desolation in the city was indescribable. The streets were piled high with rubble, and soldiers were removing unexploded shells and bombs while buildings were torn down to prevent sudden collapse. Austria had been shocking but the situation in Germany was much worse. There seemed no sign of hope. The people were spiritless and confused.

Hughes and I went to the military headquarters in the I. G. Farben building in Hörsch, a few miles out of the center of town. We found Colonel Jones in charge of the supplies we were interested in. He listened guardedly to our proposal, but he was not too difficult to persuade. The result was that we traded two hundred horses to the army for several carloads of cabbages and potatoes to distribute to the hungry people in our zone of Austria.

Our military were living quite comfortably on the supplies they had brought. The officers were preparing to move the main command to Berlin. There was captured German materiel and some supplies in our army dumps. I managed to get some of this for Austria. It was a time for bargaining and for maneuver. We in the American zone of occupation benefited by transfers from Germany. One of our most constructive officers, General Jesmond D. Balmer, made an agreement in which we gave Austrian water-generated electricity to southern Germany and received about $100 million worth of coal from the Ruhr.

Back in the State Department several years later, working on the Austrian-German desk, the Pentagon tried to get the Austrians to pay for that coal. I maintained that an authorized American signed the paper, and the Austrians did not owe anything for the coal. This developed into a contest between the State Department and the Army. The method I chose was to edit every Pentagon cable that came to me to clear, making about fifteen or twenty changes. This necessitated more meetings and then the writing of a new draft. The delaying tactics went on for about six months, until the Army got tired of them and filed the papers—the Austrians never did pay.

The occupation was so chaotic that if one really wanted to do something, maneuvering was necessary. You can trade cabbages and horses, or electricity for coal, but you must maneuver for the deal, especially if you're a woman.

After I had arranged about the food deal one of the officers in Frankfurt took me to the cellar of the Reichsbank building where the SS concentration camp authorities had stored the gold teeth, trinkets, and eyeglass frames taken before the burning of the victims of the camps at Dachau, Belsen, and others. Huge wire cages held these miserable relics, piled up to the ceiling, just as the Germans had left them.

While I was in Frankfurt, I managed to go from there to Wiesbaden, to see my brother Allen, then in OSS, later head of the Central Intelligence Agency. He had as guests two men, leaders of French and German resistance groups. They were introduced to me as Mr. Wood (Fritz Kolbe) and General Salmon. This was just before Allen went up to Berlin to attempt to verify the account of Hitler's death in his bunker. I had just learned that my children were staying in his house in Berne, Switzerland.

Back in Salzburg, I continued to explore the Austrian economic situation. The work had an unreal quality, and though we knew the time was precious we had little data to work with. We knew the establishment of a separate currency was an essential first step for reconstruction, but it was clear that we needed the help of the Austrian economists and officials who were in Vienna. Our preparations in Salzburg were not very meaningful—but we worked.

It was midsummer, while I was still in Salzburg, that I had an illness, which I am now convinced was a gallbladder attack. I was taken in an army car to one of Hitler's rest houses, Chiemsee, in Germany. There, talking to a young American doctor, I said, "I may have a brain tumor. One of my eyes protrudes." (This was a comment a doctor once made to me.)

He asked me a few questions. The pain had stopped. I was bored and talked freely. On a radio in the background a record of "Sentimental Journey" was being played over and over. I wanted to get back to Salzburg.

They woke me at six the next morning.

"Into the ambulance," they said. They put a tag on me which said, "*Operate for brain tumor.*"

In the 101st U. S. Army Hospital in Munich, one of Hitler's constructions used mainly for the SS and their girls, they took me to a ward. I objected to undressing and kept on my clothes. They put me on a stretcher, pushed me to the X-ray room, and took dozens of pictures of my head. I never knew what they showed, but I was apprehensive.

Back on the ward, I found a field telephone.

"Lucky Rear to Lucky Forward," I called. "Is this Salzburg—Mr. Denby? Please send a car to the front of the 101st Hospital in Munich. I'll be waiting on the street in two hours."

I escaped quietly through a side entrance. They may still be looking for me.

Just before I went to Vienna, I met some friends in the OSS—later the CIA—and some Austrians who had worked in the resistance. We arranged to eat in the Gablerbrau, one of the few *gasthauses* in Salzburg that had not been destroyed. One of the men invited to join the group was Karl Gruber, a member of Austria's People's Party, and later, Foreign Minister and also Austrian ambassador to Washington.

I could not find my friends and did not know where to look for the *gasthaus*. Inquiry led me to think that Gruber was in the large palace on Kapital Place. I had already met him and knew him by sight.

I explored the large empty halls of the palace and finally found a room where some forty men were seated at desks. Unnoticed, I slipped into a seat at the rear, and listened. I heard the discussion of the *Landeshauptmen*, the provincial governors, meeting for the first time with other leading politicians. This was probably the first political gathering for most of these men since the Anschluss in 1938. Gruber had led the resistance group who liberated Innsbruck in early spring. He had walked into the provincial offices of Innsbruck and defied the local gauleiter. He was a man of great courage.

They voted in September that he should be made Foreign Minister when the new government of Austria was established. Karl Renner, in Vienna, had been acting as President for some months.

After a few moments I decided I was out of place in this secret meeting and that it would be wise to withdraw. They were so absorbed in their deliberations that no one noticed me. When, an hour later, I met with Gruber and the others at the restaurant, I did not mention my presence at the meeting. I was beginning to get a feel for the situation.

In late August some of our group, including my friend, Eleanor Raynor (Burns), our legal adviser, had flown from Salzburg to Vienna. Those of us left behind were very tired of the bomb-shattered Hotel Pitter. Although Salzburg still held medieval treasures, it was tedious in its ruins. We were in limbo. For the women in our group, the game was to captivate an officer who had the use of a car. Even access to a personnel carrier made a man worth cultivating. It was the only way we could go to Berchtesgaden, to the Weisses Rössl, to the Eagle's Nest, and to the beautiful lakes and the "Fat Bellboy," as we called the glacier, Grosse Gloekner.

The Eagle's Nest, high over Berchtesgaden, was a lookout from which one could view the mountains of Austria to the East and of Germany to the West. Hitler had a winding road built up sheer cliffs. There was a door, leading to a copper-lined elevator shaft, which took us up five hundred feet, to an austere room with walls two feet thick. This was where one could look out over the mountains and where it was said that Hitler had intended at one time to hole up in a last stand against the conquering armies of the Allies. But touring around Salzburg was not what we had come to Austria for, and all of us were impatient to get to Vienna and to work.

Among the attractive young women on our staff was Dixie Davis, an amusing secretary. She joked with everyone—even with General Clark. On a day in late August she said to him, "Flying is so boring. Why don't you let all of us drive into Vienna?"

Clark, surprised at the idea, told a colonel to find one of Hitler's cars, and one of Mussolini's, liberated in May. I rode in Hitler's. It had bulletproof glass an inch thick. There were ten of us going east down the autobahn to the Enns River in the Soviet zone of Austria where the Russians had a boom across the road.

Near the zonal border American Military Police on motorcycles formed an escort for us. The Soviet guards asked, "Who are these women?"

"Mark Clark's girls."

"What a man!" they exclaimed. "Let them through."

So we drove another ninety miles through the devastated countryside, into the ruined suburbs, to the heart of Vienna, and to the Hotel Regina on "The Ring." The Ring Strasse is a wide boulevard, encircling the inner city of Vienna on three sides, the fourth being the Danube. It was edged with once glorious buildings. But when we reached it after the seven-hour drive over shell-pocked roads we were too tired to note those buildings that were still standing. We were more aware of rubble piled twenty and thirty feet high, where whole buildings had been bombed.

The entrance of the American occupation staff into Vienna had been delayed from June to September while General Clark negotiated with the Soviets about access to the city through the Soviet zone of occupation. While Clark's arrangement with the Russians proved more acceptable than that concluded in Germany by General Clay, as I noted earlier the Soviets proved easier for Clark to deal with because of Austria's lesser importance than Germany.

It is clear that the Soviets made an error in judgment in appraising the Austrian situation. They assumed that because the Austrians had a socialist President, Karl Renner, the Austrians would give them easy arrangements on the Danube and that the Western powers had virtually lost the city. They did not realize that Renner was a democratic socialist, a firm believer in freedom. Renner and Leopold Figl, the Chancellor, whom the Soviets permitted to exercise authority, would in time hold out for independence against all four occupying powers, English, French, American, and Russian.

At the time, the staff did not realize why Clark took such pains about access, or why the Soviets posed so many difficulties. We were still unaware of the Cold War, and too occupied with our local problems to assess correctly what was happening in Germany.

Clark was the dominant figure among the leaders of the four occupying powers. There were in the Occupying Commission four national Elements, as they were called. Each had a military commander who was the chief, and a political adviser, as his aide. Under the military and diplomatic there was a staff, in our case, mainly civilians. Options or choices were referred first to the lower-level committees. When agreement was reached, the papers were passed up the line. Usually a decision was made at the level just under the commanding general—in our Element, Mark Clark.

Since a shattered nation, attached to the German Reich for six years, had to be reconstructed, the work was extemely demanding. It covered the essential services, supplies of food and fuel, electricity, water, rebuilding housing, largely destroyed, and the reconstitution of the Austrian Goverment, as well as economic, political, and cultural institutions.

There was no aspect of the national life that did not have to be rebuilt and shaped to the democratic goals that had been suppressed for so long. It was the most fascinating work I was ever to do. My previous experience in general economics, industry, finance, and in Social Security helped me to make proposals. I enjoyed it, no matter how long the hours and how great the drain on my energies.

In 1945 the economic future of Austria was in question. Goebbels had called Austria a head without a body. This phrase was Anschluss propaganda to justify the absorption of the area into the Third Reich. We in the State Department occupation planning forces were dedicated to the principle that the country could survive, with a moderate amount of outside help; it proved to be slightly more than a billion dollars. Austria should and did survive. The task before us was not easy and demanded unflagging effort.

There were some excellent economists among the civilians with the U.S. Army. The late Arthur Marget, head of the U.S. occupation economic committee, was a brilliant theorist. He had been in finance classes I took at Harvard in 1924 and 1925, and I knew him to be highly qualified. I had had some twenty or more years of study and industrial experience, in addition to my research on banking and currency for *The French Franc* and for other books. I had been told that Professor Charles Warren of Princeton's economic department had suggested to Jack Erhardt that he take me with his team.

Austria was the center of my interest. Where there was a conflict of interest between Germany and Austria, the U. S. Army and Austria, or the French and Austria, I felt I should fight for my client. My specific job was to try and see that the balance of payments was put in a healthy condition, to raise productivity and reduce unemployment. I wasn't the only one doing the work, but I had the opportunity to stay with this job from 1945 to 1951, giving me continuity and familiarity, along with a certain amount of authority, which I used to the fullest extent. Since the policy for Austria developed along different lines from that for Germany, we were encouraged to constructive effort. It was agreed in Washington that, from a moral and political point of view, Germany should not be given a standard of living higher than that of France, Belgium, and other countries in the early reconstruction period and Austria was favored above Germany.

Shortly after we went to Vienna in August, I received letters, delayed for more than three months, from the children and Joan. I was granted a few days leave and drove with an embassy colleague in his small car to the Swiss border, three hundred miles to the West. When our passports were checked at St. Margarethen, north of Zurich, the Swiss border guards waved Bill back into the car.

"She can't go with you," the guard said. "We have to disinfect her."

I protested, "But we came from the same place, the same living conditions, and in the same car. I have no disease."

"We are inspecting all refugees," he said.

There was nothing I could do as Bill drove cheerfully on to Zurich. I was directed down a path to a large shed, where I was interrogated.

"What is your religion?" an official asked.

"I do not choose to answer."

"You might be Jewish," my interrogator speculated.

Apparently there was a fear of a plague from Jewish camps. I had not been near any of them.

Then they took my purse, my clothing, my glasses, and left me naked, defenseless, and waiting.

"Can't you hurry up?" I asked.

"We can't afford to disinfect a single person. We must have thirty or forty."

At last I was put in a wooden-walled room with some twenty-five women. It had chemical sprays on all sides. Then I was given a rough blanket and told to wait until my clothing had been baked. After a while soup was served at long wooden tables. My clothes were returned, I dressed, and was permitted to leave.

In a letter I wrote to the legation in Berne, dated September 21, I described the incident:

> I was cleared by the passport official at St. Margarethen at 11:15 the morning of the 13th of September. I was then sent to the immigrant camp where I was told I would have to wait several hours to be disinfected. Later, my clothes were entirely removed and, along with a group of other women, whom I had never seen before, I was sprayed with delousing chemical from head to foot. My hair was completely drenched in the solution. This process took more than an hour. I then had to wait two hours for a train.

The letter ended with a request for written indication on my passport that I was attached to the diplomatic mission. My passport indicated only that I was on the staff of the adviser to General Clark.

The Swiss later sent a letter of apology.

Three hours after the Swiss released me I arrived at Zurich and found my children, who were staying at St. Peter's Hotel. What a joy it was! I have rarely experienced such a tremendous feeling of relief. The lack of contact and communication had been from early May until September. When I left for Vienna, the children remained in boarding school, David at Le Rosey and Ann at La Combe— dependents were not yet allowed in Austria.

Our responsibility in those early September days was focused on the control agreements, a comprehensive one to follow the first Four Power arrangements. My own work, helping with the monetary reform called for careful technical planning. Our serious and apparently successful discussions with the technical officers of the Russian element, as well as with the British and French, made us very optimistic about a quick conversion of the Austrian currency. It was a shock, and a surprise, when the Soviets reneged on what we thought were agreements. We learned then that the Russians would not explain their reasons for doing anything, and were frequently inconsistent in their actions.

Only when these negations of all our work occurred did we

begin to sense the climate of relations with which the United States would struggle for ten years, until the Austrian State Treaty in 1955.

What happened is simple to explain, but it came as a shock to us. We had many boxes of occupation currency, paper money printed for Austria. Arthur Marget had gone to Vienna in August, and begun his talks with the Russian colonel who was supposed to handle currency. The British and French were soon there also.

The plan was to substitute this currency for the reichsmarks, circulating since the Anschluss. This change would permit the disengagement of the Austrian economy from Germany and the orderly budgeting of government expenses, as well as reconstitution of the banking system to aid in production.

The negotiations, which began in the summer, continued at the level of colonels of all Four Powers. Plans for the transport of the boxes of currency to local centers, and the ratio at which the new currency would be exchanged for old, went along smoothly. The complete program was put before the higher-level Economic Commission of the Four Power directorate. It was ready for action in early October. The meeting was held as scheduled and the Soviets simply said, "*Nyet.*" They turned the whole plan down.

Their representative on the lower committee had approved every step and had given no hint that a superior officer might throw out the completed plan. We were new at negotiating with the Soviets. We faced a difficult problem. I had been in constant touch, as had the other financial experts, with the Austrian national bank officers. Some of them had just emerged from hiding from the Nazis, and had avoided any type of collaboration. I worked primarily with Dr. Gustav Wärmer and Dr. Fritz Störger-Marspach, both patriotic, anti-Nazi, and competent.

Soviet unwillingness to use the occupation currency brought us face to face with the practical problem of printing the full range of currency from one-schilling notes to large units in a short space of time. The printing and engraving machinery had not the capacity to put out this volume in a period of two or three months. Delay, however, would mean serious obstacles to economic recovery as reichsmarks continued to flow in from Germany.

My proposal, as well as that arrived at independently by others, was to print schilling notes in high denomination, to the full value of the circulating notes, and retire the reichsmarks. As time went on we could gradually issue smaller denomination notes to the banks, until at the end of ten or fifteen weeks, a normal distribution of large and small currency would be in circulation. During the initial period, with the issue of high denomination notes, IOU chits and other informal pieces of paper could be used by individuals for day-to-day transactions.

When we presented this plan to the Soviets, we braced ourselves for the customary negative *Nicht demokratish*. However, we were surprised. Without any discussion of its merits, the Soviets accepted the proposal. It went into effect in late October.

The Soviets did manage a minor gain for themselves. It had been agreed by all Four Powers that the German currency in Austria would be brought to a central place and burned. The British, French, and American brought the reichsmarks from their zones. The Russians delayed from week to week without explanation. They never did bring the old currency in. There were indications that they sent the reichsmarks they collected into Germany, where the money was used to buy German goods in the black market.

The Four Power meetings of the finance committee were pleasant, orderly, and serious. The Russian member was friendly, and technical matters were developed smoothly. There were some odd discussions. For example, the Russian officer said there was no word for *profits*—there was only exploitation. If more were taken in by banks or businesses than was paid out, that was exploitation. I found the discussions a fascinating, if bizarre, introduction to postwar realities.

While the group of which I was a member worked on financial and industrial programs, others were working on political rehabilitation. The Soviets, in May 1945, had permitted the venerable Karl Renner to act as President because he was a socialist. They also agreed that there could be a central government to operate under the general tutelage of the Four Power Occupation Commission. The Austrians, with our guidance, set the national elections for November. The Soviets assumed that the Socialist, whom they thought shared the ideas of Soviet socialists, would win.

Kieselev, the Russian political adviser, had told Erhardt, his American opposite number, that if the Austrians would have an election, the Austrian Communists would get more than 20 percent of the votes, and with that number, the Soviets could control the Austrian Government—it is notable that he was not afraid of a free election at that time.

Ballot boxes were taken up into the high mountains and the valleys and, after the voting, brought down over snow and ice, to be duly counted. The resulting tally was a surprise to the Russians. The conservative People's Party won over the Socialist party. There was a small vote for the Communists, who were allotted two members in the Cabinet of fourteen.

The preponderance of conservative votes was in part the result of Russian soldiers' wild rampage when they entered the country. The raping, looting, roistering troops had terrified the Austrians. They wanted to be guarded from communist excesses and they thought that they would be safer if, through the Conservative party, they worked closely with the Western Allies.

The Western occupying elements took full advantage of this attitude and there was full cooperation from the beginning. Chancellor Leopold Figl was not only a brave resister of the Nazis but a leader determined to protect the interests of Austria against forays by *any* power, not only the Russians but also the other three powers.

Figl had refused to carry out Nazi orders, even after the SS troopers had taken him to a labor camp in the high mountains. There, he told me, he had slept in an open shed in the snow. His captors had kicked his teeth in and he had suffered other wounds and indignities. In 1945, with the elections over, he took full advantage of an Allied control agreement, cleverly drafted by Ware Adams and approved by all Four Powers. This was a great contribution. The agreement let the Austrian laws passed by the Parliament go into effect, subject only to *unanimous* veto by the Four Power Council. This stymied Soviet objections.

But Figl had to pursue a delicate course. There is a joke in the folklore that reveals something of the difficulty of his position. After a council meeting he attended, so the legend goes, the doorman called for Mark Clark's Cadillac, the French general's Citroën, the British general's Rolls-Royce, the Soviet general's ZIS, and Chancellor Figl's galoshes.

From the beginning of our work in Vienna, we were all anxious to get out of military billets and into houses and apartments. I had an Austrian friend, Leah Furthmueller, introduced to me by Quaker friends in Philadelphia. I took her to the Regina for several meals. My recourse to military rations, though limited, made it possible to give away cans of fruit, flour, powdered eggs, and other staples—

even coffee. These luxuries meant a great deal to the Austrians who were suffering from hunger.

Leah came to me shortly after my first meeting with her and said, "I have found a good apartment for you and your children when they come later."

I said, "Wonderful!"

When I saw the "apartment" I was astounded. It was the Clam Gallas Palace, with forty-eight rooms. A fine, two-story Empire building with large salons and many bedrooms, its gardens stretched between beautiful trees and bushes. It was in the center of town. I talked to the three sisters who owned the palace. I said I would pay two hundred dollars (U.S.) a month into a bank in Switzerland for them. This was the rent I was being paid for my Washington house. I told them they could use half the rooms. Twenty-four would be enough for me!

When I presented my formal request to General Keyes, Clark's deputy, I had no difficulty in getting it accepted, even though it was unusual in that I offered to pay in dollars. Most housing was simply requisitioned and not paid for.

By this time I had found Trudy—Gertrude Rotter—who was to be my mainstay for years. She was a nineteen-year-old displaced person. My assistant, Ruth Heller, asked me if I would like this young girl to work for me. Trudy's aunt, Relly (Aurelie Rotter), was Ruth's housekeeper. I knew that the two had worked in Czechoslovakia, in a district that had once been part of the Austro-Hungarian Empire. When the Russian troops had entered their village the people hid Trudy in the barn to protect her from the soldiers. She was an attractive girl. She told me she was working for six dollars a month. She was pleased when I offered her ten dollars a month.

Later, when Ruth left Austria, she suggested I employ Relly. This extraordinary cook was a fine woman and was to become well known in Washington, where she was my housekeeper until she retired in 1971. Her meals were renowned.

I had, for the start, a beautiful home, if severely cold. Eleanor Raynor (Burns), my lawyer friend, and I picked a few rooms in the palace we hoped we could warm with *Kochelofens*—porcelain stoves. Trudy would run from the big kitchen stove down the long corridors to the bathroom and pour boiling water into the tub. I had the choice of getting in it while it was steaming hot or waiting until it chilled to icy cold, with a few acceptable warm moments between. However, my new home was not only beautiful but the only palace I ever lived in.

I remember a number of parties in these cold rooms, cheered by military liquor rations and enlivened by animated conversation. At one such party I persuaded "Silver Jim" Rundel, an army colonel, to get me thousands of bales of cotton from the occupation zone in Germany to supply the idle textile mills at St. Polten, outside Vienna, and get production under way. Later, at another evening cocktail party at my home, I got tons of artificial rubber from Germany for Austrian tires to get the trucks rolling.

It was here, too, that I argued with Professor Frank Fetter from Princeton University, then with the Export-Import Bank, that Austria was viable and could build up its economic life with American help. This argument resulted in the first loan, $10 million, some months before the Marshall Plan came into operation. This capital sum was a sign and an instrument of American support.

After my niece, Joan, joined me in Austria she also lived in the palace. We were nicely settled, a half block from the office on Boltzmanngasse.

Then came an unpleasant surprise. A group of efficient-looking men arrived one day with measuring tapes, and without asking "by-your-leave," began to explore the rooms. When I asked what they were doing, they showed me a paper signed by the military authorities on instruction of General Keyes. The Red Cross was to take over the building. Nothing was said about me or my permission to rent the palace.

When I went to the military and showed them my papers, the officer in charge said:

"The General has the right to requisition and assign quarters. There is nothing we can do."

I was worried for myself, but I was also worried because I knew that hordes of GIs tramping through the halls, playing games in the drawing rooms, setting up Coke bars, and using furniture hundreds of years old would destroy the beauty of one of the most perfect Empire palaces in Austria.

David, then eleven, was spending his Easter holiday with me when the Army said it was going to take the palace for the Red Cross. He argued in favor of the Army taking over.

"Mother, here we are in a great big palace and the poor GIs are

[204]

lonely and don't know how to entertain themselves in a strange country."

David said it would be much more reasonable to make the building available to hundreds of American soldiers than it would be for the Dulles family to live there. But I was arguing with David for preservation of historic monuments. Not long after the Red Cross took over I discovered the GIs wrecked much of the furniture, lamps, and floors.

Meanwhile I made other plans. I had made the acquaintance through the OSS of a banker who had worked with my brother, Allen, in Switzerland. Kurt Grimm knew how to "manage" even matters hard to arrange. He put at my disposal a fine house at 57 Sternwarte Strasse, for which I also paid in dollars in Switzerland. The arrangement was approved by the housing authorities, though this was unusual. Most people, if they paid rent, paid in cigarettes. Those who did not pay rent just walked in and put a sign on the front door: "This house is requisitioned by the U. S. Army." It was not illegal to throw out an Austrian and take over his house as part of the "occupation."

Our new home had been lived in briefly by a group of Austrian communists. They had torn out much of the paneling for firewood and had not bothered to remove the dead horse from the garden or fill in the shell holes. The structural condition of the house was good, the rooms bright and spacious, though many windows were out. My friends and former landladies, who owned the palace, loaned me all the furniture I could take on the theory that it would get better care with me than with the Red Cross. Even if I had not been financial attaché at the mission—later the embassy—I still would not have engaged in transactions for personal profit.

Some of my supplies came from Fritz Hörlesberger, the brother-in-law of one of my Harvard colleagues. His sister wrote him that I would be in Vienna and Fritz came to see me shortly after my arrival. He took us under his wing. He was chief manager of Julius Meinl, the prestigious grocery and liquor store. Because of his dealings in Budapest and other neighboring countries, he still had contacts and managed to get supplies through the Russian lines. In fact he was on good terms with Soviet officers. He did this partly on the basis of "schnapps," a term the Russians used to cover any hard liquor. Once a Soviet colonel came to his office and pounded the

[205]

desk, demanding schnapps. Fritz went to the warehouse and came back with a bottle. After the officer left, Fritz discovered, to his horror, that it was wood alcohol. I trembled for him expecting he would be dragged away as a saboteur. The next day the officer returned. "More schnapps," he said.

At Christmas I had a wonderful reunion with my children, with Allen and Clover Dulles, who were in Bonn, and with Karl and Helga Gruber. Gruber was then Minister of Foreign Affairs in Vienna.

We stayed at the Kleine Scheidegg, a fine hotel under the towering cliffs of the Eiger Nordwand. The family in America had sent many presents and we had a very festive time. The skiing was good and suitable for amateurs as well as experts.

I went back to Austria ready for the hard work that lay ahead. I knew we had already laid a foundation for political and economic reconstruction.

# 17

# AUSTRIA'S RECONSTRUCTION

The Cold War began in Austria in 1946. While the Austrians were trying to reorganize what was left of their economy, the Soviets were taking out of the country essential machinery and valuable oil from Austrian wells. Soldiers of the Soviet Army were allowed many predatory activities, taking over housing, making the cultivation of the land difficult, and seizing fuel already scarce and almost wholly unavailable to the Austrians. Starvation and cold reduced the capacity of Austrian labor to work, and the equivalent of aid brought in from the West was taken out in the East—the value was later estimated at more than a billion dollars. Some loss as the result of the presence of the four occupying powers was inevitable, but the Russians went far beyond this natural degree of interference. In fact, the policy to exert intolerable pressure on Austrian business leaders was part of their plan to move their power westward.

I had little previous training or experience to prepare me for the realities of the Cold War. I had considerable concern and some sympathy for the Russian Revolution. I had observed various aspects of Russian behavior in the last months of the war, but I had not given up hope of cooperation with the Soviets. I may have been naïve, but I was as informed as most of my colleagues. I was not ready to accept the desperate nature of the struggle ahead. I had to change many of my ideas as months went on.

I had been warned by Nicholas in London and by some other students of Russian history that the goal of the communists was expansion. However, it was quite another thing for me to see this policy in action. We Americans had a degree of optimism about working in concert with the Russians which we were gradually forced to discard. Following the chaotic postwar weeks we came to recognize the meaning of the brutality of the Soviet occupation and to realize that it was not the result of random actions. I saw in 1945 and 1946 Austrians fall in the streets from starvation when I knew food was being taken away by the Russians. A friend told me of the kidnapping of a railroad official who never returned. I knew of cases where people were shot resisting the seizure of property. The pattern became clear to me.

The Soviet aim was clearly to reduce Austria to abject compliance with what the Russians wished and to build a communist state and strong pro-Moscow group. Since I had many officials and newsmen in my house, I learned of Soviet activities and the resulting distress. We would sit for hours drinking my army liquor ration and speculating as to how we should gain freedom for Austria. I can see the doughty Leopold Figl; urbane and well-balanced Adolf Schärf; energetic Andreas Korp; the handsome Karl Gruber, Foreign Minister; Peter Krauland, Minister of Reconstruction; the stolid Julius Raab, future Chancellor; financial expert Gustav Wärmer; the speculative editor of the *Arbeiter Zeitung*, Oscar Pollack. There were many others, glad to relax in the warm and friendly atmosphere of my paneled study. We discussed Europe's future—and the possible release of Austria from communist pressures.

The hints of obstruction and oppression that were noted in the autumn of 1945 became increasingly evident as time went on. The tough negotiations over access to Vienna in July, and final compromises between Clark and Konev, difficulties in September over the monetary conversion, and the increasing removal of goods and machinery were observed with apprehension by the U.S. authorities.

We began to work with increased vigor. We found inspiration and guidance from the local people, for they were not only competent but friendly and energetic. The conditions in the country were so chaotic after the Nazis left and the Allies came in that advance planning, though it would have been helpful, would not have been decisive. However, as we groped for first steps in rebuilding the economy, more knowledge of prewar conditions would have helped in the early weeks of occupation. I was glad I had had experience in industry.

Arthur Marget and I were baffled by the unexpected setback in our monetary program at first approved by our Soviet associates, but we did not realize clearly the obstacles we faced until 1946. We were, however, gradually aware of the impossibility of constructive economic agreement with the Soviets. Our meetings in the beautiful Schwarzenburg Palace were games of diplomatic chess.

Fred Bunting, my assistant, and I went to Paris in January 1946 to a conference of foreign service officers. We reported the many signs of Russian depredations in the Austrian industry. We said there was an evident drive to gain domination. We did not then know the term "Cold War," which later characterized the period. Other foreign service officers from England, Belgium, France, and several other countries said that our view was myopic and unbalanced. But supporting views came from the U.S. representatives in Germany and our officers stationed in Moscow. They concurred in warning of Soviet intentions.

We went back to Vienna, hoping we had shed some light on the European situation. Our only option was to meet every specific occasion with as much firmness as we could and to encourage the Austrians to develop their capacities in the Western occupied zones. After the new Austrian schillings were in circulation there was a solid monetary base on which to build, and we struggled to find raw materials and funds for imports to get the factories rolling.

With our encouragement, in spite of hunger and cold the Austrians began to have hope. The food rations provided fewer than 1,200 calories in 1946, but there was help in prospect. The leaders knew us personally and were aware of our interest in their problems.

Realizing the wider implications of Soviet policy, I wished to convince the officials in Washington of the obstacles to reconstruction. I put together a systematic study of Soviet removals and destruction of their zone of occupation and analyzed the effects throughout the country. This took the help of my colleagues and of Austrian economists.

My final paper caused debate in the diplomatic mission. Jack Erhardt called a small meeting, and for two hours, sitting on the corner of his desk, chewing gum and saying nothing, he heard the arguments for and against my conclusions that the Soviets wished to take over Austria.

After heated discussions, pro and con, he ruled that my paper should go to Washington with his concurrence. At this time, General Balmer established a committee to try and control the exports from Austria to the Soviet Union. It was not long before Washington took steps along this line which led to the COCOM (Coordinating Committee) set up to curb shipments of strategic material to Iron Curtain countries.

From my vantage point in Vienna I welcomed these efforts

manifesting a strong determination in Washington to frustrate further Soviet aggression. My paper earned me a commendation and strengthened my position in the mission. The communists' expansionist intentions became clearer some months later with the takeover of the Prague government in early 1948.

I discussed my summaries with Austrian officials in the ministries of Commerce, Reconstruction, and Finance, often sitting with them on Sunday in my house over coffee. The men I worked with on specific economic decisions became friends and I managed to get them modest gifts of bread and canned goods. They invited me to their homes and gave me tea, which was about the only thing they could offer by way of hospitality. Several of them had managed to keep their apartments, although some of their furniture had disappeared. A few had cottages in the country where I went with the children on weekends. They realized early that I had experience in the field of practical economics and that I, along with my colleagues, was genuinely interested in helping the recovery of production and in finding ways to meet the needs of the people. We were able to move faster than in Germany. There was a central Austrian government, and also the U.S. directives under which we worked called for help, whereas Germany was limited by the harsh Joint Chiefs of Staff Directive 1067.

Since I had early decided that time spent with the Austrians was more productive than the cultivation of the generals and colonels, even though the military officers seemed to hold the power and had obvious prestige, my friendships with the Austrians led to several constructive plans. I felt a tremendous sense of accomplishment as tires were produced and trucks rolled, as cotton went to the textile mills and coal to the steel mills. I had never before had a chance to exert a comparable influence. The Austrians thought I had rank—which I had not. What I had was the will to maneuver and to manipulate the power that others had. It was a serious, exacting, yet rewarding game.

In these months the problem of dealing with former Nazis could not be ignored. It was difficult to know who had a completely clean record. My friends from both the Conservative and Socialist parties helped me to avoid too close association with those who had bad histories. I knew, for instance, that the Nazis who had been interested in the valuable magnesite deposits in east Austria were trying to consolidate their position. I was able to help the American Winter family interests in Pittsburgh to maintain their participation, although the matter was not completely resolved even in 1979.

Some of the bankers had had questionable relations. One man who had compromised in 1938 and had also helped the Nazis had later given the Americans important information. He came to me late on a Friday evening asking me to help keep him out of jail. I called some of my friends in the security branch and turned the matter over to them. Their decision was that the help he had rendered to British bombing squadrons (by way of the OSS in Switzerland) about the plants making V-2 bombs at Peenemünde, in Germany, outweighed the compromises he had earlier made with Nazi financial authorities. He stayed free, although he lost most of his financial power and resources. He lived in fear and trembling, for he knew we knew his varied activities.

Since the impression grew that I had influence over supplies and funds controlled by the Army, I was offered small bribes or presents, which of course I refused. I was not able to engage in even the minor black market activities of many of my colleagues, since I was close to the financial decisions and had to have clean hands. I had bought an Alfa Romeo from an American major for $2,000 when my Dodge broke down. Willy Teufenstein offered me $4,000 or more in schillings. I had to say no. He bought it for half this price. The radio I borrowed for a few weeks I returned. The food smuggled in from Hungary by an Austrian friend I paid for in dollars. My actions were motivated not only by a sense of honor but also by the fact that once tainted with any corruption, I would be under suspicion by my Austrian friends and downgraded by my colleagues. In no way did I engage in the cigarette and liquor traffic, so I came home to the United States poorer than when I left it.

If I was poorer in money and possessions, I was richer in my sense of being able to manage the government apparatus. I knew that I had helped not only with the industrial recovery but indirectly with the state treaty assuring Austrian independence.

After the November election when I had talked with the Minister for Construction and officials in other departments including Commerce, Labor, Agriculture, and Transportation, I decided to take a more active role in stimulating industrial recovery. I had not been assigned this work and had only limited authority. Moreover, there were a number of amateur economists in the American diplomatic mission and I found their dealings with the Austrians were confusing the issues. They did not have enough knowledge of the economic potential, nor of past traditions. I decided that lacking rank the only way I could handle the situation was to upstage these men. It was a simple matter to engage them in technical conversations where they were over their heads. After a few weeks some decided to work more with the military and they left the economic field largely to me.

My new and self-appointed responsibilities were seriously threatened only once by Jack Erhardt. Shortly after the turn of the year, in 1946, Jack called me to his office. He said, "You have been talking to the Minister of Commerce."

"Yes, sir."

"You were in the National Bank on Monday."

"Yes, sir."

"You had the Minister for Reconstruction to dinner."

"Yes, sir."

"Well, don't make any mistakes."

"No, sir."

We both laughed and I went my way. I decided to make my own decisions even if there were a risk I might be sent home. It was worth taking that chance.

There were several extraordinarily competent economists with the military and I spent considerable time with them both in four-power committees and in various preparatory sessions. Among the generals, Jesse Balmer was particularly helpful. While there was some rivalry between the State Department and the military, it was not a serious problem. We all worked together with the OSS officers and were informed of the large Soviet shipments out of the country over the Easter weekend. We understood that the nationalization of the Austrian banks was not so much a socialist move as an action taken to thwart the Soviet seizure of their assets. The agreement between State Department and military officers was surprisingly effective. I was satisfied with the results. I did not expect public credit but secretly gave myself medals for the accomplishment, which I could observe as the result of our combined efforts.

For part of this time I had an assistant, Ruth Heller. She was slim, agile, eager, and high-strung. We had much the same interests. She spoke excellent German and drove a small Ford with skill over the mountain passes and through the small villages. We had to secure gray cards, issued by the Americans and approved by the Russians, to go out of Vienna since the access roads crossed the Soviet zone of occupation. We were anxious during our drive through the Russian zone. We had to keep to the main roads. Even a minor accident would bring us trouble. When we reached the British, American, and French zones, we were free to go in any direction.

We explored various industrial centers. We learned that the Austrians were not primarily concerned with drinking, dancing, and music but that they were hard workers, energetically trying to make the prostrate economy work. We were well received and sat in the cafés with local dignitaries and visited many of the factory managers. Adventuring around the country gave us a clear knowledge of what Austria could produce. With this information we tried to guide the military authorities in their disposal of fuel from Germany and raw materials from surplus dumps as well as the use of aid funds. It was fun to find new places and meet new people. We usually took army food with us to supplement the small rations the Austrians could supply and gave some of it to the innkeepers. We did not have special permission for these trips and planned them on our own.

I took some weekends off for pleasure with my children and friends. One excursion was particularly memorable. I was usually prudent but on that summer's day I took chances that nearly ended in disaster. With me that Sunday were the children, David and Ann, Fritz Hörlesberger, and an American, Matthew Marks, on temporary duty for the Treasury Department.

I knew that the Soviets had absolute power in their zone. An Austrian woman friend of mine, a high official, was taken from her car near Linz and held under arrest in Russia for six years. A man of my acquaintance had been kidnapped and disappeared forever. One of our officers, driving in the wrong zone at night, was beaten to death—but that was later.

When I picked up Fritz and Matthew in my old blue Dodge, the children were with me. We had a picnic lunch. Fritz proposed that we drive some twenty-five miles to Mayerling of romantic tradition.

"How can we get through the Russian roadblocks?" I asked.

"I'll tell you where to drive," he said. "There are small roads of no interest to the Soviets. No one will stop us."

"All right," I replied, "but keep me away from their military headquarters—Baden bei Wien."

Unexpectedly, on a small road leading to the mountains, we

came to a barrier. A short, almond-eyed, Mongolian-type soldier challenged us. I had my passport and a pink driver's license. Pink was the color of the Austrian identity card which permitted Austrians to travel freely throughout the four zones of military occupation. I showed my license, which they assumed was the Austrian pass. There was no conversation, as we had no common language. They raised the boom and we drove on, but I had become alarmed. I knew we were getting dangerously close to Baden. I asked Fritz to guide me back to Vienna.

Then, at the next roadblock, we met a Russian captain. A tall, handsome man, armed to the teeth. He was having no nonsense. In halting German he asked to get in the car. He sat in front with David between him and me. David was fascinated by his pistols, daggers, bullet belt, and medals.

We drove, under instructions, to a small, two-story school building that had been taken over as an office. He took the men first, to the left through a side door. Then he came back for me. The children stayed in the car. They had Coca-Cola and sandwiches.

I told them, "Eat your lunch and play near the car."

When I was in the upstairs room with three Russian officers, I knew I was defenseless. Their questions, in German, were strictly nonpolitical, or so it seemed. They asked about the automobile, its horsepower, cylinders, spark plugs, carburetor. Since I did not know the answers, I gave them various figures from one to twenty. They wrote them down on a piece of brown wrapping paper with other notes. I was scared but calm.

The next questions were more difficult.

Why was I in Austria?

I did not want to mention the State Department.

"I am a widow with two children. There are many men here without wives. The army soldiers are attractive. It seems a sensible place to look for a husband."

This answer seemed to convince them—I was a camp follower. They said, "Horoschow, okay."

After talking to me for some time and looking over their notes, the captain said, "Leave, and *nicht zuruck*, you must not come back."

"Yes, sir," I said, and followed him down the stairs.

The children had consumed the food and drink. They were playing with a young Russian boy. David's red Swiss Army knife had accidentally cut the boy's hand, but David bandaged it.

[214]

All seemed well, but I wondered, "What next?" Finally my companions appeared, shaken and silent. "Show me the way home," I said to Fritz. I have never been back.

By Christmas of 1946, a considerable number of dependents were in Vienna and the children were with us when we went through the American sector of Vienna, singing carols. The Russians had a big villa in the middle of the American sector. They had pigs in the garden which they brought into the house during the winter. We sang carols and four officers came out on the balcony. They were confused. They appreciated our coming, but they were suspicious of capitalist music and of the Baby Jesus. Their applause was perfunctory, as if they were not quite sure whether they should thank us or not.

Then we went to Chancellor Figl's house nearby, a much more modest residence than that of the Russians.

Whenever possible, I shared travel and social life with the children. Ann and David saw a fine exhibit of the famed Lippizan horses at Wels, south of Linz, in the American zone. I was one of a half-dozen people who in addition to General Patton, have reason to claim they saved these marvelous animals from being taken to the East. It doesn't matter where credit lies; obviously generals were responsible for official actions, but some of us helped persuade the generals the importance of saving them.

For entertainment David had resources of his own, based on an American army dependent's pass. With it he rode all over Vienna, on the street cars. He amassed an amazing array of empty shell cases and eventually a collection of twenty-eight different types of soldiers' helmets.

There were many unusual aspects to our life with the Army. Our access to the Post Exchange was new to us—so were a number of military facilities. The children reveled in the doughnut and coffee shop, drinking innumerable Coca-Colas. They could also go to American movies free by showing their identity card. They were very well treated by the soldiers and spent considerable time in the Red Cross centers. The Soviet soldiers who roamed our sector of the city were friendly. David, who was studying Russian, tried occasional conversations with them.

There was a fair amount of crime and we knew that there was some danger from desperate refugees and unrestrained soldiers. Our dog was stolen and we suffered for we knew the animal would probably be eaten. When we advertised for its return, we had telephone calls saying we should be ashamed to care more for animals than for people who might be starving.

We had many parties in our house. My economic status was a new one to me. I was postponing my income tax payments, living on rations, paying Trudy and Relly ten dollars each as a monthly wage, and had a chauffeur who also received ten dollars as a monthly wage. Our household included a cleaning woman and laundress as well. It was luxurious living.

One of the best parties in my new residence was given for the four financial elements in the Allied Commission. The guests, about thirty in all, drank, sang, and danced to the music of a string quartet until six o'clock Sunday morning. The Soviet contingent of two officers played the piano and sang. Each drank one highball and at ten-thirty they bade me good night.

I did not know until two weeks later what had happened when my Russian guests left. We continued to meet as usual in the committee and their courtesy and friendliness were unmarred. But army friends of mine told me that the night of my party a cordon had been thrown around the area and in a general sweep they had picked up all the Russians who were in the *bezirk* (district). The officers from my party were held in jail for twenty-four hours while the search went on for two Russian soldiers who had shot an American and stolen a jeep. My Soviet guests were not surprised and not resentful. They were pleased to be held no longer.

The party had been very gay. I decided to retire at about 5 A.M., when Willy, my chauffeur, came to me. He said, "One of your friends outside needs help."

I went into the street and saw a senior British official sitting on the curb, leaning against a lamppost. He did indeed need help. I hailed a military jeep coming down the street and asked the sergeant-driver if he would take my friend to the Hotel Regina. I knew that the room Joan, my niece, had there would be empty as she was staying with me. Then I called the hotel concierge and told him, "A friend will be delivered to you in a few minutes. Would you please have someone put him to bed in Miss Dulles' room?"

The next morning, when I was struggling to awaken at about eleven o'clock, Trudy told me I had a caller. I went down to greet this same British friend.

"I have to leave for England at one o'clock," he said. "But I wanted to thank you for the party. It was great fun and I'm so glad I was there. Certainly, everything was laid on."

He did not tell me how puzzled he was to awaken alone, in the middle of a room cluttered with a young girl's dresses and toilet articles.

Along with the fun, there were moments of tension and anxiety. I had driven to Munich for a meeting with some economic officers there, and although it was not far, stayed overnight and returned the next noon. When I got home I found the household in a state of great excitement. About eleven o'clock the night before, a man had climbed the balcony and tried to get into my son's room. David had let out a bellow that was heard from roof to cellar. The intruder jumped to the ground. He hurt his foot, as we knew by the footprints in the garden, and escaped over the back fence. Since there had been many kidnappings in Vienna, the army security officers decided to post an Austrian civilian in the house at night to prevent another intrusion. After ten days I decided the risk was negligible and asked the Army to remove the watchman. I did not like the atmosphere of fear his presence created, and David and the rest of our household agreed.

That winter of 1947 was the coldest in many years. It was so cold that the plans restricting wages in Germany had to be changed so there could be more mining to produce coal for reconstruction. Goods of every kind were difficult to find. Even the occupying forces felt some privation. For example, when the fuel pump on my car broke, I had to buy new means of transportation.

My new fuel pump for the Dodge was airmailed from New York. Later in my rehabilitated car, the chauffeur was driving too close to the barrier on a mountain road. He scraped the chrome strip off the side. By that time I knew nothing could be easily replaced, so I told him to stop the car and I jumped into the lake, which was eight feet deep at that point, and picked up the strip, putting it back in the car. It was summer and my dress soon dried in the warm air.

[217]

Early in 1948, before Washington's Birthday, I drove to Budapest with my son, David, and several friends. On our way back we were caught in a snowstorm. We reached a point between Hungary and the little slice of Czechoslovakia that cuts the Vienna road, and the car went into a ditch. After we had wrecked the clutch, trying to get back on the road, another American car, driven by an officer of the AID mission, John Curtis, came along. He tried to get around us, but he also went off the road. I had a heater in my car, so John joined us and I found the food in my baggage which I always carried for emergencies—cookies, chocolate, and oranges. We put on socks and sweaters. I suggested a heat and fuel rationing plan.

"As soon as the frost forms on the inside of the car, we will turn on the heater. When it melts, we'll turn it off."

Several cars passed, including a Russian truck. I ran to it and the driver allowed me to put my hands on the tailgate, then laughed and drove off, leaving me tottering in the middle of the road. At dawn, out of the fog, I saw two huge horses coming down the road, hauling a rig on which a Czech peasant sat. Since I spoke no Czech, to communicate I began showing him money. First I tried Hungarian currency, and he shrugged his shoulders. He was also uninterested in Austrian money and even Swiss francs. But when I took out some American dollars, he reacted quickly. Hitching up the horses to the car, he leaped on his rig, and we were dragged down the road to a little town called Ruzoczi, and to a café there.

As I recall the scene in my mind's eye the café was like a stage setting. It had a potbellied stove, around which were gathered a shoemaker, a forester, a policeman, a postman, and other villagers. They made way for us and as we warmed ourselves, I could hear "fascismus, communismus, dictatorship," words I could recognize. I thought that I had never been in a town where everyone was so politically minded. These simple peasants were talking politics on Tuesday morning at about nine o'clock.

We didn't know then that there had been a coup in Prague.

I decided to go to the town post office and see if I could telephone Bratislava, also in Czechoslovakia. When I got through, Claiborne Pell, now Senator Pell of Rhode Island, answered. He was consul at Bratislava and said he would send a car down for us.

After a long interval the car still had not come and again I made my way through deep snow to the post office and got the consulate at Bratislava on the line. The staff told me *their* car had started for us, but was stuck in the snow. They suggested the possibility of catching a train if one were available. Late in the afternoon we left Ruzoczi on an antique two-car train which brought us to Bratislava. The people in our consulate knew more about the coup than we did, but not much. We went to the British consulate across the street from the Russians' office. The Russians had dozens of people gathered in cars and outside on the walk. At the British consulate we listened to the radio announcement that Eduard Beneš, the President, would speak. We waited and waited but he never did. He had been taken to the hospital.

As the Czech-Austrian border was shut, it was several days before we could leave Bratislava. This was the reason for my participation in the Russian take-over of Czechoslovakia. I kept learning more each month about Soviet intentions. My car was not towed back to Vienna for ten days.

The Austrians had learned the hard way in 1945 that it was difficult to work with the Russian soldiers. It was not until 1948, however, that they realized it was not only the unruly military but the political leaders who were a threat to their freedom.

In October the leaders of the Socialist party, among them Adolf Schärf and Andreas Korp, went to Prague for a conference. They came to my house for supper the evening of their return to Vienna.

"We cannot work with the Russian socialists," Schärf said. "They have a different philosophy and different aims."

Schärf was later to be President of Austria. Now, some thirty years later I remember with real affection his speech at a farewell supper given for me by the Socialist party in October 1948, before I left Austria. He died in 1965.

Negotiations for the Austrian State Treaty from 1947 on were long and tortuous, with many frustrations. To understand how complicated and difficult they were, one has to go back to conversations of Churchill, Stalin, and Truman at Potsdam in 1945, and before that to the Yalta meeting, subsequent Council of Foreign Ministers (CFM) meetings of representatives of Britain, France, Russia, and the United States in 1946 and 1947.

Ten years and four Secretaries of State later, in 1955, Foster signed the treaty in Vienna.

My first exposure to the problem had been in December 1946, when I flew with Erhardt to London. He asked me to go with him.

We went in a C-47 through fog and snow. The pilot said to us before we reached the halfway point in our journey, "Prepare for a drop. I've got to go down several hundred feet to shake the ice off the wings."

I said to him, "If the ice doesn't come off the wings, where will we land?"

"We won't," he said.

"I withdraw the question."

A moment later he said, "The weather's closing everything down. London and Paris are out. So is Frankfurt. I'm going to try Brussels."

We put down outside Brussels with little warning to the authorities but glad to be on the ground. The Belgians thought it would have been more convenient if we had put down someplace else. It was so late that the officials had gone home and we had to send for special security officers to clear us through the airport.

The next morning we went off early to London where the Council of Foreign Ministers was meeting to discuss Austria and Germany. I saw Foster, went to one of the meetings, and had time to see my friend Nicholas, whom I had seen in 1945 in London. After two days Foster and Janet left for Paris, where Foster had conversations with two great Frenchmen, Robert Schuman and Jean Monnet. Secretary of State James Byrnes was in London and had agreed that it was a good idea for Foster to talk to Monnet and Schuman about European economic cooperation. The ideas they explored were forerunners of the Marshall Plan.

This episode was never publicized and, in fact, Foster told his colleagues that he had taken Janet to Paris to see if she could find a new hat.

After a brief visit Erhardt and I returned to Vienna.

The CFM in London requested that there be a meeting in Moscow in March. This later meeting came just after the Truman Doctrine was announced in Washington.

Foster asked General Clark if Clark would let me go to Berlin to talk to him about European conditions, before he went on to Moscow. I flew up with Clark and Erhardt and stayed with my friend, Elizabeth Holt. My friend of long standing knew Berlin well. I had several meetings with Foster and was with him on the afternoon when George Marshall, newly appointed Secretary of State, came in from Washington. I saw the two men meet at the

Army Wannsee Guest House in Berlin, not for the first time, but for the first time without several others present. Each seemed tense but pleased to have this encounter.

Foster went on to Moscow with Generals Marshall and Clark. General Lucius D. Clay, Erhardt, and other officers accompanied them. I was told later that Mark Clark asked his officers to see that Foster had little or no opportunity to confer with Marshall, but Clark admired his firmness in difficult circumstances. He did not feel easy with Foster and apparently he wanted him bottled up. He did not trust diplomats and feared Foster's ability to influence General Marshall.

During the meetings in Vienna in 1947, arranged in Moscow, practically no progress was made. One interesting step was taken, however. It had been agreed at Potsdam and Yalta that Austria would not pay reparations but that "former German assets" should be assigned to the Allies as an alternative for them. We discussed all that summer what a former German asset was—what definition could be agreed on.

The Russians, in the efforts to increase the assets they would take, claimed that if a Jew had sold his property to a German, even though the Jew had been jailed and then offered his freedom if he would make the transfer to the Nazi, he was acting freely and voluntarily. We argued that this was coercion. The issue was tossed back and forth each day. Finally, one of the men on the American delegation thought of an idea to resolve the property question. Since it had not been cleared by Washington, he decided that he would suggest this new approach to the French delegates and not raise the issue in the American delegation. This would save weeks of bureaucratic delay. The idea was that we would substitute a lump sum payment in lieu of a case-by-case settlement. One hundred and fifty million dollars was the sum chosen. The Russians would be paid this and a considerable share of the oil recently found in Austria. The remainder of the assets in Austria would be considered Austrian property.

Somewhat to our surprise, the Russians accepted this arrangement, so we entered a new phase of negotiations, even though the meetings went on debating other questions, with respect to refugees and neutrality. Following the 1947 meeting, which had accomplished almost nothing, a commission under the deputies was called and met in Austria, to be followed by 247 more meetings over the next seven years until the sudden change in the Soviets' attitude came with the ascendancy of Khrushchev.

The meetings that began in Vienna had been continued in New York. But it wasn't until the Soviets had an indication that we considered it essential to *go ahead* with the plans we had already blocked out that they finally agreed to sign the Austrian Treaty.

The explanation lay in the power struggle of Khrushchev in Moscow. In 1955 Khrushchev indicated to Foster, then Secretary of State, that he thought a summit meeting was important and would like one with President Eisenhower. Foster said there could be no possibility of a summit meeting unless the Soviets "showed by deeds" that they were willing to make some compromises. Only this would permit negotiations with some prospect of success.

Even then, there was a setback. The Russians insisted that neutrality, the neutrality of Austria, be put in the treaty. Foster objected. He did not think it was consistent with the Austrian sovereignty that the treaty was to establish. For a short time in 1955 it looked as if the Soviets were not going to sign after all. We made no moves to change our position, and after twenty-four anxious hours and without further explanation, they agreed. The treaty was signed in the Belvedere Palace on May 15, 1955.

The fact that Austria gained steadily from the first days of our work there, in spite of the large removals of capital and equipment by the Russians from the Soviet zone, is proof of the constructive nature of the Western powers' decisions. More and more factories opened. And even before the Marshall Plan began to pump resources into the economy in 1948, the signs of recovery and the hard work of the Austrians convinced the outside world that the country would be able to stand on its own feet after outside help was terminated.

Before the presidential election of 1948 the U.N. General Assembly had met in Paris and Foster was a member of the delegation. He was specifically instructed by Secretary Marshall to report anything of interest to Thomas Dewey, then the Republican presidential candidate—assumed by many to be the next President.

I went to the head of Press Affairs in Vienna and told him it would be useful to have Foster visit Vienna.

"Why?" he asked.

"He may be the next Secretary of State," I answered.

[222]

"Well, perhaps we should ask him, but I don't quite see the purpose," he commented.

He talked to the generals and it was decided to invite Foster and to set up a press conference for him. During this visit Foster learned a great deal about the Balkans and the Danube area. He had a growing interest in Austria.

I gave a luncheon to which I invited many prominent Austrian leaders and newsmen. At noon, as it turned out, Foster had to leave for Frankfurt and Berlin on the airlift, at General Clay's request. I left at the same time to fly to Paris and confer with Governor Averell Harriman about the Marshall Plan for Austria. Lunch went on without us. Later that night Foster and I met Janet for dinner in Paris. Foster's solicitude for Austria was greatly increased by this short visit and his meeting with the leaders there. The whole picture of the relations with the Soviets and the treaty struggle came alive for him.

The Marshall Plan gave a tremendous boost to the economy. I remember particularly the summer of 1948. I had been sent orders to return to Washington. I thought it a critical time for the work I had begun and found a way to telephone through to my brother Allen in Washington, explaining to him that it would not be a good thing for me to leave just then. A few days later my orders were canceled and I stayed on.

The Austrian economists and politicians were puzzled as to how to go about getting aid. I decided I must act. I called a group of Austrian officials to the office on Boltzmangasse. I asked, "How much cotton do you need? How much coal?"

"We don't know," they answered.

"Can't you calculate?"

One explained, "We have been a part of the German economy and have no experience with planning for Austrian imports."

I had a list of pre-Anschluss imports. I said, "I'll tell you how many bales, how many tons of key imports are needed."

They wrote down my figures, protesting, "Too much," or "Too little," as I called them out.

From the argument that followed, I got a list of some thirty key raw materials. These figures they agreed could be used as a basis for discussion in the European Cooperation meeting. Armed with this theoretical schedule of needs, two of the ablest Austrians went to

Paris. There they bargained with representatives from other countries, and with Paul Hoffman, Averell Harriman, and Richard Bissell. The Marshall funds were in effect a pie to be divided among the sixteen members. Priorities had to be established. Dickering between nations brought final decisions, and in a few months the paper plans brought shiploads of imports for Europe.

In October another set of orders came through from the State Department, so I packed for Washington. David had already gone back to attend school at Putney, Vermont. Ann was still with me. Trudy and Relly wanted to come, but the law with regard to displaced persons did not yet permit visas. They had to wait some months.

An important phase of my life was ending. Although the early weeks of my work in Austria were difficult and I even considered resigning and returning home, I finally arrived at a solution to my major problems which made the years there among the most satisfying of my life.

In September 1945 I found my men colleagues reluctant to give a woman a chance. They assumed they should take charge.

My solution was to think out what would be most constructive for Austria, who would be able to help in achieving these objectives, and then to go forward as if I had the power and the authority. When Erhardt realized that I was going ahead on my own, and when in his shrewd and somewhat intuitive way he recognized that I was making progress, he was amused and pleased. I took chances and he thought this interesting and useful. He was even gratified that some of the men who tried to thwart me were sidetracked. He began to give me leeway and support. I took a gamble but it paid off. My months in Austria, more than any before, gave me a chance to use my previous education, economic experience, and then after the day's work, to drink and dance and enjoy pleasant social contacts. It was a well-rounded life, supported by friends, a good family life, and an efficient household staff. It was a time when I felt excitement and pride of accomplishment.

It was strange and unpredictable that the very qualities that made me doubt at first if I could work with Jack Erhardt led to the extraordinary opportunities and mutual understanding by the end of my tour of duty. The fact that he was an eccentric and that he acted

[224]

on instinct rather than by the book gave me my chance. If I had not been willing to take risks and act on my own initiative, I would not have had the fine experience of those years. In the end my determination to do what seemed constructive made him take me seriously and added affection to our cordial official relationship.

He knew I had been transferred to Washington, so it was no surprise when I told him I was leaving. I planned to leave Friday night, October 30. Jack said, "You can't go Friday. I'm giving a party for you Saturday night."

I changed my plans.

The party was for about thirty people, most of the Austrian Cabinet, all of the senior mission officers, and a few other friends.

After the speeches that reflected three and a half years of work and friendships, the other mission officers came in and we danced. I realized, according to protocol, I must leave first. So I went to Erhardt to thank him. He took my arm and made a sweeping gesture to the others, while we waltzed. They formed a large semicircle. Erhardt danced me to the first man in line, and I danced with him and then the others in turn. Then Erhardt took me out to the courtyard where the car was waiting, and the men threw roses after me. I went home in a dreamlike haze. Almost at once I started the long drive over Austria, Switzerland, and France.

My trip from Vienna was punctuated by news flashes on the car radio about the American presidential vote. As I drove north through Burgundy, the Loire, and into Paris, I heard the French radio commentators say, "Truman is winning the election."

I thought they had their information mixed and they didn't know which was which. I was very tired when I drove over the Place de la Concorde to the American Embassy. Nonchalantly parking in the ambassador's slot, I walked over to the Crillon, carrying our poodle, Daisy, and guiding Ann with the other hand.

I got in the elevator with Mrs. Eleanor Roosevelt and Ben Cohen, United States delegates to the U.N. General Assembly. They were smiling broadly and did not notice me in their excitement.

When I got off at the suite on the second floor, I saw Janet, dressed in an evening gown, Foster, in white tie and tails.

"Is it true?" I asked.

"Yes. Dewey lost," Janet said.

She ordered supper brought up for Ann and me before she and Foster went out to a dinner party given in their honor. Ann and I went to bed, exhausted by the two days of driving from Austria.

The next morning we started for Le Havre and caught the S.S. *America*. We tied up in New York during a docker's strike and had to leave the car on the ship. Fritz Molden, Joan's fiancé, met us at the boat. We arrived safely at Allen's house on Sixty-first Street with but one minor catastrophe—the Hungarian doll that Ann had brought back with her had been stolen.

My share in Austrian history continued with two celebrations years later. I was twice invited by the Austrian Government to be their guest in honoring the State Treaty first at the tenth anniversary in 1965 and then in 1975. In 1965 I sat behind Andrei Gromyko and Dean Rusk. The ceremony was in the Belvedere Castle, its balcony overlooking fountains and gardens. It was there that representatives of the Big Four had stood in 1955.

I saw many old friends, though I missed many who had died, especially Leopold Figl— "Poldy," as we called him. He had died two days before I arrived. I went to the High Mass in St. Stephan's Cathedral. I almost wept as the mountain boys marched down the aisle with flags of the outlying regions, their ruddy faces solemn in the cathedral candlelight.

I walked in the funeral procession, feeling deeply the debt we owed this brave man. If I were to write a book about Austria, I would dedicate it to Figl. All of us in the democratic world can be proud of his courage and his deeds.

In 1975, thirty years after my slow crossing of the Atlantic in a convoy, I flew to Vienna again. My friends still remembered what I had done for the nation in the desperate times after the war's end and Foster's achievement of the State Treaty in 1955.

The city had been in ruins in 1945. It was shining, brilliant in 1975. The citizens had put aside their recollections of the Anschluss that brought the nation under the Nazis, the grim years of war, and difficult struggle for recovery. The people under forty could not visualize those times; they knew only vaguely of the struggle in attaining the State Treaty, but they gloried in the beauty of their city.

The older people remembered. They remembered and were grateful. Some came to my hotel with flowers. Many cheered at the

Belvedere Castle on the anniversary of the treaty signing. Earlier my brother, in presenting me a beautiful Austrian inlaid box on my birthday, had written, "To Eleanor with love for June 1, 1955, and in memory of another happy day, May 15, 1955, Vienna—a day which you helped to bring about. Foster."

# 18

# SEX DISCRIMINATION IN THE STATE DEPARTMENT

My years in Austria had been recognized as highly successful both by the Austrian Government and by my co-workers. As I drove through the Inn Valley, its mountains bright with golden aspen and rich with dark pine, I wondered what would come next after the months of excitement and creative work. I returned to Washington on the crest of a wave. I was glad to have my children back in the United States. I was glad to be close to my brothers and sisters. I was glad to be back in my own house.

But the months after my return in November of 1948 were to be the worst in my professional experience. They were even more frustrating than my last months at the Social Security Board. There my problems had centered on policy and personalities. Now they were to be rooted in sex discrimination.

Women in the State Department are a problem—to themselves and to the men in the department. A few women have made the grade by combining superior ability with infinite patience. A few have fought with no holds barred, knowing that many men did not accept them as equals. Some have endured in silence, some have resigned, and during the last decade, a number have protested, publicly, legally, and loudly.

My own experience was to include all the problems women face in the service. Many people jump to the conclusion that my brothers, Foster and Allen, helped me with my career. The reverse is true. While people in other countries where I worked assumed I had a higher rank than I had, in other respects, having a brother who headed the CIA and another who was Secretary of State, was not an advantage.

Of the two, Foster in his official position was more of a handicap than Allen. Those who liked Foster feared to favor me because they knew how totally he rejected nepotism. Those who disliked him told me so on several occasions, in no uncertain terms. In my working hours I saw no more of my brothers in the office than did my colleagues in similar positions.

In 1953, in his initial days as Secretary of State, Foster asked me to resign. I was working on Berlin by then. I told him I would be no bother to him and asked him to let me stay on trial for a month. At the end of the month, to the day, he called me and said, "All right. Good-bye." Permission had been granted, but the brevity of his comment indicated the amount of assistance on the job I could expect as long as he was Secretary.

But on my return from Austria in 1948 Foster was not yet Secretary. My problems were the same as those faced by most women in the Department. I was confronting a clear case of attempted exclusion from a man's world.

Professor Jeane J. Kirkpatrick, in her book *Political Woman* (Basic Books, 1975) has well described the situation that I found so frustrating. She writes of four "put-downs" used by male legislators on forty-six woman legislators who had served more than one term as state representatives. They were women who already had job experience, just as I had. The "put-downs" are categorized by Professor Kirkpatrick as (1) Excluding, (2) Killing with Kindness, (3) Emphasizing Differences, and (4) Putting Women in Their Place.

In "Killing with Kindness," she quotes a woman legislator:

> In the beginning I was submitted to the most subtle form of put-down. It is over-chivalrous, over-protected, over-courteous, and you're sort of bowed to and scraped to when you first come in. You are given first choice of seat, then other members get seats in the order of seniority. You're treated like a very bright child.

This approach I found the most difficult to combat, although eventually, I experienced all four types of "put-downs."

I knew the maze of Washington would present me with jurisdictional problems and the question of organization and rank that I had circumvented in Austria. But the sexist discrimination puzzled me.

I had been working on the Austrian treaty problem, and did not yet know I would be barred from further serious work on the treaty. My assistant was a man who said that *he* had been told by the division chief that because I was a woman, he would not have to take me seriously. This was his explanation of why he hid cables relative to my work. Shortly before, I had been told I would not be promoted to second place because the chief did not want a woman for his deputy.

It seemed a hopeless situation. Not only was I not getting advancement and salary increases, but I was not getting appropriate work.

Before I had time to search for a solution to my problem, one presented itself.

Into my office came a lean, sarcastic man who slouched in the chair as he asked me questions about copper, steel, and machinery. His name was Malcolm Slaght. After ten minutes of questions, seeming to have little to do with my work at that time, I grew impatient.

"I have work to do," I said to him. "What do you want?"

He said, "I'd like to offer you a job. I've been told by Captain Charlie Hersum in Commerce that you can make up your mind—that you are decisive."

"I don't want to leave State."

"You can be detailed to Commerce at a higher grade, and return later on."

I took the job. It seemed psychologically and financially imperative that I do so. I sometimes wonder if I hadn't, whether I could have long endured the situation at State.

My new job was at the National Production Authority, a temporary unit under the Department of Commerce. It issued priorities for export of machinery. Without these, certain items could not be sold overseas. We were protecting the industrial buildup intended to support the Korean War. Our decisions meant a great deal to a number of large American manufacturing firms, including General Electric, Caterpillar Tractor, International Harvester, and Minneapolis Honeywell. I found my work in industry helped me to understand the relative importance of products, although I admit I had never known that a Caterpillar tractor was, of all American products, perhaps the most prized by buyers abroad.

My assignments included representing NPA on the Petroleum Committee for Defense, under the Department of the Interior. I remember the confidence shown by Interior officials in 1951 in the sufficiency of oil—from U.S. reserves, Canada, and Venezuela. The long lines at gasoline stations twenty years later during the shortage of 1973 and 1979 must have come as a shock to some of the officials at Interior.

[230]

I also sat on the COCOM, which developed the list of items barred from export to communist countries. This program was in some degree the result of the report from Vienna I had written in 1947, outlining the dangers to the U.S. position in Austria caused by Soviet seizures. The banned list and the Battle Act, which refused aid to nations exporting strategic materials to communist countries, came shortly after this report reached Washington.

At NPA I was working with people largely unfettered by old-line tradition—people respectful of ability. My co-workers were highly intelligent, practical, and witty. They did their job effectively, but remained unimpressed and unsubdued by the contorted machine of bureaucracy. Work and wit were not mutually exclusive.

There was the report on *bort*. When Mal Slaght asked me to research *bort*, he was really playing a practical joke. He assumed I didn't know what it was, but I accepted the assignment without question. He really wanted to see if his assumption was correct. When I told him I had never heard of *bort*, he said, "Do some research."

I found that *bort* is a powder, a by-product of industrial diamonds, supplied principally by South Africa. It is needed to produce hard, steel cutting tools for the manufacture of defense equipment. We were in short supply but the Russians were not. They had supplemented their supplies with an alternative electrolytic process. My assignment on *bort* may have started as a Slaght joke, but it ended in the NPA's recommendation to increase stocks to meet the demands for supplying our forces in Korea.

Life at NPA was also brightened by "the battle of the windows." A perennial concern we all shared was retention of our office—one of the few with two windows. The building, now occupied by the General Services Administration, is a solid block, providing its occupants with an impression of working underground, except for a very limited number of offices on the outer walls with windows. There was a continuous bureaucratic battle to attain an office with a window, not only for the view but for the *prestige* involved in possessing anything in such short supply.

Attempts were made to wrest our bewindowed office from us. A woman administrative officer in Commerce was constantly being approached by personnel in other committees and divisions who sought to banish us to the windowless interior while they took over our territory. Slaght countered these moves, with our help, alternatively inviting her to lunch or dropping veiled threats.

While the NPA provided a pleasant interlude, it was not helping me to solve my problem of how to continue work in foreign affairs—work I had begun at State. I had other problems—to provide a decent homelife for my children, to earn enough money for their education, and to find an outlet for leftover energy (this has been a lifelong problem).

By 1950 I had decided on a new house. The idea of a swimming pool had always been attractive and I found it would be difficult under District regulations to build a pool on my sloping, heavily treed property.

After some persuasion, I got Clara Beyer of the Labor Department to sell me an acre and a half of a large cornfield outside McLean, Virginia. It was just off Old Dominion Drive, a twenty-five minute drive from the White House. A young architect whom Clara knew, Nicholas Satterlee, agreed to work with me. I told him the reason I would like a relatively inexperienced man, at the beginning of his career, to do this for me. I expected to have a lot to say about the design. Many architects insist on the building they think would do credit to them, not the one that suited their client. When I had built the house on Chain Bridge Road, I had to wait until the fine architect Gertrude Sawyer went on vacation before I added a balcony to suit my taste.

Nick Satterlee and I worked together on the design to make the one-story house embracing a swimming pool. Even before the house was started, the pool was built and in operation.

The day the Korean War broke out I was in that pool with Barbara and Covey Oliver; Covey was later ambassador to Colombia. We were shocked almost speechless as we tried to think of the future, full of apprehension on that bright Sunday, June 25. We had taken our lunch and spent the day in and out of the water.

A few days before I had given a party for the Austrian ambassador and his staff. We had a Mai Bowle, white wine, and strawberries. We undressed in the cars, and we swam, sang, and shared the strawberries. Then at dark, we went back to my home on Chain Bridge Road in the District and finished our Heurige (wine party) in the warm evening, under Japanese lanterns, with an accordion player accompanying us as we sang Austrian songs until the morning.

[232]

When it came to signing the contract for the new house with the builder, as soon as the ink was dry, I said, "Please buy the lumber, cement, kitchen, and plumbing equipment. I have arranged with a neighbor [Clara] to store them in her barn, and with a bank to borrow the money."

"Why?" he asked.

"There's a war on," I said. "Prices will go up, shortages will plague us, and the building will drag out over a long period."

This prospect had not occurred to him. Acting on my suggestion, we saved most of our price rise, although we were caught for a time by the lack of cement. But my years of financial research had saved me some thousands of dollars.

That summer I used to drive out in the evening after supper with my Polish friend to note the progress and to have a swim in the pool. I loved to see the sturdy framing of two-by-fours and two-by-eights going up. It was the house I designed, one floor, open to the sun, a simple structure. There was a detached large bedroom and bath for Trudy and Relly Rotter. There was space for a garden and some three hundred small trees and bushes, many of which I dug up in the woods and replanted myself. The whole process of building gave me great pleasure in spite of wartime difficulties.

We moved from the city on Washington's Birthday in 1951. I had hoped to have no interruption to my work at the office, but my chief quite unnecessarily asked me to write a paper over the holiday, insisting that I go in to the office. I went for four hours. Fortunately I had friends who helped arrange the books and china.

I did not immediately sell my house on Chain Bridge Road, since I was not sure the children would prefer the new one. After a year I asked David and Ann and they both agreed that they liked McLean. I sold the classical New England-style house in town to the tenants, and worked on the garden and trees in the old cornfield in McLean, where we were then overlooking the lovely rolling meadows. The pool was a constant delight, unheated, but used at least six months of the year. Foster sometimes went swimming in December and January. Here I entertained a dozen or more ambassadors and other visiting friends from Austria, Germany, Italy, France, and other far places.

Early in November 1952, I had a dream which left me very uneasy. I had dreamed that I was searching for young Allen Dulles, a lieutenant in the Marines, fighting in Korea. I woke at six and for a reason that I cannot explain, I got in my car and drove in from McLean to Georgetown to the house of my brother Allen. I knew he was alone there and that Clover was in Switzerland. I let myself in with my key and, since it was before seven in the morning, I waited until I heard him moving about upstairs. Then I went to the bottom of the stairs—he stood there with a strange distraught look on his face. "It is young Allen," he said.

He came down and told me that the CIA had sent a message that his only son had been badly wounded in the forward battle line in Korea while leading his platoon. There was no final word as to the critical nature of the wound, but it was in his head. I stayed with Allen while he telephoned various offices and called Clover in Switzerland. Plans were made to go to Tokyo, since the boy was to be taken to Japan. It was, in fact, some weeks before he would be flown home. He had been in a coma for several days and his partial recovery was a medical miracle. He had paid a tragic price, which few would fully appreciate, serving his country in the Marines.

While building a house, I sought additional income by participating in "rebuilding the inner city." About a dozen friends and acquaintances of mine joined together in what was the first private effort of any significance in renovating houses in the heart of Washington. The area we chose comprised about eight blocks of small houses near the present-day Watergate complex, close to the White House, George Washington University, and the State Department. The buildings had deteriorated, they were rat-infested, with bad flooring and rotten staircases.

There were some of us who had some professional experience in a venture of this sort, but most of us were semiprofessionals moonlighting, engaged in a financial speculation in housing which had been neglected by the owners and by the larger real estate firms and the government.

I bought five houses, on Green's Court, for $2,500 each and added $8,000 or $9,000 each for repairs and improvements. They would now sell for a probable $100,000 each. They were eleven and twelve feet wide, two stories high, and secluded from Virginia Avenue, facing an open court. Partitions divided the narrow rooms, to make two rooms for cooking and eating downstairs, sleeping quarters upstairs.

[234]

My tenants, like those in the other fifty or sixty houses refurbished by our group, included young professional people and government workers. They had the imagination to live in tiny houses, on limited incomes, and were so compatible that a neighborhood association was formed.

Of these mews houses, about half are still standing. The ones I bought were condemned by the government, since they stood in the path of a highway being built into the city, a large complex of cement spaghetti.

However, I realized a net profit of about $20,000, including rents for a few years, and the compensation that the government paid. This money, along with smaller sums I made on real estate ventures elsewhere, enabled me to send my son and daughter through college. My notes show my salary at that time was $8,500, before taxes.

Aside from the monetary profit, this project was a change from government work—I was dealing with property I could see, planning with real material, making friends with other fellow investors and tenants in the neighborhood, and learning something about the District.

Still another outlet for my energies in 1950 was a very private project. I was much interested in the growing economic strength of the Soviet Union and devoted many evenings a week to a manuscript on the future of communism competing with capitalism. I drew up comparative advantages of each approach to the universal needs and economic capacities of mankind. I sought an analysis that would evaluate the effect of each of the two competing systems on the other. This led to a judgment of what would happen in ten, twenty, or thirty years. I read books on political philosophy.

I knew a number of CIA officers. I found them well educated and alert. I talked to them at length about East-West policy. There were two men, Bill and Nicholas, who helped me on my private project. Nicholas had lived in Russia, Bill was then in the CIA. They came to McLean on different evenings and spent considerable time criticizing, arguing, and analyzing the present and future world problems. Both had individual insight into what was to be Cold War policy. I had started this project while still at State, but my energy flagged as I got fully occupied in my new job at NPA in 1951.

At this time Coburn Kidd, a very able young officer in the State Department, was one of the men who gave me suggestions on reading. He came to me one day to tell me about a Czechoslovakian family who had immigrated to Chicago. They were so grateful to the United States that they had spent their evenings for almost a year making and dressing a doll for one of President Eisenhower's granddaughters. We called the White House and they set up an appointment in the Oval Office. The family motored from Chicago. In tense and excited anticipation they went with me to 1600 Pennsylvania Avenue. The President received us with great urbanity. The doll was spectacular. Eisenhower examined the peasant dress and the braided blond hair. "What pretty eyes," he said. "My granddaughter will be delighted." We left in a mood of euphoria. The couple went back to their hotel and they told me they sat on the bed and wept for joy.

A principal pleasure in these years came from entertaining. I had a delightful house and I wanted all my friends to enjoy it. These friends came out for supper or a swim. I was in close touch with them. We talked about Berlin, Europe, and broad policy questions—never about operational details or specific current issues. Once in a while I would have a cocktail party including my friends among the ambassadors, Germany, Austria, Italy, Switzerland, and others. When the early guests had left, we would go swimming.

A party to throw other parties in the shade was one I gave for my old friend Chancellor Julius Raab of Austria, along with a clutch of ambassadors and Cabinet-level men and their wives. When the contingent of District police on motorcycles joined the Virginia police to enter my short driveway, the quiet suburb shook with the noise of traffic and flashing lights.

I had arranged my living room so the Chancellor, seated in the large, wing-backed chair, did not see the dining room table behind him and was comfortably surrounded by guests as he smoked the dark Virginia cheroots that I had been told he liked. I had also been able to provide the carefully chosen meal that suited his diet, which my Austrian helpers, Relly and Trudy knew about. We gave him the red wine and dishes he preferred. Meanwhile, Relly and Trudy fed eighteen motorcycle policemen sandwiches at the back door.

The evening was a special combination of the formal and informal. I was told the Chancellor liked simplicity and realized that a ranch-style house in the country setting could be arranged for his comfort. For me it was a *tour de force*. It also represented an end to one phase of my work for Austria.

In 1952 I went back to the State Department from NPA. The opportunity to serve was so interesting that I decided I could not refuse. The Berlin desk proved challenging, but I continued to face situations that are typical of what many women officers still face. During a particularly tense time dealing with the problem of access to Berlin by the Allied occupation forces, cables were coming in day and night. I wanted to handle these in the normal course of my work, but was told I must not come in at night. This was the "Killing with Kindness" treatment. A woman should not work eighteen hours a day. But a foreign service officer frequently does. A younger, male officer was assigned to watch those night cables. When the time came to go abroad for an international meeting on access, the young man was sent with the Assistant Secretary to help in this crisis.

Part of the responsibility is the urgent, round-the-clock work and attendance at international conferences that comes after the apprenticeship needed to train a well-rounded senior officer. I was never sent to such conferences, even those concerning Austria or Germany. Yet I had had extraordinary experience in dealing with crises, in allocating hundreds of millions of dollars, and in fostering close relationships with foreign leaders.

By instinct and design I made a special effort to get to know citizens of any country I worked with. As often as possible I invited them to my house. I did not spend much money on this—light refreshments were enough. In Austria it was possible to have more elaborate entertaining. In Berlin I invited people to Harnack House, an army club. Sometimes I would get one of my colleagues to share a cocktail party or beer evening with me. Anyway I devoted considerable time to talking informally with newsmen, labor leaders, businessmen, their wives, and people at various levels of government. This helped me in my understanding. I visited their offices. I anticipated problems that might arise, problems not yet thought important by my male counterparts. When those problems needed solutions, I was prepared. In this way, I was able to work at a level above my official grade.

Some acquaintances who did not know me as well as my close friends said, "You are lucky you can take risks because you will be taken care of," or "You have financial resources." The truth of the matter was that I was very apprehensive of what might happen when I stood up against my superior officers. I had slender financial reserves and heavy obligations for my children. I had training, energy, and experience which I wanted to put to use. I managed— but during the sixty years of my working life I took many risks. I never did engage in outright warfare with a male-dominated Department. I decided if I were not promoted I would act as if I had been. When President Eisenhower granted me the personal rank of Minister in December 1959, many people thought I held the rank of career minister. I never did. The title was to give me readier access to top-level officials in my work abroad.

Recently Carol Laise was inspector general of the Department of State. Anne Armstrong was the first woman ambassador to the Court of St. James. There have been more than eight others—half political appointees—who were ambassadors, but we have no Golda Meir, no female counterpart of Henry Kissinger. The women in our Foreign Service who achieve recognition are exceedingly able, and exceedingly few in number.

What about the rest? There are the endurers who serve well and loyally—at a lower grade and for less pay than they deserve. There are the resigners. They leave for jobs outside of State, transferring to other less hidebound areas of government. A few enter politics, businesses, foundations, universities. In the last few years there have been increasing numbers of protestors.

Best known is Alison Palmer, described here by Mike Causey of the *Washington Post* (February 16, 1976):

> In her decade-long struggle against the powers-that-be at Foggy Bottom, she's plowed new promotion ground for women; helped FSOs (male and female) get more career due process, and pay for overtime that once was a mandatory, voluntary chore at State. She has also created more gray hair and peptic ulcers among State's officialdom than anybody since Khrushchev. ... To condense a 10-year fight into this space let it be said that Palmer has won, again. Big. This time the victory is more than just a triumph of her principles. She has just got a Treasury check, for $25,768.25. That is payment for promotions denied, back pay and other things.

Women like Palmer, who seek new opportunities, must not expect old courtesies. They will not be "Killed with Kindness" either. But there is little doubt in my mind that if men think it better to slam the door or grab the taxi, it would be a small price for women to pay for increased opportunities for apprenticeship and advancement in the Foreign Service.

I understand much of the motivation that led men in State to avoid appointing women to serious committee assignments or negotiating positions. There was and is a genuine fear that women lacking sufficient discipline might get to a rank and position where they would make dangerous intuitive, even emotional, decisions. To the extent that men make this judgment about women, they are acting cautiously, but not necessarily intelligently. Women already make a large share of the decisions in business and homelife, and they can *learn*, can *be taught*, the power issues.

Not until men, who hold nine tenths of the power, are willing to train women the way they do the young men on their staffs will there be a serious chance for women to get into the hard negotiations and the critical decision making. Until that time comes and men accept it, only by chance and in rare instances will women wield power. It would not be right to shoulder on them the heavy burdens of choices for war or peace. Only if they have fought their way up through the local elective process, or have gone through a serious apprenticeship, would it be right to put them in the center of the arena. Inadvertently, tokenism may lead to some progress, but equality of treatment is still far away.

If I were to rail about my treatment, I would have to turn about and say that the men involved were splendid, patriotic officers. They were my friends. They were extremely kind to me when I had been doing less significant work. But I was to learn the difference then, which exists today, between the friendly, easy situation that often prevails, and having women share the rough and tumble of the world of Washington.

There is little question that in most of the intellectual activities that are expected, women are well suited to excel, if, as I suggest, men and other women are willing to make the effort to break in the young person. In economics, in finance, in science, in public relations, and in many special branches of the Foreign Service there is opportunity. Only, perhaps, in the field of military affairs is there any noticeable difficulty, and even this may vanish, now that women are admitted to the three military academies.

The obstacles here listed are largely psychological: the unwillingness and doubt on the part of men associates, the uncertainty and hesitation of women within a tradition-dominated department.

I have little advice to give to women in the State Department except to say the going will be rough. If possible, choose an understanding boss. That may be the key to opportunity. It was for me. Except for Bretton Woods, State never sent me to an international meeting. This fact seems strange as I look back.

At this writing, I think it ill advised for any woman to enter the service with her eye on an ambassadorship. The chances for men are not favorable, since places are limited; for women the outlook is hardly worth contemplating. If a woman enters the service, it would be with the desire to perform useful work in a field of great significance. She should consider the special skills required, the nature of the tasks within the service that are compatible with her abilities.

So we come back to the question, What do women want? Do they really care about the issues, enjoy the craftsmanship, long for the particularly exciting experiences? Do they want variety, change, and very long hours of work? If they do, in thirty, forty, or fifty years, they will get their chance—equal, or almost equal, to that offered men.

# 19

# BERLIN'S ECONOMIC REVIVAL

The "Berlin Desk" came close to being the perfect job. It was difficult. It was exciting. It put me in contact with hundreds, then thousands of people, some of whom became close friends. It gave me a sense of leadership and importance and permitted me to develop a brand of prestige based on initiative, American dollars, and the exertion of unstinted energy. I am grateful to have had this opportunity to make a basic element in United States policy more substantial. It was my opportunity, and I believe my accomplishment. What more could I ask!

My experience in Vienna and Austria in the forties, dealing with a divided country and in confrontation with the communist Soviets, was of enormous help. It contributed to the nature of the Berlin program and also foreshadowed the probable action of the Soviets. By the time I was charged with the reconstruction of Berlin and concerned with policy toward the city, I had few illusions about the Russian aims in Europe. In carrying out my mandate, I had many large-scale ideas and naturally encountered opposition in some quarters both from those who thought my ideas were impractical and from others who wished to use the funds for different purposes.

I enjoy a good fight and managed to get the money and also in most instances to get the support of the people who were needed to help carry out the plans.

The year 1953 was a crucial one from several points of view. For one thing a new administration had taken over in Washington, with Foster as Secretary of State. Then unexpectedly Stalin died and there was a shift in leadership in the Kremlin; Malenkov, Bulganin, and then Khrushchev became Chairman. Meanwhile a growing turbulence in and around Berlin brought delicate problems; the need for aid and moral support came to the surface more than had been evident for several years.

After the blockade was lifted in May 1949, the city was no longer in the limelight and its importance in the East-West struggles was forgotten to a considerable degree. As soon as I came to my new job I felt the urgency to change the situation. The success of our efforts from 1952 on, in planning and administering the many programs with more than a billion dollars and several hundred million deutsch marks, enhanced my sense of authority and accomplishment. Once again Berlin was recognized as a key element in our European policy.

Few now realize that the Berlin of postwar years was a whole city, much as Vienna had been, and that the sectors assigned to the four occupying powers, France, Britain, the United States, and the Soviet Union, were temporary and for administrative purposes as in Austria. There was no intention of, or agreement for, dividing the city. Movement back and forth was free and unimpeded. Moreover, in American policy it had been assumed that German reunification would come soon after the war's end. Nothing remotely approximating the present wall of separation had been imagined. In fact, it was taken for granted by many that the Soviet intention of cooperation in the United Nations and their appeal to uncommitted nations would tend to moderate their actions. Only a few of us realized the dangers of Russian forward movement in Europe and the menace this would be to the very existence of free Berlin. Those of us who were close to the problem in 1953 believed then, and consider now, the strength and significance of the city as crucial to withstanding the onward surge of communism.

I was fifty-seven years old when I went to Berlin for the State Department. I was sixty-two at the time of the dedication of Congress Hall in 1957, and it was then that I was called frequently by friends and the press, "the Mother of Berlin." (General Lucius Clay was sometimes referred to as the Father.) In 1959 after Foster's death I spoke at the dedication of the John-Foster-Dulles Allee. Then the crowds assembled for Mayor Willy Brandt, Secretary of State Christian Herter, and me and shouted, "Here's Eleanor!"

I was eighty-two on a recent visit in 1977. Many of my friends were still there.

It was shortly after the 1952 election and General Eisenhower's proposal to Foster that he become Secretary of State that I met my friend Jimmy Riddleberger by chance on Twenty-first Street. We stood by the flagpole near the entrance of the State Department as he asked me if I would like to come back from the National Production Authority (NPA) and work under him on Berlin. I was more than ready. I knew he was fair-minded, competent, and experienced. I knew that as head of the Office of German Affairs he would give me the opportunity to do constructive work. What he proposed to me was actually what was to become the "Berlin Desk." Although this assignment was never specifically recognized as a *desk* in the State Department, it was spoken of by many in a way that made it a recognized job that could have been put in the Table of Organization as such. It is true that others worked on the problems with me, as well as those who were my assistants, but it is also clear that all the work on the political, military, cultural, and economic aspects of Berlin were coordinated and to some extent synthesized at my desk. It was my task in 1953 to make plain to the Western world the broad political meaning that was becoming more widely evident after the Soviet blockade of access. The significance was clear to me in part because of my experience in Austria, and it became more obvious as I came to know the situation and people. After the blockade had stopped traffic in and out of Berlin, and after General Clay had mounted the airlift with President Truman's support, the will of the people to hold fast to their freedom became the salient fact. Their courage in the face of danger and destitution amply justified our determination to come to their aid. But the political importance was wider and constituted a crucial element in the resistance to communist expansion everywhere.

The Allied concept of postwar Europe had been an occupation of one or two years with peace treaties promptly negotiated and a return to normal international relations, with the Soviet Union cooperating in reconstruction. Geographic positions, roads, air corridors, and other arrangements of interest to the military garrisons seemed of incidental importance. Some of the generals, including Mark Clark, took them seriously, but few civilians or politicians in London, Washington, or Paris thought them of consequence.

In my wartime work on the planning committees and during my first weeks in Austria I can testify that little thought was given to the problem of access. My work was concerned with political and economic reconstruction and, like my colleagues, I considered military occupation a temporary and probably a delaying factor.

Observers now telescope past events. They assume that in 1945 we had knowledge that came only later.

Understanding of the precarious Berlin situation came only after we in Austria saw that the Soviets were frustrating our efforts to restore the productive system in 1947 and when the blockade was imposed on Berlin in 1948. The Allies' determination to hold fast, combined with the decision of the city's leaders to cast in their lot with the West, led to a firm policy maintained into 1977 and beyond.

Khrushchev said in 1958 what many thought in 1953, that the situation of Berlin was "abnormal." The communiqué of the sixth session of the Council of Foreign Ministers of June 20, 1949, has been expressed in a tripartite declaration of March and again in May of 1952. The American policy statement was a strong commitment:

> ... the security and welfare of Berlin and the position of the three powers there are regarded by the three powers as essential elements of the peace of the free world in the present international situation.

It was the intention of the United States to make of Berlin a showcase to demonstrate the vitality of free peoples and the readiness and ability to take risks in the name of democratic development. I was asked to develop strength and to make the showcase more visible. It was a task I welcomed and one that challenged my imagination.

Before I took over, responsibility for Berlin had been scattered. A State Department office looked after cultural affairs in Berlin. Security was largely under the Defense Department. As many as six sections were working on Berlin—usually when they had nothing more pressing—and Mr. Riddleberger felt this did not place the priorities properly.

In this new position I was determined to do everything I could. I made a list of things to be done. Every day I checked what might be added. Berlin was my client and from that time on whatever could be done I tried to do. This exciting discovery of the specific problems facing Berlin was the first phase of more than twenty-five years of concern with the fate of that city.

Foster had said to me in November that he would not approve my appointment in the Department. However, he indicated, if he found me at work, when he came in, that would be another matter. Riddleberger was aware of the situation and asked me to go abroad immediately.

In December 1952 I left New York on a two-decker Constellation, having an upper berth, and was served breakfast over the Atlantic at 20,000 feet—the beginning of luxury before the jet age. I went first to Bonn for consultation.

My friend the late Sam Reber was acting chief of mission in Bonn. He followed Walter Donnelly. We did not yet have an ambassador to the Federal Republic. Soon after Reber returned to Washington, our new High Commissioner, James B. Conant, former president of Harvard, took over the post in Bonn. In Berlin, meanwhile, Cecil Lyon, a distinguished Foreign Service officer, had taken over as chief of our Berlin mission and was shortly to be designated minister. He met the turbulent conditions in the city in 1953 with courage and style. He was quick to understand my assignment and to give me full support.

It was in the course of this visit to Germany, on January 16, that I first met Chancellor Konrad Adenauer, the builder of the new Federal Republic of Germany. This man, who had been pursued by the Nazis, mistakenly jailed by the British, and chosen Chancellor in 1949, was tall, straight, and looked somewhat like an Indian. His face had been scarred in an accident years before. He was a towering figure and an astute and indomitable politician. He became my friend.

When I told him of my first arrival in Bonn, back in 1930, in a small paddle boat, he sent to the Schaumburg Palace wine cellar for a special bottle of Piesporter. There were four of us that day: Adenauer; Heinz Weber, his able translator; the head of the American Mission in Bonn, Sam Reber; and myself. Adenauer wanted to know all he could about John Foster Dulles.

"Is he really interested in Germany?" he asked. "Does he know this part of Europe well? What are his relations with President Eisenhower? Is your brother pro-French, as is sometimes said?"

I told him that Foster had a new, but close, relationship with our President. I said that he had also been in Germany a number of times. He had recognized the evils of Nazism in the mid-thirties, and he had closed his Berlin office.

Foster had traveled widely, I said, as a churchman, a lawyer, and for our government. Foster's interest was not so much in one country as in the hope of international cooperation.

The lunch was delicious. Although there were only four of us, there was an engrossed menu, autographed by Adenauer, which I still have, listing grapefruit, medallions of veal, and chocolate soufflé. That lunch was my first encounter with this truly great man, who was to be a friend to me and to my brothers.

Whenever I returned to Bonn I saw him—at the Palace, and later, when he was no longer Chancellor, in his study in the Bundestag.

When I reached Bonn, I had been welcomed and told of the situation. This was appropriate since the United States High Commissioner along with the other three High Commissioners and subsequently the four ambassadors to the Federal Republic were responsible for policy and action in Berlin. When the contractual agreements were drafted, it was stipulated that Berlin was covered by the reserve clause, which meant that the Federal Republic would not govern the city, nor of course would any single power acting alone such as the Soviets. The military occupation ending elsewhere in the Federal Republic was to continue in Berlin then, as now in 1980.

I found great curiosity and, even from some people who did not later show much friendliness, an anxiety to express enthusiasm for all Dulleses.

In the course of the briefings in Bonn I received much information both as to funds that might be available in deutsch marks and also with respect to the political relations of the city and the government of the Federal Republic. One interesting session was with the political section, headed by John Paton Davies. He had under him some brilliant and sophisticated Foreign Service officers. If I remember correctly Davies himself put forward the proposition that the city should become a garrison post, with the evacuation of women and children and the transfer of civilian-type industry to other parts of the Federal Republic. I do not recall that any person under his direction supported this idea, and it seemed to me to go counter to the accepted policy that we should maintain the *security and welfare* of the city.

Berlin as a whole was frequently referred to as an island of freedom in a red sea. It was not until 1961 and the building of the wall that we recognized that the physical presence of the Soviets in the eastern sector and their power could make it two cities.

I have written three books and many articles telling of the problems and accomplishments of those days. The world has taken a bright, prosperous, productive Berlin for granted. Its distant future is shrouded in mystery.

Recently the Berlin Wall, that most evil expression of the political anomaly, has been punched full of holes. Thousands of people go through it every month. *Berlin, bleibt doch Berlin*, it remains.

Flying into Berlin, in 1953, we skimmed the rooftops and saw the sheep grazing on the turf by the runways of Templehof. (The French sector airport of Treptow is now used.) I was met there by some Berlin officials and our minister, Cecil Lyon, and his wife, Elsie, daughter of the distinguished ambassador, Joseph Grew. They were the delightful hosts of the parties for refugees where we sang and danced to cheer those who in desperation had sadly left their homes in East Germany. The refugees came west by the hundreds. There was no official prohibition.

At these gatherings Elsie played the piano and sang. Cecil sang and danced. They entertained me at 66 Miquel Strasse in the room known for years as "Eleanor's room." After the hurry and scurry of the day we had late evening discussions.

A series of appointments were made with bankers, educators, and government officials. In Berlin a government council called a Senat was appointed by the Abgeordnetenhaus, an elected body. The head was Mayor Reuter, a big man with a deep rich voice—wonderful in his frequent broadcasts. He had lived in Russia, turned against communism, and left for Turkey, where he remained during World War II.

A luncheon with Berlin economists was given by Herbert Higgins, head of the Economics Section of the mission. Herby invited key industrialists and leaders of the economic community, among them Paul Hertz. Paul had been called back to Berlin from a comfortable life in the United States, where he had made money in the stock market. Reuter had told him Berlin was fighting for its life. He returned. I worked long hours with Paul, arguing against some of his socialist views, but agreeing on basic plans. He literally worked himself to death, straining his heart, and died just as Berlin was gaining genuine industrial strength.

It was impossible to have twelve men and twelve wives to what was a working lunch, so women were not invited. Mrs. Higgins—Ann—could serve the lunch, but she could not join us. She has since accused me in her usual humorous style of boycotting the women. Actually I was not conscious of sex discrimination, but only of the significant role the men had played in the impressive work of the city. I needed their cooperation, their advice, and their wisdom.

The reconstruction of Berlin was very different from the efforts to develop the nonindustrial nations. The foundations could be traced, once the rubble was cleared away. Managers and technicians were there; some of the records and plans remained. Skilled workers were available and the export markets were presumed to be like those in the past. It remained to rebuild the plant and to supply raw materials.

The system was set up under the Industrie Bank, a special institution, not a commercial bank. It is still in existence. The bank would advance funds and when those loans were repaid, the money was reloaned.

Under the counterpart system, for example, the United States would send free grain to Germany. The government would sell it, and this money went into the counterpart fund and much of it went to the Industrie Bank.

In the early fifties unemployment was more than thirty thousand workers—this was about one third of the labor force. By rehabilitating the basic production—iron and steel, electrical, and garment industries, for example—it was possible to create thousands of jobs and to reduce unemployment to a few hundred with empty job places equal to the small number still out of work. Thus unemployment came down to zero. This was accomplished in approximately six years before the end of the decade. Unemployment, which had been a sign of weakness and a cause of unrest, was eliminated. The effective instrument was loans by the Industrie Bank and also planning by the industrialists. Production increased and shipments out of the city grew in volume.

Berlin is one of the largest industrial cities in the world— probably one of the first three in the scope of industrial capacity within the city limits. Its garment industries accounted for about one quarter of the city's GNP. Siemens Halske, an electronics company, has factories extending over a wide area. The General Electric factory is also large. I visited dozens of factories, breweries, heavy industries, garment centers, chocolate factories, and others.

At that time, workers from East Berlin could work in the western sector and many did. The West Berliners also worked in East Berlin, notably in the telephone company. A total of more than fifty thousand Berliners worked in one sector and lived in another.

They were called border crossers. They did not need special papers and were seldom challenged by police or soldiers.

Getting the allocation for new funds in Washington out of a total annual aid package appropriated for the Marshall Plan countries took a great deal of maneuvering. I enjoyed the infighting. I made friends and, also, enemies in Washington, where I got new dollars to add to funds already in Germany in counterpart money.

I was never posted in Berlin. I went back and forth from there to Washington almost as a commuter. During a typical visit, I would be on a work schedule of ten to twelve hours a day. At my request they made a large chart with days across and hours down. If I saw an empty hour on it, I asked them to fill the space with a visit or interview. Having explored the needs, I would then consult with the U.S. minister. With his approval, I would write cables to Washington, making suggestions and proposals. All this would take a week or ten days, then I would fly back to the United States.

Before the cables were decoded and acted on in Washington, I would be back at my desk where I was responsible for drafting the answers. I would prepare a favorable answer to my own cable and write a brief, defending the request. These I would "buck up the line." I usually got quick approval in the department. I had some trouble with the agency set up to administer the aid, and sometimes would have to go to Congress to argue a point with a subcommittee.

In my contest for Berlin, the city had a favored position because it was considered a security problem. This placed it closer to the political and military and not so close to commercial and trade committees.

Everyone was fighting for a larger slice of the pie. I struggled to meet challenges with a tone of conviction. Once I had approval of a project, I could stand firmly on my plans and usually managed to hold on to the money.

There was an interesting consistency between the foreign post requests that I often wrote and the responses from Washington— since I made the requests and engineered the responses. And I managed to shoehorn out of the aid administrations more money than they wanted to give, but they were never sure who had done it, and how. Not counting counterpart funds, I secured approximately a billion dollars in AID funds for Berlin. I also got considerable German money from Bonn for Berlin.

In February 1953, after I was back in Washington, there were three thousand refugees a day coming over from East Germany—travel was relatively easy, before the Wall was built in 1961. I had seen them sleeping on straw in abandoned factories.

As the numbers increased, I sent a cable from Washington to Germany. It was on a holiday and I cleared it by telephone. There were about ten different names on the cable and under each was written, "Clearance ELD." Ambassador Conant didn't realize the system of handling cables. My cable went out "urgent" and his came back, "Eyes only, Dulles." It came to me. It was destined, normally, to go to my brother. I thought, "If Foster sees this cable to me and the outgoing with my name initialed ten times and his name initialed by me, maybe he'll fire me."

I called up one of his aides and said, "You know, there's an Eyes Only cable that has come in. I think you needn't bother the Secretary with it."

I never knew whether Foster saw the cable or not. Nothing was ever said. In any case we got $15 million for refugee aid.

I visited the refugee camps. When "accepted" the refugees were given tickets to fly out to West Germany, unless they had relatives in West Berlin. They were asked why they had left East Germany and most said they could not bear the oppression. They also resented being forbidden to listen to Radio in American Sector (RIAS). Although the East Germans have always considered that everything on RIAS was propaganda, even the music, the management has always taken great pains to give the news straight and to see that the music, the humor, and the drama were as devoid as possible of political slants which would justify criticism by a serious listener. I spoke over the system a number of times.

I visited the refugee camps for East Germans and the receiving center at Marienfeld. I can still remember the woman doctor in charge of the refugees there. Looking after them was Dr. Elizabeth Gerhartz, a tall, square, determined woman. She was gruff and outspoken, but kind. It was not long before she became a close friend, entertaining me in her one-room apartment in Corbusier Haus. The suggestion that we build a hospital—eventually the splendid Klinikum—was hers. Because she was so blunt and politically inept, I did not feel it wise to bring her into planning that hospital, and she has never got the credit she deserved for the idea.

The refugees were all examined for possible disease. The fleeing East Germans were also examined for political motivation.

There was a committee of three that decided who was to be accepted in the West.

One of the means of protecting our position in Berlin was the accumulation of food and fuel stocks. This was known as the stockpile. Although Ernst Reuter spoke of it in a broadcast in 1953, it is, in some of its aspects, still top secret.

After the 1948 blockade, the U. S. Government determined that it would never be caught short. Started in 1950, the stockpile was well under way by the time I took over the Berlin job.

The quality of the stockpile was maintained by rotation. Every year a part of it was sold off and replaced. There was also an effort to diversify—to include medicine and baby foods for instance. The Germans paid for part of the operation and we paid for part.

Thus one of our tasks was the expansion and diversification of the Berlin stockpile. The decision to build up a stockpile did not determine exactly how big to make it. But it was thought that coal and grain were very hard to fly in; they're very dusty and dirty and difficult to handle. It would be wise to accumulate them in Berlin, since you know they can be used and are durable. Other items could be added.

When in Berlin I had visited the large buildings where wheat, canned meat, sugar, and butter were stored. I surveyed the large piles of coal. I had talked to my brother Foster a little about it. Foster didn't talk to me much about Berlin, but he would sort of look at me in an amused way and say, "Well, how is your city?" and I was usually ready with one sentence that I thought would be good for him because I couldn't impose on him with three or four sentences if he came out to my house in McLean to swim. I would try and flag his attention about one or two things; and, as a parenthesis, I think the one thing that the younger people don't learn soon enough is that they can't have thousands of words and hours of time of a man who's making big decisions.

Once I said to him, "I've been working on the stockpile." He asked, "What do you mean, the stockpile?" And I said, "We've got coal and wheat and some other things in Berlin," and apparently I caught his attention, because one day in June 1954 (I think this was the year) when things were pretty tense in Berlin, he called me in my office and said, "I got you some money today." I said, "That's fine." He said, "I got you fifty million dollars today." I said, "Where'd you get it?" and he said, "I got it from unobligated defense money, end

[251]

items, money that was going to lapse to the Treasury, and I got them to give it to me for your stockpile." So I had a new $50 million.

When we cabled Ambassador Conant about these funds, his economist asked to have $15 million of it diverted to industrial investment, which I thought was all right.

The Industrie Bank invested in Berlin industries, and they wanted some more money for that. Although there was a sizable revolving fund, I thought it was still a reasonable proposal.

So we had $35 million for the stockpile. And then we went through one of those government rigmaroles that nearly drive you crazy. This was in early June, and what we had to do was to get it irrevocably committed before the end of the fiscal year; if not, we would lose it. It might seem that three weeks is a lot of time, but by the time we communicated with the field and explained to them the urgency of committing this money and got them working, they had to call a meeting of the properly constituted authorities, because this stockpile is basically German-owned, and then they had to work out a formula for getting this money allocated to certain purposes, to certain categories, so that it was legally *obligated*. I remember rushing around from office to office on June 30, 1954. If I had failed, we would have lost all the money. We had to go to get clearance at the Pentagon, we had to go to the aid organization, and we had to go through the Budget Bureau. After I had the clearance from the different divisions and agencies on June 30, the "action paper" had to be signed by the President. I called the White House. I could not get the papers in before six so I telephoned one of the President's aides to see if the President would actually sign between six and seven. I thought the President might have gone to Camp David or somewhere else. I finally cleared this last hurdle. We didn't get the cables cleared until a few hours before the end of the fiscal year.

It was typical of Foster's handling of foreign affairs that when he knew I was well versed in Berlin's problems and had the support of the officers in the field, he assumed I was handling the Berlin Desk competently and did not concern himself. He did not intervene or question me about my work; only on those special occasions such as the chance to get this money, and when Khrushchev or others raised problems of major significance in international relations did he call on Riddleberger or others in the State Department or abroad to help him formulate the United States policy. As a matter of protocol he also had us participate on such occasions as visits of Mayor Reuter,

Mayor Brandt, and other high officials. I also worked with men from the CIA, both in Washington and abroad, but I rarely discussed Berlin problems when I saw Foster socially.

On June 16, 1953, on the second visit of my Berlin assignment, I was attending a meeting of the committee for the stockpile near the sector border. We were discussing additional purchases and also the rotation of some stocks. A member of the committee came in, looking very agitated, and said, "The plasterers and other construction workers in white smocks are running into the British sector across the line from East Berlin! There is trouble!"

We broke up the meeting and went into the streets. The crowds were gathering in the neighborhood of the Brandenburg Gate and Potsdammer Platz. I stood on the fringes and heard the shouting. "We want freedom." "Get Ulbricht out." We were told by men from radio RIAS that eighty laborers working on Block 40 of Stalin-Allee had thrown down their tools and marched up the street. Soon hundreds of other workers had joined them at the Brandenburg Gate. I decided to go back to the mission and talk with the other officers.

I had lunch with David Maynard, deputy to Cecil Lyon; Richard C. Hottelet, the commentator; and a Swedish diplomat. A head of the German Red Cross was there. Our mission chief, Cecil Lyon, along with U. S. General Timberman, and the French and British political and military advisers were in a closed meeting.

One question arose immediately. Should we allow Ernst Scharnowski, an important labor leader and a dynamic man, to go on the air, calling for the workers in the East to rise against the communist regime.

After lunch I went with the German Red Cross official to the sector border in the center of the city. The crowd was raging. My friend told me not to speak but to carry his briefcase. He was afraid if they knew I was American, they might mob me. They came to him shouting, "Why don't the Amis give us guns? We could take over their guard posts. We could free the city." He joined with the unarmed Berlin police who tried to get some of the young men coming from the construction sites to a large warehouse. There soup was being served. The excitement was intense. The Vopos, East German police, were not at that time in evidence. We went back to headquarters in the U.S. sector to report.

By midnight on June 16, the basic decision for restraint had been made by the three commandants and their political advisers. Bonn concurred. Washington was far away and not really in the picture at the first critical moments.

One hour of high excitement in the revolt came on June 17 when two young men climbed the Brandenburg Gate and tore down the hammer and sickle flag. They were caught up by the crowd and carried on their shoulders—the cry was "We won't be slaves." Almost at once four Russian tanks rolled down Unter den Linden. Willi Göttling, an innocent bystander, was shot. Others were killed and wounded. Martial law was declared and the streets were gradually cleared. A temporary wire barricade on the sector border was patrolled by Soviet and Vopos as many sought to escape to the West.

Mayor Reuter had been in Munich but returned as soon as possible. Scharnowski was allowed to make a short speech over RIAS, but he was strictly limited in what he could say. In addition to radio, telephone and railroad workers spread the news of the revolt throughout the zone. In spite of cautions, some scores of cities and towns rose up and threw the communist leaders out of the town halls.

A fact we had to take into account in making policy was that the revolt had no leadership and no formation. We knew there were no outstanding resistance leaders in the zone. Those who might have played this role had escaped to the West. We were stirred by the gallantry of those thirsting for freedom but we feared they were doomed to defeat. It had been a spontaneous and unprepared reaction to increased demands of the workers. The revolt had spread throughout the Soviet occupied zone to several hundred towns and cities. By the time we knew this, Soviet tanks had crushed the uprising in Berlin.

The Berlin revolt and the Allied reaction have been cited by some as evidence of lack of contingency planning and weakness; they assume we might have supported drives for freedom. The charge is made particularly in connection with the Hungarian uprising in 1956 and also on the occasion of the 1968 efforts to gain independence in Czechoslovakia. I was there in 1968.

Actually the lessons from the three episodes had a profound meaning. They revealed the Soviet's firm position and the Kremlin-proclaimed Brezhnev doctrine. The U.S.S.R. cannot retreat or permit the Western powers to gain a military and political dominance in Eastern Europe. They consider the Warsaw Pact Nations a "vital interest." However regrettable, it is a fact that the leaders in the Kremlin now and for some time to come will not tolerate any violent rebellion in their satellite nations.

The issue during the 1952 election campaign of "rollback" and the hope for liberation from communism was brought into focus by these events in Eastern Europe. The risk of nuclear war and the Soviet firmness in holding on to restive areas made clear that any action to help those in revolt would bring imminent danger of World War III. Berlin and the eastern provinces must live with this situation.

Those on the Senat and in the Allied command who knew the Russians were certain that the Soviet Union could not let these workers prevail. If the revolting workers had been given arms, in their wild bid for freedom, a bloody confrontation would have resulted.

When I returned home, a few days after the riots, Allen called me. "What can we do for the East Berliners and those in the zone?" he asked. "They are willing to risk everything for freedom."

I said there were a few things we could do, but that they were not of great significance.

"If there is anything, try to work out a plan."

I got "through channels" to Foster. Foster spoke to Allen, who called me back. By then I had thought of some action. I said, "Let's give them food as a demonstration."

I assembled a committee representative of Agriculture, Commerce, Treasury, Defense, CIA, and one or two other agencies. I explained the plan. We would borrow food from the stockpile, package it, and give it to anyone with an East German identity card who would come to get it.

I said, "We must act quickly. What we agreed today can be worked out in detail and I will clear the cables by telephone. We do not need another meeting."

They all agreed. Germans were recruited at various stations in Berlin to give out the packages, and the distribution began in a few days. At first the people who came were from East Berlin and nearby communist towns. Then the word spread and people came from more than a hundred miles. The packages were worth about fifteen dollars—a week or more's supply of food. The cost of travel for some

[255]

was more than the value of the packages, but they came to demonstrate their solidarity with those in revolt. There was a stream of people.

The communists faced a dilemma. They hesitated to prevent people getting the food, but they did not like this demonstration of courage. Finally they decided this was an insidious attack on the system in East Germany and began arresting those on the trains coming over.

After careful consideration we decided that the confrontation occurring was hazardous to the people getting packages. We agreed to end the program. The remainder of the $15 million was distributed in the East zone through other means. All the food went East.

The demonstration of thousands of East Germans in their continuing attachment to the West did not go unnoticed. The working conditions of the German Democratic Republic were eased by the communist masters. The harassment was lightened and the confidence of Berliners—though mixed with cynicism—was solid enough to permit economic recovery at a steady rate. We had done a good deal by this simple program.

Economic reconstruction and rehabilitation of Berlin was a natural for me. I had a keen awareness of the importance of reducing unemployment that had risen to 33 percent—and then fell to zero. The increase in production was of especial interest and we were very successful in the loans extended.

# 20

# A SHOW WINDOW TO THE EAST

Once the Western sector's production was on the track, and loans flowing into the proper channels to increase the output of an industrious citizenry, more attention was devoted to the question of the image of the city abroad and the morale of the population. This was a phase of the psychological warfare in which the publisher C. D. Jackson and Nelson Rockefeller in the White House were concerned. The actions undertaken were *impact* programs.

I knew the people by 1956 and sensed their need for stimulus and interest in their circumscribed conditions. I figured also that fine buildings would carry the message of a long-range commitment by the United States and other NATO countries to the Kremlin. I directed substantial portions of our aid to build the Congress Hall, the Klinikum, and social housing and student dormitories. The communists built the wall! This was Khrushchev's answer.

The most spectacular and least expensive of our major projects in Berlin was the Congress Hall which stands on the banks of the River Spree, and is used almost every day by hundreds of people. Modern in design, and cleverly planned with telephones, snack bars, a restaurant, multilingual translation, press rooms, and other facilities, it is a model for a conference of between one thousand and two thousand people.

My work, from the first concept to the final festive opening, represents one of the most satisfactory experiences in my working life. This modern building, nicknamed "The Pregnant Oyster" or "Frau Dulles' Hut," stands in my mind as the best representation of those years.

We decided to set aside $1 million out of the year's total of $4 million, for this project. A committee under the American Institute of Architects was set up. We chose a Boston architect, Hugh Stubbins. With Ralph Walker, a leading architect in the AIA, as chairman of our committee, we went to Berlin.

Facing financial restriction which meant the relapse of funds not spent in the fiscal year, I resorted to the device of founding an institution, or *Stiftung*, under the laws of Berlin, to which the money could be irrevocably allocated.

Our exploratory trip was in the summer of 1956, and our first stop was in Bonn. When I got off the plane with five handsome upstanding men, the Germans said, "See, this time she comes with a bodyguard." At the embassy we had a talk with Ambassador James Conant. We had drawn up fifteen or twenty possible projects to consider—everything from a monument to an individual or small "Disneyland," a special clinic, an art school, and other proposals. We presented the list to Conant. He looked it over, walked to the window, and peered out. Then he said, "The best thing in America is the kitchen. I suggest you put an American kitchen in the center of Berlin."

We thanked him and said we would add it to our list. Later, when we reported back to the ambassador, his only remark was "So you didn't take my kitchen."

From Bonn we went to Berlin to consult with Mayor Otto Suhr and his colleagues. We toured the city to see what had already been built and discovered there was a great, barnlike auditorium called the Deutschland Halle, which would hold more than twenty thousand people, affording no particular comfort or anything to please the eye or ear. There were also a few small places for meetings, but they had no adequate conference hall.

Several questions were raised by the Germans. One was about the management of the project, another about the location. With respect to the setting up of a *Stiftung*, the Germans thought it a good procedure, but said members must be government people. No one in our group was a government person. I did not belong to the *Stiftung*. I just ran it. Legally, I didn't belong. The German members were all government personnel.

The American members said they expected the land to be donated, as well as the water, electric, and sewage systems. The Germans consented.

In order to reach conclusions about the building plans we had a "beer evening" with Mayor Suhr in his home. We wanted to build the hall in the Tiergarten. Suhr said emphatically that no buildings were to go in the Tiergarten.

We answered that we wanted it near the eastern sector border with a lot of land surrounding it. Maps of the city were spread out on the floor and Ralph Walker, a hot-tempered man, said to me, "Well, if they don't want the building, let's go home."

Suhr's English was poor and Walker's German, nonexistent.

The Americans stood up, ready to leave. I was distressed, and said to them, "The location is a very delicate matter. The Tiergarten has a long tradition. Have a glass of beer. We can't leave abruptly."

They sat down. Meanwhile I looked at a place on one map, near the Spree River, and said, "What's this place? Is there any building on it?"

"Couldn't we have that? It's near the Siegessäule [the Victory Column] and just across the river from the eastern sector. It isn't far from the old Reichstag. Could we have it?"

"Certainly," Suhr agreed.

The location had been settled. Time had cooled tempers. The crisis over.

Although my job did not involve negotiations of the Henry Kissinger type, I did have to negotiate many things, and I was tremendously pleased with this resolution, because for five minutes the whole project was in jeopardy. This was a kind of work I enjoyed.

We had only a year in which to develop the architectural drawings, get them approved by the city and the State Department, and build the hall at Im Zelten, where Romans had pitched their tents.

The hall was to have assembly rooms, ranging in capacity from 1,200 to 500, 300, or 200 persons, and even several rooms for 30, plus a hall for exhibits.

On my return I went to Boston. Stubbins showed me three sketches. One looked like the Jefferson Memorial, but was trite; another was a rectangle. I was always interested in architecture and here was my chance to express my views. I wanted to influence the design.

"I like the water around this one, but the building is rather dull. If you would put this element of sketch one with this in sketch two and add the external elements of sketch three, you'd have something."

What he came up with was a cantilever roof over a main hall, and under this, conference rooms with a restaurant on the lowest level, facing the river.

I had also told him, "The Germans love to have turnstiles, where they collect pfennigs. I want to have open areas for them to enjoy."

So Stubbins included a large open deck, bordering the Spree with a plaza which was reached by steps over a reflecting pool. Anyone could walk on the plaza, sit on the benches, and purchase hot dogs and soft drinks at a stand. It became like the Washington Mall, a gathering place, and it had an atmosphere of freedom and accessibility.

Before any payment for admission was required, people could go in the front door, buy postcards, and read the Benjamin Franklin plaque. This plaque commemorated the bicentennial of the birth of Franklin, which coincided with the year the hall was to open. We called the *Stiftung* the Benjamin Franklin Foundation.

I insisted that we not attach an American name to the building. For that, we settled on the simple title of Kongresshalle (Congress Hall). I knew there would be times in the future when tensions between our government and the Berliners might be aroused. An American name would tend to provoke the unruly to throw stones.

On the marble plaque were the words of Franklin, in a letter he had written to David Hartley:

> God grant that not only the love of liberty but a thorough knowledge of the rights of man may pervade all the nations of the earth so that a philosopher may set his foot anywhere on its surface and say, "This is my country."

Under Franklin's words is the dedication:

> To these ideas and to the man who spoke them and lived them this Kongresshalle is dedicated.

A friend of mine looking at the plaque one day heard a little boy say to his mother, after reading the words, "Mother, I want to go to America. I would like to live in the country where this man lived."

Our plans developed rapidly under the Benjamin Franklin Foundation. It is the most comfortable hall I have ever sat in. The tedium of sitting in ballrooms on little, gold folding chairs was eliminated. So were the frustrations of dark theaters, never intended for the business of a conference. The pitch of the floor afforded a good view of the stage. It was designed for its main purpose, not for music and ballet. The pleated plyboard walls ensured fine acoustics. In addition to the great hall there is a little theater, seating more than five hundred.

The building had to be completed in time for the 1957 exhibit. The 15-person *Stiftung*, with its American chairman, had to make contracts with forty-five different contractors—a terrific job to contend with. But it was done.

I had the apparent authority, which I sometimes played to the utmost, of withholding money. No funds could be approved without my okay. But if I had refused the money and they had chosen to make an issue of it, I might have been in trouble.

A little later, on July 4, there was a thunderstorm, and lightning struck the roof, at that time just a tar skeleton on scaffolding. It didn't cause much damage, but it is interesting to contemplate that on the Fourth of July a building in Germany, dedicated to Benjamin Franklin, brought lightning from the sky.

Since Berlin was to be a symbol of freedom on the continent, we tried to get a special allotment for the celebration at the opening of Congress Hall. Ralph Walker, chairman of the *Stiftung*, became interested in the celebration and under him we set up an Events Committee. We also solicited the help of Virginia Innes-Brown, a leader of the American National Theater and Academy (ANTA).

Foremost among the entertainers was the late Thornton Wilder, a small bouncy man, gentle and charming, who gave us permission to present three of his one-act plays without charge, one of which had never been produced, and directed the plays and acted in them himself.

Later, when I asked him if he would write the introduction to my book *Berlin: The Wall Is Not Forever*, he wrote saying he would like to, but felt that he did not know Berlin well enough. He said he loved the city but he recognized his own limitations.

In addition to the three Wilder plays, others written by Tennessee Williams, Eugene O'Neill, and William Saroyan were presented by the ANTA group.

Another person especially charming and generous was Lillian Gish, who had starred in her youth in D. W. Griffith's film *The Birth of a Nation*. She was recently working on promoting the celebration of the hundredth anniversary of Griffith's birthday.

Ethel Waters, who wrote a fine autobiography, *My Eye Is on the Sparrow*, was also in the ANTA group. I still have a beautiful picture of her embracing the opera star Eileen Farrell, who sang for the opening. Miss Waters went to East Berlin and told me on her return, "I talked to a lot of people there and they said conditions are terrible in Berlin. What's all this fuss about two Berlins? I don't understand."

We told her it would be best if she stayed with the group and did not talk much in East Berlin, since some might seek to make her say things she might regret.

Others in the group included dancer-choreographer Martha Graham; Billy Allen, one of the successful black actresses; Eileen Heckart, who had won acting awards for her performances in *The Bad Seed* and *Picnic*. The Juilliard String Quartet was included in the week's program.

The day of the opening, I held an early session with the local people who were going to work in Congress Hall during the first week. I had seen on shipboard how the young men and women lined up every day to receive instructions. So I lined these people up and told them in my fairly good, but not perfect, German that they were there, not to prevent people from seeing and doing what they wanted, but to make them feel at home and to show them as much as possible of the hall. I also did this on the second day of the opening. After dismissing the group, I discovered that somebody had hung ten-pfennig signs outside the toilets. I called one of my aides and told him, "As long as this is in American hands we are going to have free toilets."

So we went through the place and tore down the signs.

The opening was one of the first really gala days of postwar Berlin. Few thought of the sad ruins of the Reichstag nearby. Most wore their best clothes and widest smiles. And for me this was one of the most exciting days in my career. Not only the management and financing of the construction but all the legal and cultural arrangements I had managed gave me satisfaction. The fine spirit of cooperation made me feel that I had accomplished something significant.

When they put the names of the *Stiftung* members on the outside wall they included my name.

After Foster's death, the broad, tree-shaded street near the Tiergarten and Congress Hall, paralleling the river, was named the John-Foster-Dulles-Allee.

The most costly and perhaps, in the long run, the most valuable project we initiated was the Klinikum. Dr. Gerhartz, whom I had met when visiting the refugees, and I had discussed Berlin's problems frequently. One evening after dinner I said to her, "I know that the great general hospital in Berlin used to be the Charité, which is now in the eastern sector. What has been done in West Berlin to make up for the loss of access to the Charité?"

"Nothing," she replied.

"What is the most modern hospital in West Berlin?"

"I believe the one the Americans are using—the Martin Luther Hospital, where they treat the soldiers—is one. And I think the Rudolf Wirchow, built on the cottage system with fifty-odd pavilions is fairly modern—it's only forty years old. But nothing has been built since the war and nothing for years before the war."

"Something should be done about the health problem," I told her.

"I don't think the Berlin Senat wants to act," she said. "There isn't any money. There's a lot of rivalry among factions whenever anything like this is started."

After my conversation with her, I went to Bernard Gufler, the chief of the U.S. mission and told him, "I think Berlin needs another hospital."

He said, "Nonsense. There are plenty of beds. They have lots of hospitals."

I knew that this man was well acquainted with conditions in Berlin, but rather worn down by all the planning necessary for the Congress Hall. He knew that arrangements for a hospital, if they were to be made, would be even more complex.

I went to some of the existing hospitals and saw the way the cottage system was run with patients brought through a series of wards, down stairways, often outdoors and down the road, into the surgery pavilion.

I noted the lack of privacy, the crowding of patients' beds under the stairways and public areas. It was then that I made up my mind that I would get a scientific study of the conditions and an assessment of what was needed. It seemed to me that American money should go into projects that met real needs and also demonstrated to the Soviets our long-term interest in Berlin. It was

[263]

important to build buildings that would last longer than the resolutions or statements of one President or one Secretary of State.

The construction of Congress Hall through the Benjamin Franklin *Stiftung* had been so successful and led to such fine cooperation that I felt a longer and more complex project could be designed and completed by them.

Knowing that the hospital project would be controversial, I suggested to my colleagues that we send a commission of American experts to Berlin to study the hospital situation. So we sent two architects, a hospital expert from Johns Hopkins University, a lawyer, and two other men to Berlin to make a survey. They came up with a report that recommended a hospital with five hundred or more beds and stipulated what modern facilities should be included.

The length of time that elapsed from the survey to the completion of the project was considerable. The Klinikum was officially opened on October 9, 1968.

After approval of the report, the question of architects arose. It was agreed that we would try to choose an American. The *Stiftung* members chose Arthur Davis of New Orleans, an expert designer of hospitals. Doctors and architects were also chosen to form the Klinikum committee, which worked with the *Stiftung* on the details.

We asked the heads of departments at the University of Berlin's Medical School what their needs were. Department heads all offered plans for the quadrimeters needed for their teaching. We worked together all one Christmas holiday.

The best way to conform to the city code without losing space was to build an eight-story, X-shaped structure, its wings slanting northeast and northwest, southeast and southwest, so the rooms received maximum hours of sunlight. At the center of the "X" on each floor were operating rooms and research areas. There is no hospital design of which I know with such a short distance between the patient's room and the surgical, X-ray or testing areas.

My interest in details of hospital construction was heightened by several stays in the austere and unattractive rooms of several hospitals. I had already been in Philadelphia and Washington institutions and was destined to be hospitalized for six major operations, four on my eyes, two for gallstones. Even in 1957 I was beginning to be aware of the logistics that required long, jolting rides on stretchers, the weariness of the nurses, and the bedside bell that disappeared when one needed help. If I saved patients and nurses in

Berlin some anxious and uncomfortable moments, it was because of my various experiences. The nurses' stations were at the middle of each wing so that no nurse had to walk more than fifty or sixty yards in any direction to reach the patients in her charge. There was an emergency generator, with capacity for several weeks.

For medical students, there were amphitheaters to observe surgery, with one-way glass for the observers. The grounds were landscaped. There were both a therapeutic swimming pool and a decorative one.

The Berliners decided they wanted to build the entire hospital with four wings at one time, since it would cost less than if it were built in two stages. We told them we recognized that fact, but we could not commit enough money. If they wished to go ahead with the complete hospital, they would have to find more German money.

Meanwhile, I was working on both the city of Berlin and the Federal Republic of Germany to get them each to match, dollar for dollar, what we put in. In the first instance, we put in $4 million, the city put in the equivalent of $4 million, and the federal government, $4 million, for a total of $12 million.

As time went on the Germans added certain features that we considered desirable, but not necessary. The German economy was in good shape. We eventually managed to get a total of about $85 million from the city and federal government and the total U.S. contribution was about $16 million. Our plan to get money out of the German Government wasn't easy to carry out. The operation had to be a joint American-German one. We paid only a small part but it had been our initiative.

In my Berlin work I found that in order to take an authoritative position one has to arrange an invisible promotion. Regular promotions are few or nonexistent. When experience increases, therefore, one must act with the air of a person at a higher grade even if there has been no corresponding administrative action. When you know what you are doing, you should push with energy. You should assume responsibility.

One technique I developed in carrying out my unusual assignment worked for the duration of my tour of duty on Berlin. When I came upon a need in the reconstruction of the city, I would write a request from the governing mayor to the minister or ambassador. This letter became the basis for a conference with the mayor.

Otto Suhr, who was the governing mayor for much of the time I was working on these programs, willingly took my draft as a basis for his action. When the request came through from the mayor's office, I was on my way home, ready to advise the Secretary in Washington with regard to a constructive response. This strategy was satisfying to develop and made me feel I was accomplishing my mission.

We wished to help the universities, but it was not easy. The Free University was going into the radical sixties at this time and there was trouble between the administration, involving the president and faculty of the university. There was a new scope of activities for the governing board as well. The hospital suffered from this. When I was there in 1972, I asked what was going on and was told they had meetings of the board every so often and that the meetings lasted for hours.

"What do you talk about?" I asked.

"The war in Vietnam."

"When you get through talking about the war in Vietnam, what do you talk about?"

"We talk about the war in Cambodia."

Health matters were seldom discussed.

Because the university had fallen into disrepute at that time and was run to a considerable extent by extremists, some of whom were avowed communists, the hospital was underused. I was told in 1977 that conditions are much improved.

The building of the Student Village as housing for the students in the Free University brought different problems. It had been initiated before the Klinikum. We thought it would be a good thing to have a campuslike development for young people who were living in attics and cellars and that it would give them facilities for group activities.

It was decided to use a German architect and to accept a German plan. At the same time, we injected some of our ideas. We thought it would be good to have small buildings—we found an open four-acre plot.

When I went to the mayor of the district of Zehlendorf, Wille Stiewe, and asked if we could have the land, I had already made my rounds in the morning. He asked me if the Senator for Education approved. I said yes, I had been to see him. He asked if the Senator for Construction agreed and I told him I had just come from the

Senator's office. So the mayor saw no reason for objecting. I enjoyed the maneuver.

Ambassador David Bruce was skeptical. This attractive and well-liked man was one of our most able ambassadors. He was the only one who was in London, Bonn, and Paris as chief of mission. His wife was friendly and charming. They did a good job. Bruce thought the Germans would dislike the idea of a campus project. I told him I had them in my corner. He was not sure the Americans would like this use of funds. I offered to defend it on Capitol Hill if it were attacked. He said, "Go ahead. It is your responsibility."

The whole complex housed more than seven hundred students. There was a small auditorium and a cafeteria, with pleasant grounds surrounding the group of buildings.

After it was built, I went out several times and made speeches. The last time I was heckled. As it happened, this was during the radical phase of the student movement and some have thought that living together on a campus accentuated the trend toward rebellion. I don't know whether this was the case or not. I am convinced that the student village was needed, but it was not an unmixed blessing. The concept was new to German universities and it seemed to me a good gamble. There is little doubt, however, that it was a hotbed of radicalism.

We also built Siegmundshof, a skyscraper student housing project for men at the Technical University. This was in the center of town. From my desk in Washington I continued to seek funds for the city.

It was while I was still working actively on Berlin in the State Department that Foster and Janet invited President Eisenhower and Mamie to come to Foster's birthday dinner on February 25, 1958. It was usually not considered proper to invite the President, since it put him in an embarrassing position. He could not be entertained by all or by a favored few. In this case Foster explored the situation and found that the invitation would be appreciated. The President and Mamie came, both beautifully dressed and in a relaxed mood. I think the only other nonfamily guest was Clare Boothe Luce. Allen and Clover and I were there. None of his children were in town. It was a delightful friendly evening. I do not remember any speeches and I don't think there was a birthday cake—it was simple, easy, and pleasant in the charming house on Thirty-second Street. The decorations in the living room were predominantly Chinese from my grandfather and grandmother's time in Asia. Many of the jades and panels are now in the memorial rooms at the University of Texas at Austin. Janet and Foster had a fine feeling for these antiques.

This evening was a pleasant interlude.

Berlin was not well restored by the fifties. There was still overcrowding in living and working centers. We devoted considerable money to new structures because they were not only needed but also symbolized a long and enduring interest.

Other projects were undertaken for the same reasons. In my trips to Berlin I got to know many interesting people. Every September there was an international industrial fair. At these fairs, themes were chosen to increase the interest of Berliners in the United States. One of these exhibits, which later toured many countries, was "Atoms for Peace." We gave the exhibit to show the uses of nuclear fission in construction and medicine. There was also a Kalamazoo exhibit, featuring the small American city with typical industries and homes.

We showed our interest and our presence in Berlin in many ways.

My job, as I saw it, was to forward to the Kremlin through various means the message that our commitment to Europe was a long-range policy and that Berlin stood as the central and continuing manifestation of our engagement. The buildings were concrete signs of this policy.

Stalin had died in March 1953. Clover Dulles, Allen's wife, called me at three o'clock in the morning, March 5, to tell me that he was dead. I was back from Germany. I knew the workers in the Soviet zone had been watching the doctors' trial in Russia. The flow of refugees had become overwhelming. Thousands left the eastern zone over the weekend of February 14. I felt that night that world history had taken a turn. I did not clearly understand the direction.

The change in leadership from Stalin to Malenkov and Bulganin, and then to Khrushchev in 1955, brought a period of uncertainty. This doubt was to end with Khrushchev's ultimatum of November 1958.

The ultimatum was serious, following a period during which no practical confrontation of consequence had taken place. There was, however, still the danger of miscalculation. Some of the specialists in the German department had prepared position papers. I thought that the policy being developed in 1959 was dangerous and that it became doubly so when leaked to outsiders, who then considered it to be the basic position of the United States.

I knew that the funds for Berlin projects along with other European aid were being eliminated. In various ways I found this treatment to be discouraging and lacking in imagination and scope. It seemed to me that I was being put in a position of carrying out a weak policy which would only become strong in case of military attack or serious threat by armed forces. I could not see, in the new situation, that there was anything I could do in the period when conditions were reasonably benign to prevent growing complacency, both in Berlin and in Washington. New conditions seemed to tie my hands and to frustrate me.

I was pleased that the Intelligence and Research Bureau wanted me to work on developing countries. It was my hope that my friends in Berlin would realize this did not signify any loss of interest in their fate, but that my official activities would, for a time, be different.

The Berlin and German officials have continued to invite me to celebrate various events, even as recently as 1977, and have given me honors, which convinces me that what I did was understood. In 1980 I am still eager to add to Berlin support.

# AND THEN THE WALL, 1961

It was in the late summer of 1958 that Foster took his last cruise. We had word at Henderson that he might come into the harbor on that early September afternoon. My son, David, was out in his little motor boat and we had a meal planned. The sloop sailed into White's Bay at about five o'clock. Bob Hart rowed Foster the half mile of quiet water to the cottage where Margaret, Nataline and I were waiting. Foster asked to go down to Georgia Belle's for fresh corn. We had a fine traditional evening ending early, so, at dusk, he went back to the boat for a last night aboard. He was due in Washington for a series of important decisions on China, NATO, Germany, and, as it developed because of the Pope's death—the funeral in Rome.

Not long after that Khrushchev issued his ultimatum on Berlin on November 27, 1958. Eisenhower and Dulles had replied promptly within hours reaffirming the United States position of solid support for the security and welfare of the city. Khrushchev had said at a reception at the Albanian Embassy in Moscow a few days later that he had not intended an ultimatum. In 1959 it was agreed to have a conference of foreign ministers in Geneva in the late spring.

Foster was dying of cancer in Walter Reed Hospital. He was concerned about the Berlin situation and asked me to go to Berlin on a trip already planned for April 1959. When I returned from Europe, his condition had deteriorated but he asked me to report to him on what I had found. He was particularly interested in the possibility of Ludwig Erhard or Franz Etzel taking over from Adenauer as Chancellor. This possibility was being discussed in Bonn. We talked for a half hour, then he tired and I left. This was May 10.

Meanwhile, the German experts in the State Department were discussing position papers for the meeting scheduled for Geneva. Many of the ideas being brought forward seemed to me unnecessary retreats from our strong position.

After Foster's death my work with the German office was to

terminate. I was faced with a real dilemma. It was clear that I was not going to attend the Geneva meeting. It was also clear that some of the position papers contained fallback positions which were substantial concessions to the communists and which I did not consider either wise or necessary.

I thought my separation from the German group would underscore the doubt and hesitations on the Berlin policy which was being discussed and rumored in Washington and abroad. Some observers had noted the situation and concluded that the changes being considered would effectively end the Allied position in the city.

When Secretary Herter was invited to Berlin for the dedication of the John-Foster-Dulles-Allee, he was impressed by the enthusiasm of the people and by conversations with those who knew Berlin's vulnerability. When he returned to Geneva, the proposal of the West was improved somewhat. However, the Russians rejected it since they were presumably suspicious of a trap, and the meeting broke up without any conclusion. The ultimatum of November 1958 was forgotten.

These affairs of state were relevant to my position in that my advice was not used, and my transfer to another division was in the works. Much later I was to learn that Foster had worried about what my position would be after his death. He had asked one of his aides to follow my situation, and if possible to see that I was not placed in an untenable position. He knew that some of my associates opposed my views. I did not know until much later that before his death he had tried to protect me. The result of my situation and his concern was that I was transferred to the Bureau of Intelligence and Research (INR).

Thus my official responsibility for Berlin ended, although in the future I was given friendly assistance in the State Department when on several occasions the Germans invited me to Berlin as their guest. This connection with the work was occasional and not a day-to-day matter.

There was no notice in the press of the change in my job. Many people considered it characteristic of the Department of State to change assignments, and I accepted this solution of my problem.

When in 1961 the momentous decisions that led to the building of the Wall were taken, I was not working on Germany, and in fact was not in Washington on the critical days. In studying the situation after August 13 when the city was divided, I felt that the first signal to the Soviets of increasing American weakness had been in Geneva in 1959. A further stage of uncertainty that led to the Soviet decision to build the Wall was reached after President Kennedy's meeting with Khrushchev in Vienna of June 1961. It is true that Kennedy showed his concern for European strength by increasing our preparedness, but his July speech was thought in many quarters to be limited to local reaction rather than to suggest that NATO would assert Berlin rights. The sum of these events from 1959 to early August 1961 was to convince the Soviets that the division of the city would be safe to carry out at this time.

When on August 13 barbed wire was strung along the sector border, it was an attempt on the part of the communists to test the firmness of the new President in Washington. At that time I was far from Berlin. I have explored the situation and the arguments between two groups of experts. The old German hands in the State Department advised a strong statement to Moscow and some countermeasures; some even advocated demonstrations in Berlin. However, a combination of caution in Washington and inertia in Bonn, particularly in the U. S. Embassy, combined to delay and smother most efforts to convince the Soviets of the inhumanity and the illegal nature of the separation of the city, not at first called *West* Berlin.

Kennedy did not want to act and did not do so until five days had passed. Then he asked Vice-President Johnson to go to Berlin and ordered a battle group of approximately fifteen hundred soldiers to march into the city. He was desperately afraid of a possible revolt in East Germany which would have resulted in bloodshed and perhaps war.

In a conversation with General Lucius D. Clay on October 5, 1970, I asked him his opinion as to whether we could have prevented the Wall going up. He replied, "All we would have had to do was to get the troops out of the billets. As it was, they remained inside. If I had been in Berlin, I doubt if the Wall would have gone up. I would have had the trucks [personnel carriers with unarmed soldiers] drive back and forth in the city."

It would be ostentatious to link this major political event to my personal situation. I had tried with success to keep my transfer inconspicuous. There is no doubt in my mind that my tendency to take a strong line accounted for a degree of isolation from some of my colleagues. In moving quietly to INR I believe I did what was most constructive; any other action would have flagged some of my reporter friends. It would not have been possible to prevent the division of the city once the flow of refugees became a torrent in 1961. It might have been possible to make the communists pull back the dividing barriers and to impress them with the danger they were incurring.

I think my personal life was more interesting as the result of my new assignment. However, it is my conviction that I should have been kept on the German work. I should have been called in or consulted when the Wall went up. And I could have been more useful to the government if they had kept me on as a part of the "loyal opposition."

There is no doubt that the Wall presented President Kennedy and other Allied leaders with a difficult decision. It would be unwise and futile to pass harsh judgment on the course of action they took. However, in this case, as in other instances, the importance of quick response and clear-cut decisions is evident. The result of these sad days has been the tragic fate of many in East Germany and the weakening of the defenses of the NATO countries by the exposure of uncertainty and hesitation in a time of crisis. It is because of this unhappy circumstance that the work I was able to do for Berlin is clouded in my mind by the shadow of the Wall.

# · 22 ·

## THE FOLDED FLAG, 1959

Foster and Adenauer stood together in the rain at the Cologne airport. They had questions of NATO, national security, and economic recovery to explore. It was then Foster told the "old man" that he would survive the coming operation he was to have on his return to the United States, for it was not for cancer—that was over, he said. But Janet knew otherwise. Foster with his will to live thought he could keep on fighting.

When Foster returned to Washington, I met him. I had telephoned David in Swarthmore to join me and we both went aboard the plane. Christian Herter was also there. Foster went home without stopping at the State Department. There Janet gave a formal lunch for Frau Brandt which I attended and the doctors called at the house while we were at lunch. Then Foster went for two short meetings at his office, one with Willy Brandt, mayor of Berlin, and the other with Bruno Pitterman, a political leader in Austria. Following the meetings, he left by the Twenty-first Street door, as some construction work was in progress blocking his elevator. Waiting for the chauffeur, he asked the receptionist if he could sit on one of her chairs. He was alone. He never returned.

It was about two weeks later on February 13 that Clover, Janet, and I stood with two doctors in a room of the Presidential Suite in Walter Reed Hospital after the operation for hernia. The doctor beside me said very quietly, "We can keep him comfortable for some weeks." Then I knew. Clover, standing nearby, had not heard the remark. She said, "How wonderful that the operation is over."

It was after the doctors told him the results of the biopsy that Foster sent for Allen. He wanted to get word to Adenauer immediately that he had not known that the cancer had returned when they stood together that rainy day in Cologne. Allen telephoned *der Alte*.

Realization comes slowly and the knowledge that life itself can waste away is not an easy thing to understand. We visited him often while he lived out those last weeks—working, thinking, and showing a courage that was not easily found. On February 25, his birthday, there were three cakes with candles. One was brought by some of his staff. I was there in the afternoon. During these weeks Churchill, MacMillan, Eisenhower came. His sisters, Margaret and Nataline, family, and friends found him clear of mind and interested in their welfare as well as concerned with events outside even as he slipped away. He had refused sedation until the very end so he could continue working.

Early on May 24 I stood with Janet and Allen in the darkened room as the nurse with her hand on his pulse counted slowly; when she stopped counting, we knew it was over. Janet said, "My life, too, has ended." Allen and I left her and went out hand in hand to sit in the outer room.

Allen immediately called Eisenhower. The President asked if we were willing to have a state funeral. It was in that dark morning hour that the decision was made to accept Dean Sayre's offer to have the service in the Washington National Cathedral. Word went out to the world's capitals. We learned that many Heads of State and Foreign Ministers were coming from East and West. We had to think of the larger meaning as we hid our sense of personal loss. The majestic music echoed through the vaulted arches and sounded in far places from Germany to Japan as the white horses drew the caisson up the hill of Arlington Cemetery's green slopes. The road was lined with thousands of silent mourning people for the long miles from the cathedral to the grave. The prayers were full of Bible blessings and words of glory. Taps were sounded. As she turned to leave, Janet took the folded flag.

# 23

# SOVIET ACTIVITY IN ASIA, 1960

In 1959, for the third time in my life in government, a major change seemed requisite. I found the conditions of my work unacceptable, and I was puzzled as to how to shift with a minimum of disturbance to my friends and longtime associates in Berlin and Bonn.

My brother Foster's death in May came as a great shock, even though it had been anticipated.

In spite of the recognition by the new Secretary of State, my position in the German Office was troubling me. I found the trend of policy was one I could not influence significantly. Ever since my brother's resignation in April I had found less opportunity to express my views on the position to be taken in Geneva. This meeting had been scheduled after Khrushchev's November threat to sign a peace treaty with East Germany and change the status of Berlin. I felt that the papers being prepared were offering too many concessions. I did not like the proposals regarding refugees from East Germany or relating to RIAS, the American-sponsored radio station.

I knew already I would not be taken to Geneva. No woman had participated in any international Berlin conference, and even some of the more important preparatory meetings in Washington were closed to me. Of course I worked on the papers, but I was increasingly overruled.

The question in my mind was how I could disassociate myself from the policy without disturbing my German friends or giving the press a hint of a weakening in our position. A resignation could not be quietly accomplished.

A rescue was effected by Ambassador Hugh Cumming, who had a feeling that my position was difficult. He knew that Foster had not been a major source of my influence on German affairs, but he also knew that the way was open for anyone to box me in if that were considered desirable. So I was offered a job in the Bureau of Intelligence and Research. The transfer did not seem abnormal to those who knew the State Department's many shifts of personnel. It was only noted in Berlin in one or two newspaper articles.

Although my work on Berlin for the State Department was ended for a time, I continued to keep up many of my German contacts and went to Berlin about a dozen times after this change in my relation to the German Office. I went on my own when I was writing the book on Berlin, *The Wall Is Not Forever,* and I went officially several times including the occasion when the State Department requested my participation in the opening of the Klinikum in 1968. The Germans invited me as their guest three times in recent years, so my contacts have continued.

The Geneva Conference in 1959 had a strange outcome. Since the American position became known to the Soviets, they hoped we might concede further. Gromyko turned down the proposals that I had feared he might accept. There was thus little significance in the conference, and the Khrushchev ultimatum faded away.

The department issued a Press Release, No. 662, on September 21, 1959:

> Mrs. Eleanor Dulles is being assigned in the near future to the staff of Ambassador Cumming, Special Assistant to the Secretary and Director of Intelligence and Research, where she will be engaged in a special project concerning economic and financial aspects of foreign aid to newly developing countries.
>
> Until she assumes her new duties she will continue in her present position as Special Assistant to the Director, Office of German Affairs, responsible for Berlin matters.

My new work was interesting and had some value for those who were guiding policy. I was asked to examine conditions and problems surrounding our aid and the programs offered by communist countries. This was shortly before people generally were aroused by the readable and unsubstantial book *The Ugly American*, a fictional criticism of the American program. It was easy to criticize what was being done, but there had been little attempt to study what the Russians, the Chinese, and other communist countries were doing abroad. Many myths had developed about our foreign aid aloofness, lack of language competence, mismanagement, and bungling officials. The contrasting legends often described sympathetic and skillful operations of the Russians and others—these had not been examined.

[277]

While the plans for my survey were being developed I had valuable experience serving on committees reviewing the *National Estimates*. These periodic reviews, prepared in conjunction with the CIA experts, summarized all major foreign situations with indications of the direction and probable nature of future developments. They involved sensitive issues and happenings in remote areas as well as those in nations I had worked with for many years.

The plans for my research were far along in the autumn of 1959. The itinerary was worked out in consultation with the missions abroad. Just as I was ready to take off I was forced to enter the Washington Hospital Center for a gallbladder operation. The resulting delay was only for a few weeks and did not call for any drastic change in plans. I was still in the hospital on January 1, 1960, when I learned by the radio that President Eisenhower had given me the personal rank of minister. I was pleased by this act, which definitely gave me added authority to carry forward my inquiries. I was up and about in January and left for Japan the end of the month, glad to undertake this challenging work. My research was under way.

Although considerable time has passed since the publication of *The Ugly American*, for reasons not easy to understand we continue to repeat some of the misstatements and castigate ourselves for performance that is alleged to be stupid and wasteful. A balanced view admitting mistakes and revealing accomplishments would be of more service.

The book, by William J. Lederer and Eugene Burdick, gives a glowing account of sympathetic and successful communist aid carried out by teams well adjusted to the people they aimed to help. In contrast, with one interesting exception noted, the Americans were said to have bungled and slipped, creating hostility and misusing funds. I looked at the programs in many nations and found this fictional portrayal of Russian projects not to be the real situation. I could refute from direct observation the thesis of the book. My tour of the aid countries and our programs as well as the communists' efforts was the basis for a clear picture of the good and the ineffective. It was never publicized and thus only served to inform a limited number of government officers, charged with major responsibilities. Now I will give my assessment to the public for the first time.

I visited some forty-seven countries in three separate trips and talked to many hundreds of people. I saw on location many communist projects and many more American. I also learned considerable about American health, educational, and civic programs, which, though inconspicuous for the most part, were designed to build a stable and productive society in scores of lands. My choice of countries to visit was determined by what we knew of communist efforts. My trip was also conditioned in some cases by inadequate transport which made it difficult, particularly in Africa, to cover more ground.

I stayed for hours and days according to the problems to be viewed and the people to be interviewed. The countries I visited were varied and gave me a wide perspective of the communist effort as well as a comparative view of our own.

ASIA AND MIDDLE EAST, February–May 1960

| | |
|---|---|
| Japan | Thailand |
| Taiwan | Burma |
| Hong Kong | India |
| Indonesia | Nepal |
| Singapore | Pakistan |
| Malaya | Afghanistan |
| Vietnam | Iran |
| Cambodia | Turkey |

AFRICA, October 1960–January 1961

| | |
|---|---|
| Morocco | Mozambique |
| Algeria | Angola |
| Tunisia | Congo, Leopoldville |
| U.A.R. | Congo, Brazzaville |
| Sudan | Nigeria |
| Ethiopia | Togoland |
| Kenya | Ghana |
| Uganda | Ivory Coast |
| Madagascar | Liberia |
| Tanganyika | Guinea |
| Zanzibar | Mali |
| South Rhodesia | Senegal |

LATIN AMERICA, January–February 1962

| | |
|---|---|
| Brazil | Peru |
| Uruguay | Panama |
| Argentina | Mexico |
| Chile | |

There were a number of general conclusions that I would stand by as substantiated both by hosts of conversations and by direct personal observation. For instance, in Burma, Indonesia, and India the Russian and Chinese workers were segregated from the general population, housed in compounds, kept largely apart from the general population. In most cases the workers and supervisors did not speak the native language, though in many cases they used English with fair proficiency. One characteristic of Soviet projects that would have caused us serious damage was the fact that many workers were killed or injured on the job. The inadequacy of building machinery and the flaws in the planning were more apparent in the communist construction than in those undertaken by the Western nations. In some instances, notably in Indonesia, Burma, and Guinea, they were asked to leave before the time of planned operations had expired. My overall conclusion was that the Soviets in particular and some of the other communist governments undertaking aid found the conditions baffling and the relations with the recipient governments very difficult. In fact, they met the same difficulties that we met and had actually less versatile resources. The situation in the Congo (now Zaire) was perhaps extreme, but it was interesting since it led to a reversal of the new communist adventure and reduced to a very low level and limited categories the scope of communist foreign assistance in Africa.

In thinking back to my survey, I conclude the Soviet projects were not particularly designed to increase living standards or to benefit the less advantaged. The Asian games stadium and the road in Afghanistan were first spectacular and only secondarily useful. The Soviets did little that was educational and seemed unaware of the desperate need for the training of civil servants. They were less concerned with transport and communications than were the American aid missions.

I found little indication of comprehensive planning and more of one-shot efforts like the steel mill in India, the hotel in Burma. We made mistakes in our programs, but I found these were paralleled, and in most cases outweighed, by errors in the communist projects. The evidence that my findings were valid is that in most countries they curtailed their efforts or withdrew entirely. That was the situation in 1960 and 1961. Present conditions are undoubtedly different in considerable degree.

As I flew the Pacific I reflected that I was facing conditions that I knew only from books and talks with visitors—my economic and diplomatic work for more than fifteen years had focused on Europe.

I had launched on a voyage of discovery, educational but demanding hard work. My inquiry into communist activities in Indonesia, Burma, India, the Congo, Guinea, Nigeria, Ghana, Tanganyika, Zanzibar, Mozambique, Angola, and elsewhere gave me a vivid picture of their efforts. They were copying some of our early activities and they were repeating many of our mistakes. Since they were not restricted by anything corresponding to congressional concern or press criticism, they could paint the picture for observers as they wished it to be seen. Only gradually was a balanced assessment possible. What I reported in 1961, and later in 1962 in Latin America, has not been altered by any study made since then. The leaders in these countries were eager to get any development help that was offered and did not at first notice the possible entrapment. Experience was their teacher. The Burma "gift projects" offered by the Soviets were among the most interesting examples of their efforts. The governments of Congo, Indonesia, and Guinea, for instance, were among those wanting to get the Russians out. For various reasons, after 1961, there was a marked decline in Soviet nonmilitary aid to developing countries.

There was no reason then, nor is there now, for the United States to oppose genuine offers of communist aid. No matter how hard we try, our resources are insufficient to meet the need. If shipments from Russia, East Germany, Czechoslovakia, China, or elsewhere increase the capital available, without undue interference in the political system of the receiving countries, such contributions can be helpful. What the policy makers from Washington have told government leaders in the developing countries is to avoid improper obligations and watch for excessive infiltration from outside nations.

It would be of little use here to trace my entire journey in the course of this inquiry. My findings were of interest to the officers back home, and in some cases I was able to look into local problems in a way that was helpful to the officers abroad. The account of a few episodes indicates the kind of information I acquired. The days in Burma were particularly enlightening. I was in Indonesia in a critical time when Sukarno was being challenged and the Russians and Chinese were seen to have overreached themselves. The relations of India with China then were strained.

I set out on my journey early in February. The Asian trip included sixteen countries and twenty-four cities. On the trip to Africa I visited twenty-four countries and thirty or forty cities. In

[281]

most of these visits I saw the Chief of State, the Economic and Finance Ministers, the ambassadors of Britain, France, Germany, Nationalist China, and other countries. I spent a large part of my time with the American ambassador, the head of our AID mission, and others on the staff. It was possible to check and cross-check. The lesson was the importance of patience and selectivity. The experiences I had were exciting and exotic. If I were writing a travelogue and not a story of my life, it would be dramatic, highly colored, and full of adventure.

To give a feeling of this chapter in my life and of how educational it proved to be, I shall cover only a few of the many unusual episodes. To do more would be to tackle material that has been more recently and more fully covered by others.

In Japan I explored particularly the relations of the nation's industrial output to the needs of the countries receiving reparations, including Indonesia, Burma, and Malaysia, and the probable manner in which Japan could export finished products to areas rich in raw material, thus developing a fruitful exchange. In Japan I found great intelligence and a realistic view of future economic development. My days were full of conferences in the various ministries and in the embassy. I was treated with extraordinary courtesy and everyone was anxious to help. I realized that here the memory of my brother Foster, and his preparation of the treaty, meant a great deal.

With a schedule filled with appointments and interviews, I had little time for sight-seeing but I did have a weekend drive to Kamakura.

My talks with Japanese officials about aid, investment, and reparation payments gave me a considerable understanding of the resources and needs of the Pacific area. The economists stressed the fact that Japan's productive capacity could be dovetailed into the international trade patterns of the raw material areas and that an active and varied commercial exchange could result.

After a week in Japan I went on to Taiwan, where I was met enthusiastically by Minister Haraldson, who said, "You must come to a party."

So from the airport we drove to dinner where several Americans and a clutch of Nationalist Chinese Generals were toasting each other *gambei* ("bottom's up") fashion. When challenged, one must down the entire glass of spirits without hesitation. I managed to keep above the table, but just.

I found in Taipei a Joint Commission on Rural Reconstruction (JCRR). This organization proved to be an efficient device for funneling economic aid in the most effective manner. It deserves the credit for the speed with which the reconstruction and expansion of production occurred. Taiwan advanced from a low level of production to being one of the most prosperous and financially stable countries in Asia. In many ways Taiwan is a model for the use of aid funds. From the point of view of my inquiry it was not a prime target since there was no communist aid there, but I talked with many experts on the problems of the Pacific area.

My afternoon with the Generalissimo and Madame Chiang Kai-shek was memorable. His dignity and presence made a lasting impression, as did the quick and shrewd way in which Madame picked up the translation from the official charged with the task. There were only six of us in the spacious, beautifully furnished room. In every direction I looked at the large moon windows, banked with flowers planted outside—mainly chrysanthemums, a different color for each window. Chiang spoke of religion, destiny, and gratitude to the United States and to my brother Foster—or at least this was his wife's version of his comments.

Later I had a much less formal talk with his son and successor, Ching-kuo. He spoke of the next twenty-five years with a considerable optimism. I gathered scores of impressions largely borne out by more recent developments.

Hong Kong was another listening post. I was able to consult with John Lacey of the consulate and his well-trained group of officers. They analyzed information from refugees, from the British governor, Sir Robert Brown Black, and other sources. The British told me that their closer official relations with Peking had not noticeably increased the quantity or quality of the information they were assembling. Their pessimism struck me as suggesting a longer time for normalizing relations than some of my friends forecast.

The weekend there gave me a chance to sail and picnic with the John Hortons while talking over with them what I had heard. Sailing in a junk for the first time, I took the helm. When we anchored, I borrowed a bathing suit which only went two-thirds around, for a swim. We went ashore in Picnic Bay in a sampan, poled by a six-toed woman. The area opposite Aberdeen was bleak. Like other visitors I went shopping in Kowloon and had a lovely suit made. Since the thread was weak as spider webbing, it fell to pieces a few weeks later in Burma.

I had a chance to review my travels so far with real experts, Consul General Julius Holmes, the Hortons, the John Laceys. The prevailing drought, typical of Hong Kong weather, meant that the water was turned off in the hotel most of the time. I thought of the millions crowded in shacks on the steep hillsides of the colony and wondered at their ability to survive.

One of the posts visited was Singapore, where I stayed at the well-known Raffles Hotel. I had a fine briefing from the British intelligence service, located outside the city in Phoenix Park. They were full of information, although some of their pessimistic opinions then, about Lee Kwan Yew, later proved to be unwarranted. This strong and intelligent man was not entrapped by the communists and was to guide the small nation through troubled times.

The crowded stalls of Change Alley brought to mind stories of Somerset Maugham and made me aware of long years of British imperialism and long-gone pirates.

I left Singapore for Indonesia. My plane circled over Djakarta for an interminable time and I wondered why. I found when we landed that an insurgent attempting to shoot President Sukarno through the palace window had been using the same air space. Djakarta was hotter and damper than I anticipated, but I was in the air-conditioned house of Minister John W. Henderson. He was deputy to Ambassador Howard P. Jones. The Americans were disturbed by Sukarno's erratic rule and thought the Indonesians should throw Sukarno out. Our political activities were limited, but the Americans gave a modicum of help to the newsmen in the opposition.

I learned to know a number of Indonesians. The women seemed more competent than the men. The officials would accept dinner invitations and then, without explanation, fail to come. The main ministers were friendly and accessible, but the resentment over past European imperialism was striking. It was not an easy country to assist; the Soviets discovered this and they and the Chinese were ejected about the time I went there.

It was interesting to see how the Russians sought psychological credit by giving a spectacular amphitheater for Asian games. They had difficulty completing it. Their projects were imposing but not for the most part successful, and here, as well as elsewhere, many workmen were killed in the course of construction. I visited the cement plant in Surabaya. I did not see the sugar mill, but I heard a great deal about it, since it was erroneously constructed for beet instead of cane sugar and had to be altered. I also learned considerable about their agricultural efforts and ours.

Indonesia was one of the countries where we extended large-scale aid of various types. We made mistakes, but the final outcome of our effort was good and we came off the winners in the competition with the communists. We not only helped the economy but improved the character of the government. I had to work long and hard to get a clear picture.

Before I took the plane to Surabaya I went with one of the embassy staff to a mass meeting for Sukarno in the large palace, and as the speaking went on and on I saw with alarm it was close to departure time. My escort said, "You can't leave." I said, "I must. I'll be temporarily pregnant." So, clasping my raincoat over a sixty-year-old extended stomach, I bowed my way down the aisle.

Because I had been scheduled to be more than twenty-four hours in Surabaya, on the east end of Java, it was decided I could visit nearby Bali. Unfortunately, the plane was delayed and I did not reach Bali until late in the evening. However, I had a swim in the mysterious lagoon where the men were harvesting shellfish, snails, seaweed, and many-colored fish. This catch they take back to their communes to share in a spontaneous form of communism. My drive to the airport at dawn was a lovely colorful experience. We passed columns of beautiful dark-haired young women with large baskets of fruits and vegetables on their heads, walking through the forest in slanting sunlight and shadows.

Going north and west I visited Kuala Lumpur in Malaya, an attractive town with a good hotel—the Merlin. The city was surrounded by dark, overshadowing forests with many rubber plantations. I found the people of Malaya looking forward to an opportunity to rebuild in peace. They had recently halted the guerrilla forces in the north and the people who were fleeing south before communist attacks. Our aid, not large in scope, was significant in raising productivity.

I found the Prime Minister, Tengku Abdul Rahman, in fine form and optimistic as to the economic and political future. He was, however, afraid of Chinese pressure—over one third of the population was Chinese. His Finance Minister had me for supper with him and one other guest. They were well informed not only in domestic affairs but also about the whole Pacific area. I concluded our aid was being well applied and the Soviet communists frustrated.

My brief stop in Saigon was to mean much in giving me a quick foreview of history. I had an appointment with Diem, but he canceled it when Nehru appeared on the scene at the time scheduled for me. I was in the palace. I saw a number of streets later to become famous and infamous. I can still remember the women in the streets with long, bright, silk dresses, pedaling their bicycles briskly. I stayed with the administrator of AID, Arthur Gardiner, and Emily, his wife.

It was in the Saigon airport before takeoff that I had the first of a series of severe attacks—which I learned two months later were caused by gallstones left in the common duct after my 1959 surgery. The trouble was to continue, but I completed my journey despite seven painful seizures in as many weeks.

On to Cambodia, I found the King ill when I reached Pnom Penh, so the young Prince canceled his appointment with me. However, I was given a fine banquet in the marble palace. There was a long table, seating forty persons. I could only talk to the Foreign Minister on one side and another government official on my right. After the meal we were seated in two long rows against opposite walls. Conversation was almost impossible.

My main source of information was the embassy staff, members of which told me of the political ferment and described aid projects. They also showed me a Soviet aid project—a hospital that was being built.

Since I had largely recovered from my attack, I enjoyed the drives through the villages with small houses on stilts. One afternoon we had a flat tire and took refuge in a Buddhist community. I am not sure that it was according to the religious rules, but the monks showed no annoyance as we waited.

My main interviews completed, the mission in Cambodia arranged for a car to take me and an escort, Ann Thomas, to Angkor Wat. It was a long drive to the border of Thailand, where I was to go next. The primitive hotel where we spent the night was on the edge of the jungle. I woke to see an elephant under my window. He was roaming free.

Fortunately I was able to rent a small Land-Rover so we could go not only to the large temple but to several smaller ones where milk trees and jungle vines struggled to bring the elaborate structures down. The carvings were magnificent. They were not so much beautiful as awe-inspiring. I fear these carvings have not survived the fighting in this jungle.

Going on from Angkor Wat to Bangkok I was received by Ambassador U. Alexis Johnson, and put up in his guest house on the embassy grounds. As in other countries, I saw various projects and I was driven down roads that had been built with U.S. aid money. These were designed to open up the jungle for the remote villages. The main road in Thailand was one much criticized because it does not end in a city, but rather gives access for a large number of scattered small towns. I had some enlightening conversations with the experts at the headquarters of the international economic organization known as EFTA. They were concerned with developing trade for a wide area in the Far East and had conferences bringing together many experts and government officials.

The city of Bangkok was fascinating with its golden temple and emerald Buddha. It was a privilege to be included in a boat trip with the Foreign Minister and his distinguished guests. The river, teeming with life and bordered by thousands of huts on its banks, was alive with fishermen and women and crowded food markets.

I was warned of the uncertain future and of the large degree of intrigue within the government of Thailand, instigated both by communists and by rival native factions.

Burma, my next port of call, was especially interesting in connection with my inquiry. The Soviets, with the combined motive of gaining an economic as well as a political advantage, had offered the Burmese government six "gift packages." The government had reluctantly accepted three and postponed decision on the other three indefinitely. I visited the three projects that were then under construction. Marshall Wright, a young staff officer who spoke excellent Burmese, escorted me first to the dormitory, where a large building offered students cell-like rooms with no doors or windows. It was on the university grounds. Then we went to the site of the hotel, which was half finished. A Soviet overseer was most interested in our visit. He apparently spoke no Burmese, but he let Marshall translate what the local workmen and foremen said, since he understood English. We were told it was a project of uncertain value—too big for its purpose and expensive to run. The Russian was most curious about our survey.

After seeing these two "gifts" we decided to go overnight to Taunggyi, northeast of Mandalay. It was the time of the water festival, April 1—and no serious work could be done in Rangoon that weekend. Thousands of people crowded the streets with bags full of water and bottles with which they doused each other. We were able to get the U. S. Navy to fly us up to the province.

It was at the Taunggyi airport that my Hong Kong suit fell apart. Fortunately, the airport was closed so that only Marshall, the pilot, and the control tower were witnesses. I explained to Marshall that I always traveled with safety pins and that I could manage some repairs. By the time the town's police chief had arrived to take us into town, I was reasonably well covered and with the first peril behind me ready for the second—a horrendous drive through the hills on two wheels of a four-wheeled vehicle. The chief took us to his house, where family and friends were sitting solemnly against the wall of a large room, open on one side, staring at us while we tried to talk to our bold and brave host. After a little time he took us to the government house, a hostel built simply with unscreened openings for doors and windows and much mosquito netting over the beds. Here we found our friend from the Russian hotel site in Rangoon waiting to see what we were up to. He had driven hard all night to get there and he followed us around all the next day.

That evening Marshall and I had a fine ride in a long, narrow boat with a small outboard engine. A Burmese boatman guided us to Inlay Lake, weaving our way through the water hyacinths and avoiding submerged water buffalo. The moon was mellow as we came in the large shallow lake to the islands where the Hansa floating villages were. It was a beautiful sight in the golden light, perhaps the most exotic of my trip.

The Russian-sponsored hospital, already half built, seemed singularly ill adapted for medical services. There was no elevator and there seemed little provision for laboratory or surgical facilities. However, they have planned the doorways to thwart the germs, providing several sharp turns for exit and entrance; these were designed to baffle the evil diseases. The Soviet program manager stayed with us. It was his first visit to the hospital, and he profited by Marshall Wright's translation from Burmese. (I have been told it was turned into a hotel.)

Back in Rangoon, I learned of U.S. efforts that were moderate in scope. I also learned of our concern over the political outlook, which seemed to be moving fast toward dictatorship.

Because of the geographic proximity to Burma, I first went to Calcutta and Nepal and later to New Delhi in India. In Calcutta I was appalled by the hordes sleeping on the sidewalks and crowding the open spaces in doorways. Moreover, I did not expect to see so many wretched cows wandering at large.

The consulate was well staffed and well informed. An officer took me to see a large, fairly modern truck factory and then to some small cottage industries which I thought were badly planned. There was a group of buildings for unrelated products—batteries, bicycles, and crockery—too small to make a dent on either employment or production.

I went from Calcutta far north to Nepal in the Himalayas, before turning back to New Delhi. Nepal was a land of mystery and adventure for me. I was fascinated by the villages and the people. Here there was a primeval lake, long gone dry. It was being "mined" for peat taken out in large chunks and used as fuel in village houses.

Here I had an extraordinary opportunity. At my first dinner a young man came in and asked if I wanted to fly to Mt. Everest for twenty dollars. I said yes and he told me to be up at six in the morning. He explained that two hitchhikers had come to the hotel there and had persuaded a wealthy Californian to induce a Nepalese pilot to fly to the mountain paying him several hundred dollars. We could join him if we shared in the expense.

It was a brilliant blue and white peak as we saw it when we were at 19,000 feet. The plane was nonpressurized. I blacked out just after the splendid panorama came in sight, but I came to when we dropped 10,000 feet and found a tolerable oxygen level.

It was in Nepal that I had another severe gallbladder attack. Dr. Miller, one of two brothers running a Methodist missionary hospital, came to help. He drew a map of my ailing insides on the back of an envelope and told me what he thought was wrong. Later I showed this envelope to Dr. Chatel, the surgeon at the Leahy Clinic in Boston who eventually operated on me. Dr. Miller was very modest, but proved himself in this instance a first-rate diagnostician—I had stones in the sphincter of Oddi and had a bad case of jaundice before I reached home six weeks later.

United States aid in Nepal consisted mainly of technical assistance. The people were pleasant and the royal family were attractive and intelligent. They were wary of Soviet communist activities and worried about Chinese aggression.

I was taken to see the Dalai Lama in his small temple. There was one Dalai Lama who was real and one who was said to be a fake. I sat beside the real one on a bench in his retreat and shared tea with him. He had an air of calm and patience and seemed to believe everything would come out all right. The fake one gave out cards and signatures. Both had escaped from the Chinese in Tibet.

When I reached New Delhi, our plane landed in a large airport where, not long before, President Eisenhower had been greeted by several million enthusiastic Hindus and taken in a triumphant parade. I do not know whether it was mainly because of the grain the United States had sent—millions of bushels—or because of some instinct about his personality. In any case I was told Eisenhower's reception had stunned Khrushchev and caused him to doubt the wisdom of the proposed visit to Moscow—even before the U-2 incident of May 1960.

I stayed at the Ashoka Hotel and found it comfortable. But no one had prepared me for the terrible dryness of my throat, which made me feel as if I had tonsillitis all the time I was in India.

I remember well when I talked to Jawaharlal Nehru, who sat looking out a window turned away from me. I felt that if he could spare me the time, he could also give me his attention. I said as much in diplomatic language and my escort, the deputy chief of the U. S. Mission, was highly amused. He told me afterward that I was the only person who had made the arrogant Nehru turn around. I asked Nehru about the prospective relationship of the public to the private sector and what his long-range planning for the economy might be. I said there seemed to be barely noticeable improvement in agricultural methods.

At the time when I was in India the politicians were very upset by the Chinese invasion of the north. Krishna Menon was under attack. Nehru was on the defensive. When I went to the Loch Sabra to hear the debate, the Socialists and the Communists got into a real physical fight and the Communists withdrew from the hall in a body. Nehru sat there wringing his hands. Then he got up and said in English, "What do you expect me to do? I am trying to do my best for you. You just abuse and criticize me."

I thought he was going to burst into tears. It was a strange performance. It did not have the ring of leadership or the feeling of power that Nehru really had. India was a strange world for me. I did not fully understand it. I felt that there was a great distance between the leaders and the people—sympathy but, perhaps, not enough understanding.

I worked hard at all the stops on my journey. The missions were satisfied that I brought some questions to the surface which were hard for them to uncover. In discussion with those in charge of local aid programs, I heard many frank comments on the difficulties of the local authorities in working with Soviet experts. Everywhere I found a scarcity of Russians who spoke the foreign language, though many spoke English. The famous Russian steel mill was a large undertaking. In India, as in all other places where I visited, the Soviet workmen were largely confined to barracks, although some of the native workmen visited them in their quarters. The importance of the enterprise was widely recognized, but the comparisons with the German and the American mills was not apt, since the processes of steel production was different.

The American Embassy in India planned well and made it possible for me to visit the Taj Mahal. On my way there, I was accompanied by a woman who was half Hindu, half American. I stopped to see a number of small villages, each a group of mud huts with tiny rooms and no furniture except beds made of rope on wooden frames, with one or two copper cooking pots, and a broom. The oxen toiled slowly around the wells, drawing water for the scrawny, parched gardens. The people seemed listless and discouraged, uninterested in me or in anything around them.

When I added my days in Calcutta, Delhi, Agra, Bombay, and other places, I had clear impressions of need but nothing to raise my hopes for the future. I saw some spectacular places from the old days, including the Red Fort, but nothing modern to lead me to expect progress or constructive adjustment to the present age. There were a number of experienced bankers, some of whom I had met in the United States, and they knew how to invest their money, but the scope of India's problems was too much for them to deal with. During this trip, when I attended the inauguration of the Maharastra state by Nehru, I realized more than I had before the divisions between areas and ethnic groups. I had almost accepted the easy assumption that foreign nations are monolithic and spared some of the problems of local divisions and difference in race, religion, and political tradition from which we suffer. In India, however, I saw immediately a host of divisive influences.

I met Nehru several times in Washington and I never knew if this mystic approach was genuine or whether it was an act.

Pakistan was a nation where we had been very active, investing in various new businesses. Mr. Fancy was one who had benefited.

[291]

He had already developed his large shrimp production and was doing a booming business. Other industries were also increasing their exports. The plans were to move the capital inland to Islamabad, but it was still in Karachi by the sea. I enjoyed a midnight sail on a Bunder boat, as well as a sailing race at the yacht club. My visit presented me with a painful problem. I had my most violent attack of jaundice. I was really ill and had to leave the reception in my honor. The State Department physician threatened to put me on the plane for New York. I bargained with him saying I would go home in two weeks if he would give me that additional time.

Meanwhile, world events were to catch up with me. While I was planning to go to Peshawar in Pakistan and to make the trip from there to Kabul in Afghanistan by car driven over the Khyber Pass, Francis Gary Powell was shot down over the Soviet Union. He was flying a U-2 mission.

I was staying with my friends Fred and Jane Bunting, who knew a great deal about Pakistan and its economic leaders. At breakfast they told me of the newspaper reports. "Isn't it strange the propaganda the Soviets put out," they said. I knew of the U-2 flights—that the planes had been flying over the Russian territory—but I said, "Yes, their stories will never cease." I was not surprised. No Dulles was in Washington on that May 1, and no one of us was involved in the first denial or in the later explanation. The State Department and the CIA cabled frantically for me to avoid Peshawar and not to go into the Soviet Union.

I had to fly back to New Delhi and then on to Kabul in Afghanistan. On the way the plane stopped briefly at Amritsar. We were told to get off for breakfast. We had twenty-five minutes, they said. I sat down with two traveling companions and then went to the primitive washroom. To my horror I saw the plane taxi down the apron to take off. I rushed out. My passport was on the plane. I had no baggage, no money, and no language to help me if I were to be stranded there. I got in front of the plane. The pilot had seen me before in Nepal and, anyway, he did not want to run me down—he stopped and a boarding ladder was brought to the great relief of my breakfast companions.

Outside Kabul I met an "ugly American." He was making simple pumps by hooking up bicycle chains to pipes, to be operated by pushing pedals. He wore a western hat and chewed on a straw in a nonchalant way. He was from Oklahoma. Carelessly, and with little understanding, the critical issues of foreign aid have been packed by some into the phrase "ugly American." In using this term, some indicate their view that the American abroad blunders and struts through native societies with little sympathy for peoples and cultures. They accept the tone and misunderstand the story of the book by that title. The result is a false cartoon.

I flew over deserts and mountains to Tehran. In Iran I was invited to a dinner party at the British Embassy, where prominent Iranians were present in extraordinary fine clothes and with fabulous jewels. I have never seen a more spectacular group of women. As I drove through the city I was aware of the poverty. I talked to a man who was very important in their program and learned they were making an effort. They had employed American engineers. The man I saw has probably been assassinated since then. I had this rumor. Quite a number of people I talked to in Asia and Africa were arrested or murdered, according to reports. I was very much impressed with the inequality in the distribution of wealth. The city was exciting and full of ancient treasures, turning slowly toward a modern world with food and water and even developing a middle class.

On to Turkey, I found Ankara dense with tear gas and roaring with rebellious students. I was there on the first day of the revolution. There were many signs of Soviet exploitation and tentative efforts, nowhere any substantial communist achievements. There was suspicion of foreigners, doubts as to the future.

Then I flew to Paris. I was there in May when Eisenhower came. I saw the original movies of Khrushchev's simulated anger and his outburst when he was cutting off the projected summit conference. The story I was told was that after Eisenhower's triumphant visit to India, Khrushchev did not dare risk the President's visit to Moscow. Khrushchev thus used the U-2 incident, which was no surprise to him, as an excuse for disrupting the talks. The real picture of his press conference was a revelation—a man acting a part and turning on his anger, then turning it off, a phony temper tantrum.

My first trip was accomplished by the end of May. I passed my sixty-sixth birthday in Washington. I was not able to go to Bryn Mawr to receive in person an award from the college. I was hustled to Boston's Leahy Clinic for the removal of the villainous stones that had plagued the later part of my trip. The Bryn Mawr citation was to me as an "Economist and Diplomat." It said I had "a unique place in the hearts of West Berliners" that my "imagination conceived The Congress Hall, a memorial to Benjamin Franklin and a monument to free speech." A friend received it for me as I lay in the hospital.

My view of Asia had been a marvelous and revealing experience, visions of old civilizations, revelations of enormous problems—it was educational and discouraging. I knew the communists would have problems and that there could be no easy conquest of poverty. The future, when the best of science and knowledge could be shared, was indeed distant. I turned in my report and prepared for my coming exploration in Africa.

# 24

## COMMUNIST PENETRATION OF AFRICA,
## 1960—1961

I was hardly out of the hospital following my July 1960 operation and was still bandaged and equipped with various mechanical devices when I started on my twenty-four-nation journey. Before leaving the United States I spent several days at the United Nations conferring with some of those who knew Africa. It was then I saw Nikita Khrushchev jump to his feet and rush to the front of the Assembly Hall to embrace Fidel Castro who had just come to New York.

The first segment of the trip in the autumn of 1960 was prefaced by a chartered flight with Radio Free Europe to celebrate the donation of the Freedom Bell in Berlin. This had been the gift of thousands of American schoolchildren contributing pennies. We flew to Portugal, where, at Gloria, outside of Lisbon, the large transmitters picked up the beams from the Munich research center and sent them across the Iron Curtain in Russian, Hungarian, Romanian, Czech, and other languages. Our group went from Portugal to Munich. There we were flown in twelve or fourteen helicopters along the border between the Federal Republic of Germany, Czechoslovakia, and East Germany. It was a strange sensation as the flock of army birds flew low over the blockhouses stationed every few miles along the barbed wire and "dead strip" that cordoned off the Soviet-dominated area.

It was some hours later when we landed in Berlin that I knew I was the subject of an East German diplomatic protest.

My greeting at the Templehof airport was from a large Berlin Bear who towered over me, giving me carnations as he overwhelmed me with a hug for the cameras.

I was hustled to a bus. Did I want to go to East Berlin? Minister Allan Lightner asked me.

"Yes," I said.

"Come now," he said. "The East German authorities are to get you, but not today."

Then he told of the formal diplomatic note from the German People's Republic to our embassy in Prague, threatening dire consequences if I stepped foot on "their territory." It was unlikely that the communists would kidnap me, but the warning added extra interest to my trip through East Berlin, surrounded by stalwart, protecting Americans.

After a short stay in Berlin I went on to London and Paris to be briefed by colonial experts before flying to Morocco, to the northern lands where the Romans and the Phoenicians had left their imprint and where Europe had been cradled in the warm shores of the Mediterranean. In Tunis, Algiers, and then in Egypt I had a chance to see the relics of the early civilization of the Mediterranean and the Nile and the archaeological finds of a type of life that predated the societies I was to find farther south.

My trip to Africa was at a time when both the Chinese and the Soviets were trying to win friends by exporting their techniques. The Russians knew we Americans had several strikes against us because of the age-long white exploitation of the blacks. They hoped they could go in as brothers, as teachers, and as political allies, but they found they, too, had difficulties.

This was the subject of my inquiry.

My visit in 1960 came after the independence of most of the sub-Saharan nations was well under way. That development did not eliminate tribal feuds and animosities, but did project a number of black leaders onto the world stage. I was able to meet a score of the outstanding personalities, some now dead—Nyerere, Keita, Haile Selassie, Nkrumah, Senghor, Tsombe, Olympia, Houphouet-boigny, M'Boya, Tubman, and others. Their obvious ability made them rise above tribal leadership to become notable figures in the United Nations and in the Economic Commission for Africa, as well as other international organizations. I met with various groups discussing aid and economic problems and recognized that the extent of their education abroad had helped prepare them for participation in world problems and at the same time it had increased their distance from the millions of Africans for whom they wished to provide leadership. I was rarely conscious of ethnic differences when I talked with them, but I was somewhat overwhelmed by a surge of primeval forces and dark superstitions when on various occasions I joined in large groups of workers or merchants. In a drive outside

Nairobi, along with an African chauffeur, I was swept along by a tide of demonstrators seeking the freedom and reinstatement of the late Jomo Kenyatta, imprisoned by the British for nine years.

My imaginary journeys as a child were as vivid as many of the sights I witnessed in later life. In my journey in 1960 I found the rivers swarming with reptiles, jungles with monkeys hanging from the trees, the lions lurking in dim, tangled bush, and pampas familiar to me for I had known them many years earlier. I found lions in the park north of Nairobi, I found the reptiles in the rain forests, and the baboons leaped from limb to limb under the slopes of Mount Kenya. I looked over the wide reaches of the great Riff Valley and I wondered how much longer this world would be alien and even hostile to our civilization—we had gone a different route with our more rigorous climate and in our drive to expand capitalism.

Everywhere I went—to some twenty or thirty cities—I was overwhelmed with the sense of urgency and impatience, the hunger for tangible freedom, progress, and technical miracles among the leaders. Nowhere did I find in the areas I visited a sense of the time ingredient in capital development. They sought packaged development, modern airports set up overnight. Yet in the Nigerian jungle, north of Lagos, the paramount chief in green face mask and brilliant robes sat in his small hut, proud of his position but inarticulate. The contrast was striking. The men gathered in the palaver huts in many countries had scant material to discuss, but they talked of future economic miracles. The sense of pace and even of direction in these countries did not follow the textbooks. I could see that there was a long, long journey ahead. Now, twenty years later, we have only gone the "first mile."

The grandeur of the landscape, the magnificence of the wildlife, I found stunning. More important and more meaningful was the emergence of leaders in some of the nations—men of power and imagination. Some had surmounted the tribal ideas and traditions of the past and were moving toward creative statesmanship. Unfortunately the problems have an immensity that is not brought into the framework of familiar Roman law or of northern European arts and sciences. We cannot fit the continent of Africa into any systems with which we are prepared to deal. It is beyond what we know and understand.

It did not take me long to realize the scope and sweep of the forces, the dark abyss, the lofty heights, and the uncertain conflicts, the wars within wars, with which the next generations will have to deal. We have our plans for development but we have neither the insight nor the power to impose them in a vast and restless world of thousands of tribes, age-old strife beyond and beneath anything Europe has experienced in recent centuries.

I would have liked to complete my trip to Africa with a more optimistic view of the future. I would have found the strength of the land and of the people a tremendous element in the reshaping of the human relations and the hopes for the rich potential of mankind. Unfortunately, I came away from my journey with my hopes receding to the distant future, which I personally would never know. I realized that decades of time and human suffering and expenditure of blood and treasure would be required.

In North Africa I was aware of the increasing thrust for independence. I talked with a number of the leaders in Morocco, Tunis, and Algeria. There was no significant Soviet activity at the time, so I did not find much to survey except our aid program. Our efforts were not spectacular, but at the same time they kept us in contact with the economists and added to our understanding. Cairo with its teeming population and staggering poverty was difficult to comprehend. I was glad to be able to have an intimate conversation with the former Egyptian ambassador to the United States, Ahmed Hussein. He was the man who had received the denial of the financing of the Aswan Dam from my brother Foster. I did not find any lingering resentment, but rather admiration for Foster. He spoke so frankly against Nasser that I worried for fear he would be overheard on the next balcony, or perhaps by a bugging device.

Going on to Khartoum and then to Ethiopia, I began to get a comprehension of the enormous problems of these regions, which seemed so far from Washington and in which the Soviets did not have a strong position. Ethiopia was beginning to feel the tremors that were to shake it in the next decades. Many of the cabinet members were thrown into jail at about this time. Our aid program here was substantial, and this was also a country to which the Germans had sent a capable team and were working out a coherent program.

I was very excited to get to Nairobi. It is the most appealing country I visited. The people, the landscape, the animals, are all attractive. Tourism is a major source of income and I could readily see why. The excursion I took on a weekend to Treetops, the house above the water hole, is more vivid to me, at this date, than my interviews on aid programs.

I was also very excited about going to Zanzibar. This place was famous because David Livingstone went there several times on his journeys. It was also infamous because it was a major center for the slave trade. I heard the Communist Chinese had an interest in this small island, not yet joined to Tanganyika. I was entertained by the British Commissioner, Sir George Mooring, and had some fine swims.

It was in Dar es Salaam that my journey first overlapped that of Teddy Kennedy. There the embassy gave us a joint briefing. The young man seemed pleasant but somewhat uncertain as to what he was supposed to do. This was some twenty years before he was considered the Democratic front-runner for the presidency. We flew on together to Rhodesia, where again we were briefed on local problems already assuming significant proportions. In our two days together I had a feeling that he wanted to act like the brother of the President of the most powerful nation, and that it would be inappropriate to offer to carry my briefcase.

I was glad to go to Mozambique because it was in a transitional stage. Beira was a main port for the shipment of metals from Central Africa, the Congo, Rhodesia, and elsewhere and was striving to use its key position to gain independence of Portugal.

Here William Howard Taft and his charming wife were my hosts. I knew his family, particularly his aunt, Helen Taft Manning, and had written him, about my prospective visit, a personal letter, "Dear Bill" and "Love to Barbara." He wrote back to me: "My dear Mrs. Dulles. If you want to come I can't put myself in the way of it...." It was clear he did not want me. I replied, "Dear Consul General Taft. I am under instructions from the Department of State to review certain problems in Africa. I am planning to spend eight days in Mozambique." He replied, "We would love to have you stay with us but the hotel is more comfortable than our house." I stayed in their house. They were extremely nice to me. Bill told me that he had written a dispatch to the department saying he did not want them to send anyone else—but he had torn it up after he found my conversations with the other consuls and various African officials had been helpful.

The Tafts drove me on a fine short trip to Kruger Park, where we spent the night and nearly collided with a herd of giraffes.

In Angola I saw more of the Portuguese than in Mozambique. A very smart young captain took me upcountry about one hundred miles and showed me a large power project which they were building at Kabinda. There they took me through a long tunnel in the mountain which would soon be flooded by the river. They were changing the course to produce a tremendous wattage. My guides showed me towns that had been reported as the scene of massacres and pointed out that they were not destroyed and seemed tranquil.

William Gibson, the consul, was a man of ability and courage. He was to live through dangerous riots soon after my visit. He seemed to have a balanced view of the situation, which was fortunate since it was indeed explosive. The officials gave a fine banquet for me and made an all-out effort to convince me of the improving relations with the blacks, the *evolués* who had become Westernized and the Portuguese who were there in large numbers.

When I came to leave, we found the plane departure was postponed an hour. "Let's go swimming," Bill said. We drove to Luanda, jumped in his boat, and went to a beach across the bay. It was a lovely spot with crystal-clear water. I swam in my slip, we ate a sandwich and then rushed back to the airport. The door of the plane was closed and it was about to take off. They stopped and let me climb aboard. I was off to the Congo.

In Leopoldville I heard much of the recent riots and the passion for freedom. Clare Timberlake, the American ambassador, had shown great courage—facing the mob on the terrace of the glass-walled new embassy. The times had been desperate and there was still unrest. When the economic officer, Daniel Margolies, took me to one of the work sites where several thousand workers were digging on a drainage project in a swamp by the river, we had a narrow escape. We drove up in an embassy car and the workers thought we were bringing their payroll, which was several days overdue. They crowded around the car—indignant when they found we had no money. Dan had the car turned around and got quickly down the road to the town.

As I continued along on my journey talking to many leaders, I found there had been many things to puzzle me in the Congo, in Togo, in Nigeria, in the Ivory Coast and tropical Africa in general, since the time of Livingstone and Stanley—the mid-nineteenth century. There were airports, but the dark forest loomed thickly over the roads. The wilderness is retreating slowly. Unfortunately, the number of animals diminishes as man develops techniques for killing them and crowding out their lairs. The lions I saw watched us languidly in the park north of Nairobi—we had to stop to change a tire. I stood guard between the driver and the pride, since I thought they might be stimulated to attack by human and car smells. At Treetops I had been lucky to see three herds of elephants. The last came just as we were preparing to leave and the white hunter told us to hurry down the ladder above the water hole. If we did not get away quickly, he said, we might be held there for several hours until the elephants left.

All of us who have been to Africa can remember the tremendous sweep and majesty of uplands and surge of herds of zebras and impalas, the lumbering rhinos skirmishing in comic attacks with each other. The rivers seethed at times with hippos, and elephants sprayed each other in the sun. There were flocks of cowbirds riding the backs of galloping buffalo and a scurry of small beasts almost underfoot. I was not able to go on a safari for I was there on business, but I did have rides into the wilds and parks. I had near views of Mount Kenya and Kilimanjaro. I knew that there were vast riches in many lands, but I saw the reluctance of the tribal leaders to change their customs and ritual. Their desire for the benefits and prestige of Western society was in conflict with their allegiance to ancient traditions.

I found that neither Western aid nor the communist programs had at that time made a noticeable dent in the primitive conditions in most of the areas. Here and there an irrigation project, a power development, a school, a seaport, or an airfield has been constructed with funds from abroad. New techniques of agriculture or of construction are visible occasionally.

I am pleased to have seen so much in Africa, North, the Sudan, Ethiopia, Kenya, Tanganyika, Zanzibar, Mozambique, and the West, Angola, the two Congos, Nigeria and Togo, Mali and coastal nations. I saw an immense variety of scenery and of economic conditions. Everywhere I looked for the communist influence I found less than I had been led to expect. I did not study the larger economic problems that were to be of such concern in the years to come. Nor did I have time to consider the many political changes except in a general way as I learned about the major issues from

[301]

others who were more deeply involved. I did get considerable exposure to the restive Portuguese territories and gained an impression of developing revolt.

My stay in Rhodesia was extremely short, but the U. S. Mission gave me a good briefing. I saw the Belgian Congo in turmoil. I found Ghana in a transitional state. Nigeria was quiet. Guinea was beginning to reject the considerable communist presence. Mali was in economic trouble, unable to sell its peanut crop.

I was told of many insoluble problems. The strenuous travel and constant demands on my previous knowledge of economics and aid techniques was exhausting, but the help of old and new friends made it possible to keep an exacting schedule. I enjoyed the days even though they taxed my energy. Only on Christmas 1960 in Nigeria did I find myself lonely and with a great longing to be at home. This was one of the few Christmases when I have had no family and no word from relatives at home. I went to the cathedral in Lagos, where a friendly black couple invited me to join them in their pew.

I had been in many countries and had learned something of what was going on in other neighboring areas I did not visit. This information was to be supplemented later by a short trip to Latin America.

My search had convinced me that the Soviet Union had not yet learned the lessons of how to deal with the governments and the people in the noncommunist nations. While some of their projects had made a favorable impression, a close look showed that they had encountered serious difficulties. In several cases they had withdrawn to reconsider and even to terminate their programs. The relations with leaders in Indonesia, Burma, Guinea, and the Congo (Zaire), for instance, were tumultuous and even antagonistic. The mistakes they made indicated the obstacles that we had found earlier and that we were beginning to overcome.

There was little if anything that we could learn from the Soviet conduct of their programs. They had perhaps a better way of publicizing their accomplishments, some of which were worthwhile, and they never published their mistakes. Apprehension that they would make great strides in gaining public sympathy by their gifts and loans was not justified. Their alertness to the kind of political turmoil, at a later date, that they would take advantage of in such places as Angola, Ethiopia, and elsewhere was already obvious.

Whereas they gained by unrest and rebellion, our policy sought to increase stability and maintain calm, with emphasis on dependable progress.

The questions I had been asked to consider were thus covered by my reports of facts and opinions that I gathered, all pointing in the same direction. Some twenty years of history since my trip indicate that the conclusions reached then were valid.

The communists did less in the less developed countries in the 1960s than in the 1950s. What they have done since then has had a political-military emphasis. The few gains have been mainly in rebellious areas and where conflict has stirred up trouble.

My journeys were seen as a one-shot assessment, as a guide to decisions, but could do little either to expedite our progress or to meet the basic needs of these nations. It established with reasonable certainty, however, that the difficulties we faced were not the result of Soviet activities, nor did the Russian effort offer guides to better solutions. Our problems were inherent in the enormous extent of the political and economic needs of these nations, their continuing tribal conflicts, and their lack of experienced governmental personnel. Neither the United States nor Europe was quick to understand the problems and importance of the Dark Continent.

# · 25 ·

## FIRED, 1961

My return from Africa in January 1961 plunged me into the snowy inauguration of the new President, John Fitzgerald Kennedy. The next few weeks government was much occupied by the turnover and soon by the catastrophic failure of the Bay of Pigs landings in Cuba. This distressed my brother, Allen, who had laid the whole problem and plans—pro and con—before Jack Kennedy in November and then in more detail in January. Allen himself was in Puerto Rico in April when the arrangements were changed in the White House and the signal given to launch the expedition.

This failure of the American-sponsored attack on Castro was the cause of Allen's leaving the CIA in the summer, some months before he had intended.

It was also the indirect cause of my leaving the Department of State soon after.

Early after his election Jack Kennedy said he was going to keep Allen and Edgar Hoover. Allen was willing to stay. He knew Kennedy. He played tennis with him. They had mutual friends in Palm Beach. Allen spoke to me in the summer about the Bay of Pigs. He had concluded that some of the Kennedy advisers didn't really want Castro overthrown. It would not be right for me to quote him directly—this is only a remembered impression. It has always seemed to me ridiculous to blame Allen and Dick Bissell for the disaster at the Bay of Pigs. The final plans and execution were made by the Kennedy group. The men around Kennedy were not pleased that Allen was still head of CIA. If he did well, he would get the credit—for failures Kennedy would be blamed.

Allen was out of office when I was planning my trip to Latin America. My program, as outlined in the Intelligence Research Bureau, was to visit sixteen Latin American countries to survey the Alliance for Progress and make some comparisons with aid in Asia and Africa to their development. I was scheduled to leave in mid-

September and did a quick language job at the department—getting easy Spanish phrases and a respectable vocabulary which later served me well.

Two days before I was supposed to leave, Roger Hilsman, who had succeeded Ambassador Cumming as the head of INR, called me to his office. I thought he had turned against Allen. There was no hint of what was to come for me an hour later. We talked of my trip. He had been smooth and, I thought, friendly. Then the Secretary, Dean Rusk, summoned me to his office and said, "I am sorry but you have to leave. The Kennedys have said I must get you out."

"What shall I do?" I appealed.

"You can stay—legally you have the right."

"But I can't sit and twiddle my thumbs—I'll have to look for another job. Can I use some of my leave to go to New York and other cities in the search?"

"Yes," he said. I left without further comment. The shock to me was greater than anyone realized. Many thought I had a comfortable income. It was easy to assume that at age sixty-seven I could and would retire.

But I did not have enough income with pension credits ($10,000 a year) to meet my family obligations, nor had I finished my job on aid programs.

It may be coincidence but my telephone was disconnected twice. I thought some of my friends avoided me. I had lunch with a colleague in the Executive Dining Room of the State Department. Her chief called her in and said, "That woman is poison," or so she told me.

My notebooks about my interviews and travels in the next weeks, after September 20, 1961, show some 117 names. Most of them represented friends and other people who could either give me a job, sponsor me for a grant, or give me practical advice as to where and how to look for work. I knew from long experience that the unemployed have a much harder time in getting a job than the employed. Therefore I felt considerable pressure. I also had an unfinished story to tell on my aid survey and it seemed to me that the Rockefeller Foundation, which had work under way in that field, might give me a grant for a few months.

I went to New York six or seven times, to Philadelphia, and to other places where I thought I could find suitable employment urging my industrial, statistical, aid, and foreign service experience as assets. I had more than sixty interviews. A representative of the Rockefeller brothers' organization said to me, "We are fresh out of money."

I was offered one job, or so I thought, by a friend who used to be in the State Department but who was then a high executive in a major oil company (Esso). He asked me what salary would be acceptable, when I could start work, which of two divisions I would prefer, and other practical questions. I never heard from him after that day.

I don't know which got worn down first—my shoe leather or my spirits. In 1961 no one seemed inclined to help. No friends, no relatives had fruitful proposals. Some asked why I didn't retire and live on my pension. I still had dependents and my pension was smaller than they assumed. My outside income could not permit me to continue to live in the house I had built in Virginia. I was full of working energy and interests. I could not imagine sitting back and doing nothing. Reading, yes. But not an inactive life with so much to be done and so many years of preparation for doing it.

I had not intended to resign soon after Rusk's word. He had said that legally I could stay for more than two years. But a queer episode determined the date of my resignation. An associate in the State Department said something to a *Washington Post* reporter, and a short article in the newspaper said I was resigning. The article gave no reason. My first instinct was to deny it. Then I thought it would be foolish to make a fuss and perhaps a few weeks later, resign. I decided to tell the administration that I was leaving that week. My departure was not one that anyone could be proud of. I carried and pushed my boxes of books along the corridor and managed to get them to the elevator. A friend's station wagon was in the basement. So the curtain came down and I was out in the cold.

My first assumption was that I could get a job in a corporation that was working abroad. I had friends and I had experience. I did not think of myself as old. There were many years ahead of me for work, at least ten I assumed.

My years in industry and government gave me practical experience in handling large funds and launching complex and important programs. It was a surprise to me when I got negative reactions. Many thought that at sixty-seven I should be content with retirement.

It never really occurred to me to stop working. Somehow I must get a job. If a hundred interviews were necessary, I would have a hundred interviews. Someone would be persuaded to take me on. I felt a little bitter but was not willing to retire.

# 26

# ON MY OWN, 1962

The months after leaving the State Department in 1962 were a prolonged crisis. My financial situation was not desperate if I could earn some salary. My son was already a lawyer in New York, my daughter was employed by an insurance company in Syracuse. Psychologically the framework in which I lived was less definite. I was less able to make a contribution to international affairs, but I kept my contacts in Berlin and in Austria, and my interest in European and other foreign areas did not flag.

I was relatively free. I decided at once that I must round out my research on the aid survey by a trip to Latin America. I took the schedule as prepared at Intelligence and Research and cut it in half. I reduced the number of countries to seven. I drew down my savings account to pay for my ticket and set out for Brazil. I had already visited the Caribbean area, Cuba, Haiti, and Guatemala. I informed the embassies of my new status and told them my interests were the same but that I was coming on my own. The foreign service officers gave me every courtesy. I asked one of them why they were so helpful. She said there were three reasons:

"You can help us by asking some questions we hesitate to ask, we admired your brother, and, after all these years of working together, we consider you one of us."

I saw many statesmen and newsmen as well as those associated with the new program, the Alliance for Progress. One of the men I made a special effort to talk to was the reputed communist Lionel Brizola, who was then in el Rio del Sur. He showed great interest, considering me as an agent and a message bearer. Political antagonism forced him to flee from Brazil; he was active in the extreme Left.

I found that the Alliance for Progress had not developed any momentum. There was a sense of disillusion among leaders. There was a different feeling from what I had encountered in Africa. Here there was a great sophistication and specific awareness of economic possibilities. The recent international conferences at Montevideo in Uruguay had held out very definite hopes. But nothing had materialized. There had been widely publicized U.S. promises, but these did not make it easier for the government leaders to handle the problems of development.

I had not thought that there would be great economic changes and I had no basis for encouraging the economic leaders. There was unrest and a sense of oncoming political troubles in all the countries I visited—Argentina, Uruguay, Chile, Peru, Panama, and Mexico. There were signs of impending government upsets. I had frank conversations with local authorities. The experts in the American embassies were troubled. In Chile I came in direct contact with pro- and anti-Allende factions.

I was glad I made the trip, even though I had to take it at my own expense. It helped to balance and round out my views of Asia and Africa.

After my return from Latin America, I was still unemployed. A friend, Jack Patterson, recommended that I go on the lecture circuit. Jack, who had been in the public relations branch of the State Department, told me that W. Colston Leigh, Inc., was an excellent agency, and introduced me to them. Colston Leigh's agents in New York asked me for some lecture subjects and I gave them Germany, Austria, Social Security, the European Common Market, and Foreign Aid, along with some other suggestions.

The schedule of appearances in some twenty states was demanding, but I was in good health. The brochure they put out ornamented with a photograph described me as "The distinguished economist, diplomat, and educator whose career in the U.S. Department of State spanned four administrations." (I was to span another five, but neither they nor I knew it then.)

The brochure continued,

> ... she earned worldwide respect and admiration for her achievements in the fields of international economics and diplomacy. In 1960 she was granted the personal rank of Minister, one of the few of her sex to be accorded this signal honor.

To assure the lecture-goer that he or she would be getting the best, I was further described:

[309]

> ... A woman of great personal charm and warmth, Mrs. Dulles is the last member of the Dulles family in Government ... A graduate of Bryn Mawr and holder of doctorates from Radcliffe and Harvard, Mrs. Dulles taught for eight years at her alma mater, at Simmons College and the University of Pennsylvania. She undertook her first public service at the request of President Hoover when she made a study of unemployment insurance in England in 1931.

The brochure unabashedly went on right through Social Security, postwar planning, Bretton Woods, Vienna, Germany, the Benjamin Franklin Foundation, and my recent travels.

Having accepted their scheduling, I chose the financial option—I had them buy the tickets and arrange the transportation while I assigned them half the fees. The lecture program was referred to in the trade as "the flesh market." It proved to be more strenuous than at first appeared.

In anticipating this rigorous program I knew that I would never give the same speech twice. I often used a salient paragraph or an illustration over again, but I reoutlined and rethought each speech so that it was fresh and interesting to me and I was not bored with my own conversation. This approach meant hours of work. At that time, the fee was $1,000 or less for the main speech, but this was only a part of the whole schedule. Usually I was met at the airport and asked if I would stop at the television station on the way to town. After that I would be told that a few newsmen would like to talk to me before lunch, and would I mind making a few remarks at the luncheon.

Then I would be offered a rest for an hour, or a drive around town before cocktails, dinner, and the main speech. In Phoenix, Arizona, I made two full-length speeches in one day. In Utah—Salt Lake City and Provo—I also made two. The audiences varied from about two hundred to several thousand. The towns included some small ones like Napa, California, along with big ones. The listeners varied from college alumni, women's clubs, international associations, to city clubs and business groups. It was a stimulating experience but exhausting. I enjoyed the travel and the contacts. I netted approximately $15,000, for about twenty-five speeches, not a big take.

I was in agreement with my agents on most of their arrangements, but I would not accede to their request for more speeches.

*Eleanor and Allen Dulles, retired Director of Central Intelligence Agency, looking at Eleanor's new book,* Détente

*Eleanor with Willy Brandt, Chancellor of West Germany, in Bonn, September 13, 1972. (Copyright by Presse-und Informationsamt der Bundesregierung)*

*Eleanor and Gerald Ford, then congressman, later President, and Jerem Carvalles, YFU student from Brazil, in Grand Rapids, Michigan, May 11, 1973*

*Eleanor dancing beside swimming pool as guests continued to celebrate wedding after Ann and her husband had left*

*Eleanor's house and swimming pool in McLean, Virginia*

*Juliet, Frederic, and Edward Dulles, Eleanor's
grandchildren, circa 1972*

*Ann Dulles Joor and her children (Eleanor's
grandchildren) Billy, Susie, and Chris, 1979. (Photo
taken by Edith Hayward Edwards)*

*Cutting cake on 80th birthday at farm in Sandy
Spring, June 1, 1975*

*Patriotic pantomime at Henderson Harbor. Standing
(left to right), Foster Manning, Allen Jebsen, Matthew
Buresch, Clover Jebsen, Joan Buresch; in middle,
Alexandra Buresch, Eleanor; front, Edith Edwards,
Michael Mimno, Joan Jebsen (Eleanor's nieces and nephews)*

*60th Bryn Mawr College reunion, 1977. Standing
from left: Eleanor Dulles, Anne Davis Swift, Caroline
Stevens Rogers, Esther Johnson, Mary Glenn, Frances
Johnson, Hildegarde Kendig Simboli, Dorothy Shipley
White, Mildred Willard Gardiner. Seated from left:
Martha Willetts, Florence Iddings Ryan, Helen
Harris, Bertha Greenough, Margaret Feurer Plass,
Constance Wilcox Pignatelli, Margaret Scattergood*

*Eleanor in Peking, April 1979—she had been invited 78 years before*

*Eleanor receiving honorary degree at Clarkson College,*
*June 1979*

They said they lost money unless I made at least fifty speeches a year. I still don't understand their arithmetic, but they had to charge the rent of their Fifth Avenue offices and staff salaries to someone, so I was one to pay. I was not willing to give more than thirty lectures a year. More appearances led often to repetition and uninspired accounts of complicated problems. I learned that some of the speakers who had preceded me and gave more lectures a year had bored their audiences, and since they were able commentators, I thought it might be because they spoke too often.

In the course of my tours I got to parts of the United States that I had not visited before and came to know many charming people. In spite of the stimulus and a little fillip to my vanity I decided it was not to be a continuing way of life, and terminated my contract after about eighteen months. My later speaking was arranged on a separate basis. I have always liked to speak, although as my father once said to me, "A good speaker is bound to be nervous." The last major speech I made was to the Commonwealth Club of San Francisco where I followed many distinguished people in the series of lectures. One of the most difficult ones was at the dedication of a new firehouse in the village of Henderson, New York. The longest one I made—and the only one I ever read—was at the University of Berlin, where I knew they wanted the message serious and long, and that was what I gave them.

It was still my goal to return to regular professional life. My first break came by chance. I went to a cocktail party at the F Street Club, given by the late Mary Lord (Mrs. Oswald Lord). I met my friend the late Ambassador George V. Allen, a fine foreign service officer. George was on the board of trustees at Duke University in Durham, North Carolina, so I said jokingly, "Duke could do worse than offer me a job."

He said, "But you have a job."

I explained what had happened to me.

Two weeks later I was invited to Duke to meet Professor R. Taylor Cole. We liked each other then, as we do now. Taylor offered me a temporary job at Duke and I felt I was back in the working world.

It was at about this time Harcourt Brace, later Harcourt Brace Jovanovich, had approached me to ask me to write a book about Foster. The publishers offered me a small advance. So with these new tasks it was easier to adjust to my situation.

In the early summer of 1962, I drove with my friend Dorothy Burch to Gettysburg to interview General Eisenhower. I had not seen him since Foster's funeral. He had agreed to see me and his aides welcomed me warmly, since they had known me over the years.

I went to a large house, set back among the trees in the center of the town. Colonel Jack Goode talked to me and Dorothy while we waited for the General. Eisenhower came in from his appointment a little late and full of apologies. He had been at Walter Reed and had breakfasted with General Heaton, his surgeon and also Foster's. I asked if he would speak to Dorothy, a former WAC officer. He was very gracious in his greeting to her.

General Eisenhower took me up to the small study on the second floor looking out over the pleasant tree-shaded yard, which he found more cozy than the larger rooms. He was easy to talk with. I could see that his frequent late talks with Foster, after a hard day's work—perhaps three times a week—would have been a help. He was comfortable to talk with, not urgent or overly analytical. In his conversations with Foster there would have been no timidity on either side but mutual respect and affection.

I told him that I was writing a book that would be published in 1963. I felt at ease and recognized Eisenhower's desire to be helpful. In commenting on their working together he said he thought Foster showed him every speech he wrote. He spoke in particular about a note he asked Foster to give to David Ben-Gurion before the time of the Suez crisis in 1956. He asked Foster to deliver it exactly as he phrased it—he stated emphatically that the coming election and the Jewish vote did not matter to him in comparison with what was right and he would not condone Israeli aggression in Egypt (he suggested I look for this note in Foster's papers).

In speaking of the 1955 conference in Geneva, I asked if he thought Bulganin had any authority. He answered that like Malenkov he thought he was a stooge and a mouthpiece. He said Khrushchev rebuked him in public. Eisenhower described how he had presented a rough draft proposal for open skies inspection as a means to further disarmament. The proposal was at such an early stage that he felt he must apologize to the British and French for not having shown them a draft but he wanted to put it before the meeting without delay. He said as they went out for cocktails—"bad cocktails"—Khrushchev and the interpreter walked out with him and they encountered Bulganin. Khrushchev said the proposal had "no merit and would not be considered."

I asked about the origin of the idea. He said it had grown out of his wartime experience with aerial reconnaissance and his knowledge of the technical advance in photography. In the inspecting of planes would be both Russian and United States technicians so they could share that knowledge. "The Soviets know what we are doing anyway," he said.

He thought he had the plan first; he had talked to Foster about it. He said, "Others might have thought of it." I spoke of the possibility that the idea came from Nelson Rockefeller. He laughed and said, "Nelson never thought of that" —then in a minute— "though he might have." Nelson had certainly talked with the military, Admiral Radford, and others.

There was some discussion of neutrality; Eisenhower said Foster had changed his mind to some extent but that the neutral nations bothered him. The General thought that we would have impossible responsibility if we brought many neutrals into defense pacts. To supply them with arms or help in their defense if their borders were violated would bring serious problems. We would rather have India put money into their five-year plan than into arms.

Eisenhower said he had argued with Nehru that he should not criticize us. He knew, however, that the neutrals were really scared of the communists. Nehru had once resigned and Eisenhower had pleaded with him to resume office, insisting that chaos would result in India without him.

With respect to "liberation" and "roll back" he said Foster never faltered in his belief that right would triumph and that morality would be victorious. But in the immediate circumstances, it is important to "keep our powder dry." Foster realized that holding our position was a matter of power. We could influence events and keep the spirit of freedom alive behind the Iron Curtain. In saying *containment* was too static Foster had in mind other physical and military elements and education, exchanges and information as influences. Eisenhower thought criticism of brinkmanship foolish— all international relations involved a demonstration of power.

The importance of summitry to the Soviets was the need to have a good propaganda base with their own people. If they could get a good dateline, like Geneva, they could get useful articles in the free world press.

The Soviets, the general said, planned, ever since Bulganin and Khrushchev had gone to India, to break up the Paris meeting in May 1960—their reception had been cold. They used the U-2 flight as a pretext. There had never been any doubt in Eisenhower's mind that he was and should be responsible. He had approved the flight on the basis of a time span. When the weather was favorable they picked a certain number of days to carry out a number of flights. The last flight was to be on the last day of the approved period; then there was a halt.

Only a few very high ranking officials knew what was going on. Eisenhower said if he had been in town the day the plane was reported lost he might—he was not sure—have smoothed over the relations with the public. Foster thought that the Soviets would be embarrassed to acknowledge the flights had been going on and they could not shoot them down. However, once a plane was down, the whole operation was over.

The general said Foster was worried because operational detail made his job difficult and thinking almost impossible. He had discussed his idea of a first secretary to coordinate all the matters relating to security. He indicated the Secretary did not like the idea at first but came to think better of it as time went on.

He said he and Foster were "an ideal combination." He quoted Foster as saying, "You have come to know all the heads of state in Europe and most significant countries. I have studied the techniques of diplomacy all my life. We complement each other in a remarkable fashion."

Eisenhower said that after the death of Chief Justice Vinson he had offered Foster the Chief Justiceship. Foster said, "I have worked all my life on what I am doing now. I think I can be more useful if I continue. I have studied the techniques of diplomacy and the causes of friction between nations."

The general spoke with both respect and affection. He asked about Janet and others of the family. He discussed at some length his consideration as to who should take over when Foster resigned in April 1959. The three that he favored most were Douglas Dillon, Livingston Merchant, and Christian Herter. He said he had talked to Foster about them and found it hard to make a decision. All were qualified. In fact, Herter was chosen. He indicated the importance of having a Secretary that he could rely on.

Many retired government officers want to teach. They realize they have something to say and like the idea of being in touch with young

[314]

people. They also think that the life of a professor is dignified and pleasant. I knew that there were many obstacles to finding a good post and that the work involved was exacting. It was fortunate that I had considerable experience in teaching before I went into government in 1936. When I once got back in harness at Duke and then at Georgetown, I already knew the ropes.

I knew that for every hour of teaching about four hours of preparation are necessary to keep the material alive. After Duke I was called to Georgetown University and taught there for seven years. The students were responsive and challenging. I allowed for considerable discussion but I exercised my right to put my own ideas before them. I said that I had fifty years of experience and that there was no reason for a student to take my courses unless he or she wanted to hear the conclusions I had drawn from these years of work.

After resigning from Georgetown to leave more time for writing, my contacts with students at the undergraduate and graduate levels have diminished in recent years, but I talk with some from time to time. They seem more interested in the content of their courses and anxious to find a useful career than they did in the late fifties. They are not so concerned in politics and do not follow the policy of the federal government as much as they did fifteen or twenty years ago. This change is partly the result of the ending of the draft and the fact that the Vietnam War is over. It is also related to the serious need of having a skill and the capacity to earn a living. Economic realities affect most of them.

The different tasks I undertook and places I visited after being dropped from government broadened my horizons. I do not think I was using my past experience to the full, but I did enjoy a considerable amount of freedom, and I picked up enough money from these efforts to maintain my standard of living.

During my years of partial retirement I had five eye operations. All affected my writing and reading speed and kept me out of circulation for some weeks. I had always suffered from poor eyesight, and in 1964 I had my first of two retina detachments. I was busy teaching and anxious to finish the story I had to tell my students. I tape-recorded lectures for my assistant which she then turned on for the students. I talked about these recordings with her

[315]

so she could answer questions. The students called this "canned Dulles," and if they were sorry that they had no vacation while I was in the hospital, they did not complain.

It was in 1965 on June 1 that the Germans honored me by a series of telegrams on my seventieth birthday. Among them were messages from Chancellor Ludwig Erhard, State Secretary of the Foreign Office Carl Carsten, Minister of Foreign Affairs Gerhardt Schröder, President Heinrich Lubecke, Willy Brandt, and others. The Washington embassy gave me a silver tray engraved with fourteen names, all of them old friends. I was particularly pleased because it was genuine friendship when I was no longer dispensing funds for the benefit of German reconstruction. I remember the fine summer evening when, at the farm of my cousins, the Francis Allens, in Sandy Spring, Jock Dean, my colleague in the department, brought the cables given him by George von Lilienfeld. It happened that I was just back from Vienna—a journey as the guest of the Austrian Government for their celebration of the tenth anniversary of the Austrian State Treaty.

Here in the glow of the evening, under the large oak trees, I enjoyed the company of my friends. I shared with them the thought that my efforts in Austria and Germany had been recognized and that friends from far away wished me well.

It was also in this year of 1965 that I began my work for the Center for Strategic Studies of Georgetown University, work that continued for more than three years.

The Center for Strategic Services, later adding the word "International" to be CSIS, was feeling its way when I joined them. They asked me to help edit and also to contribute to the book entitled *Détente*. I worked with Robert D. Crane on the editing and I wrote the chapter "Berlin—Barometer of Tension." The center had various discussion sessions with members of Congress and senators, including several times then Congressman Gerald Ford. The reports differed in format and covered a wide variety of subjects. In addition to the *Dominican Report*, which I initiated, I worked on the Panama Canal problem along with a panel of political experts and economists.

After some twenty years of activity, under the leadership of the much admired Admiral Arleigh Burke— "30 knot Burke" —and

[316]

David Abshire, the center developed a quarterly report and other publications and recruited able scholars and experts who wrote and led discussion meetings which I often attended even after I stopped regular work for the organization.

In 1966 I had a bright young student from Guatemala in my class at Georgetown, who wished to write his term report on the Dominican crisis of 1965. His family had entertained a refugee general from Santo Domingo and his father had known a great deal about happenings on the island. I was impressed by the story he wrote and the soundness of his references and conclusions. I told David Abshire and we agreed it would be a good idea to have a Center Report on the subject. At that time there were many rumors and too few facts available in Washington. We called in the late Jeremiah O'Leary, the well-known correspondent, to consult with him, using his wealth of knowledge on the Latin American situation. We found also that Thomas C. Mann in the State Department had wanted a more accurate description of events to be written. He was personally hampered by his official status, but he would welcome the opportunity to have an account published and would give us material on which we could depend. So the work that began in my office expanded and ended in our second report, *Dominican Action, Intervention or Cooperation*, 1965.

In order to check the details of the timing of the orders to the navy ship *Boxer*, which took the helicopters in for action, and to confirm the orders given from Washington, Abshire sent me to Norfolk, where I conferred with Admiral Thomas Moorer and others. I had a fine day there with them. I was invited to the admiral's mess for lunch, "the first woman," he said, and I added, "perhaps the first boat builder"—for I told him of the two boats I had built in Washington and later floated on Lake Ontario. He agreed he knew few who had used hammer and nails in that fashion.

The final story had a considerable impact when it came out. Several people changed their views, even in public statement. It was a careful piece of research, and, though it did not deny a degree of impulsiveness on President Johnson's part when he gave his radio speech the night of the rescue of the Americans from the embassy, it did show in clear terms the many requests for help which the ambassador, W. Tapley Bennett, and the State Department had received. I enjoyed this work, which was in a new field for me. Since

[317]

Jeremiah O'Leary and I wrote the text—which of us did most of the writing is not important—I have noted it as one of my publications.

My student got an A in the course and I learned about the Navy and about Latin American dictators.

In the summer of 1967, as a private citizen, I had taken an eight-day automobile tour of communist East Germany. I was spending some weeks in Berlin working on my book *Berlin: The Wall Is Not Forever*. Marc Catudal, a student friend of mine, drove me. I did not want to be trapped by some official for any alleged traffic violation, which might give an excuse for holding me, but from the time I checked into the German Democratic Republic's tourist office I was followed by official agents. A man in a small white car did most of the shadowing. At one time in Jena four agents in four cars followed me around. When I stopped to enter a building, the watchdogs would park a short distance away and then speak to the concierge or guard of the building to find out where I was and what I was doing.

We had to stay in assigned hotels and keep to the route I had indicated when I got my visa. I was told I could take photographs but in parts of Thuringia where there were several hundred Soviet soldiers in barracks there were signs posted against trespassing, and also against taking pictures.

I saw some housing projects; although these were modern in appearance, there were few if any with elevators and not many conveniences. I saw some of the tiny, crowded apartments where chairs jostled tables and there was little room for even the most elemental personal possessions.

As we drove through small towns we looked for places where we could sit and drink a beer. There were few, but when we did come upon an inn or terrace we found the people often eager to talk and some even spoke out against the regime. Several times on the street someone would come to us and say, "You are American. I wish I could go to America."

Many of the older people said that they hated the Russians, but the young indicated they were trying to accommodate themselves to the regime, trying for better jobs and more education. The universities were free but the courses limited largely to technical subjects. Students knew there was no way of getting better housing or applying for an automobile, unless they were good party members and supporters of the system. Above all, they said, life was dull.

Since my visit thirteen years ago, I am told that the physical standard of living has improved substantially, but there is not much more personal freedom.

Until the last two days of our trip, I avoided contacts with officials. Then I decided to venture further and I called on a remarkable man, Dr. Manfred von Arden. He lived in the Weisse Hirsch, a suburb of Dresden. His house on a hill above the river was beautifully furnished with rugs and portraits. Dr. von Arden claimed to be able to cure cancer and said he could have saved Foster's life. In his garden was a small observatory; he was an astronomer as well as a biologist and politician.

He gave Marc and me tea. There were two other guests—one an American—who asked about our journey. I complained about the agents constantly at my heels. Dr. von Arden disappeared from the room—to telephone—and when he returned he assured me I would no longer be bothered. After we left his house the followers stayed farther back, but still in sight for the next few days.

My trip to more than a dozen East German cities convinced me that the people in the GDR were persistently German, that they disliked the Russians, but that they were accommodating to the system. Above all, in the hotels, on the street, and in the countryside, I felt the pall of the heavy and uninspiring atmosphere of the communist regime.

The academic year of 1967–68 I spent at the Hoover Institution in Stanford. I had been given a fellowship enabling me to write a book, my seventh publication. It was entitled *One Germany or Two: The Struggle at the Heart of Europe*. The year in California was pleasant. I saw old friends in the San Francisco area, and made some new ones. But I also recall shocking events of the times. I remember just where I was standing when I heard that Martin Luther King had been shot. I know where I was at midnight when Robert Kennedy was assassinated in Los Angeles.

My manuscript on Germany was well along and I finished another, correcting the galleys of *American Foreign Policy in the Making* (Harper & Row). My surroundings were ideal. My office looked out on a beautiful sequoia tree. There was both peace and stimulation in the institution. Up and down the halls and in the stacks there were scholars from other universities, from Russia, Hungary, and China. I had enough social life, both in Palo Alto and in Berkeley, to keep me stimulated.

Not only students but professors also were troubled by national policy in these years. It was never wise to have engaged ourselves in a ground war in Asia. I am not competent to judge all facets of the Vietnam struggle, but the original involvement was regrettable. However, any conflict once begun must be taken seriously even at great cost. It seems to me that most of what was said by those on either side of the controversy was erroneous. I do not feel free of guilt nor do I feel burdened by decisions to which I did not contribute at any time. Poor judgment, prejudice, undependable estimates of strength and weakness must be shared by many and cast a dark shadow on our international image and our reputation in foreign parts. Many nations err over the centuries and this Vietnam War will always be a black mark on our international reputation.

Thinking over my earlier travels, which had taken me far and wide, I felt my perspective was incomplete unless I visited communist Russia. A friend, Kay Brown, was able and willing to go with me. We made our plans in a conventional manner through Intourist and set out for Leningrad via London and Helsinki on June 30, 1968.

Leningrad interested me especially. My mother had lived there as a girl of seventeen when my grandfather John W. Foster was our chief envoy at the Russian Court of St. Petersburg. Ninety-seven years ago Mother had left Paris for Russia on August 16. From the family apartment on the Moskaia Prospekt she could see the Cathedral of St. Isaac, she wrote. I could see it from the hotel room in the Astoria where Kay and I stayed but I could not identify her apartment because the street names were in the Cyrillic script.

The collection of French impressionist paintings at the Hermitage was superb, as were the splendid palaces outside the city. Our Intourist guide was helpful but did not wish us to vary the routine. I wanted to see schools, hospitals, and factories. I was told I could not.

"It is enough," the guide said, "to see the city, and the people in the streets."

"I will go back home," I told her, "and say all I saw in Leningrad was the French impressionist paintings and the palaces of the czars."

The guide was not amused.

Moscow is impressive in many ways, particularly the Kremlin, not far from the Metropole Hotel. Red, towering, high-walled, it is unique in appearance and tradition. We walked often in the great square. But I did not like Moscow. I did not find the atmosphere pleasant nor the people cheerful. The subway was interesting and monumental, with its large halls deep down and decorated with frescoes. At the time of our visit the ballet was not performing, so we missed one of the real treats. Our sight-seeing in and around the city gave me vivid impressions but offered nothing to lure me back. Kiev, which we visited after Moscow, had a much more pleasant atmosphere.

Yalta, to the south, was especially exciting to me because of the crucial summit meeting held there in 1945. I thought then and I believe now that what Roosevelt said to Stalin was disastrous and that Roosevelt and Churchill gave away a large part of Europe to the Soviets in that fateful meeting.

From this tropical port, Kay and I took a Soviet ship across the Black Sea, disembarking at a dock on the Danube in Romania. It was a neat, well-run ship and we had frequent conversations with some of the Soviet passengers—particularly a teacher who talked to us about education in Russia.

Romania was much more free and easy than I had expected. I took a day's trip into the mountains to visit a large truck factory. It made a good excuse for a long ride in the country, through the oil fields of Ploesti and many farms and villages. The truck factory was well organized and I learned that the managers bitterly hated the Russians, although they did not go into details as to why.

From Bucharest I went on to Prague and arrived as the revolt of 1968 was brewing. Dubcek, the political leader in his search for party independence, had gone too far for his own good. My schedule was quite demanding and not easy to change, so I did not stay long enough to see the later stages of the clash. I left before the Soviets brought in their tanks. I was back in the United States by mid-August.

When the news came of the sad culmination of this strike for partial political freedom, Allen and I were walking on the road by Lake Ontario. Johnny Johnson, who ran the *Watertown Daily Times*, met us and brought us the news. Allen said the Soviet Union could not tolerate the flaunting of their power; the Soviets considered the uprising to be a direct affront so their reaction was inevitable. The declaration referred to as the Brezhnev Doctrine was a natural expression of Soviet policy. It was, however, a discouraging outcome for the lovers of liberty and the brave Czechs when their attempt to increase their independence was suppressed.

The impressions I gained from this trip, as well as others made previously, helped me to understand the deadening effect of dictatorship and the loss of inspiration that comes with a communist regime. There had been some improvements in food and shelter for the masses as a result of comprehensive planning, but the lack of initiative and absence of variety resulted in the closing of the walls and a darkening of the ceiling so that shining hopes for human development often spoken of are shrouded in gloom. There are varied ways in which different nations adjust. The situations in Yugoslavia, Poland, Romania, Czechoslovakia, and Hungary differ markedly. I know that I could not live in any of the communist countries I have visited. I wish that more people would visit communist lands to get a feeling of what is happening and experience the repression and fear. They could then reassess the values of life in our flawed but struggling democratic capitalist system. I think we could go forward with more spirit if there was a more widespread understanding of the contrast between communism and democracy.

A short but interesting participation in student international exchange matters came at this time, stimulated by my good friend Arthur Collingsworth, one of their chief officers. My introduction came with an ocean voyage on the S.S. *Aurelia*. The year 1969 was the summer of tropical storm Anna. The passengers were mainly foreign students, returning home after a year attending American schools and living with American families. Their plans had been made and, in a few cases, paid for by Youth for Understanding, a private organization, then based in Ann Arbor, Michigan, now in Washington, D.C. I worked part-time with them for several years.

That summer I had been asked to join the returning students and to share in the program by giving lectures during the voyage. Also speaking on U.S. foreign policy and programs were Ambassador Allen and Ambassador Joseph Satterthwaite. Our trio talked about foreign relations while other lecturers covered different subjects, including English and art. We also led small discussion groups for the students.

In spite of Anna's huge waves tossing us about, I managed to keep my sea legs and enjoy the evening entertainment as well as the daytime meetings. I was asked to be one of the judges of a dance contest and the handsome German who won the competition nearly danced me off my feet as the boat rolled and pitched in the storm.

I left the group at Rotterdam. There the parents of many of the students had come to meet them. I went north to Bergen in Norway and over the mountains by train to Oslo, then on to Berlin. Back in Hamburg, I joined some other YFU students bound for the United States.

Youth for Understanding moved from Michigan in 1978. The organization is more than twenty-five years old. It began when the State Department asked the Rotary Club of Detroit if it could take care of forty or fifty non-Nazi students from Germany and Austria. During the first two years, when the State Department financed the program, the department had difficulty in finding families with whom the students might live. To solve this problem it asked Rachel Andresen to find families. She was then with the Council of Churches in Detroit and was able to help. Rachel took over and found homes for all the students, first for the department and then independently as she expanded the program.

The outgrowth of the first two years of this work led to the present YFU operation in which the foreign student, or a friend of the student, provides money for transportation to this country, plus incidental expenses. The family with whom the student lives pays the cost of room and board.

Further expansion of the program included a plan for American students to go overseas. The program arrangements for Americans is mainly for the summer months, in Europe, Latin America, and Asia. During the last twenty-five years, American student participation has been about one third of total, with two thirds of the students coming from other countries to the United States. The reason for the difference is a reluctance among Americans to take time off from a regular school year and also the dollar payments requested of the parents of American students. There is also a great desire on the part of the foreign students to learn English.

The total number of students involved in YFU up to the present is about 75,000. Fellowships are offered to about 20 percent. Beginning in 1976, American students were offered loans through the Eleanor Lansing Dulles Student Loan Fund. This fund was set up by YFU, making available $300,000 in low-interest loans to qualified students.

Not long after my first journey with YFU they asked me to go to Ann Arbor, where I attended many of their meetings. I agreed to act as consultant for a small fee and make speeches both to incoming students and to gatherings of people who might have an interest in supporting the program.

During the summers of 1970 and 1971 I spent some weeks at Saginaw Valley College in Michigan, which YFU took over for the orientation of incoming foreign students and also to prepare Americans going abroad. The groups from Latin America, Europe, and the Far East came to Saginaw for three or four days. The orientation helped give them a start at using English as they ate together, played games, and listened to instructions.

Rachel, the head of the organization since 1952, had a farm near Ann Arbor in South Lyons. Here we joined her for consultation and refreshment. She gave the spirit to the organization, convincing the young people that we sincerely wished them to feel at home and explaining the opportunity of family life in a new land. Of course some were homesick and bewildered, a few even wanted to go home, but by and large they made a smooth adjustment.

The president was John Richardson, assistant secretary for State Department Cultural Affairs. I became convinced by observation that the high-school-age students, the age group we handled, were best suited for this experience—here and abroad. They were not as arrogant as some of the older college students and were willing to stay with their adopted families. We did not want them to wander about. There were always problems, although among the 7,000, more or less, that we sent abroad and brought here each year, the number of serious difficulties was actually low. There were one or two cases of drug smuggling, a few pregnancies, and two or three accidental deaths.

The students did a little traveling, but this was not a major part of their experience. We considered it most important for them to become intimate members of the families and towns where they lived—to join the clubs and play on the teams and in the school bands. The students made speeches before local groups about their home countries and about their impressions of America. In all, over the twenty-five years, the program has brought young people from more than forty countries. The American students going abroad were for the most part on shorter time schedules; some for three months, a few for a year.

The financing of YFU was well devised and was a part of the

[324]

program on which I spent considerable effort. I went with another member of the staff to Houston, Philadelphia, Toledo, Detroit, and California, to solicit funds from foundations and individuals. In San Francisco, where we had friends among the foreign consuls and local Californians, we set up a special committee.

The consuls for Finland, Sweden, Germany, and Switzerland in California were most helpful. They gave parties to which we could invite host families, students and other interested persons. The aims of the California Committee were to help find families to take in students, to interest American boys and girls, and to raise funds for scholarships.

In 1971 I went with Rachel to the Philippines and Japan. We had a large number of Filipinos in the program. We were invited to the barrios of Lourdes Cruz, the head of the local committee and a prominent lawyer-judge. The Lourdes family had a large plantation—sugar, I believe—and dominated the area. There was a gathering of about four hundred young and old, and three large pigs were barbecued for twenty-four hours. After eating the meal of pork and rice, we danced. The Filipino children started and then we all joined in. The celebration to thank us for sending old English textbooks to their schools went on in the warm night for hours of singing and dancing.

From Manila we went to Japan. We landed on a Sunday morning in an almost empty airport. I passed customs and official checking quickly, only to look back and see Rachel sitting, tired and sleepy, on a narrow wooden bench—she had no visa. I persuaded the officers to let me go back to her and then to telephone the watch officer in the American Embassy. The officer cajoled the Japanese into letting us enter the country. Once through the barrier we found our committee chairman, Mr. Shinohara, and his wife waiting to take us to International House.

I had other journeys for YFU. The most informative were two trips to Yugoslavia with Dr. Oliver Rose, one of the staff, in 1971 and 1972. There we had the delicate problems of dealing with the communist youth organizations. We had friends in the country, since students had already come to the United States on the program. One was a fine football player who said his claim to fame was kicking a sixty-yard field goal. Because of the currency restriction, we had to agree to pay all the dollar expenses of students coming to the United States, but we negotiated to have some of the dinar expenses of our American students visiting Yugoslavia paid by the communist youth organization.

Ollie and I went south by train to Skopje in Macedonia, which was a somewhat exotic part of Yugoslavia. The territory had been invaded in 1371 by the Turks, yet the city had preserved its strong Greek atmosphere. It was more Oriental than I expected, with ancient churches and monasteries. One was underground, with hidden areas where Christian refugees had evaded capture by the Turks. All these ancient buildings, rich with mosaics and turrets, are being shouldered by the new buildings, square, boxlike structures. Some of our foreign exchange students lived in these new apartments. They told us their Yugoslavian friends were eager to join the program. I was fascinated by Oriental buildings and enjoyed particularly a noisy, crowded market where cooking utensils, clothing, and fruits were spread on the ground—the salesmen shouting and jostling each other—the people more Asian than European.

In the train going back to Belgrade we went through rugged mountain passes. Plans for this first journey had been made by a handsome former exchange student, cooperating with a lovely Yugoslavian woman, who worked part-time at the U.S. Embassy. Michael Toon, then the U.S. ambassador to Belgrade, later in Moscow, was an old associate of mine in German affairs. We consulted with him. It was agreed that it was best politically to deal directly with the Yugoslav youth officials. We made considerable progress with plans and also had a chance to visit Yugoslavian homes. On one occasion we went to a family celebration where there was a sumptuous meal with three main meat courses and six salads followed by three enormous cakes. The older people ate in one room and the young, including three of our American exchangees, in another. The wine flowed freely as we toasted each other in mixed languages.

Our arrangements with the Yugoslav youth committee for the selection of exchangees were a compromise but still acceptable. To tighten up our plans with the other committee we went to Zagreb and Ljubljana by train. We were impressed to see many small farms—we were told that they were privately owned. In Ljubljana the Austrian influence was still apparent. The region did not seem to have absorbed much communism.

When we went to Zagreb, where our recruiting committee had been almost dissolved, we were told of a student revolt. We saw streets barred but did not actually witness the violent rioting. I was to leave from there for London to return to the United States. A violent snowstorm intervened. After some delay I was flown back to Belgrade and then on to London. There I missed my flight scheduled to go over the pole to San Francisco. I settled for a flight to New York and then on to California, spending four hours mellowed by a scotch in the London airport Clipper Club. I arrived very tired in Berkeley in the early morning and slept three hours before a Thanksgiving dinner with Emily Huntington. This was in November of 1971.

Some months later, in March 1972, Ollie and I returned to Yugoslavia. We asked for our old friends, but they seemed to have disappeared. A formal governmental youth management was very rigid.

I was able to take a weekend in Dubrovnik, a city I had not before visited. I went alone. All my life there had been many solitary excursions taken in intervals between working appointments. In the ancient port city I stayed in a castlelike hotel, high on rocks over the Adriatic Sea. I walked down to the open plaza between the monastery and the palaces. I sought out, using sign language, a place where I could eat the renowned local oysters. I found a small open stall with tiny tables and few customers. Since I was there out of season, I had the popular jazz center almost to myself.

My experience with YFU students was stimulating. We had arguments in my room at Saginaw Valley College. I danced with some wild Brazilians and Chileans. We drank beer together and discussed the State Department and the CIA. I told them some of my life story in foreign service work and varied bits of history. Some of these students have come to see me when they returned, as many do, to the United States a second time. I am convinced that they gained much insight and realized that the quiet small-town living that most of them experienced was different from the stereotypes of American luxury and extravagance they had been shown in the movies. They were given a vivid experience of how the American teenager lived. Some few among these foreign visitors could not adapt and had to be sent home, but the majority fitted well into the new environment.

The American youngsters found a special quality of understanding which comes with walking the streets of a foreign city, visiting its churches, eating in its restaurants, watching its sports. This I had first experienced in 1909 when I was fourteen years old, the year I went to Paris to join my family. At this impressionable age one realizes that the sunlight has a different angle, the air a different quality of scent and sound, the food, a new taste, the greetings— "Hi," "Ciao," "Bonjour"—a special resonance. I was too young to get all the nuances but I was awakened to the fact that people could be very different, though have similar pleasures and sorrows. Custom and tradition are important and add a special tone and color to all experience.

These new perceptions, which came to me early in Paris, are, I think, typical of the meaning of our student exchanges. After their time here none of these students would ever be the same. All the bright and malleable young would have wider horizons and would cherish more meaningful human values in the years to come.

Not long after these journeys, in the spring of 1971, I had my first cataract operation. It was followed by a second detached retina. The first had been in 1964. So I was in and out of hospitals. In 1975 my other lens was clouded so I had to undergo another operation, making it my fourth eye operation—my sixth major surgery.

After the third operation I knew I would not get a driver's license and I decided I must sell my house in Virginia and move to Washington. This was a hard decision.

I loved the house and garden. I had lived there since 1951. The swimming pool was only a few feet from my living room. Rain or shine, I was in the water twice a day, on weekends more often. Though it was not heated, I used the pool from April through October and occasionally in the winter. The house was everything I wanted for a home and gave great pleasure to my family—a gathering place for Austrian, German, French, Italian, and other friends from abroad. The view over the hills was not obstructed by houses and I felt I owned the countryside. I planted more than three hundred small trees and large bushes in what had been a cornfield. It was an unspoiled part of Virginia, about twenty-five minutes' drive from the center of Washington. I said good-bye to it before I was fully recovered from my third eye operation. I have never been back.

I missed the country living, but I still had summer sailing at Henderson, and on the Chesapeake Tim has his boat, *Julie*, for cruising. Tim—Ambassador Clare Timberlake—says he met me first when I picked him up on Pennsylvania Avenue in Washington. He had come out of the State Department in the rain. I saw him as I drove by. "Get in," I said. "I am Eleanor Dulles and who are you? It's drier inside."

We were to meet often after that. I visited him and Julie in Bonn, Germany, when he was Minister and in Leopoldville, the Congo, where he was Ambassador.

But the most fun I had was in 1976 when I met him at Falmouth-Foreside in Maine, and we launched on a cruise down the Maine coast. We took four days to reach Marblehead where I left the crew of four. They continued south in a hurricane and I envied them the stars and the winds. The *Julie* was a lovely 50-foot sloop made in Hong Kong. The next September I joined Tim again for three days, taking off from the Solomon Islands for the Chop Tank and the Chesapeake. I liked the pitch and roll and the good seagoing companions. Perhaps I can sail the seas again.

# 27

# THE FUNERAL OF KONRAD ADENAUER, 1967

Allen sat in an easy chair smoking his pipe in the sunny alcove of his Que Street house on April 21, 1967. He had asked me to come for lunch. I drove in from McLean. "Sit you down," he said, with his usual warm welcoming gesture. "You are to go to Adenauer's funeral with the President." I answered, "I think you should go." "No," he said, "I have just talked with the President. He said, 'I am taking care of your sister,' and we agreed you are the person the Germans would want to see there as their friend. I may go too, but I am not sure."

Allen did not know it, but I had planned to go on my own at my own expense. I wanted to pay tribute to Konrad Adenauer. I felt we owed a great debt to this man who had made a monumental contribution in the restoration of Germany to political decency and comradeship in the society of free nations. I had talked to the German Embassy and to the German Office in the European Bureau. The Germans offered to pay my way but I said, "No, that is not proper." However, everyone I consulted approved of my idea of going. I had a reservation on Lufthansa. My State Department colleagues said, "Hold everything—you may be sent officially," and that is the way it worked out.

In the end Allen and I both went. I packed my bag that afternoon. On Saturday the White House sent a car to get the bag to look it over for security reasons, and the driver got lost. The next morning, Sunday, I looked out of the window at 6 A.M. A car had stopped on the quiet road within sight of my bedroom. It was a black official car and stayed by the lane for an hour. The driver had evidently been afraid of not finding my house in the countryside off Spring Hill Road, so he set out early. Lyndon Johnson would not brook a five-minute delay.

On April 23 some ten or twelve people were assembled in the lower room under the Oval Office before I arrived at eight in the morning. Presidential aides offered us coffee and we waited for the helicopter to land on the south lawn. I knew most of those who had been invited. Many of them had been concerned at some time with Germany's reconstruction. All were persons of national reputation. Secretary Rusk was there and George Meany, head of AFL-CIO, John J. McCloy, former High Commissioner and prominent banker, also Viola and Volkmar Wentzel; she was the daughter of Chancellor Kiesinger in Bonn. There were half a dozen others including German Ambassador Knappstein, General Lucius D. Clay, Marvin Watson, special assistant to the President, Walt Rostow, special assistant to the President, and Ambassador Symington, chief of protocol.

I talked with Viola Wentzel, whom I had come to know. I had invited her to my house several times and she had talked to her father, the Chancellor, about me. My acquaintance with her was one reason he had given a small dinner party for me in the spring of 1966 just after he had taken over the chancellory.

In about twenty minutes the President came down with several aides and security guards and went to the helicopter just outside the door. We flew to Andrews Air Force Base and there boarded his plane. There were thirty or forty newsmen and others besides our official group. There was a comfortable lounge and a working area with several typewriters, code machines and telephones. We were given coffee, sandwiches, and before long, highballs. The meal when we had it was good, steak and potatoes and ice cream and pie. After lunch the President went to his compartment just off the lounge. A short time later he came out and sat with us. He said, "I didn't sleep. You see this partition just behind you? It is thin. My head was only a few inches away—your conversation was very interesting." He spoke with some irony. We were somewhat chagrined and wondered what had been included in our uninhibited exchange of views.

We were given a twenty-nine-page printed agenda with names, schedules, instructions, and maps. It told the President how many paces it would be to stand before the honor guard, when to turn left and when to turn right to the helicopter, who would follow whom, where we were lodged, and who our escort officers were.

One of the messages coming in from Bonn annoyed the President. He was informed that he was having lunch with Kiesinger on Monday. He did not wish this appointment. It was the only chance to entertain the ambassador, the minister, and some of the staff—he had it canceled. Although his displeasure was evident, he did not lose his temper. In fact, he behaved as Foster or Allen would have—but he had his way. An appointment with Kiesinger was set up in the morning.

The landing at Cologne-Wahn Airport was dramatic with flashbulbs lighting up the darkness and six or more helicopters with their blades flashing. There were no speeches. We were in the air again in less than five minutes, bound for Plittersdorf across the Rhine.

The President's party was about two hundred people. Some of them flew the Atlantic in a jet following ours. Tickets for the cathedral and for the ceremonies in the Bundestag were hard to get for this large number. Some high-ranking officers in our Bonn embassy could not attend either ceremony.

Allen and I were guests of Ray and Marjory Cline. Ray was a leading officer in the embassy. This was very pleasant, since we both knew them well and could enjoy comfortable conversations with them. On the flight over I had talked with General Clay. I told him confidentially that I was worried about Allen's health. Allen had had more than one small stroke. I said I did not think Allen wanted me to hover, but I thought if Clay would walk into the cathedral and keep close to him as he went up the steps, it would be a good precaution. General Clay was most tactful and kind in keeping close to us on the following day. He assured me that there would be no embarrassment.

In the Bundeshaus in Bonn the speeches and eulogies took place. There were none in the cathedral.

I sat about fifteen rows from the front of the Parliament. I saw Harold Macmillan and Harold Wilson come in. Ben-Gurion was there. Charles de Gaulle had arrived at the airport just twenty-five minutes before the ceremonies began. I could see his head above everybody else's. I could also see Johnson's head. Kiesinger was also tall—the three men were handsome and impressive.

Of the speeches the one I found most interesting was by Eugen Gerstenmeier. It gave a sense of the power and the stature of Adenauer.

After the ceremonies we went to different places for lunch. McCloy and Johnson went to the President's house. Johnson and De Gaulle were in separate dining rooms—each dominant in his own group. Allen, Meany, Clay, and I, with a few others, went to the lunch given by the Foreign Office, with Willy Brandt the host.

Everything was fully regulated and carefully planned. Many of the German leaders were with us. I saw a number of old friends, including Ludwig Erhard and Karl Blessing. There was good political and economic conversation.

After lunch the motorcade was formed. The President, in driving to Cologne, was escorted by several dozen "white mice." These were handsome, tall German security police in white leather coats, a motorcycle guard. He also had his own guard. This annoyed the Germans, who were well prepared. The autobahn to Cologne had been cleared of all other traffic and we drove with speed, which Adenauer would have liked, reaching the cathedral in twenty minutes.

The cathedral with its soaring columns is gray and austere, but the red and gold vestments brought color and the casket was covered with the brilliant flag. The massed flowers were spectacular. As I saw the silent crowds surrounding the cathedral, I thought of the time in 1963 when I stood on Connecticut Avenue at President Kennedy's funeral in St. Matthew's Cathedral. The mood then was very different. The people, more visibly excited, had been scrambling to climb the boxes they had brought to see the visiting potentates and to take photographs. The mourners in Cologne were solemn, some tearful. They had been more respectful. Perhaps there is a difference in the nature of the German people.

Adenauer was revered. He had kept his capacities to the very end. He had been working in his study at Rhöndorf a few days before his death. In a letter to me in connection with the introduction he wrote for my book on Berlin (*Berlin: The Wall Is Not Forever*), he said he hoped to see me in June.

After the Mass was concluded and the clergy, the President, and the Chancellor had left the cathedral, Allen and I walked along with General Clay and one of our escorts, Ralph Brown, who had found us in the crowd. I saw President Johnson up ahead on a platform overlooking the crowd and the barge that was to take the casket up the Rhine. There was a reception after the procession had left and then we went back to the Clines' house. The emotional pressure of the ceremonies and the crowds had been exhausting. We did not go to the formal evening gathering.

The next morning on the helicopter to the airport Johnson was talking very emphatically to Rusk about his conversation with Chancellor Kiesinger. It had been satisfactory. The Chancellor's daughter sat close to him, but he did not seem to notice that she was listening to the conversation. I gave a sign to Secretary Rusk but he did not pass it on to the President. He talked for some minutes after we reached the airport where the presidential plane was parked. On the plane we settled in the lounge and Rusk came to me. He pulled a small notebook out of his pocket and said, "My staff told me that yesterday I had passed the time record of Foster Dulles as Secretary of State."

Soon we had lunch and afterward Johnson turned to me and said, "I think you are a little sleepy. Wouldn't you like to take a rest?" I was not sure which bench was most suitable. The President said, "Come with me. Let me show you. There is a bunk up forward here. In fact, there are several bunks. Take your skirt off, take your shoes off, and get under the covers. You'll rest better." I said, "Thank you, Mr. President. This is the first time I have ever been put to bed by a President."

When we got off the plane later, he said, "You mean to say you have never been put to bed by a President before!" He showed both sensitivity and humor. I recalled that Foster had once said to me when Johnson was senator he was good to work with.

I did not have much substantive conversation with Johnson. The only policy matter I remember talking about was the Punte del Esta meeting in Uruguay. I told him I was favorably impressed with what had gone on there. Perhaps we had made some progress in Latin America. I thought he was quite pleased that I had said it.

The same people were on our plane except for McCloy, who had gone on to London for a meeting. Walt Rostow was with us but for some reason not in the lounge except for a few minutes. I did not have a chance to talk with him.

On our return we were told to hurry to the helicopter. It was rather fun coming down over the White House to see the day's traffic clogging the streets and to see the lovely flowers and the trees on the lawn. I said, "The trees are surprised to have us come in. They are bowing under the draft from the choppers."

I went from the White House with Allen to his house in Georgetown. I told him of my conversation with Clay. He had wished for a harder line on Berlin. Allen and I discussed De Gaulle and Adenauer. We agreed that both had built into their personalities certain prejudices and symbols, that these elements could become a kind of straitjacket with time. Adenauer had not had the words of Churchill but he had taken a degraded, humiliated, broken population, living in smoking rubble and, by applying strength, inspiration, and constructive ability, had built a really amazing nation.

I felt affection for this great man, but I never felt completely informal with him. The pressure of his personality was too great. I was glad I could be one of those who honored him at his death.

# 28

# DAVID AND ANN

When I was young, at the turn of the century, most women wanted children. It was the tradition. We all considered having a family a personal justification and a triumph. Few thought of professional work as a substitute or as an important part of self-fulfillment. I personally did not give the matter much thought and was more interested in short-time developments which took me into professional life without any conscious choice of career versus marriage, or the possible combinations of the two major concerns. It was not long before the problem became a real one.

In deciding to have children and agreeing with David about having a family, I did not feel matriarchal. It never occurred to me that my children would enter politics or that they would have an unusual chance to become famous or leaders in the times ahead, in a world of rapid change. I did expect them to be honest and literate, to be family-oriented, and to be attractive. If they were to write or teach, that would be fine, but I did not feel that they had "to follow in the family tradition." I was not sure what I should teach them as religion, but I wanted them to feel at home inside a church. The extent to which I succeeded is evidenced by my extraordinarily fine grandchildren. The extent to which I failed with my children is that I have not always been able to communicate with them as friends. I am glad I had both of them and I know that they have contributed in recreation and serious discussions to the family of some fifty or sixty young people with whom I now keep in touch. Some of the nieces and nephews are professors, some parents, some lawyers, some pastors, some doctors, and some attractive vagabonds.

What sacrifices I made to create a warm homelife for my children were well worth the price and the good times I had with children. My pride in their development and my sense of joy as they acquired those characteristics that made them unusual human beings were worth every effort I made. What would have been different in my professional life without them I cannot picture. I know that they have been of the utmost importance to me, and I have been grateful to them for the qualities they have added to my life. Anyone else who has had children can understand their importance to me. It is not easy to describe a complex parent-child relationship, but I owe them much—they owe me little.

I knew my working potential could only be developed by cultivating a strong power of concentration. This capacity meant the optimum use of my mental resources which were limited in serious respects but which could be applied usefully with a high degree of intensity. This conscious exertion on my part led to a compartmentalization of my thoughts. The sharp focus led to cutting off extraneous interests when such elimination seemed necessary. This control of my attention has sometimes led to misunderstanding as I pressed at the moment for the issues that seemed to require my whole concern. This segmentation of my behavior was important when, in my late thirties, I undertook to combine homelife and working responsibilities. This combined way of life is not easy, but it can be immensely rewarding.

The birth of my son in October 1934 was an experience of unequaled excitement. The adoption of my daughter in 1937 was a matter of comparable joy. I felt that the three of us could have many good years. I was sure that there would be problems, but I knew the struggles would be outnumbered by the many satisfactions. I had to work, for I had almost no income, but the time left for children would be equal to that of most mothers or fathers. I would give them a good house and home—relatives and friends, schooling and recreation.

I remember well the time of David's birth. I was in the labor room for about twenty-four hours. Although I was healthy and normal, the obstetrician did not take account of the special circumstances—not only was I thirty-nine years old but I was a widow. When I came out of the anesthetic that October 6 I thought I heard the nurse say, "We saved the mother but the baby is dead."

In the elevator, still groggy and exhausted, I heard my sister Margaret say, "You have a fine baby boy."

"But he is dead," I answered.

[337]

"No," she told me. "He is perfectly healthy and handsome!"

I burst into tears. My joy when I saw him and held him was boundless. Yet I longed to have his father there.

Every phase of David's development was of keen interest to me. He seemed slow in speaking and then his conversation came out in long sentences. I now think he did not have enough to eat as an infant. In those days babies were not given solid food for months after their birth. The Pablum seemed to be uninteresting and unsatisfying. I was able to get home from work in time to play with him and used to sing him to sleep. After some months of this he said to me, "Mother, you can't sing."

He was right. My talents in that direction were limited. We turned to the radio for more professional music. I did not mean to have him precocious, but by the time he was three I realized he was developing intellectually at a rapid rate. His vocabulary was extraordinary. He listened intently to the friends who came to the house to discuss Social Security, economics, and foreign affairs. As time went on I would actually talk with him about events of the day and my work in the office. It was an irresistible sharing which I alternated with listening to the Lone Ranger and "Hi-Yo, Silver," and reading the comics with him. It was all fun and I was happy to be a mother.

David, my husband, had said, "If we have children, we must have at least two." After his death, and our son's birth, I thought it unlikely that I would remarry or have another child of my own. Adoption seemed to be the right course. I talked to friends and got advice.

As soon as I saw Ann I knew she was a superior baby. The shape of her head, the spacing of her eyes, and all her physical attributes were charming. I claimed her at once.

I set up my household with a nurse, Helen, to take care of Ann, in addition to a housekeeper who was partly occupied with three-year-old David. When Ann and the new nurse came, my housekeeper went berserk. I was in my office when Helen called me to come home at once. I got to my house in Cleveland Park to find Helen and the baby locked in a third-floor room and the distraught housekeeper shouting she was going to throw the baby out the window. I went across the street and got my friend Michael Straus. He was big, strong, and friendly. The excited woman told him that I was *illiterate*. I suppose she meant illegitimate. He said, "You wouldn't want to spend the night in the house of an illiterate woman, would you?"

She said, "No! I'll get my boyfriend to pick me up."

She borrowed a suitcase of mine and packed her things to disappear forever. The two children and I were at peace.

Not long after, I moved into the house I had built at 2824 Chain Bridge Road. Then I found Kitty who was competent, loyal, and friendly. She served as the children's nurse for several years. Then the devoted Irene also joined the household as cook.

It was at the time of my adoption of Ann that I came to know Nicholas. He did not approve of my adopting Ann. This is one of the reasons I did not marry him. He and I were interested in many of the same things and he became an important part of my life from 1937 to the mid-fifties. He liked the children and was very kind to them, but he considered them a hindrance to the full enjoyment of adult life and work.

It was lucky for me that I had Kitty and Irene. They stretched my budget to the absolute breaking point, but they could be relied on—and there were a number of emergencies. David had eye problems from birth. I noticed early his lack of control over his left eye. He was operated on at the age of three. His eye troubles were different from mine and his father's. They were not hereditary. Partly because of imperfect vision he fell and cut his face on three different occasions. Several times, I had to rush home from the office to take him to the emergency hospital and have his cuts sewed up—his chin, his nose, and the side of his head. These scars are not visible now.

Ann had an emergency appendectomy when she was about six years old. She had her surgery on Washington's Birthday, so I was away from the office only briefly.

My secretary had standing instructions to find me immediately if there was a call from home. The problems of the children were on my mind during my working day. Although I was not unduly distracted, I frequently wondered when the phone rang if there was a call for help.

Conditions became more difficult to manage after the United States declared war in 1941. My working hours were extended to Saturday afternoon at 5:30. Shopping was difficult and gasoline rationing made tight planning essential.

I was healthy and did not mind the hours. Fortunately, I had few illnesses. The children stayed up until I came home so we could play together.

Next door in a large open lot Viney and Joe and their two grandchildren, Ducky and Claudia, lived in a small shack. They drew water from our outside spigot and were often in my kitchen with Irene. Ducky and Claudia played with Ann and David. They were not concerned with race or color and found each other congenial. There was plenty of room in the field and the woods for games.

Ann always knew she was adopted. We had a celebration when she was a little over a year old on adoption day and then again the next year. This was in addition to birthday parties for both children. These children's parties required serious effort and planning. Was there enough ice cream? Were the plans for the games enough to keep them amused? I lived through them, but just barely.

Even in those days, schools and colleges were costly and always a cause for worry. Were they the best for each child? I think I did better than average in my choices but my budget was strained. This was one reason for my moonlighting in real estate.

Our lives were often refreshed by guests and relatives who visited us. Toddy, Allen and Clover's daughter, whose parents were then in New York, spent a winter with me while working on Yugoslavian problems in the OSS. Robert Edwards, Margaret's son, spent one winter with us when he was assigned to military intelligence. The comings and goings of various relatives and friends were good for the children and added interest to their lives.

After the children were in bed I would go to the basement and work on carpentry. I made a dollhouse for Ann, about four feet square with stairs and windows, and a doghouse for Bimbo, our shelty dog. I made several tables and, with the help of a friend, a log cabin on the slope in the woods below our house. It was sixteen by twelve feet and very correct with its diagonal flooring, covered by random-width boards, its shingled roof, and its fireplace. This work took about two hundred hours, mostly under a strong light which we wired down from the house. I had selected the logs at a farm in Virginia and stripped them myself, with a drawing knife. I also used chinkum and caulkum between logs and stained them with protective oil. This cabin was a place where we sometimes picnicked and where the children played. The trees hid it from the house and provided them with a refuge. I made two boats of marine plywood. They were light and maneuverable. I took the boats on the top of my car to Lake Ontario. I have pictures of the children rowing in the boats I made in the basement.

Carpentry was so absorbing that I stayed up too late at night and became almost an addict. I had to stop it completely to save time for more important things. There were always many things to do.

Since we lived across the street from Fort Kemble Park, we had a nearby picnic ground. We could even ski occasionally there. Henderson was very important in summer. I usually took a month off.

Then in 1945 we went to Austria.

Mrs. Ruth Shipley, the Czar of Passports, did not want me to take the children to Austria. She refused to give us our passports after they were issued. Four times we were assured by her staff that we should pack and dress for the train for New York. Four times at the last minute we were told that they could not give us our passports. By the beginning of April I had rented my Washington house and moved with the children to the Roger Smith Hotel. They were in and out of school. The British and Swiss ambassadors heard of my predicament and said they would give me visas on separate pieces of paper and that we were welcome in their countries. Clover and Allen were both in Switzerland, where Allen was responsible for the OSS. They were expecting to have the children for a while. Finally Mrs. Shipley yielded and with the proper papers we set out on our journey. We took the train for New York.

We sailed on April 25 on the S.S. *Marine Fox*. We met other ships and were in a convoy of about seventy-six.

Unfortunately the workings of the State Department and the section governing travel responded to Mrs. Shipley's request at that time and made it impossible for the children and Joan to go to the Continent with me. I had to leave them in England and was only reunited with them four months later when I saw them in Switzerland.

When shortly after my departure for Italy to join the State Department group Joan and the children took off, they were among the first American civilians to cross France and enter Switzerland. There they were received joyfully by Clover and Allen, who shortly arranged for their schooling. They were entered in schools near Lausanne, La Combe for Ann, Le Rosey for David. Both of them

[341]

were homesick but adapted reasonably well to the new environment and became highly proficient in French in a matter of weeks.

For me the separation was hard. I was used to being concerned night and morning with their welfare. It was particularly difficult during the first two months when I did not know where they were. I felt desperate when all attempts to get in touch with them or with Allen and Clover were fruitless. It is now incredible that communications were so mixed up that letters, telegrams, and telephones failed to go through. I sought the help of ambassadors in Rome, London, and Berne. The fact that we were shifted from one military outfit to another was partly to blame. Anyway, it was not until I got to Wiesbaden and met Allen in July that the ten-week blackout ended for me. Soon the delayed letters reached me and I arranged for my September trip to Switzerland to see the children.

It was not until July of 1946 that they could both join me in Vienna. For the next years our family life seemed normal and comfortable. I was fortunate to have Relly and Trudy as my full-time helpers. From then on they have done many things for the children, watching over their welfare and contributing to their pleasure in life as well as to their training.

The schools the children attended in Vienna were military and seemed to be hastily put together. We in the American occupation contingent did not feel that it was possible for our children to go to the Austrian schools. They were often closed because of the inability to heat them and the children were so pitifully underfed that we felt it would put an emotional strain on our young.

We had some fine weekends in 1946 and 1947 in the American zone of Austria. We went often to the medieval castle, complete with moat, owned by Willy Teufenstein. He was one of the officials in the Austrian treasury with whom I worked, who was very hospitable to us. Some of our outings were extraordinary. The children were aware of the tension of driving through the Soviet zone and always exclaimed with joy when we crossed the dividing line. In Vienna we had gala celebrations at Christmas, Thanksgiving, and birthdays. The children went to the opera and also frequently to the movies put on by the Army. David traveled the city at will, on his military pass, looking for souvenirs.

In 1948 I decided that David would be better prepared for college if he went home to school. When we were on home leave, we had looked at several schools and we both decided on Putney in Vermont. He left Austria in the fall, flying on his own. I was at Igls in the mountains and waited anxiously for word that he had landed. There was a delay en route. The hours before I heard from him were among the longest of my life. I decided to telephone Clover in New York—she said at once, "I'll put David on the line." I was over-whelmed with relief and joy.

Ann went back with me in November 1948 on the S.S. *America*. She went briefly to the Cathedral School and then to Mount Vernon, then a preparatory and finishing school. There, both as a day scholar and later as a boarder she made her mark. Her particular talents were in design, painting, and sculpture. She could have gone far if she had wished an artistic career. In any case, the same talents helped her as housewife and mother.

It was possible, though not easy, to send both children through college. At that time my salary was just at the cutoff point to preclude scholarships. I knew that many thought I had more money than I had and I decided to make do somehow. My real estate ventures added substantially to my resources, and looking back over my records I note that I borrowed several thousand dollars. David was at Swarthmore and Ann at Syracuse—they rewarded me for my efforts. Both institutions seemed to fill the bill, and I think they were satisfied.

As children my Ann and David responded to the accepted formula of a good house, pets, exceptional cooking, pleasant neigh-bors, schools, friends, relatives, and a considerable variety of activity. Early they showed, as most children do, individual dif-ferences. Ann was more visual and artistic, David more articulate, argumentative, and passionately interested in foreign affairs. They both had talent. They were good-looking, attractive, and well mannered. They were at table with adults from early years and entered into general conversation in an agreeable way. I was proud of them and enjoyed their company.

It has seemed to me in later years that they somewhat resented my having a job. Although I spent a great many hours with them, they knew my work was important to me and in competition for limited time.

When they were back from Austria, they were able to take advantage of Henderson. They were interested in sailing and swimming and became very fond of life at Linden Lodge. This was a place where they saw a good deal of other branches of the family, and came to know their cousins well.

With the two children married, I felt my main job had been accomplished and was delighted to have in fairly short order six grandchildren, fine young ones—Chris, Susie, and Bill, Fred, Edward, and Juliet. They are my hostages to the future. I count on them and find my confidence in them well placed.

As a mother I did all the traditional things; as a grandmother I am still in there pitching. There is a contribution of faith that can count for something to them as the years go by.

# 29

# CHINA'S WELCOME, 1979

I always wanted to go to China. Before leaving in March 1979 I reread the account of my grandparents' visit to Tiensin and Peking in 1894 in *Diplomatic Memoirs*. I had always wanted to see the country where Grandpa had served. I was fascinated by the Yangtze, the deserts and mountains, the cypress and dragon, palace and pagoda.

At the age of six I told some Chinese dignitaries calling on General Foster in 1901, to express their thanks for his service to their government, that I would see them later in their country.

"I hope you will treat me well," I said, thinking of the Boxer Rebellion.

"Yes," they said, "you will be welcome."

I had told the silk-gowned ministers that I would come as a medical missionary and hoped to see them. They said they would be glad to greet me, and in March 1979 their great-great-grandchildren gave me, an unknown American, a warm and clamorous welcome. Without this journey my world view would have been incomplete by a large segment.

My trip was seven years after that by President Nixon. His trip was unexpected. Our Presidents have been a mixed bag. There have been good and bad and the accomplishments of some have been surprising. Richard Nixon was not the sole creator of a new China policy, but he was an active agent and is recognized as such in the People's Republic of China, where his picture is sometimes posted along with Mao and Deng. His sending of Henry Kissinger secretly was an important first step. His personal journey in February 1972 advanced the process and, from then on, recognition was almost inevitable. There is no doubt that the establishing of formal relations with Peking has made for easier communication and for increasing commerce. Travel from America to China is growing rapidly and this tends to increase public interest. I did not expect to learn a great deal from a short trip, but I knew I would be a better reader of reports on this enormous, changing nation if I saw and experienced the life of some of the cities. If I saw the countryside and watched the people at work and in the streets, I would gain some understanding.

My plans for my journey to China were precarious. Dr. Stephen Pappas, my opthalmologist, had given me a laser treatment on my right eye in February. He said, "I want to see you again on March 22."

But I said, "I'll be on my way to China then."

"You can't go to China unless I say so," he said.

"Can't you see me sooner," I begged.

"The soonest is March 21," he said. "We may have to operate on the twenty-third."

So I hung on the ropes for several weeks, uncertain as to the future. I packed, I bought travelers' checks, I made my arrangements to leave on Thursday morning.

Wednesday evening at 5:00 Dr. Pappas examined my eye. He said, "Are you a good gambler?"

"Yes," I said, "I'll go if it is possible."

"The laser treatment may hold," he answered. "If you think it worth the risk—go ahead."

I shouted for joy and went home and gathered up my things. In a few hours I was off to see the unknown world.

My trip was planned by President Victoria Schuck of Mount Vernon College in Washington. We flew in via Anchorage, Tokyo, and Hong Kong, about nineteen hours in the air. We walked over the Chum Lung Bridge at the border. After winding through various inspection points, up and down stairs, we were in the People's Republic of China. They told us we were among the last groups to follow this tortuous route, since they planned before long to have the train go through. At the bridge on the Chinese side we were served an excellent lunch.

During our whole journey of approximately two thousand miles by train and plane we saw a great deal of the countryside from Canton, Sian, and Taiyuan, Peking (only from Sian to Taiyuan and Peking to Tokyo by plane). It was less than a two-hour ride to Canton and we were hungry for the new sights and sounds, seeing the fields being planted, the laborers hoeing and digging, glimpses of the sea and fishing boats, assorted beasts and bicycles on the road beside the track—"a better roadbed than Amtrak," remarked one of my companions.

There were twenty-five in our group and we were linked with another twenty-five to fill the quota Japan Air Lines wished to program. We were usually on two buses for our special trips—the green, mostly friends, we considered ourselves the choice group, and the blue, people whom we got to know as time went on.

The arrival at Canton was typical. We had a short briefing in the station, and then walked to our buses. The path had been cleared through a horde of waiting Cantonese—perhaps two thousand— eager to see the visiting "Friendship Tour" of foreigners, strange white people visiting them. We were greeted with waving and clapping hands, grown-ups and children. At the large but somewhat cavernous hotel across from the Trade Fair grounds, we were assigned two to a room.

There I began my fabulous search for Paul Geier. He was an old friend from my Vienna foreign service days and we had met briefly in Hong Kong, expecting to get together for dinner in Canton.

It was there that I discovered that the men at the desk in the lobby did not know who was staying in the hotel. They did not have my name nor Geier's. They gave some possible room numbers and I knocked on six or seven, surprising the unknown guests. I did not find Paul for ten days, though we both looked frantically for each other. In Peking the embassy helped us end our search. We had dinner together.

Our glimpse of Canton was brief. The Chinese guides who stayed with us determined what cities we would visit. Their decision was probably based on the availability of hotel rooms. We did not know.

It was dark and rainy as we drove through the streets—crowded with bicycles, people, and ramshackle trucks. The rule in China is not to use headlights except in emergencies—then I suppose it is too late to see what hit you. This made the late night streets we saw from our hotel seem very empty as the bicycle riders went home.

The guides took us out early in the morning for Sian. We were going west through dun-colored mountains and crossing sluggish streams.

We found the landscapes were interesting but the mountains bleak and dry. There were no forests and few trees. Patchy areas were planted in rice with some evidence of irrigation. In the northern provinces there was wheat. Bullocks and camels dragged the rickety carts. There was little mechanization. Most of the men and a smaller

[347]

number of women leaned on their hoes and shovels—they rested, at least while we were looking, and seemed almost as tired as the shaggy horses drawing the carts. There were few motorized trucks—practically no private cars—bicycles always in large numbers, almost no cows, a few goats, and fewer pigs than I expected.

The shape of the mountains—the porous volcanic rocks—gave variety to the landscape. The sheer cliffs were pierced with caves, and though we did not see many people it was clear that they were inhabited.

We were delighted that we were going to Sian. We knew it would be a high point of the trip and we knew few tours did get there. New diggings of several years were a major discovery in 1974.

When, on our first main excursion, we walked around the gallery in the shelter that protected the eight-thousand-year-old village of Pan P'o, we felt as if we were participating in these discoveries. This forty-five-house village surrounded by a protective wall was discovered by chance in 1953 in building foundations for a factory. Bones, cooking utensils, and tools of great interest were in the small houses. The artifacts were displayed in museum cases set apart.

The most recent, and little known, digs were those revealed when a stone prepared by the Qin Emperor describing the gravesite was found. At this impressive memorial to the long-dead potentate, we watched the workers removing the earth from centuries-old life-size terra-cotta statues of courtiers standing in rows to honor Emperor Qin. There were more than one thousand men and horses and chariots. The whole tomb was under an extremely large hangar-type structure erected to protect the relics.

Near Sian there were the Hot Springs and small lake resort where Chiang Kai-shek rested with his wife and followers when he was kidnapped in the mid-thirties, a place the guides showed us with some pride, as if it, too, were a shrine.

The city was the first capital of a united China and remained the center for some centuries. It has many pagodas and museums and was a place of unparalleled interest for us.

There we went also to the university and talked with the director and some of the professors, going to classes and several laboratories. We saw the struggle they are making to overcome the losses in twelve years of lack of teacher training and the destruction of textbooks during the cultural revolution. In this city we went to an opera of a classical Chinese love story and another night we had a fine banquet with fourteen separate dishes of meat, fish, and vegetables in a special restaurant outside the hotel.

It was in Sian that we began the postal card routine. First you buy the cards, then the stamps, then you go to your room to write, and then back to the post office—when it is open—to line up at the glue pot. None of the stamps have glue on them. It was a special task.

We could have spent weeks in Sian, but we were glad to get on to Taiyuan, an unknown and unexpected stopping point. Here we found some wonderful museums—old Buddhist temples, courtyards, and fascinating buildings in groups, with marvelous exhibits of vases, stone dragons, lions, elephants, and always the people in crowds watching us and applauding us as we climbed in and out of the different pavilions.

The hotel at Taiyuan was better than at Sian—but both were endurable although lacking in charm. They were examples of the modern Russian style of architecture.

Our trip to Taiyuan was by sleeper—an interesting and not unpleasant experience. We were four to a compartment—two up, two down—and we slept a fair part of the night, arriving at our destination in about eleven hours. We were becoming used to five o'clock rising, though we never enjoyed it.

The countryside from the border to Peking had large barren stretches and bare rock pierced with caves. There were long lines of bullocks, camels, horses, and bicycles. We saw tractors, but they were not, for some reason, in the fields. There were many shoulder-pole-carrying farm workers—men and women usually indistinguishable, some working in groups, some leaning on their shovels and hoes. Rice at first, farther north, wheat and a few vegetable plots. Scattered patches of green on the brown mountain sides, in many places—sheer rocks.

There was little water, and the rivers we crossed in almost two thousand miles of travel were shallow and full of silt. Snow lay on the upper slopes of the mountains. We traveled east and north. Peking lies on the latitude of Philadelphia.

Here and there a factory chimney of recent construction belched its chemical pollution. Coal lay in haphazard heaps beside the rails. Our overnight ride—four to a compartment ("soft")—was quite comfortable. The meal on the train was good, even practical to eat with chopsticks, and the beer was excellent.

To me one of the finest experiences was the climb to the temple of Xuan Chang near Taiyuan. Here in a notch, high in the steep mountains between cyprus and pine, was a Buddhist temple with several smaller temples and picturesque red and green structures where five old monks lived. In this holy place from which Buddhism is said to have been carried to Japan, I found the perfect shape and form of the misty Chinese print. I have walked up these paths and sat in the sun on these venerable rocks. I have touched the colored timbers of the shrines. All the artist's lines and shadows are now mine to recall and review in sun and wind, between waterfalls and beside rugged cliffs—they are mine.

In the drive back to the city of Taiyuan we asked about the reports of bomb shelters for a million people. The guides showed us ventilators over almost a quarter-mile area.

The old and the new we saw are clear signs of a terrific effort to catch up with modern times. Years have been lost in internal struggle. The "cultural revolution" destroyed much of science and art for a reported ten or twelve years. Feverishly the intellectuals—thwarted by some of the communist glorification of manual labor at the expense of intellectual achievement—are striving to reconstruct universities and schools. Two years have been devoted to this turnaround. Textbooks, teachers' equipment, buildings—all must be renewed and reconstructed.

We went to several schools and were impressed with the alertness of the young children. Questioned by their teacher in each group, the little hands shot up in the fraction of a second. The child called on stood and answered—in several classes—in English. When we came in and when we left, they clapped and smiled, charming in their colored blouses which were mingled with the prevailing blue—some with ribbons in their hair and seeking the eye-to-eye contact they seemed to cherish.

In none of the forty or fifty countries I have visited were young ones so attractive. Along the streets fathers—more often than mothers—held the toddlers and waved with them. To all appearances they were glad to see us.

We reached Peking on Wednesday, April 4, and left for Tokyo Monday, April 9. We visited the Imperial City, the Summer Palace, the vast Tien An Men Square and Mao obelisk, Peking University, and many other important institutions and buildings. A dust storm led to the cancellation of the planned visit to the Temple of Heaven.

At the time of our visit they were limiting the expression of criticism by posters. I was struck by the scarcity on the traditional walls. It was clear some had been recently removed.

In the universities, schools, communes, and factories in Peking and elsewhere there was always some conversation and tea was served. There was a chance to ask questions, and the answers were straightforward but not always revealing.

Our conversations with our Chinese guides were informative, but if we got beyond the obvious and factual they were puzzled and, though I think they meant to be frank, they often did not understand what we were asking. Everywhere we watched the people—the fields, the buildings, the temples, the traffic, bicycles, bicycles, bicycles. We wished to engrave the impressions of present-day China on our minds, as a moving dramatic pageant. We wanted to anticipate the future and understand the present, but we were overwhelmed by the past. It is impossible to bridge the gap between present construction and the towering pagodas of former centuries. The ancient treasures are overwhelming. The new products have little relation to the art of the past.

Those who knew the situation well—some Americans I talked to have been in Peking more than four years—seemed to believe Deng was firmly entrenched. The absence of his photograph from the wall displays was the result of his desire not to encourage the "cult of personality." I saw almost no photograph of him. Portraits of Mao and sometimes Chou En-lai were in the schools and public buildings and in museums everywhere.

The news circulation is very sparse. A double sheet was available, I was told, to the cadres and communes but not widely disseminated. I heard only two or three radio broadcasts.

The people showed no signs of restiveness, although we had no way of knowing their thoughts. They referred to Mao more than to Deng. I was not able to get a clear impression of the political atmosphere.

The Wall loomed through the mist and rain—dark and formidable. Our luck was not good on this trip. The weather was abominable. There were steps and a steep slope as the way led up the ridge. The Wall was wide and strong and disappeared in the distance, curving out of sight. We were thrilled to share in a century-old experience; the evidence of the fear and the resistance of armies against hordes from the north and west. We were glad to witness this fabulous barrier, though we were cold, wet, and shivering in the murky clouds.

We could not see the mountains, although we knew they were there. The stones underfoot were slippery and rain drenched the crenellated parapet. It was cold as ice as we leaned on it. We were glad we had climbed the Wall even though we could only see about twenty or thirty feet—but we have been there. We had traveled back into the past to explore this ancient drama.

Surely the Wall is the high point of a trip to China. It takes the visitor back through the centuries long past.

After we climbed down, wet and cold, we boarded the train and went south, according to our rigid and unchangeable schedule, to the Ming tombs. Here we again waded through mud and slush to climb up and then down some sixty steps to the vaulted chambers where the Emperor's coffin with those of two of his concubines was placed. Since the rich jewels and crowns had been moved to the nearby pavilions, the underground tomb, the only one of several now open, was bare and lacked embellishment. The others are not open to the public yet and not fully excavated.

This impressive historic monument was more massive than attractive, but the visit to the site was worth the extra effort because the cavernous vault was approached by the "avenue of the beasts"— elephants, tigers, horses, camels—twelve fascinating life-size statues. We returned to the hotel exhausted to be revived by hot baths. We had a sense of accomplishment, since we had seen the special relics and testimonials of a long span of human endeavor and had brought these impressions of the past into the present.

What did I learn? I came to realize as I could not have imagined the immense task of governing these 990 million people—transplanting technology, building new factories, changing methods of work.

I realized as I had not before the tremendous loss of the decades of strife and the cultural revolution. I was convinced that Deng was solid in his job and was entrenching himself more firmly and curbing criticism—down with wall posters.

I realized that transport and distribution problems would hamper the flow of investment.

People I saw—millions, friendly, eager, and many struggling to create the modern world. People with enough to eat—but not enough protein for energy. I was not sure they were aware of the outside world. We were foreign friends—but what was America? Could we help them create miracles?

I will not see or even read about what is going to happen in perhaps thirty years. The China I wanted to see—as a child of six— is still there. The new China I can only vaguely imagine.

Can equality, such as the Chinese foster it, permit a real, effective drive to modernization? At the hotels no one seemed in charge—neither management nor leadership seemed to be a factor.

Building of worker dwellings is a major activity in Peking. We visited a large commune outside Peking—they said 43,000 people lived and worked there. The roads were usually good though not subject to heavy traffic. Factories poured out smoke and fumes, giving evidence that industry is growing.

Nothing that I saw among the new products gave me hope they would soon find artistic inspiration. There is no substitute for religion—Buddhism is left to the museums—and politics have not permeated the masses. The task of providing subsistence and housing is immense. Food can scarcely suffice. Steel is in short supply. Farms are only partially modernized. The question constantly demanding answer was how can the system provide for a billion people. A quick answer is only by a firm rule and dictatorial controls. To this answer one puts the further question, will the people tolerate such controls? Several decades will reveal what is possible.

The trip is an exciting one for all those who want to look to the East and to the future, and for those who can still climb a hundred steps, rise at five in the morning, and enjoy Chinese food. Others can read in books but they will never have the feeling for these hundreds of millions young and old—a large seething population struggling with vast plains and mountains. To feel the pulse of a changing world one must go there.

# 30

# PERSPECTIVES

After more than eighty years of wondering and questioning, I have come to a number of conclusions. I learned early that men took a position of leadership. On the boat they held the tiller and started the engine. On shore they built the campfires and pitched the tents. As a small child I became accustomed to this situation. It was easier in my family circle because my two brothers were older, stronger, and always ahead of me in experience. When I got into the outside world of camp, of school, and of college, it was harder. I realized that women were often first with the ideas and strong and skillful with execution. There was no reason why they could not be the first in business and in finance. I plunged forward in these directions in my early postcollege years. What I found was that men had got there first. They were entrenched and had solidly established their position and had a tacit agreement to hold the top positions and the instruments of control. This dominance was being exercised, usually in a benign way.

My response to the conditions I found in the early twenties was to choose my own job and win total independence of my brothers. I found my career and only asked for advice in situations where I had the possibility of making my own decision even if different from ones my brothers favored. There was never a spirit of hostility and I knew they were warm in their intent. In the case of my study of the French franc, I asked advice. In my work on the Bank of International Settlements I sought counsel. In my move to Washington to work for the Social Security Board, in my subsequent transfer to the Department of State in 1942, I conferred with them but I made my own decisions.

Even in those early years some men, including my husband, David, in Paris, James Bourne, married to my cousin Dorothy, Jack Erhardt in Austria, Jimmy Riddleberger in Washington, Cecil Lyon in Berlin, and a few others felt a woman's imagination, drive, and clear-sighted motivation worth nourishing and exploiting.

The situation I found sometimes meant I had to shift jobs when, as in 1950, I came up against solid walls of discrimination. Women are not alone in the need to move from dead-end jobs; men, too, must develop the courage and the ingenuity to seek new kinds of work, new ways of life from time to time.

My conviction is that as the steady increase of numbers of children of working mothers changes the general attitude, there will be more even distribution of the daily and weekly responsibilities.

I do not think the belligerent female is a substantial help in this civilized process. In my own experience, in Austria, in Berlin, and elsewhere, I used the techniques of gradualism and persistence.

Social life is an aid to both men and women in their struggle to understand, to create and win allies. I have had many an interesting conversation at a cocktail party. I have planned some small dinners and swimming parties with a purpose. I have cited, earlier, the time in 1951 when I had the German military committee in my swimming pool with their American counterparts.

There are in 1980 old methods and new problems to be taken into account. The much talked of generation gap is not a new phenomenon. It is older than Moses. The approach to the young is to listen. The approach of the young to the old is also to listen. There is much to be learned and little to gain in imposing a will, where communication has broken down. The young are a handsome, healthy lot. I can trust the future to them. They will not make more mistakes than we did, or our parents. If they will learn from us, they can avoid some errors. They have a bewildering lot of tools, an overwhelming mass of data, a horrendous set of problems—let them take these on with our blessing. I am not sure I envy them, but I am glad they have the stamina. In some strange way each generation runs faster, vaults higher, dives cleaner; let them use their amazing mental skills and scientific discoveries—perhaps I shall rest for a time.

Let no one think that government can do it. Whatever *it* is, you will do it—the oncoming men and women, boys and girls. The most dangerous thought that can infect the public is that somehow what government does is costless, easy, and leaves them free to relax. Nothing from health care to intelligence and national security can be shifted off our shoulders onto a giant called government. In some cases a joint effort, a pooling of assets, helps as in recourse to insurance. In other cases it merely increases the complexity and adds to expense.

Special care must be directed to the mystery and the magic.

[355]

Will the method chosen conceal the real cost and cultivate the illusion that the miracle of creation has brought society a free lunch at last? The trick financial solution ends—or rather begins—with inflation. Inflation, for its part, is the surest road to disaster. Nothing except war can wreak greater havoc. Sophistication in the world of finance is needed, and perhaps a little wisdom among economists will save us from impending doom. It is not the reliance on mathematical formula but the perception of human nature and the denial of the sugarplum of credit that can keep us on the right course. If we would consume more, we must produce more.

In all these choices and application of effort, it would be well to recognize that the difference that many scientists attribute to the brains of men and women does not spell inferiority, but rather diversity and opportunity. No sex, race, or type of person should be burdened with the stigma of incapacity or doomed to failure. In the demanding times we face, all people must be used, all must be given opportunity so there will be universal hope and cooperation.

When I look out from my apartment on the hill called Mount St. Alban, I see the city where much of the world's foreign policy is made and where a great deal of foolishness originates from time to time. The politicians and the voters know little of the past and cannot predict the future. I must tell my story not because I can solve the mysteries or foretell what is to come, but because it is about people. The nature of individuals is a deep mystery but significant and relevant to our unraveling life's quandaries. If we who are older try to advise and guide those who are malleable and who are searching for understanding, the possibility of creating a better world will be brighter.

In my life there have been scores of unanswered questions and many unsatisfied desires. I could barely tolerate the restrictions of working for government, but by staying within the system I could direct power to creative ends in Austria, in Berlin, and elsewhere. Power was there to be used and I managed to grasp the controls on various occasions which made it seem as if the power was mine. This accomplishment could only come by working with others and seeing the opportunities that money and planning could bring, if used where they would be effective.

Wisdom is a rare commodity and can only be gained slowly and painfully.

[356]

I do not know how the political life of the United States will develop in 1980—I know we are slowly awaking to the needs for energy programs and the critical dangers of inflation. I do not know the future of Central Europe, but I have witnessed the strong racial feelings of the Germans in various countries, which leads me to think there will be some kind of unity for German-speaking people. I cannot forecast the pace of constructive cooperation of the European communities, but I have followed with interest and understanding the progress since World War II, which few counted on in 1945. What will happen in China is an enigma that baffles the experts, but I was impressed on my recent journey by the vast regional differences which might suggest political divisions to come at a later date. Africa, which discouraged me by its chaotic tribal life and lack of understanding of systems of production, has advanced further than I would have thought, since 1960, but the obstacles to rapid development are still enormous. The nuclear potential of large and small powers has awed millions so that they shy away from large-scale conflicts—but still stumble on the road to lasting peace. Education of a kind is spreading, but its overemphasis on technical proficiency delays the growth of more perceptive handling of the democratic process and the cooperation of people. I have learned something from years of work, travel, success, and failure. I have an immense sense of gratitude for a thousand chances to see and hear and feel. Now I can pass along to those who take up the burden some sense of responsibility and awareness of the flaming glory of life.

We have reached a stage in human affairs when complete disaster is possible. Mistakes in the fields of population, of drugs, of finance and of nuclear fission may destroy all that has been created over the centuries at enormous cost. But we have reached a period when there is *time*, no World War, no overwhelming disaster impends. I could be pessimistic about the threat to our survival, but I am optimistic. The oncoming generation has some years in which to tackle these enormous problems. If they can improve education, raise the standards of behavior, insist on a high level of honesty, and establish values which we can hold in a will to cooperate within and between nations, our resources can bring us through the coming years to the dawn of a new world. The resources and the inspiration, as well as the overwhelming need is there. Now there is a call to action.

[357]

# APPENDICES

# Chronology*

| | |
|---|---|
| 1884, Aug. 25 | Husband, David S. Blondheim, born |
| 1886, Jan. 13 | Parents, Allen Macy Dulles, Edith Foster, married in New York Avenue Church, Washington, D.C. |
| 1888, Feb. 25 | Older brother, John Foster Dulles, born in Washington, D.C. |
| 1889, Apr. 25 | Older sister, Margaret Josephine Dulles, born in Watertown, N.Y. |
| 1892, June 29 | Grandfather, John W. Foster, appointed as U.S. Secretary of State by President Benjamin Harrison (resigned Feb. 23, 1893) |
| 1893, Apr. 7 | Brother, Allen Welsh Dulles, born in Watertown |
| May 24 | Allen Welsh Dulles to Philadelphia for operation on foot |
| | Grandfather Foster starts building Underbluff cottage at Henderson Harbor, N.Y. |
| 1895, June 1 | "Little Eleanor born about six a.m." (Line-a-Day) |
| July 30 | Minister Yang Yu, Chinese statesman, visits family at Henderson Harbor |
| 1896, Nov. 6 | William McKinley elected President |
| 1898, Jan. 22 | Younger sister, Nataline Dulles, born in Watertown |
| 1901, Sept. 14 | Theodore Roosevelt inaugurated after President McKinley's assassination |
| 1903, June 1 | Eleanor in Washington, D.C. (Mother in Lausanne, Switzerland) |
| 1904, Mar. 4 | Theodore Roosevelt inaugurated |
| June 1 | Birthday present—a bicycle—ordeal of learning to ride |
| Sept. 19 | To new home in Auburn, N.Y. (67 South Street) |
| Sept. 21 | John Foster Dulles to Princeton University |

*The sources used for this chronology include diaries I kept sporadically and my parents' "Line-a-Day." The "Line-a-Day" has 366 pages with entries for the years 1886 to 1919 and beyond. These are delicately written and compact and give much information. Other sources include books and almanacs.

| | |
|---|---|
| 1907, June 15–<br>Oct. 18 | Foster to Hague Peace Conference with<br>Grandfather, John W. Foster |
| Oct. 5 | Margaret Dulles to Bryn Mawr College |
| 1908, June | Foster graduates from Princeton—valedictorian<br>Eleanor at Mount Vernon Seminary, then at 12th &<br>M streets, Washington, D.C. (family in Europe) |
| Sept. 17 | Orville Wright's plane crashes, Fort Myer (Lt.<br>Thomas E. Selfridge killed)—Eleanor visits the<br>field |
| Nov. | William Howard Taft elected President |
| Dec. 20 | Father returns from France and joins Eleanor at<br>Englewood for Christmas |
| 1909, Mar. 4 | Eleanor watches President Taft inaugural parade,<br>heavy snow |
| May | Eleanor to Paris with father—S.S. *Rotterdam*—to<br>join family in Paris |
| Sept. | Golden Wedding Anniversary of Mary Parke and<br>John W. Foster (James Brown Scott, international<br>lawyer, congratulates Eleanor on poem) |
| 1911, Sept. | Eleanor at Auburn Academic High School |
| 1912, June 2 | Foster returns from BWI—early international trade<br>effort for Produce Exchange |
| June 7 | Margaret and Deane Edwards engaged |
| 1912, July 8 | Eleanor to Alford Lake Camp, near Camden, Maine |
| Sept. | To Wykeham Rise School, Washington,<br>Connecticut |
| Nov. | Woodrow Wilson elected President |
| 1913, June 13 | Graduates from Wykeham Rise School<br>Receives First New England Scholarship for Bryn<br>Mawr College |
| 1914, Aug. | World War I—Germans cross into Belgium Tuesday<br>the 4th |
| 1915, June 23 | Uncle, Robert Lansing, appointed Secretary of<br>State (ad interim June 9-23) |
| 1916, Jan. | At Bryn Mawr College |
| June | Volunteer counsellor at Fresh Air Camp at Long<br>Beach, New Jersey |
| Nov. | Woodrow Wilson re-elected President |
| 1917, June 7 | Bryn Mawr, AB |
| June 9 | To France, S.S. *Espagne*—to work for Shurtleff<br>Relief Committee in Paris |
| Sept. 11 | To Berne, Switzerland, to visit Allen W. Dulles |
| Nov. 15 | Grandfather Foster died |

| | |
|---|---|
| 1918, Nov. 11 | Armistice signed in France |
| | Works with American Friends Service at Mareuil-le-Port, Marne, France |
| Dec. 14 | President Woodrow Wilson to Paris—saw him enter Place de la Concorde |
| 1919, June 16 | Returns from France—to Henderson |
| Sept. | Awarded Fellowship in Social Economy and Psychology—student at Bryn Mawr |
| | Meets Emily Huntington at Bryn Mawr |
| 1920, July | Employed by American Tube and Stamping Company, Bridgeport, Connecticut, as Assistant Employment Manager |
| Sept. | S. Glemby and Company, Long Island, New York, Payroll Clerk and Employment Manager (to June 1921); lived on Staten Island |
| Nov. | Warren G. Harding elected President |
| 1921, June | Sails to Europe, S. S. *Homeric* |
| | Walking trip in Black Forest, Germany |
| Sept. | London School of Economics—student—report on home workers for Toynbee Hall, factory survey |
| 1922 | Flies the Channel, from Croydon to Brussels |
| June 18 | Grandmother Foster dies |
| 1923, Aug. 3 | Calvin Coolidge inaugurated after death of Harding |
| | Student—Economics at Harvard and Radcliffe (1923-1926) lived in Boston (Mount Vernon Street, Charles Street, West Cedar Street) |
| 1924, June | M.A., Radcliffe and Harvard |
| July | Simmons College—taught economics to June 30, 1925 |
| Nov. | Calvin Coolidge elected President |
| 1925, June 24 | Ship to Europe—Paris—research on French franc |
| Dec. | Met David S. Blondheim |
| | Takes Greek ship from Marseilles to Constantinople to visit Nataline Dulles |
| 1926, Jan. | Returns to Paris from Turkey |
| Mar. | Returns to Boston with thesis on French franc |
| June 23 | Ph.D., Harvard-Radcliffe |
| July | Aunt Eleanor Lansing gives her namesake a small sailboat |
| 1927 | Returns to Paris |
| July 1 | On teaching status—Simmons College to June 30, 1928 |

| | | |
|---|---|---|
| 1928 | | To Bryn Mawr—teaching Economics and Social Economy |
| | Oct. 30 | Robert Lansing (Uncle Bert) dies |
| | Nov. | Herbert Hoover elected President |
| | | *The French Franc, 1914–1928* (first book published) |
| 1929, Sept. | | To California, visits Emily Huntington in Berkeley |
| | Sept. 10 | Nataline marries James S. Seymour |
| | Oct. 29 | Stock market collapses in New York (Black Tuesday) |
| | | Teaching—Bryn Mawr College |
| 1930, July | | Voyage by *faltboot* on the Danube, Ulm to Passau, visits Vienna, Austria |
| | Aug. | To Bonn |
| | Sept. | To Berlin |
| | Sept. | To Basel, Switzerland, research, Bank for International Settlements |
| 1931, Apr. | | London—research for Report on British Unemployment for President Hoover (associated with George Woods) |
| 1932, Jan. | | Teaching Bryn Mawr (after return from Basel) |
| | | On staff of Wharton School, University of Pennsylvania |
| | Nov. | Franklin D. Roosevelt elected President |
| | | Teaching—Joseph Willit's Seminar and at Pennsylvania Women's College |
| | | *Bank for International Settlements at Work* published |
| | | *The Evolution of Reparation Ideas*, monograph, published |
| | Dec. 6 | Marries David S. Blondheim |
| 1933 | | Teaching at Bryn Mawr and Pennsylvania |
| | Mar. 4 | Franklin D. Roosevelt inaugurated; Cordell Hull, Secretary of State |
| | | *The Dollar, the Franc and Inflation* published |
| | | London—Economic Conference (attended one session) |
| | | To France with David |
| | | Brittany—bicycling with Emily |
| 1934, Mar. 19 | | David S. Blondheim dies |
| | Oct. 6 | David Dulles born |

| | |
|---|---|
| 1935 | Bryn Mawr College and Wharton School, University of Pennsylvania |
| | Consultant for Carl D. Montgomery and Louise Watson, Investment Management firm |
| | Elected HonoraryMember—Phi Beta Kappa, University of Pennsylvania |
| 1936, Apr. | *Depression and Reconstruction* published |
| | To Washington—economist at Social Security Board, Bureau of Research and Statistics, head of Division Financing Old Age Insurance |
| | Rents house on 33rd Place |
| | Starts building house at 2824 Chain Bridge Road |
| 1937 | Speech in Defense of Financing Social Security before Vandenberg Commission |
| | Baby girl born February 26, Ann Welsh Dulles, a member of the family by adoption |
| | Moves into house—2824 Chain Bridge Road |
| 1938 | To Geneva, Switzerland—for conference on Financing Social Insurance |
| | Work on amending the Act—defense before Ways and Means Committee |
| | Writes report—*Financing the Social Security Act* |
| 1939, Sept. 1 | World War II, Poland invaded by German forces |
| 1940 | Continues research with Social Security Board |
| 1941, May 8 | Mother, Edith Foster Dulles, dies in Auburn |
| Dec. 7 | Japanese launch attack on Pearl Harbor and Philippines |
| Dec. | Speech to American Economic Association—New York meeting, *War and Investment Opportunities* (in Civil War) |
| 1942, Apr. | Transfers to Board of Economic Warfare |
| Sept. | Transfers to Leo Pasvolsky's Division on Postwar Planning, State Department, Economic Officer |
| | Finance Committee work on White Plan and Keynes Plan |
| 1943, Nov. 9 | Works on agreement on UNRRA—United Nations Relief and Rehabilitation Administration |
| | Planning for postwar Germany, Austria, France, Belgium |
| 1944, Apr. 22 | White and Keynes financial plans published |
| July 1–22 | Appointed to International Secretariat Conference of 44 nations at Bretton Woods, New Hampshire |
| Dec. 1 | Edward Stettinius, Secretary of State |

| 1945, Apr. 12 | Harry S Truman sworn in after Franklin D. Roosevelt dies |
|---|---|
| Apr. 25 | Sails for England on S.S. *Marine Fox* assigned as U.S. Financial Attaché in Austria |
| May 5 | Weymouth, England, early landing ordered because of submarine threat |
| May 8 | VE Day |
| June | To London; Caserta, Rome, Florence, Verona, Italy and to Salzburg, Austria |
| June 29 | Short trip to Berchtesgaden and Hitler's Eagle's Nest on mountain top |
| July | To Frankfurt, Germany (to exchange 200 Hungarian horses for food for Austria—arranged with U.S. military) |
| Aug. 18 | Ill, sent briefly to Munich hospital |
| Aug. 29 | To Vienna, Austria, in Hitler's automobile (see photograph) Moves from Hotel Regina into Clam Gallas Palace, Vienna, then to Sternwartestrasse |
| Oct. | Monetary conversion begins—reichsmarks withdrawn |
| Dec. 20 | Kleine Scheidegg, Switzerland, for Christmas with Allen, Clover, Joan, David, Ann, Foreign Minister Karl and Helga Gruber |
| 1946, Jan. 26 | To Paris, France, for Conference of U.S. Economic Officers |
| Feb. 3 | To London to confer with Foster and Janet |
| Feb. | Austrian monetary conversion program completed with distribution of small notes |
| Mar. | Arranges grant of cotton from military stockpile Secured Export Import Bank Loan |
| Apr. | Soviets seize large portion of Austrian industrial plant Eleanor briefs Walter Lippmann on his visit to Vienna Negotiates purchase of Konsular Academie building for Embassy—using surplus U.S. credit |
| July 3 | James R. Byrnes, Secretary of State |
| Sept. 6 | Secretary Byrnes' and General Clay's speech given at Stuttgart—Germany to be helped |
| 1947, Jan. 21 | George C. Marshall, Secretary of State |

| | |
|---|---|
| Mar. | To Berlin to confer with Foster on his way to Moscow negotiations on treaties for Germany and Austria with Mark Clark and Secretary Marshall |
| July | U.S. Treaty Commission comes to Vienna to negotiate |
| Aug. | Soviets hold Eleanor for interrogation in Baden, Austria |
| Oct. | To Trieste for visit—head of mission, Robert and Jane Joyce |
| 1948, Feb. 20 | To Budapest, Hungary, for weekend |
| Feb. 22 | Stuck in blizzard at Ruscozi, Czechoslovakia |
| | Bratislava, Czechoslovakia—visits Consul Claiborne Pell |
| | Communist takeover—Prague government |
| Mar. | Sails on S.S. *America* to Washington with children on home leave |
| May | Returns to Austria via England, motoring through Europe |
| July | Rents villa on Travensee Lake near Linz |
| | Marshall Plan—(pressure of work prevented extensive vacation) |
| Sept. | David, thirteen years old, flies to United States for school |
| Nov. | Sails with Ann on S.S. *America* |
| | Returns to Washington—reassigned |
| Nov. 4 | Harry S Truman elected President—defeats Thomas Dewey |
| | Returns to house, 2824 Chain Bridge Road, Washington |
| | Reports to Department of State |
| 1949, Jan. 21 | Dean Acheson, Secretary of State |
| | Assigned to German Austrian Division—Department of State |
| May 30 | Niece, Edith Edwards, dies |
| | Gertrude and Aurelie Rotter come from Austria to the U.S. |
| | Eleanor buys Six Town Point Island in Lake Ontario from Foster for $600 |
| 1950, June 12 | First honorary degree, Dr. of Laws, Wilson College, Chambersburg, Pa. |
| | Swimming pool built, McLean, Virginia |

| | |
|---|---|
| June 25 | North Koreans invade South Korea |
| | Foster in Tokyo after visit to Korea—preparations for Japanese peace treaty |
| July 3 | Starts building house on Spring Hill Road, McLean, Va. |
| 1951, Feb. 22 | Moves to McLean, Va. |
| June 11 | Detailed to National Production Authority in Department of Commerce, grade GS15, salary $8,800 |
| 1952, July 25 | Transferred to Commerce NPA GS15, $10,800 |
| Nov. | Dwight D. Eisenhower elected President, defeated Adlai Stevenson |
| Dec. 17 | Reemployed—State Department Office of German Affairs under James W. Riddleberger |
| Dec. 27 | Survey trip to Germany—Bonn, Berlin |
| 1953, Jan. 16 | Lunch with Chancellor Konrad Adenauer |
| Jan. 20 | Eisenhower inaugurated President |
| Jan. 21 | John Foster Dulles sworn in as Secretary of State |
| Feb. 14 | Large refugee flow to Berlin, secures $15 million for programs of aid |
| Mar. 4 | Stalin dies |
| June 16, 17 | Uprising in East Berlin and East Germany crushed by Soviet military (Eleanor at the Brandenburg Gate) |
| | State Department initiates food package program for East Germans |
| July | Mayor of Berlin Ernst Reuter visits Washington, confers with Secretary Dulles |
| Sept. | Mayor Reuter dies |
| 1954 | Continues work in State Department—German office |
| Apr. | Berlin visit |
| | Working on houses in Foggy Bottom in Washington, D.C. (moonlighting) |
| | Speeches for State Department—(see list in Appendices) |
| 1955 | Continues work in State Department |
| May 15 | John Foster Dulles signs Austrian State Treaty in Vienna |
| | Eleanor visits Berlin |
| June 11 | Granted Distinguished Achievement Award by Radcliffe Alumnae |

| | |
|---|---|
| Sept. | Berlin visit |
| 1956 | Continues work in State Department |
| Jan. | Berlin visit |
| March | Visits Haiti |
| Sept. | Berlin visit |
| Nov. | Eisenhower reelected, defeated Adlai Stevenson |
| 1957, Jan. | Berlin visit |
| Feb. 23 | Dr. Honoris Causa—Berlin Free University Political Science faculty |
| Apr. | Berlin visit |
| June 3 | Doctor of Literature, Western College, Ohio |
| Sept. | Berlin visit |
| Sept. 19 | Dedication of Congress Hall—"Pregnant Oyster" |
| Sept. 27 | Awarded Carl Schurz Plaque in Berlin |
| Oct. 19 | John Foster Dulles dinner for Queen Elizabeth and Prince Philip, Pan American Union, Eleanor there |
| 1958, May 8 | Arranges Berlin visit for John Foster Dulles Eleanor in Berlin |
| Nov. 27 | Khrushchev ultimatum on Berlin delivered to U.S. Embassy, Moscow |
| Nov. 27 | Thanksgiving dinner, Foster, Allen with Eleanor in McLean |
| 1959, Feb. | Willy Brandt visits Washington |
| Apr. 22 | Christian Herter, Secretary of State |
| May 24 | Foster dies—funeral in Washington Cathedral, May 27 |
| Oct. 18 | Transferred from German Office to Intelligence and Research (INR) |
| Oct. 21 | Laying of cornerstone, the Klinikum, 1500-bed hospital, Berlin |
| Oct. 21 | Awarded Ernst Reuter Plaque by Governing Mayor Willy Brandt |
| Nov. 3 | CIA cornerstone laying, Langley, Virginia |
| Dec. | Gall bladder operation |
| Dec. 31 | Eleanor accorded by President Eisenhower personal rank of Minister |
| 1960, Jan.– May | To Asia, Japan, Taiwan, Hong Kong, Singapore, Indonesia, Malaya, South Vietnam, Cambodia, Thailand, Burma, Nepal, India, Pakistan, Afghanistan, Iran, Turkey, London, Paris, U.S. |
| June 4 | Bryn Mawr citation for distinction, received in absentia |

| | |
|---|---|
| July | To Lahey Clinic for abdominal operation |
| Oct. | Trip with Radio Free Europe to Portugal; Munich, Germany; Berlin |
| | London and Paris, Africa, Morocco, Tunis, Algeria, Egypt, Sudan, Ethiopia, Kenya, Uganda, Tanganyika, Zanzibar, Southern Rhodesia, Madagascar, Mozambique, Angola, Congo (Leopoldville), Congo (Brazzaville), Nigeria, Ghana, Togo, Ivory Coast, Liberia, Guinea, Mali, Senegal |
| Nov. | John F. Kennedy elected President, defeated Richard M. Nixon |
| 1961, Jan. 20 | Dean Rusk, Secretary of State |
| Aug. 13 | The Berlin Wall erected (Eleanor was not on the ·Berlin desk, research on developing countries in INR) |
| Sept. 21 | Secretary Rusk requests Eleanor's resignation from the State Department |
| Dec. 27 | Pamela Forbes and David Dulles married in Boston |
| 1962, Jan. | Eleanor resigns from State Department |
| | Eleanor to Latin America on her own, to Brazil, Uruguay, Argentina, Chile, Peru, Panama, Mexico |
| Mar. 26 | Visit to Germany |
| | Adenauer presented decoration, *Das Grosse Verdienstkreuz* |
| May 26 | Ann marries David Joor |
| Nov. 8 | Doctor of Law—Mount Holyoke College |
| autumn | Teaching—Duke University, Durham, N.C. |
| Nov. 17 | Attends Dulles Airport dedication |
| 1963 | Duke University—teaching |
| | Lecturing for Colston Leigh Speaker's Bureau |
| | Teaching—Georgetown University, to 1971 |
| Nov. | To Bonn as guest of Adenauer for retirement reception (see photograph) |
| Nov. | *John Foster Dulles—The Last Year* published |
| Nov. 22 | Kennedy assassinated |
| | Lyndon B. Johnson sworn in as President |
| 1964 | Research for Center for Strategic Services— Georgetown University |
| Mar. 30 | Operation on detached retina—right eye |
| June 23 | Christine Joor born |
| June 27 | Frederick Dulles born |
| Nov. | Lyndon B. Johnson elected President |

| 1965 | | Teaching at Georgetown University |
| | May 15 | To Vienna, Austria, guest of the Austrian government |
| | June 7 | Awarded Litt. Dr., Duke University |
| | | *Détente*, Dulles & Crane, published by CSS |
| | | Interview for Princeton Oral History—on John Foster Dulles |
| | July 19 | Susan Joor born |
| 1966 | | Teaching at Georgetown University |
| | June 29 | Edward Dulles born |
| | | Work at CSS (Center for Strategic Studies, later CSIS, Center for Strategic and International Studies) |
| | July | *Dominican Action 1965—Intervention or Cooperation*, CSS |
| 1967, | Apr. 24 | To Adenauer's funeral with LBJ in President's plane |
| | July 11 | To East Germany (GDR): Leipzig, Weimar, Dresden, Eisleben, Halle, Karl Marxstadt |
| | Sept. | To Stanford, California—Hoover Institution (lived in Palo Alto) |
| | | *Berlin: The Wall Is Not Forever*, The University of North Carolina Press |
| | | *Berlin und die Amerikaner*, translation Wissenschaft and Politik, Koeln, FRG |
| 1968, | Apr. 25 | William Joor born |
| | | Research and writing at Hoover Institution |
| | July 19 | Wins a small sailboat at Henderson Harbor Yacht Club drawing |
| | July | To Helsinki, Leningrad, Moscow, Bucharest, Prague |
| | Oct. 9 | Klinikum Dedication, Berlin, included as part of U.S. delegation |
| | | *American Foreign Policy in the Making*, published by Harper and Row |
| | Nov. | Richard M. Nixon elected President |
| | Dec. 24 | Allen to Georgetown Hospital |
| 1969, | Jan. 1 | Allen in Georgetown Hospital |
| | Jan. 20 | Nixon inaugurated as President |
| | | William R. Rogers, Secretary of State |
| | Jan. 29 | Allen dies (Allen Welsh Dulles) |
| | Mar. 30 | Attends Eisenhower funeral at Washington Cathedral |
| | Apr. 6 | Charleston, S.C., personal visit (Dulles ancestral house) |

| | |
|---|---|
| May 14 | Janet dies (Mrs. John Foster Dulles) |
| June 16 | Juliet Dulles born |
| June 23 | Speech at High School, Henderson Village |
| July 25 | Bretton Woods agreements celebrated at dinner—25th reunion |
| July 31 | To Europe on S.S. *Aurelia* with Youth for Understanding group.* YFU consultant (1969–73) |
| Aug. 18 | Visits Bonn, Berlin—return from Hamburg |
| Dec. | Joor and Dulles grandchildren come to McLean for Christmas |
| 1970, Jan. | Consultant, Department of State, Bureau of European Affairs |
| | Teaching at Georgetown University |
| Feb. 18 | To San Francisco for Youth For Understanding (YFU) |
| Feb. 25 | *One Germany or Two*, published by Stanford University Press |
| May 29 | Margaret Edwards (sister) dies |
| June 14–24 | Lecturing at Saginaw Valley College, Michigan, for YFU |
| July 3 | Reverend Deane Edwards dies (brother-in-law) |
| July 14 | George V. Allen (a Director of YFU) funeral in Washington |
| Aug. 13 | To Detroit and Ann Arbor for YFU |
| Sept. 9 | YFU Board Meeting—Ann Arbor |
| Dec. 9 | To San Francisco for YFU |
| 1971, Jan. | Consultant, State Department |
| | Teaching at Georgetown University |
| Jan. 14 | Lecture for YFU, Battle Creek, Michigan |
| Feb. 10–25 | To Philippines with Rachel Andresen, head of YFU, to Tokyo, Japan |
| May 4 | Left eye operation for cataract |
| June 9 | Left eye operation for detached retina |
| June 29 | Consultant to Bureau of European Affairs, Department of State—continued reappointment until August 1977 |
| July | Moved from Virginia to 3900 Watson Place-B, Washington |
| Nov. 12–25 | Yugoslavia, Belgrade, Ljubljana, Zagreb, Skopje—trip for YFU |

*International Teenage Exchange Program
Headquarters: Washington—formerly Ann Arbor, Michigan

| | | |
|---|---|---|
| 1972 | | Consultant, Department of State |
| | Mar. 21–28 | Belgrade, Dubrovnik, Yugoslavia |
| | Apr. 17 | *The Wall—A Tragedy in Three Acts*—University of South Carolina, Columbia, S.C. |
| | Apr. 18 | Berkeley and San Francisco (YFU) |
| | June 9 | YFU Board Meeting, Ann Arbor, Michigan |
| | July 23 | Evansville, Indiana (YFU)—visits Foster house |
| | Aug. 24 | Association Island Association Board meeting— Conservation (Henderson Harbor) |
| | Sept. 11 | To Berlin, Bonn |
| | Nov. | Richard M. Nixon reelected President |
| 1973 | | Consultant, Department of State |
| | Feb. 23 | Speaks to Commonwealth Club, San Francisco, California |
| | Apr. 15 | Church at White House (Nixon) |
| | Nov. 30 | Austin, Texas, University Dedication Memorial Rooms (Foster and Janet Dulles)—(see brochure in Appendix) |
| | | Henry A. Kissinger, Secretary of State |
| 1974 | | Consultant, Department of State |
| | Apr. 15 | Clover dies (Mrs. Allen W. Dulles) |
| | | Princeton with Doris Rich—to consult Dulles Diplomatic Library |
| | May 8–11 | Berlin for celebration end of blockade—guest of German government |
| | June 16 | Princeton, Dulles Library, for research |
| | Aug. 9 | Richard M. Nixon resigns as President |
| | | Gerald Ford sworn in as President |
| | Nov. 16 | To California—YFU |
| | | Working on Acheson and Dulles manuscript |
| 1975, Apr. 1 | | Cataract operation, right eye |
| | May 15 | To Vienna, Austria—20th anniversary of State Treaty |
| | June 1 | Doctor of Literature, Mount Vernon College, Washington, D.C. |
| | | 80th birthday party—Amersly, Maryland (the Frank Allens) |
| | July | Henderson for second birthday party |
| | Sept. | Cruise from Maine to Marblehead with Tim (Ambassador Timberlake) |
| 1976, Feb. | | Speaks to Historical Society—Watertown, New York |
| | May 16 | Visit to Bonn, Berlin |

| | |
|---|---|
| May 21 | Frankfurt—at bicentennial celebration—Nelson Rockefeller spoke—Eleanor guest of *Atlantik Bruecke* and Carl Schurz Foundation |
| 1977, Jan. 20 | Jimmy Carter inaugurated President Cyrus R. Vance, Secretary of State |
| June | 60th reunion of 1917 class Bryn Mawr College, Bryn Mawr, Pennsylvania |
| Sept. | Cruise with Tim on Chesapeake and Chop Tank |
| Sept. | Berlin |
| 1978, Feb. | Florida |
| June 23 | Eyelid operation—bi-lateral ectropion repair |
| Sept. | Stopped consultantship at State Department |
| Nov. | Trip to Hawaii, Fiji, via Berkeley, California |
| 1979, Feb. 14 | Laser treatment to right eye |
| Mar. 23– Apr. 12 | China trip via Hong Kong and Tokyo |
| May 27 | Doctor of Literature, Clarkson College, Potsdam, N.Y. |
| 1980, Apr. | Publication of autobiography (Prentice-Hall) |

# SPEECHES OF ELEANOR DULLES
## 1956—1961

| DATE | PLACE | SUBJECT |
|------|-------|---------|
| June 14, 1956 | Hunter College Commencement Exercises, New York, New York | The Impact of the United States on Europe, Press Release #317 |
| June 21, 1956 | Second Summer Workshop, International Legal Studies, Berkeley, California | European Payments Union—and Financial Adjustment |
| June 26, 1956 | World Affairs Council of Northern California, San Francisco, California | Berlin—Today |
| June 28, 1956 | Zonta International Convention, Sun Valley, Idaho | The Meaning of Foreign Affairs to the Average American, Press Release #352 |
| October 29, 1956 | Cosmopolitan Club, Philadelphia | Berlin and Germany (Refugees) |
| January 17, 1957 | World Affairs Council, League of Women Voters, Bryn Mawr Club, Albany, New York | Meaning of Berlin, Press Release #27 |
| February 23, 1957 | Free University, Berlin | The Arithmetic of Occupation in East Germany |
| March 27, 1957 | 52nd Annual Convention of the Buffalo Federation of Women's Clubs, Buffalo, New York | The Soviet Occupied Zone of Germany, Press Release #174 |
| May 17, 1957 | Conference of the Women's Organization of the Dept. of State, New State, Washington | Divided Germany and the Western Alliance |
| May 22, 1957 | National Home Fashions League Inc., Willard Hotel, Washington, Luncheon | Berlin's Recovery in Changing Times |

| DATE | PLACE | SUBJECT |
|---|---|---|
| May 22, 1957 | Women's National Republican Club, New York City | Berlin and Soviet Methods in Germany, Press Release #311 |
| June 3, 1957 | Western College for Women, Oxford, Ohio | Education—Communist Style, American Style, Press Release #333 |
| August, 1957 | Article in *Madame Magazine*, Berlin, Germany | Women in the Free World |
| September 27, 1957 | Carl Schurz Seidlung, Berlin, on the occasion of receiving the Carl Schurz Plaque | Working Partnership Between the U.S. and Germany |
| November 8, 1957 | Auburn Community College, Auburn, New York | West Germany Today and Berlin, Opportunities, Signs of Danger |
| November 19, 1957 | Georgetown University, Foreign Service School | My Career in the Foreign Service |
| March 20, 1958 | Indianapolis Council on World Affairs, Inc., Indianapolis, Indiana | U.S. Economic Policy and Postwar Germany |
| March 21, 1958 | International Relations Council, Inc., South Bend, Indiana | Labor Rejects Communism—East Germany, Press Release #134 |
| March 22, 1958 | Kalamazoo, Michigan | Kalamazoo Exhibit in Berlin—importance to establish contacts |
| April 9, 1958 | Radcliffe Alumni, Radcliffe Club of Washington | Problems of Postwar Germany—Anticipated in 1944, Reviewed in 1958 |
| April 17, 1958 | American Women's Activities in Germany | The City of Berlin and Our Position There—Wiesbaden |
| February 21, 1959 | Third Annual Institute on United States Foreign Policy, University of Wisconsin, Milwaukee, Wisconsin | The Challenge to the Western Policy for Germany, Press Release #125 |
| March 2, 1959 | Women's Bond Club of New York, New York | Germany and the Berlin Crisis |

| DATE | PLACE | SUBJECT |
|------|-------|---------|
| March 2, 1959 | League of Women Voters of Norwalk and League of Women Voters of Wilton, Norwalk, Connecticut | German Problems |
| March 3, 1959 Afternoon and evening speech | Department of Political Science, Mount Holyoke College, South Hadley, Massachusetts | Europe and Germany |
| March 23, 1959 | Indianapolis World Affairs Council and YMCA of Albert Lea, Minnesota, Department of State Auditorium, Washington | Berlin Situation |
| March 25, 1959 | American Foreign Service Association, Shoreham Hotel, Washington | Diplomacy in Time of Crisis—Berlin |
| April 9, 1959 | Harvard Club Luncheon, Washington, D.C. | Berlin—What We Have Done There |
| May 4, 1959 | Amerika Haus—Berlin | The Story of Developing Diplomatic Methods |
| September 22, 1959 | Senior Officers' Course, Foreign Service Institute | The Role of an Ambassador in Foreign Policy |
| November 12, 1959 | League of Women Voters, Watertown, New York | The Meaning of the Division of Germany, Press Release #784 |
| January 20, 1960 | International Center, University of Louisville, Louisville, Kentucky | Progress in Foreign Relations (and you), Fifty Years of Foreign Relations (techniques) |
| March 6, 1960 | The Sunday Evening Forum, University of Arizona Auditorium, Tucson, Arizona | Berlin—Challenge and Opportunity |
| February 19, 1961 | The Rye Forum, Rye, New York | A World Divided, Press Release #73 |
| April 18, 1961 | Bryn Mawr Club | The Importance of the Problems of Underdeveloped Countries |
| April 27, 1961 | Cazenovia Junior College, Cazenovia, New York | Africa—New Trends and Problems |

[374]

| DATE | PLACE | SUBJECT |
|------|-------|---------|
| April 28, 1961 | The 100,000 Club of Oneida County, Yahnundasis Golf Club, New Hartford, N.Y. (American Association of University Women, Utica, New York) | Africa—Hopes and Contradictions |
| May 11, 1961 | Student Officers' Wives, Military Assistance Institute, Arlington, Virginia | The American Abroad— Foreign Service |
| May 22, 1961 | Auburn Seminary Alumni Luncheon, Union Theological Seminary, New York, New York | The Impact of the United States on Africa |
| May 25, 1961 | Senior Reserve Officers, Detachment #51, Mobilization Designation, Department of Defense | Understanding Africa |
| July 19, 1961 | Old Louisville Association, Inc., Urban Renewal | Renewal Housing |
| August 3, 1961 | Girls Nation 1961, Washington, D.C. | Problems of Present Day Africa |

# IN REMEMBRANCE OF THINGS PAST
## FOSTER and JANET DULLES*

*Eleanor Lansing Dulles*

It is a strange phenomenon that a vase, a jewel, a desk, a picture can survive and bring a message for years, even for centuries after many spoken words have been forgotten, after voices have been silenced, after the world has revolved many times on its axis with a feverish rush of events which has made us forget the thoughts and deeds of the past.

Here in Austin, Texas, two rooms, modest in size and well furnished, have been reconstructed. They are an enduring manifestation of the life and spirit of Foster and Janet Dulles. They can show to hundreds of people, visiting them in decades to come, the interests and personalities of these two individuals, indicating in some measure their extraordinary talents, character and charm. Foster and Janet travelled much in far places but they also had a feeling for home. They nourished family traditions and were glad to come back to the houses they had furnished and filled with memories. Their possessions, some rare, some simple in their functional nature, were chosen to make a harmonious dwelling place. Many of these objects are now placed as they were when Foster died in May 1959, and as they were, still in much the same order in 1969, at the time of Janet's death.

The first half of the twentieth century was momentous and Foster, in partnership with his wife, made a lasting imprint. The critics of the man as Secretary of State, as well as his admirers, recognized his statements and his actions, in office and before, as shaping United States policy and power in this century. His relationship with President Eisenhower has been considered a model of effective government operation in the field of foreign affairs. The strength of leadership is widely considered as placing him among the great men of his age. In these rooms we see signs of his interests, his character, his feelings, his lighter moments. We see something of the clarity of his nature, his unvarying good taste. It was the same in his house at Cold Spring Harbor and in his home on 91st Street in New York City. The same tone was set in his small log cabin on Duck Island and even in his sturdy yawl the *Menemsha* for his sailing vacations. While he liked comfort in living and working, his possessions never exceeded what was useful or artistic.

The reality of things that we can see and touch now, the projection from the past into the future has an extraordinary importance as it helps us to recall ideas, personality, aims which tend to become dim with the passage of time. The pictures, books, furniture, *objets d'art* have been more than background: they have been part of the living choices of two people and thus are a continuing expression of former lives. This memorial will last into coming centuries with its message.

The rooms on 32nd Street in Washington were moderate in size, quiet, remote from traffic or tumult on a curving road in a hilly wooded section of the city, not far from the British Embassy on Massachusetts Avenue and the Belgian Embassy at 34th and Garfield. The terrace which lay in the angle between the study and the living room was cool under large trees, planted with surrounding magnolia and laurel in somewhat the same fashion as the terrace on Long Island. There was always a sense of privacy even when groups gathered for a reception or in small circles for consultation. The house was only fifteen minutes from the State Department and the White House by Rock Creek Parkway, yet the contour of the land was such as to make it seem almost alone in the country, far from the bustle of impatient motorists. Thus the silence in these rooms now is like that of past years.

They were rooms for two people who liked to have their friends around them, and were furnished ideally for small gatherings, family and close associates. The study was ample. Foster was a big man, broad shouldered, tall, relaxed when not on public display. The sense of humor, which was occasionally evident in news conferences, was characteristic of his evening hours in his home. The living room was not overly formal. Here Foster and Janet would pause, she in evening dress, he in white tie and tails, waiting for the car to take them to a dinner with Churchill, with Chancellor Adenauer, or with a President or a Prime Minister, Janet beautifully dressed, fine boned, slender, with "bubbly hair"—Foster once said he loved her

[377]

hair—with simple jewelry, in dignity and charm. The walls of the living room were a soft green, set off by the spectacular black teakwood panels from China, priceless jade ornaments, and vases from France.

Here, once on a birthday evening, President and Mamie Eisenhower, a few chosen guests, Allen and Clover Dulles and Eleanor Dulles celebrated the twenty-fifth of February. It was on that day, in 1888, the day of the great blizzard, that Foster was born at the home of his maternal grandfather, John W. Foster, 1405 Eye Street, Washington. Perhaps this room reflected more of the spirit of Janet. She leaned more to the fine and delicate, Foster preferring the strong and masculine, but their tastes were complementary and compatible.

Foster spent much time when away from the office, in the study in Washington. It was down a few steps and through a narrow archway. Near the entrance leading up to the bedrooms there was a staircase. It was possible for Foster to use these stairs when Janet had company and he could retreat this way if there were reasons to avoid some untimely visitor or interruption to his work.

Almost every thing that was in that room is now here in Texas. Only a few things have been added, notably the portrait of Foster which he did not have in his study. The reconstruction has been faithfully carried out. Thus the atmosphere and the tone of life are clearly evident and the hours and days here can be vividly recaptured.

The desk with its telephones and the long yellow pad was used when Foster talked with the President or with the State Department. After his death, Janet put there the photograph of Foster at work with the globe before him. The couch which stood under the window was where Foster sat for small conferences, where he wrote many of his speeches longhand on the legal pad and where on quiet evenings at home he sat to mix a martini or drink a highball of Overholt rye whiskey. Foster wrote every speech that he gave. He read and considered the texts put before him by his staff but the final result was essentially his writing. He could call to his home experts from his office and advisers. No one who worked with him could be sure that a weekend would pass without a conference, except when he travelled abroad. This participation in his thinking and writing was treasured by those who were close to him. The hours spent in the study were informal, stimulating and highly educational. Foster liked to hear the views of his staff. They soon learned that he wanted them to be succinct and to have clearly expressed ideas. The calm and friendly atmosphere of this room made such exchanges natural and easy. There was often time at the end of a discussion for an anecdote and a drink. Janet would join in the relaxed moments at the end of a hard working session.

In front of the couch and between the easy chairs there was a table of unique design. It was said to be from the Orient. It stands with the strength of the primitive tree from which it was cut many years ago. The cross section with its many rings of growth glows like the skin of a lion. It stands firm on its convoluted, twisted root-branches, as hard as granite, but as soft to the touch as satin. The substructure is intricate, circuitous, pleasing to see and feel, polished, broad, useful, difficult to imagine and describe. Perhaps this table from some distant forest had something of the same beauty as the broad, wind-tortured oak that grew by the log cabin on Duck Island. The glistening wood, circling around the tiny inner core with a century of growth from a small seed, combining the light of the sun, earth's minerals and drenching rain, created a massive trunk with wide-spread branches, one of the many mysteries of life and growth. In such phenomena there are marvels of creation which drive us to seek the meaning of the strange and manifold forces of nature which are only partially understood. Foster was always drawn to these things and in their contemplation he found deep satisfaction.

At the ends of the couch there were two bold and brilliant roosters which held the reading lamps. Sharp of outline, their combs crisp and red under the lights, they are thoroughly French in their posture and alert to give a tone of European independence to the setting. Janet found them in Paris. She and Foster loved to visit France. She had gone to a boarding school there, living on Avenue Henri Martin, where the chestnut trees added to the special beauties of spring. She was still in hair ribbons, a simply dressed youngster, when in 1908 Foster took advantage of a prize fellowship won for his essay on "The Theory of Judgment" at Princeton to go abroad. Most of the family went to Paris and took an apartment on Boulevard Raspail. He studied in Spain and in Germany as well as in France. It is said that he met Janet briefly then, though the difference in their ages at that time meant that they did not spend any considerable time together. He was a mature nineteen, she was a shy fifteen. It was several years later that he met her again in Auburn, New York, where the family then lived. The story goes that they fell in love at sight. Foster was studying for the bar examination which he was to take in Buffalo more than two hundred miles away. He had invited Janet to go canoeing with him on Owasco Lake near Auburn. He did not want to miss this chance to see her. Therefore, when he had finished a considerable part of the examination, he calculated that he would pass. He left the room and returned to Auburn to find Janet. This was one of those "calculated risks" which were later to become an element of his foreign policy. Soon they were engaged and in the spring of 1912 they were married. Their lifelong bond of intellectual companionship and deep affection brought many happy hours in Paris and elsewhere abroad. Among their mementos and books there are many signs of their shared taste for things that are French.

The books in the room in Washington and now here in Texas include many French books, novels, essays, poetry, English classics and modern books of exotic types. Janet was alert to new publications and read more than most people in these busy days; biography and novels were probably her favorites. Foster had many serious books of reference, political science and history. Here there is one of his eight copies of Stalin's *The Problems of Leninism*. He kept the other copies in various places where he worked. To the books written by his close family, Janet added some after his death. Originally there were those by his two grandfathers. The one by John W. Dulles, *Life in India*, written almost 140 years ago, tells of his adventurous trip round the Cape of Good Hope, a six months' voyage to Madras where he served as missionary. *Diplomatic Memoirs* by John Watson Foster, along with the other books on diplomacy, was frequently consulted. They were concerned with urgent problems of foreign affairs and included much analysis of Grandpa's negotiations in the Orient as well as his experiences as Chief Envoy—we did not have Ambassadors then—in Mexico, Spain and Russia. He had been Secretary of State in 1892 and Counsellor at the State Department for several decades. Robert Lansing's books—we called him "Uncle Bert"—were also there and recalled much of Foster's experience in Paris when he worked on the Treaty of Versailles—which the United States never signed. Uncle Bert had been Secretary of State chosen by President Wilson but was never in close sympathy with his chief, who was impatient with his precise legal approach to the problems of neutrality and peace.

Other family books included *The True Church* by his minister-father Allen Macy Dulles, several by his brother Allen, by his two sisters, Margaret Edwards and Eleanor Lansing Dulles, and those by his sons. There were several by Avery, his son whose installation as a Jesuit priest he attended in 1956, and several written by his son John on Mexico and Brazil and published after Foster's death. The collection was varied from atlases, reference books and the Federalist papers, which he used frequently, to several shelves of mysteries and detective stories, which he found better than sleeping pills—he said he could put an adventure story down in the middle of a critical scene and turn off his light. Among these books one can trace many strands of influences and thoughts which formed his intellectual background; through them the past influenced the future.

The pictures brought here from Washington have specific historical meaning and were cherished by Foster and Janet. Unique among them was the parchment cartoon which pictured Grandfather Foster in his role as negotiator of the Treaty of Shimonoseki which in 1895 brought an end to the war between China and Japan. John W. Foster had come to know the Chinese leaders in the course of his diplomatic exchanges and during a two weeks' visit in Peking in 1894 when he was received by high officials. His closest friend was probably Viceroy Li Hung-chang and he maintained his official and unofficial association for years, including his service on the Chinese delegation to the Hague Peace Conference in 1907 when he took his grandson Foster as his aide.

A balancing picture, more conventional in type, shows Foster among the delegates of forty-nine nations signing the Japanese Peace Treaty in 1951. The drafting of this treaty was profoundly influenced by Foster's disillusion over the negotiations in Paris which resulted in the Treaty of Versailles. He sought to give the greatest possible opportunity for political and economic reconstruction. To do this he concluded that he must avoid the multiple compromises which paralyzed constructive action in the large assembly in Paris in 1919. I saw him one Sunday working on the first draft—triple spaced and of few pages—in his house in Washington. (He then lived temporarily on Dumbarton Avenue.) The brief but comprehensive statement which emerged he took with him to England, France, Australia, New Zealand and elsewhere, taking account of suggestions, accepting some, putting aside others until there was a revised draft to be submitted to the signatory powers. This work, arduous and delicate in nature, was completed in approximately a year. The Russians protested, attended the conference, but did not sign the treaty. They had not been

[381]

permitted to stop the progress toward peace. The conference in San Francisco was convened to approve and not to debate. The task was completed on September 4, 1951.

Another picture relating to the Treaty of Versailles is the portrait by a celebrated artist, Johul Johansen, that Janet saw painted when she accompanied Foster to Paris in 1918. It shows the main United States delegates consulting together in the Hotel Crillon on the Place de la Concorde, the room one of the most elegant in Paris, with long rose-colored draperies, beautiful furniture and the atmosphere of the palaces of ancient France. Lansing and his associates are shown in contemplative mood, sober, and they were faced with the dual problem of crippling proposals by the French and British and the inability to gain access to a frustrated and already ailing President. The inability to exert our power on the practical issues, the absorption of Wilson in the plan for the League of Nations and the bitter struggle between the main participants brought cruel disappointment to Lansing and the main delegates from the United States.

Besides the portrait of Foster Dulles, that was not in the two rooms in Washington, there have also been added in these rooms in Texas the charts showing voyages of Foster's yawl, the *Menemsha*.

The forty-foot, gaff-rigged yawl *Menemsha* was an important part of Foster's vacation life. It was bought in 1933, after he had done adventurous cruising in open boats on Lake Ontario in former years. His boyhood sailing, often with his brother Allen, sometimes out of sight of land, had taken him to Canada and frequently to the Canadian island of Main Duck. The charts show the log of several cruises down as far as the western end of Lake Superior, and twice down the St. Lawrence to Nova Scotia and to Anticosti Island. The waters there were cold and the winds strong. Lines were rigged around the deck to lessen the likelihood of being swept overboard. "It is not probable that we could come about quickly enough to rescue you," Foster said. In spite of the cold, however, there was a daily swim. Heavy weather and frequent fog in the upper St. Lawrence off Newfoundland left the sailors cold and wet much of the time and limited the cooking to a bare minimum. The pitch and toss of the boat and the strain on the rigging tested the mettle of a man. The log of almost twenty thousand miles notes a shroud parted, whales sighted and an unplanned run of the rapids in the St. Lawrence and other happenings.

When the United States was swept into World War II, Foster sold the *Menemsha*. He knew that the kind of sailing he loved would no longer be possible. At about this time he was able to buy the Main Duck Island which had always been a favorite camping place. Here he arranged to bring down some Indians from northern Canada to build a log cabin, one room with a small kitchen and dressing room, on a bluff looking north over the wide stretch of Lake Ontario, above a quiet swimming beach. It was a very private refuge, and here with Janet he went for rest and contemplation as often as he could get away from the scheduled responsibility as Secretary of State.

The tracings on the charts show his longer navigation and his return to anchor at Duck Island. His last cruise in 1958 was in a chartered boat some months before he was hospitalized. He had cancer. On this cruise he stopped at Henderson Harbor where his sailing days had begun and had Sunday supper with the family in one of the cottages in which he had lived years ago. In speaking of sailing in a speech at Sodus Point in 1956 he said the captain of a boat, like the diplomat sometimes when the wind is against him, has to do a lot of tacking to reach his goal.

The variety and changes in his experience are well reflected in the objects he chose to have around him. The number of Chinese and other oriental treasures is notable. There is a beautiful grey silk screen which was a present to Janet from Mrs. Syngman Rhee, wife of the President of South Korea. The four teakwood panels with the jewelled figures making their way up the branches of oriental trees to some mythical heaven came from his Grandfather Foster, gifts from his early days in China. The jade pieces were partly from the grandparents' house, some were bought by Janet. She went with Foster when in 1938 he took a personal trip to China endeavoring to get a better picture of the political situation than he could get from American sources.

On this trip he had a hazardous airplane trip to Chungking through fog and wind in a small plane. His flight across the Pacific in 1938 was also vastly different from the present jet flights. His conclusions on United States relations with China then and later need to be viewed in the light of contemporaneous military and political events. He twice stated before he was Secretary that mainland China should be in the United Nations if the government showed the capacity to govern without serious popular opposition. The question of recognition was more complicated. The record is clear as reflected here that he had a keen awareness of the importance of that nation. This interest in China was a factor leading Foster in 1958 to urge Chiang Kai-shek to turn his attention to his mission as custodian of honored cultural values.

The beautiful objects in these two rooms, the mementos and awards shown here as well as those in the Dulles Diplomatic Library at Princeton University, testify to the broad range of Foster's interests. So do his own books also here, *War, Peace and Change* (1939) and *War or Peace* (1950). They reflect his concern for worldwide problems, security and NATO, Germany and Austria, the Middle East, the rejection of colonialism and the support of small nations. The story behind the material things, the gifts, the honors, is the story of the lives of Foster and Janet, crammed with action, rich in friendship, illuminated by thought. These had been years of church leadership, law practice, diplomacy, family, sport and travel. A biography can select and recapture some of the living reality, recount vivid incidents, but there are many facets to the human personality. No written account is likely to reveal the man, his inner warmth, his deepest convictions and his intimate desire for harmony and understanding.

Here among these cherished possessions one can imagine frosty mornings, golden afternoons and Foster and Janet as gracious hosts, informal and humorous in moments of relaxation, calm, thoughtful and at peace. Foster and Janet have left these rooms—there is no voice, no sound of living here. But something of their spirit lingers on. So in remembrance of things past this dwelling place has been re-created.

ELEANOR LANSING DULLES
July 19, 1973

# INDEX

Abshire, David, 316
Acheson, Dean, 182
Adams, Samuel Hopkins, 22
Adams, Ware, 202
Adenauer, Konrad, 182, 245
  funeral of, 330–335
Africa, tour of, 296–303
Agency for International Development (AID), 249
Allen, Billy, 262
Allen, Francis, vii, 316
Allen, George V., 311
Allen, Priscilla, vii
Allport, Harriet, 46
Altmeyer, Arthur, 147, 157
*America*, S.S., 226, 343
American Field Service, 58
American Institute of Architects, 257
American National Theater and Academy (ANTA), 261
American Tube and Stamping Co., 78–80
American University Union, 113
Andresen, Rachel, 323
Applebee, Constance, 43
Armstrong, Anne, 238
Asia, tour of, 278–93
Aswan Dam, 298
Atlantic Refining Co., 77
*Aurelia*, S.S., 322
Austria, and Marshall Plan, 223–24
Austrian State Treaty, 200, 219, 222, 226–27

Balfour, Arthur James, 74
Balmer, Jesmond D. (Jesse), 192, 209, 212
Bank for International Settlements (BIS), 122, 126, 170, 174, 354
*The Bank for International Settlements at Work* (Dulles), 96, 122, 131
Baruch, Bernard, 66
Battle Act, 231
Bay of Pigs affair, 30
Bean, Louis, 167–68
Beneš, Eduard, 219
Ben-Gurion, David, 312, 332
Benjamin Franklin Foundation, 258, 260, 262
Bennett, W. Tapley, 317
Bergson, Henri, 28
Berlin
  blockade, 184
  Congress Hall, 242, 257–60
  Klinikum, 257, 263-65
  postwar visit, 183–85
  revolt, 253–54
  stockpile, 251–52
Berlin Desk, 184, 241, 243–56
*Berlin: The Wall Is Not Forever* (Dulles), 261, 277, 318, 333
Berlin Wall, 247, 272–73
Beveridge, Sir William, 88
Beyer, Clara, 232
Bezanson, Anne, 76, 78, 139
Bigge, George, 147
*The Birth of a Nation*, 261

Bissell, Richard, 224, 304
Black, Sir Robert Brown, 283
Blake, William, 37
Blank, Theo, 185
Blessing, Karl, 129, 333
Bliss, Robert, 52
Bliss, Tasker H., 67
Blodgett, Katharine, 46
Blondheim, David (husband), 26, 48, 104–105, 108–13, 338, 354
  dies, 143–45
  marries, 138–43
Blondheim, Grace, 110
Blondheim, Hillel, 110, 138
Board of Economic Warfare, 158, 167
*The Boer War* (Dulles), 15
Bolten, Seymour and Stacey, vii
Bourne, Dorothy, 354
Bourne, James, 58, 354
*Boxer*, U.S.S., 317
Bradley, Robert, 78
Brandt, Rut, 274
Brandt, Willy, 182, 184, 242, 316, 332
Bretton Woods Conference, 133, 134, 171–73
Brezhnev Doctrine, 254–55, 321
Briand, Aristide, 179
Bristol, Mark, 107
Brown, Bernice (Cronkhite), 92
Brown, J. Douglas, 152
Brown, Kay, 320, 321
Brown, Ralph, 333
Bruce, David, 267
Bruere, Henry, 152
Brunel, Clovis, 113
Brunsdale, Anne, vii
Bryn Mawr College, 33
  award from, 293–94
  fellowship at, 75–77
  teaching at, 115–19
  student years at, 34–37
Bulganin, Nikolai, 241, 268
Bullitt, William, 69
Bullock, Charles J., 92
Bunting, Fred and Jane, 209, 292
Burch, Dorothy, 312
Burke, Arleigh, 316
Burns, Arthur F., 88
Byrnes, James, 176, 182

Cannan, Edwin, 88
Carnegie Foundation, 142
Carsten, Carl, 184, 316
Castro, Fidel, 295
Caterpillar Tractor Co., 230
Catudal, Marc, 318
Causey, Mike, 238
Center for Strategic International Services, 316
Chase, Lucia, 46
Chatel, Dr., 289
*Cheaper by the Dozen* (Gilbreth), 76
Chew, Samuel, 41
Chiang Ching-kuo, 283
Chiang Kai-shek, 283, 348

[385]